South of the South

SOUTHERN DISSENT

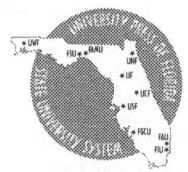

Florida A&M University, Tallahassee
Florida Atlantic University, Boca Raton
Florida Gulf Coast University, Ft. Myers
Florida International University, Miami
Florida State University, Tallahassee
University of Central Florida, Orlando
University of Florida, Gainesville
University of North Florida, Jacksonville
University of South Florida, Tampa
University of West Florida, Pensacola

SOUTHERN DISSENT
Edited by Stanley Harrold and Randall M. Miller

The Other South: Southern Dissenters in the Nineteenth Century, by Carl N. Degler,
with a new preface (2000)

Crowds and Soldiers in Revolutionary North Carolina: The Culture of Violence in Riot and War,
by Wayne E. Lee (2001)

*"Lord, We're Just Trying to Save Your Water": Environmental Activism and Dissent
in the Appalachian South,* by Suzanne Marshall (2002)

The Changing South of Gene Patterson: Journalism and Civil Rights, 1960–1968,
edited by Roy Peter Clark and Raymond Arsenault (2002)

*Gendered Freedoms: Race, Rights, and the Politics of Household
in the Postemancipation Delta, 1861–1875,* by Nancy Bercaw (2003)

Civil War on Race Street: The Civil Rights Movement in Cambridge, Maryland,
by Peter B. Levy (2003)

South of the South: Jewish Activists and the Civil Rights Movement in Miami, 1945–1960,
by Raymond A. Mohl, with Matilda "Bobbi" Graff and Shirley M. Zoloth (2004)

* * *

South of the South

* * *

Jewish Activists and the Civil Rights Movement in Miami, 1945–1960

RAYMOND A. MOHL

with Matilda "Bobbi" Graff and Shirley M. Zoloth

University Press of Florida
GAINESVILLE · TALLAHASSEE · TAMPA · BOCA RATON
PENSACOLA · ORLANDO · MIAMI · JACKSONVILLE · FT. MYERS

Copyright 2004 by Raymond A. Mohl
Printed in the United States of America
All rights reserved

First cloth printing, 2004
First paperback printing, 2005

Library of Congress Cataloging-in-Publication Data
Mohl, Raymond A.
South of the south : Jewish activists and the civil
rights movement in Miami, 1945–1960 / Raymond A. Mohl;
with Matilda "Bobbi" Graff and Shirley M. Zoloth.
p. cm. — (Southern dissent)
ISBN 0-8130-2693-8; ISBN 0-8130-2922-8 (pbk.)
1. African Americans—Civil rights—Florida—Miami—History—20th
century. 2. African Americans—Relations with Jews. 3. Jewish women—Florida
—Miami—Biography. 4. Jews—Florida—Miami—Biography. 5. Civil rights
workers—Florida—Miami—Biography. 6. Civil rights movements—Florida
—Miami—History—20th century. 7. Miami (Fla.)—Race relations.
8. Miami (Fla.)—Ethnic relations. 9. Miami (Fla.)—Biography.
I. Graff, Matilda. II. Zoloth, Shirley M. III. Title. IV. Series.
F319.M6M75 2004
323'.092'39240759381—dc22   2003057911

The University Press of Florida is the scholarly publishing agency for the State
University System of Florida, comprising Florida A&M University, Florida Atlantic
University, Florida Gulf Coast University, Florida International University, Florida
State University, University of Central Florida, University of Florida, University
of North Florida, University of South Florida, and University of West Florida.

University Press of Florida
15 Northwest 15th Street
Gainesville, FL 32611-2079
http://www.upf.com

For Sai Sai

Contents

Foreword ix
Acknowledgments xi

Introduction: Interpreting the Civil Rights Movement in Miami 1

PART I
South of the South: Jewish Activists and the Civil Rights Movement in Miami, 1945–1960 11

PART II
Matilda "Bobbi" Graff and the Civil Rights Congress 63

The Historic Continuity of the Civil Rights Movement, by Matilda "Bobbi" Graff 71

PART III
Shirley M. Zoloth and the Congress of Racial Equality 123

Civil Rights Correspondence and Miami CORE Reports and Minutes, 1957–1960, by Shirley M. Zoloth 133

Notes 205
Bibliography 229
Index 255

Foreword

By choosing *South of the South* as the title for this volume on Jews in Miami's civil rights movement, Raymond A. Mohl emphasizes his subject's ambiguous relationship to southern culture and history. Incorporated in 1896, Miami had no physical link to the Old South's political economy based on the enslavement of African Americans. The city, during the years covered by *South of the South*, was expanding as a resort and retirement center for northerners. Yet, as Mohl's book indicates, Miami during the post–World War II years was still southern in its formal commitment to racial segregation and in its toleration of anti-black terror generated by the Ku Klux Klan. It was a city that simultaneously could attract northern Jews who were sympathetic to black aspirations *and* a city that could react viciously to their work in behalf of the civil rights movement. That the Jews involved were women whose activist backgrounds included ties to labor unions and communists made them even more threatening in the minds of those who defended Miami's racial status quo.

Mohl rightly insists that events in Miami cannot be understood apart from the broader context of the black freedom struggle, the repressive Cold War era, and the complicated relationships between African Americans and Jews inside and outside the South. But Mohl especially points to Miami's uniqueness. No other southern place was so much affected by large-scale migration of northerners, many of whom were Jews familiar with labor and social justice causes. Such people did not take well to southern ways. Also, Miami was more dependent than other southern places on cultivating and maintaining a good national image. It was a place where the Old South met the first burst of the Sunbelt South. Therefore the possibility for social change in the city was a critical factor in the dynamics of civil rights.

Into this milieu came two remarkable women, Matilda "Bobbi" Graff and Shirley M. Zoloth, whose stories—told in their own words—about their work with the Miami branch of the Congress of Racial Equality (CORE) and the Miami chapter of the Civil Rights Congress (CRC) are the substance of this book. Jewish radicals from the North, they became in postwar Miami the epitome of outside agitators. That they were white women working with black men to change race relations could not have been more threatening to local myths and customs concerning sexuality and race. Facing reactionary and repressive elements that were quite capable of violence, Graff, Zoloth, their families, and their black allies demonstrated steadfastness in their progressive commitment to human rights.

In *South of the South,* Mohl takes readers inside Miami's civil rights movement. There is Bobbi Graff's autobiographical account of her work with the CRC and related social justice organizations. There are Shirley Zoloth's eyewitness reports, sent regularly to the national CORE office, on sit-ins, activism, and civil rights meetings in Miami. Together, Graff and Zoloth bring the daily dynamics of social justice reform to light. They also point to the organizing role of women within the civil rights movement. Men gained attention by speaking publicly for organizations, but women such as Graff and Zoloth built and sustained the infrastructure. Along with the men, they stood up for social change by marching for freedom and by desegregating restaurants, accommodations, and other public places.

Although Mohl recognizes that most southern Jews, as well as most Miami Jews, were not active supporters of black rights during the 1940s and 1950s, his book is an important reminder that many Jews *were* active in the civil rights movement. Since that time the black and Jewish communities in America have tended to disagree on such issues as affirmative action, support for Israel, and economic policy. Outlandish charges by black intellectuals associated with the Nation of Islam that Jews were responsible for the Atlantic slave trade mark an extreme in the recent deterioration of relations between the two groups. But it is not surprising that Graff and Zoloth, in the wake of the Holocaust, would sympathize with African Americans in their quest for racial justice. American Jews themselves faced discrimination in housing and education, which made them natural allies of African Americans in seeking to change Miami, the South, and the nation.

The goal of the *Southern Dissent* series is to publish books that explore and analyze the complexities of southern dissent on a broad, multi-ethnic plane. Mohl has achieved that goal in an admirable fashion in presenting a complicated but very human story of interracial cooperation in behalf of human rights. That the story unfolds in a city that is south of the South makes it all the more intriguing.

Stanley Harrold and Randall M. Miller
Series Editors

Acknowledgments

Writing a book is an adventurous journey, with many unexpected encounters, discoveries, revelations, and pleasures along the way. Historians spend a lot of time alone as researchers and writers, but a book such as this one relies upon crucial assistance from librarians, archivists, other scholars, and those who can provide oral testimony. Thus, it is gratifying to be able to acknowledge their help in researching, writing, and interpreting the role of Jewish activists in postwar Miami. My greatest debts are to some of the main participants in Miami's early civil rights movement. Shirley and Milton Zoloth provided essential information during several long interviews and remained enthusiastic supporters of this project from its inception. At the end of one interview, Shirley Zoloth gave me her clipping scrapbook, stuffed with yellowing clippings from Miami newspapers dealing with school desegregation issues. Despite her harrowing experience in Cold War Florida, Bobbi Graff has demonstrated an admirable determination to tell her story. In the decade I have known her, she has submitted to innumerable interviews, permitted me to examine her FBI file and correspondence and clipping files, and patiently awaited completion of the project. Involved in just about every phase of postwar activism in Miami, Jack D. Gordon offered great information, insights, and interpretation in several long telephone interviews. Others who supplied important information during interviews include Thalia [Stern] Broudy, Marilynn Bloom, Cindy Thorner, Libby Strauss, Ruth Greenfield, Leonard Turkel, and Robert Kunst.

The historical paper trail on Miami's civil rights movement has provided the essential framework for narrative and interpretation. Research in the archived papers of the Civil Rights Congress (CRC) and the Congress of Racial Equality (CORE) revealed the inner workings of Miami's early civil rights organizations. Interlibrary loan librarians at Florida Atlantic University and the University of Alabama at Birmingham facilitated the loan of CRC microfilm from the Schomburg Library in New York City and CORE microfilm from the

Wisconsin State Historical Society. Research in other important archival collections was assisted by archivists and librarians at the U.S. National Archives, the Library of Congress, the Florida State Archives, Florida International University, the University of Miami, the University of Florida, the University of South Florida, Emory University, Georgia State University, the Atlanta University Center, and the Swarthmore College Peace Collection.

This book began, in modest fashion, as a conference paper at the Southern Historical Association meeting in Atlanta in 1992. In his role as commentator at that SHA session, John Bracey provided an incisive critique. I also want to thank several friends and colleagues who work on similar subjects and who read and offered suggestions on that early version of the Miami civil rights story. They include Sarah Hart Brown, Gregory Bush, Henry A. Green, Cheryl Greenberg, Deborah Dash Moore, and Leonard Dinnerstein. Subsequently, I sharpened the analysis and interpretation in presentations at other conferences and in seminars at several universities, where audience questions and commentary proved helpful. After additional research and several revisions, an article version of "South of the South," summarizing the present volume, was published in the *Journal of American Ethnic History* (1999). I appreciate the valuable commentary and suggestions provided by those who responded to different versions of that article manuscript, including Gerald Horne, Kim Lacy Rogers, Ronald H. Bayor, and several anonymous reviewers. Kenneth W. Goings and Mark H. Rose, two of my former colleagues at Florida Atlantic University, read several versions of the article manuscript and provided detailed comment and critique. Mark Bauman and Leonard Dinnerstein, reviewers for the University Press of Florida, read and critiqued the book manuscript, providing excellent suggestions for improving the text and sharpening the interpretation. Randall M. Miller and Stanley Harrold, editors of the "Southern Dissent" series, have worked through two successive versions of the manuscript and contributed in innumerable ways to making it a better book. Finally, the subject of this book cuts across a number of substantial scholarly literatures: civil rights history, women's history, modern Florida history, the black-Jewish relationship, and communism and anticommunism in the postwar era. Writing history is a cumulative endeavor, and I am indebted to dozens of scholars and writers who have analyzed, interpreted, and worked through these subjects in their books and articles—a scholarship, reflected in the bibliography, that has informed and helped shape this work.

Introduction

Interpreting the Civil Rights Movement in Miami

THIS BOOK TRACES the emergence of civil rights activism in postwar Miami, Florida. It focuses on the work of progressive and left-wing Jewish women, originally from northern cities, who built local organizations in Miami to challenge racial segregation. In the midst of the anticommunist hysteria of the McCarthy era, these Jewish activists demonstrated a level of commitment to civil rights that was rare and unusual at that time in the American South. They connected with national civil rights organizations, but for the most part they pursued their own local agendas and followed their own timetable for action. They also worked effectively with local black activists, suggesting new dimensions to the much-studied black-Jewish relationship in modern American history. Their stories stand at the center of this book. But the book also interprets the Miami experience in the context of an extensive scholarly literature on southern Jews, the civil rights movement, and the postwar surge of anticommunism.

During the postwar years, from the mid-1940s to about 1960, a small, committed, and Jewish-led civil rights movement emerged in Miami. The movement was reflected in the social activism of Matilda "Bobbi" Graff, a young woman, originally from New York City, who migrated to Miami from Detroit with her husband, Emanuel, and their daughter in 1946. In the late 1940s and early 1950s, Graff played an instrumental role in the Miami chapter of the Civil Rights Congress (CRC), a left-wing group that boldly confronted racism and fought for civil rights and civil liberties in the midst of the repressive McCarthy era. Miami's early civil rights activism can also be traced in the work of Shirley M. Zoloth, who arrived in Miami from Philadelphia with her husband, Milton, and their children in 1954. In the late 1950s, Zoloth helped organize and then provided the driving energy behind the Miami branch of the Congress of

Racial Equality (CORE), which conducted dozens of sit-ins at downtown lunch counters in 1959 and 1960. The organization ultimately forced the desegregation of public accommodations in Miami. Newcomers to the South, Graff, Zoloth, and others like them with leftist or progressive political leanings found Miami's racial segregation intolerable and decided to do something about it.

This book presents the stories of these two women, mostly in their own words. Through autobiographical writings, reports, and correspondence, Graff and Zoloth provided contemporary accounts of Jewish civil rights activism in postwar Miami. These documentary materials are reproduced here and form the heart of the book. Numerous first-hand accounts of civil rights activity have been published in recent years, but there are no such accounts by Jewish women from South Florida during the hard, early days of the civil rights movement and, indeed, few such accounts anywhere.[1] Thus, the Graff and Zoloth writings offer new ways of learning about, understanding, and interpreting civil rights in the mid-twentieth century. At their most basic level, these materials demonstrate the centrality of local action and individual agency in the movement for racial reform. They also challenge traditional views of Jewish involvement in the early struggle for civil rights in the South.

Bobbi Graff and Shirley Zoloth never met. Although they had friends in common, their civil rights activities in Miami did not overlap in time. By the time the Zoloths arrived in South Florida, the Graffs had already departed, driven out by local McCarthyites and FBI harassment. However, the two women separately helped shape Miami's early civil rights movement—a movement notable for its assertiveness in a region where few white people spoke out for civil liberties or defended the right of black people to vote, ride a bus, attend integrated schools, live in racially diverse neighborhoods, or sit down for a cup of coffee in a restaurant.

The work of Miami CRC and Miami CORE, as well as the activist leadership of Graff and Zoloth, provides a unique angle of vision on the postwar civil rights movement in the American South. Miami in 1950 was still very much a Deep South city where segregation and anti-Semitism were entrenched. But powerful new migration streams from the North, especially Jewish migration, had begun to alter the city's population patterns and social dynamics. The Miami area's Jewish population surged from a few thousand in 1940 to around 140,000 in 1960, comprising by that time about 15 percent of metro Miami's total population. Both Graff and Zoloth were Jewish, as were almost all of the white activists in Miami CRC and Miami CORE. Not surprisingly, most of them were also recent migrants to South Florida. They left the big cities of the North behind, seeking new opportunities and pursuing tropical dreams in the Florida sunshine. They abandoned familiar and insular ethnic communities of the urban North for the uncertainties of the new urban South.

Not all was left behind. Miami's Jewish newcomers brought with them important elements of their communal and religious culture, a culture that shaped their adaptation to the unfamiliar ways of the South. It was a culture that valued human dignity and supported social justice, a culture that found segregation and racial discrimination deeply troubling. Beyond traditional elements of Jewish culture, however, some Jewish migrants to Miami also brought oppositional traditions of progressive, activist, and radical politics. These traditions were very much in the minority among Miami Jews at the time. Nevertheless, this leftist political culture—trade unionist, progressive, socialist, and communist—informed, inspired, and motivated Miami's early Jewish civil rights activists.

The mid-century activist tradition among Miami's newly arrived Jews simultaneously found expression in various other movements, causes, and organizations on the radical and progressive (or nonsocialist) left. Some of these groups were exclusively Jewish, such as the Emma Lazarus Federation of Jewish Women's Clubs, the Jewish People's Fraternal Order, the Workmen's Circle, the National Council of Jewish Women, the Jewish Veterans Committee, and the American Jewish Congress. Left-liberal Jews dominated other activist organizations, as well, including the American Veterans Committee, the Florida Progressive Party, Southern Women for Peace, the Women's International League for Peace and Freedom, the Florida Civil Liberties Union, the National Committee for a Sane Nuclear Policy, and Women Strike for Peace. Taken together, these varied activist organizations energized a powerful thrust for progressive social change in postwar Miami.

The struggle against racial segregation that engaged Miami's activist Jewish women reflected larger trends and shifting roles among postwar American women. During World War II, American women served in the armed forces and filled war-production factory jobs as men went off to fight in Europe and the Pacific. The determined image of Rosie the Riveter, contributing essential labor to the war effort, trumpeted the power of women on the home front. But once the war ended, women were expected to yield their places in the labor force to returning veterans and resume their traditional roles in the home. Recent historical research has demonstrated that many women did not follow that path back into the home and the kitchen. Indeed, activism on numerous fronts absorbed the time and energy of women in the late 1940s and through the 1950s. Black and white women, for instance, assumed prominent roles in the civil rights movement throughout the nation.[2] Bobbi Graff, Shirley Zoloth, and many of their coworkers in Miami CRC and Miami CORE exemplified these new postwar roles for women, as they balanced family life with civil rights activism and other progressive causes.

Interracialism marked Miami's early civil rights movement from the beginning. Both Graff and Zoloth had engaged in interracial reform efforts in New York, Detroit, and Philadelphia before pursuing new lives and activist careers in Florida. The movements they led in Miami were interracial from the start. William L. Patterson, a well-known African-American communist and labor lawyer, led the Civil Rights Congress on the national level. In Miami, the work of the CRC branch appealed to a tiny group of whites and blacks on the left, including some local black communists who had earlier been members of the black nationalist Universal Negro Improvement Association led by Marcus Garvey. The Congress of Racial Equality had few chapters in the South before 1960, but Miami CORE's membership mirrored the organization's northern interracial pattern. Thus, blacks and whites worked together in Miami's civil rights organizations. They alarmed Miami's segregationists and provoked fierce resistance and opposition. Led by Jewish women on the left, Miami's early civil rights movement assumed an interracial stance that challenged the fundamental practices of white supremacy.

The significance of Miami CRC and Miami CORE can be evaluated in the context of the evolving historiography of the civil rights movement. In the 1960s and 1970s, civil rights historians emphasized the importance of well-known national leaders, the work of national organizations, and the achievement of national civil rights legislation. This top-down history, historians now recognize, presented a misleading and incomplete picture of the larger struggle for civil rights. In the 1980s, several new books began shifting the focus of attention to the many local civil rights battlegrounds.[3] This more recent and still dominant grassroots interpretation contends that freedom struggles at the local or community level took place independent of national activities and leaders in response to local circumstances. This interpretation also suggested many different civil rights *movements,* rather than a single unified movement with a common agenda. Such community-oriented interpretations have provided a new appreciation of the role of local agency in achieving civil rights victories. As historian Charles W. Eagles has noted, "The local community approach to studying the civil rights struggle has in fact nearly supplanted the earlier emphasis on great men and big organizations operating on the national stage." The work of Miami CRC and Miami CORE, in which activists such as Graff and Zoloth took the lead, paralleled community struggles for civil rights in many other cities and states.[4]

Newer analyses of the civil rights movement have emphasized the continuity of the African-American struggle for civil rights over a long period of time. With a few notable exceptions, traditional civil rights narratives focused heavily on the period after the mid-1950s. The crucial 1954 U.S. Supreme Court decision in *Brown v. the Board of Education of Topeka, Kansas* outlawing school segregation and the transforming events of the 1955–56 Montgomery bus boycott seemed to many to mark the beginnings of the modern civil rights crusade. To be sure, new strategies, alliances, and leaders emerged in the 1950s and after. But earlier narratives of the movement often assumed that those events had few precedents and little history behind them, or that that history was relatively unimportant in light of the major advances of the mid-1950s. It was as if there was no civil rights movement in America worth writing about before *Brown* and before Montgomery. However, historians have pushed back the battle against racism, segregation, and discrimination by many decades and even into the nineteenth century. Civil rights scholars have come to appreciate the cultures of opposition and resistance, agency and activism that have characterized the long span of African-American history.[5]

This book places the activism of Bobbi Graff and Shirley Zoloth within the context of the interpretive insights advanced by recent historians. Miami blacks contested segregation on many fronts long before the 1950s. In 1919, for example, they formed the militant Negro Uplift Association to protest police brutality and demand better treatment. In the 1920s, large numbers of Miami area blacks, especially immigrant blacks from the Bahamas, joined Marcus Garvey's even more militant Universal Negro Improvement Association in another early challenge to white supremacy. In the late 1930s and early 1940s, black editor and activist Sam Solomon organized the Negro Citizens Service League, which carried out successful voter registration campaigns in Miami's black community. In 1944, Florida civil rights activist Harry T. Moore established the Progressive Voters League, which conducted similar voter registration work among blacks in Miami and elsewhere. Baptist minister Edward Graham, head of the Miami branch of the National Urban League, directed Atlantic Ocean wade-ins in 1945, successfully gaining beach access for African Americans for the first time. In the late 1940s, housing pressures encouraged blacks to buy and rent houses in white neighborhoods, despite house burnings, bombings, Ku Klux Klan marches, and other hostile threats from white terrorists. Local NAACP legal challenges on issues of police brutality, public accommodations, and other points became more frequent by mid-century. These confrontations with the rigid system of southern segregation emerged spontaneously in the local community, without assistance from any national leaders or organizations. Driven by local issues, the civil rights movement in Miami had an important history prior to the mid-1950s, but few white people were involved in these activities.[6]

The large Jewish migration to Miami in the postwar years brought white people into the local civil rights movement for the first time. These cooperative efforts were rare and unusual, given the time and place. Indeed, the active role of some Jews in the Miami civil rights movement provides a new perspective on the black-Jewish relationship in the South. Jews and blacks often found common cause in the North, working together in a struggle against racism and anti-Semitism. In most of the South, Jews represented a tiny, identifiable minority in a biracial society. Historians of the subject generally have maintained, with considerable supporting evidence, that most southern Jews held back from the civil rights struggle and never developed activist alliances with African Americans to challenge white supremacy. Although sympathetic to the goals of racial justice, the argument runs, most southern Jews maintained an uneasy silence, quietly accepting segregation. To be sure, some leading rabbis in southern cities spoke out against segregation. But most southern Jews worried about jeopardizing their own marginal role in southern society and feared a violent anti-Semitic backlash that would endanger their families and businesses. Some others, small in number, actually supported the southern racial system. These views have been elaborated by several historians of the southern Jewish experience, including Mark K. Bauman, Deborah Dash Moore, Cheryl Greenberg, Leonard Dinnerstein, Marc Dollinger, and Clive Webb, whose book, *Fight Against Fear: Southern Jews and Black Civil Rights* (2001), provides the most substantive treatment of the subject.[7]

Webb's book focuses primarily on small, stable, established Jewish communities in urban centers in Alabama, Georgia, and Mississippi—Birmingham, Atlanta, and Jackson. By contrast, Jewish Miami was an upstart community and a postwar phenomenon. Most of Miami's Jews migrated from northern cities after the war, an enormous migration that produced a Jewish community much larger than anywhere else in the South. Jewish newcomers to Miami with leftist leanings and activist backgrounds rejected the acquiescent racial attitudes of their southern brethren. In their new subtropical home, they built a vibrant network of activist organizations promoting civil rights, school integration, civil liberties, world peace, and political reform. In fascinating ways, Miami's Jewish activists of the 1940s and 1950s continued their political advocacy roles into the 1960s, 1970s, and after, moving on from civil rights to other issues, organizations, and programs as the times changed. For instance, virtually all of the Miami activists participated in the antiwar movement of the 1960s and early 1970s. They energetically supported reform movements within the Democratic Party, including Eugene McCarthy's 1968 primary challenge to President Lyndon B. Johnson and George McGovern's 1972 presidential run against Richard M. Nixon. Within the Florida Democratic Party, they posed an annoying challenge to the party's conservative old guard, eventually forming their own separate reform organization called Florida Concerned Democrats. Many Jewish CORE activists participated in the War on Poverty, taking key positions in the mid-1960s in Miami's antipoverty agency, Economic Opportunity Program, Inc. (EOPI). For the Jewish activists, working with EOPI served as a means of continuing the civil rights work they began with CORE. Thus, Jewish activism in Miami, and its persistence over several decades, offers a new and different perspective on the role of Jews in the postwar South.

The left-wing political orientation of many Jewish and some African-American activists, as well as the intensity of local anticommunist hysteria, shaped the civil rights struggle in Miami. These issues, too, are matters of debate among civil rights scholars. To what extent did the left influence civil rights activism? Did association with the left damage the movement or postpone its ultimate success? The red scare, unleashed by Senator Joseph McCarthy and others on the political right, dominated the domestic politics of the postwar era. For many Americans, fear of communism outweighed commitment to such liberal values as civil liberties, civil rights, and racial integration. At the national level, mainstream race advancement organizations such as the NAACP and the National Urban League, as well as leading Jewish agencies such as the American Jewish Committee and the American Jewish Congress, backed away from left-wing associations. In Miami, too, local branches of these organizations adopted a low civil rights profile for a time in the 1950s, seeking to avoid the smear tactics of the politically potent and popular South Florida McCarthyites.[8]

The challenge to segregation in mid-century Miami sparked a powerful white opposition campaign. To the defenders of white supremacy, the local left-wing civil rights coalition of blacks and Jews, small as it was, represented a threat to what was revered as the southern way of life. Strong currents of anti-Semitism and anticommunism characterized white Florida's defense of racial segregation in the era of McCarthyism. The Ku Klux Klan and the White Citizens Councils offered a persistent, powerful, and often violent resistance to change. At the same time, official investigatory bodies contributed to the climate of fear and conflict. The U.S. House Un-American Activities Committee and later the U.S. Senate Internal Security Subcommittee both held hearings in Miami in the 1940s and 1950s, ostensibly searching out left-wing threats to

American security in the Sunshine State. In addition, in the mid-1950s both the Florida legislature and the Dade County state attorney's office launched investigations of their own. They held hearings in Miami to stave off the supposed communist threat to Floridians and to white supremacy.

The civil rights movement in postwar Miami, in short, became caught up in the anticommunist hysteria of the late forties and fifties. Many civil rights activists, and especially Miami's Jewish advocates of racial reform, became targets of segregationists during the congressional and local investigations. Pensacola civil liberties attorney John M. Coe, who defended many of the Miami activists during the period, starkly summarized the situation in 1954: "The local McCarthys have set up a reign of terror in Miami." Civil rights attorney Frank J. Donner charged in 1954 that Florida's "grass-roots" McCarthyites developed their own "Miami formula" for neutralizing the left-wing civil rights crowd. It seems clear in retrospect, as Carol Polsgrove has suggested in her book, *Divided Minds: Intellectuals and the Civil Rights Movement* (2001), that "resistance to racial change accounted for much of the energy behind the domestic assault on communism." This explanation holds particular salience for the vicious opposition to civil rights activism in Miami and in the South generally.[9]

Despite Miami's repressive atmosphere, civil rights activists challenged segregation in the decade and a half before 1960. Bobbi Graff and Shirley Zoloth, de facto leaders of their respective organizations at a crucial moment in time, stood at the center of this early campaign for racial change. They nurtured interracial movements that by their very existence threatened Miami's dominant political and racial cultures. Their activist work exemplified an important aspect of the history and character of Miami's civil rights movement. Along with others with similar goals, ideologies, and backgrounds, they confronted the city's system of segregation and forced change. Their stories are central to a larger narrative about racial reform in Florida's emerging Sunbelt city.

* * *

The research for this book has unfolded over a decade. It grew out of a larger and still ongoing study on the history of race relations in twentieth-century Miami. As I surveyed studies of the city's history, it seemed clear to me that the full story of the civil rights movement in Miami remained untold. Preliminary research in Miami newspapers revealed the leading role of Jewish women in civil rights activity throughout the 1950s, suggesting a civil rights history that might be different and more complex than that of most southern cities. Newspaper reports on Miami's 1959 CORE sit-ins documented Shirley Zoloth's involvement in those challenges to racial segregation in downtown Miami. In September 1991, I met with Shirley and Milton Zoloth at their home in Miami Beach in what was the first of several lively interviews about the pathbreaking civil rights action initiated by Miami CORE. Several months later, in early 1992, I met Bobbi Graff at the home of my friend Greg Bush, a history professor at the University of Miami. During this first discussion with her, we learned of her work with the Miami branch of the Civil Rights Congress beginning in 1948. Nearly fifty years later, Graff still had vivid memories of the vicious harassment and red-baiting experienced at the hands of various defenders of the segregationist status quo. Subsequent interviews with both women, as well as with other participants, provided essential first-person details and insights into the early civil rights movement in Miami.

Interviews alone cannot tell the whole story. Traditional historical research in the microfilmed papers of the Civil Rights Congress at the Schomburg Library in New York City and the Congress of Racial Equality at the Wisconsin State Historical Society provided a revealing paper trail. In each case, extensive files of Miami branch correspondence and reports complemented the interviews. The CORE records, in particular, had a complete set of Shirley Zoloth's lengthy first-person reports from Miami CORE's 1959 sit-in campaign at downtown lunch counters. In addition, Bobbi Graff shared with me an unpublished autobiographical account that she wrote in the early 1970s about her activist work in 1950s Miami.

Assimilating these varied materials and thinking about their importance led to the idea for this book and accounts for its present form. Part I represents a historical analysis of the Miami civil rights movement between 1945 and 1960, placing the movement in its local and historical context and incorporating the concepts and interpretations mentioned earlier in this introduction. In Part II, Bobbi Graff's autobiographical memoir recounts her work with the Miami branch of the Civil Rights Congress and other groups such as the Florida Progressive Party in the mid-century years. Part III contains the many reports Shirley Zoloth sent to the national CORE office immediately after sit-ins and meetings, as well as some of her correspondence and published articles. Taken together, the primary materials written by Graff and Zoloth provide unusual and revealing documentation of the Miami movement for racial change. They also demonstrate a level of Jewish activism, especially Jewish women's activism, unique for the postwar American South.

PART I

* * *

South of the South

Jewish Activists and the Civil Rights Movement
in Miami, 1945–1960

* * *

APRIL 15, 1959: Activists from Miami CORE—two Jews and two blacks—entered the Woolworth store on Flagler Street in downtown Miami. The lunch counter was nearly full. Shirley Zoloth and Alice Barr took the first available seats, then Milton Zoloth and Ishmael Howard sat down a few seats away. The waitresses suddenly disappeared. "We were left sitting there," Shirley Zoloth later wrote. Soon an assistant manager came over and announced that "they did not serve colored here." The CORE activists asked to see the store manager but were told that he was out. The four discussed CORE and its objectives with the assistant manager, gave him a copy of CORE's leaflet, *This Is CORE,* and promised to be back. This brief and seemingly uneventful encounter on Flagler Street—one of dozens of lunch counter sit-ins in Miami during the spring and fall of 1959—marked the beginning of an activist phase of the civil rights movement in South Florida that within a year had cracked the color line in Miami. Blacks and Jews working with CORE assuredly and effectively challenged segregation in the Sunshine State a year before the more celebrated 1960 student sit-ins in Greensboro, North Carolina.[1]

Much has been written about the relationship between blacks and Jews in twentieth-century America—a relationship marked both by cooperation and conflict. Since both groups were outsiders, marginalized by race and religion, blacks and Jews had a mutual interest in challenging discrimination and struggling for civil rights. During the formative years of the American civil rights movement, the argument runs, blacks and Jews forged a notable civil rights alliance. As James Farmer, who worked with both CORE and the NAACP, remembered it in 1992, "Wherever in the United States there was a driving force for equal rights for blacks, American Jews were a part of it.... Wherever there was a fight to be fought, American Jews joined hands with African Americans to wage that battle." In 1994, Hugh Price, president of the National Urban League, recalled that among "whites of good will" no group "matched the Jewish community as long-distance runners in the civil rights movement." Stuart Svonkin's recent book, *Jews against Prejudice* (1997), makes a powerful case that at the national level the three major Jewish defense organizations—the American Jewish Congress, the American Jewish Committee, and the Anti-Defamation League—took strong positions supporting African-American civil rights and pushed for improved intercultural relations after World War II. In his *Portrait of American Jews* (1995), Samuel C. Heilman wrote of Jews that "except for African Americans themselves, it would be hard to find another ethnic group that so embraced the cause of civil rights." For civil rights activist and scholar Julian Bond, the civil rights movement represented "the highest and best collaboration between blacks and Jews toward a common goal." Most scholars working on the history of civil rights and ethnic relations have assumed the essential correctness of the views expressed by Farmer, Price, Svonkin, Heilman, and Bond.[2]

Yet these generalities about a historic black-Jewish alliance or coalition have never been subjected to detailed examination at the community level. Was this postwar period a "golden age" for blacks and Jews, as some have contended, or has the black-Jewish relationship been "romanticized and considerably exaggerated," as others have suggested? Have blacks and Jews always been "strangers to one another, more than popular liberal sentiment would suggest," as sociologist Peter I. Rose has written? Was the presumed black-Jewish alliance merely an expression of the positions taken by national organizations such as the American Jewish Congress and the NAACP, or did the idea of cooperative struggle filter down to activism at the community level? How did the black-Jewish relationship play out in the South, where segregation was deeply embedded in the local culture and where Jews were considerably less numerous than in the urban North and West? And how did the anticommunist hysteria of the McCarthy era affect black and Jewish civil rights activism? An examination of the civil rights movement in postwar Miami provides a unique vantage point for engaging these interpretive issues.[3]

In the postwar era, racial troubles threatened Miami's reputation as "America's playground"—the nation's top tourist destination at the time. Racial hatred and religious bigotry seemed powerfully intertwined in the South Florida city. The influence of the Ku Klux Klan prevailed in the Miami area into the 1950s. Institutionalized racial discrimination pervaded all walks of life. Similarly, anti-Semitism and patterns of Jewish exclusion persisted even as Jewish migration to South Florida surged and even as Miami Beach was becoming a predominantly Jewish resort. White supremacists and anticommunist redbaiters targeted both blacks and Jews in South Florida throughout the postwar period. In a southern city such as Miami, where both Jews and blacks remained outside the mainstream, one might expect to find significant evidence of common struggle against racism and bigotry. Miami, after all, was thought to be "south of the South" in more than just geography. Not surprisingly, Miami became an important civil rights battleground for blacks and Jews in the postwar years.[4]

JEWS AND BLACKS IN THE POSTWAR ERA

Most Americans think of the civil rights movement as coming to fruition in the 1960s, when the movement became increasingly militant and as the U.S. Congress enacted national civil rights and voting rights legislation. Less well known is the fact that by the mid-1940s, as historians Robert Korstad and Nelson Lichtenstein have written, "civil rights issues had reached a level of national political salience that they would not regain for another fifteen years." Historians now attribute the emergence of this early civil rights activism to a number of dynamic changes taking place in the nation at the time. For instance, the surging black migration from the rural South to the urban North during and after World War II loosened the constraints imposed by southern Jim Crow patterns. Participation in the war itself initiated major social transformations on the home front, as returning black veterans pushed for completion of the "Double-V campaign"—victory over totalitarianism abroad and victory over racism and segregation in America. Progressive CIO labor unions began organizing black industrial workers in the late 1930s and 1940s, encouraging black activism. President Franklin D. Roosevelt and the national New Deal stimulated urban liberalism and pulled most black voters away from the Republican party. The NAACP grew rapidly from fifty thousand members in 1940 to five hundred thousand in 1946, as the organization successfully challenged the legal bases of racial segregation in the courts. The African-American press and some black advocacy groups such as A. Philip Randolph's March on Washington movement demonstrated new levels of black militancy. Finally, specific federal policy decisions, such as the creation of the President's Fair Employment Practices Committee (FEPC) in 1941 by Roosevelt, the establishment of the President's Committee on Civil Rights in 1946 by Harry S Truman, and the desegregation of the armed services in 1950, also by Truman, had an important impact in setting the stage for civil rights activism in the 1950s. Signifying the postwar political drift toward a more liberal stance on race relations, the Democratic Party included a strong civil rights plank in its 1948 political platform. Moreover, President Truman addressed civil rights issues during his second term, but opposition from southern Democrats and conservative Republicans in Congress made any legislative advance virtually impossible at the time. In retrospect, Truman's most lasting legacy on civil rights may have been his several appointments to the U.S. Supreme Court, helping shift the Court's balance toward judicial activism.[5]

Important advances in civil rights took place during and after World War II, but the postwar period also brought renewed racial bigotry and anti-

Semitism. Discrimination against Jews seemed on the increase, declared the National Jewish Community Relations Advisory Council in a 1946 study of fifteen cities. In the early years of the Cold War, as the *American Jewish Yearbook* put it in 1947, the old line pro-Nazi groups were "involved in their own post-war reconversion," seeking now to link Jewish liberalism and black civil rights activism with communism. Ku Klux Klan leaders, in particular, had developed close connections to American fascist groups in the 1930s and early 1940s, documented at the time by investigative journalists such as John Roy Carlson, Stetson Kennedy, Carey McWilliams, E. A. Piller, Dorothy Roberts, and Harold Preece. It did not take long for these extremist groups to reorganize after the war, focusing on white supremacy, anti-Semitism, and anticommunism. As Jesse B. Stoner, a Klan leader from Tennessee put it in a 1945 interview with Preece, "Anti-Semitism and white supremacy go hand in hand."[6] Cold warriors spouting white supremacy and religious bigotry became especially prominent in the South, where politicians and race-hate groups targeted the NAACP and other organizations working for improved race relations as representative of all that was dangerous and threatening to white, Christian America.[7]

The powerful anticommunist campaign of the early Cold War years helped to undercut the promising civil rights gains of the 1940s. In his book, *Nightmare in Red* (1990), historian Richard M. Fried put it bluntly: "The rise of anticommunism inspired a new caution among mainstream civil-rights leaders." The FBI, according to legal scholar Frank J. Donner, played an especially important role in the 1950s in discrediting the civil rights movement "by linking it with subversion." As historian Athan Theoharis has written, in reports to President Eisenhower in the mid-1950s FBI director J. Edgar Hoover portrayed the NAACP and the civil rights movement generally as being manipulated and influenced by communists in significant ways. Government and public support of domestic anticommunism gradually declined in the late 1950s, but the FBI continued its own form of "underground McCarthyism" into the 1960s, with civil rights activists remaining prime targets of investigation and harassment.[8]

To defend themselves against red-baiting, the national offices of the NAACP, the Urban League, and CORE took strong anticommunist positions during the 1950s. These groups refused to work with alleged communist-front groups, and in some cases they adopted lower profiles on civil rights and civil liberties issues. Similarly, as Edward S. Shapiro has written in a study of American Jews since World War II, "the Jewish establishment was careful to distance itself from the Jewish left and to make sure that Jewish communal leadership rested safely in the hands of staunch anti-communists." Stuart Svonkin noted that each of the major Jewish defense organizations adopted an "aggressive anti-communism" by 1950 and initiated anticommunist purges of their own ranks. These moves increasingly marginalized the Jewish left after 1945 both nationally and at the local level. Whether these mainstream black and Jewish groups served as "the left-wing of McCarthyism," as has been suggested, is debatable, but the anticommunist surge slowed "the momentum of change" and retarded the early civil rights movement.[9]

The civil rights alliances between African Americans and American Jews extended back to the beginning of the twentieth century. Prominent Jews were among the white liberals who helped organize the NAACP in 1909 and the National Urban League (NUL) in 1911, although white Protestants predominated in those early years. By the 1920s, however, increased levels of anti-Semitism motivated liberal Jews to take a more active role in civil rights organizations, especially evident in financial support for the NAACP. During the 1920s and into the 1930s, moreover, some black and Jewish leaders challenged racial stereotypes and developed, as historian David Levering Lewis has noted, "strategies of overt and covert mutual assistance" to achieve group acceptance and assimilation. These impulses led, for example, to NAACP legal challenges to segregation in schools, housing, and public accommodations, and to NUL campaigns for black economic advancement. Throughout this early period, the "civil rights Jews," as Lewis calls them, had become an integral part of the movement for racial betterment.[10]

The modern civil rights alliance between blacks and Jews built upon two other historic traditions. During the 1930s, CIO industrial unions began organizing black workers. Left-wing Jewish activists dominated interracial labor organizing in many industries. Jewish-led unions such as the Amalgamated Clothing Workers and the International Ladies Garment Workers Union took strong stands on civil rights issues. The Jewish Labor Committee, founded in 1934, worked with labor and with black organizations such as the NAACP to promote interracialism. Leaders of major CIO unions such as the United Auto Workers in Detroit committed their unions to racial equality and shop-floor integration. The CIO packinghouse, rubber, electrical, and steel worker unions took similar positions on fair employment practices. By 1942, the CIO had established its own Committee to Abolish Racial Discrimination in organized labor, although it had little authority except moral suasion. During World War II, the National Maritime Union conducted a campaign against racism among its members. When the CIO launched "Operation Dixie" in the late 1940s, left-wing organizers unionized southern black and white industrial workers *and* promoted black civil rights. In Philadelphia and New York City, although some white bus and streetcar workers resisted, the Transport Workers Union supported black hiring and pushed for civil rights legislation. Especially in New York City, writes historian Clayborne Carson, "an Afro-American-Jewish-radical community survived occasional internal conflicts during the 1930s, 1940s, and 1950s to become a seedbed for civil rights activism during the 1960s." Black leaders such as A. Philip Randolph and Bayard Rustin helped to hold this interracial alliance together during those decades.[11]

The black-Jewish civil rights alliance also stemmed from the decisive embracement of equal rights by the mainstream Jewish defense organizations. As Cheryl Greenberg has written, the "overlapping goals and interests" of blacks and Jews "converged in a particular historical moment" at the end of World War II. The 1945 report of the politically moderate American Jewish Committee, for instance, asserted that discrimination against any group in America represented a threat to all. Anti-Semitism could not be eliminated, the AJCommittee contended, until all forms of "anti-minority and illiberal attitudes" had been extinguished. This linkage of anti-Semitism and racism was a powerful motivating force for liberal Jews throughout the nation. In Los Angeles, a local Committee for Negro-Jewish Relations made the same point in a 1953 report: "The oppression of the Negro people, economically and politically, is a main prop for the anti-Semitic forces in our land. It must concern us because the gospel of racism and the brutalizing of the Negro people brutalizes in turn those who allow such things in their midst." Similarly, the Anti-Defamation League (ADL) in the late 1940s and 1950s intensified its efforts to combat all forms of discrimination and bigotry, as did the National Jewish Community Relations Advisory Council, an important umbrella group representing many Jewish mainstream organizations. In 1947, the Central Conference of American Rabbis, through its Commission on Justice and Peace, took a public stand against racial hatred, advocated FEPC legislation at the state and national levels, and called for federal laws outlawing lynching and poll taxes. In many cities, Jews took the lead in neighborhood fair-housing committees and in supporting open-housing legislation. By mid-century, both locally and nationally, the campaign against racial injustice emerged as a major effort among leaders of Jewish organizations.[12]

Few such agencies were more energetic in this postwar campaign against racism and segregation than the left-leaning American Jewish Congress. In the immediate aftermath of the Holocaust, the AJCongress seemed determined to challenge all expressions of minority-group discrimination. In 1944, the AJCongress established the Council on Community Interrelations to fight anti-Semitism and promote better relations with other groups. A year later, the organization founded its Commission on Law and Social Action, which aggressively challenged all forms of intolerance and discrimination. The commission worked through the court system, especially at the state level, to achieve precedent-setting judicial decisions on civil rights and civil liberties. The AJCongress and the NAACP worked together after 1945 in making annual studies of civil rights and group relations, as well as in pursuing legal strategies to combat segregation and discrimination. In the early 1950s, when the NAACP came under attack from political right-wingers, and when southern legislatures sought local NAACP membership lists in the hunt for alleged communists, the national AJCongress rushed to defend civil liberties and the freedom of association. During this period, the AJCongress had more attorneys working on civil rights issues than the entire Civil Rights Section of the U.S. Department of Justice. The intensification of anti-Semitism and racial bigotry in the early Cold War era brought the major Jewish agencies into the forefront of the civil rights movement.[13]

National Jewish organizations actively worked for civil rights goals, but aside from cooperative work of the NAACP, black groups generally seemed less committed to supporting the Jewish struggle against anti-Semitism. As Robert G. Weisbord and Arthur Stein have noted, blacks "spoke not with one voice, but with many" on black-Jewish relations. Indeed, historian Leonard Dinnerstein has documented a deeply embedded anti-Semitism among some African Americans dating back to the nineteenth century. However, some influential blacks recognized the mutual interests of the two groups in the postwar era. Blacks and Jews clearly experienced different degrees of oppression, but black writers in the 1940s such as L. D. Reddick urged cooperative alliances in the common struggle against racism and bigotry. In 1946, in an influential article in the Jewish monthly *Commentary*, black psychologist Kenneth B. Clark pleaded for "candor about Negro-Jewish relations." Clark noted the many "real or imagined grounds for mutual antagonism" between blacks and Jews. Hostilities often stemmed from poor relationships between landlords and tenants, and between storekeepers and consumers. In the South, Jewish merchants and businessmen accepted segregation, and Jim Crow policies applied in Jewish hospitals and other institutions; even many northern Jews held stereotypical attitudes about blacks. Nevertheless, Clark urged blacks and Jews to move beyond narrow group loyalties and combine their efforts "to rid society of the virus-like affliction which is one man's hatred of other men."[14]

The black press often echoed Clark on the commonality of black and Jewish domestic concerns. For instance, in the decade after World War II the *Chi-*

cago Defender and New York's *Amsterdam News* urged cooperative struggle against racism and discrimination by members of the two groups. Similarly, *Pittsburgh Courier* columnist Joseph D. Bibb often praised Jewish support for the black civil rights struggle in the late 1940s. "The Jews are the best friends that the colored man in America has," Bibb wrote in 1947. "We seldom see the Swedes, the Poles, the Italians and Irish people projecting themselves with the same active interest into our problems as we see the Jews." Despite real mutual antagonisms and patterns of black anti-Semitism, a multifaceted but loosely linked black-Jewish civil rights alliance involving national organizations, local community leaders, intellectuals, and journalists seemed well-established by the postwar era.[15]

ANTI-SEMITISM AND RACISM IN POSTWAR MIAMI

During the decades spanning mid-century, Miami developed something of a schizophrenic character. The city exhibited many aspects of Deep South views on issues of race relations, labor organizing, and federal power. The city's tourist economy and its many transplanted northerners conveyed the sense that Miami was more politically and socially liberal than the rest of Florida. Nevertheless, white supremacy and anti-Semitism remained deeply embedded in the South Florida metropolis. In the 1930s, the Miami area had at least three active anti-Semitic organizations—the American Defenders (1934), the National Citizens League of America (1937), and the White Front (1939). These groups embraced Nazi ideology, attacked the New Deal (often referred to as the "Jew Deal"), denounced communism as the "Red-Jew menace," and supported American fascists such as William Dudley Pelley and Father Charles E. Coughlin. One of these Miami anti-Semites was Frank Pease, the self-styled "commander" of the ultra right-wing and militaristic American Defenders. From his home in Coral Gables, Pease published anticommunist and anti-Semitic pamphlets in the 1930s, developed links to the Ku Klux Klan in the 1940s, and, according to one "informant," hung a photograph of Hitler in his living room. He sought to "keep America white," called for abolition of the Fifteenth Amendment to the Constitution, and supported the criminalization of the "atrocious crime" of interracial marriage. Anticipating anti–civil rights strategies of the 1950s, Pease's fanatical American Defenders program combined anticommunism, anti-Semitism, and racial superiority and separation.[16]

Miami's White Front mirrored Pease's American Defenders and described itself as "a militant anti-Jewish society, defending the White Race and the Stars and Stripes." Modeled on Hitler's storm troopers, the group's uniforms included brown riding boots, khaki shirts and riding breeches, and wide Sam Browne belts. The Khaki Shirts of America, a proto-fascist paramilitary organization from the early 1930s with strength in Philadelphia, New York, and Baltimore seems to have provided the inspiration for Miami's White Front. William Blanchard, the group's leader and editor for a time of an anti-Semitic magazine called *Nation and Race,* boasted to reporters of "a 24–point program one of which stresses the fact that Jews are one of the nation's principal problems." In March 1939, a White Fronter distributing literature and staging "a one-man anti-Semitic demonstration" was slugged with a lead pipe during a street-corner confrontation with Jewish opponents. Blanchard's White Front articulated an aggressive anti-Semitism in the 1930s, but restrictive real estate covenants and widespread discrimination against Jews in Miami hotels and clubs suggested a much more widespread pattern of anti-Jewish thought and behavior.[17]

Miami's White Front had anti-Semitic allies in the local Ku Klux Klan. Florida investigative journalist Stetson Kennedy contended in the 1940s that the White Fronters and the Klan were one and the same in Miami. A few months after the White Front street battle of March 1939, Miami's John B. Gordon Klan, named after a Confederate general from Georgia, publicly opposed admission to the United States of twenty thousand Jewish children seeking refuge from the Nazis. In the early 1940s, the Klan's national newspaper, *The Fiery Cross,* approvingly printed a list of "Gentiles Only" hotels on Miami Beach, hinting that "there must be good reason for the policy." The anti-Semitism of the Klan had deep roots in the organization's past, but it also reflected a wider pattern of discriminatory action that continued for years in the Miami region.[18]

Miami area hotels routinely discriminated against Jews in the mid-century decades. "Always a View, Never a Jew," one ocean-front Miami Beach hotel promised in the early 1940s. In 1949, after lobbying by Jewish war veterans, the Miami Beach city council passed an ordinance outlawing such discriminatory signs, but discrimination continued in more discreet ways. By the early 1950s, according to an ADL survey, hotel discrimination in Florida had declined, especially in Miami Beach. Yet, the ADL survey revealed that 20 percent of Beach hotels still prohibited Jews. In 1960, the *Jewish Floridian* published a list of Miami area hotels that continued to bar Jews. Even as late as 1969, these patterns of anti-Semitism persisted, as demonstrated in a report on the subject published by the Greater Miami Chapter of the American Jewish Committee. However, the fact that even in the mid-1950s most Miami and Miami Beach

Jewish hotel owners barred African Americans suggested the contradictions involved in the black-Jewish relationship in South Florida.[19]

An organized white terrorism campaign designed to maintain the color line paralleled the anti-Semitism directed against Miami's Jews. Using violence and intimidation, the Miami police department enforced white supremacy throughout the first half of the twentieth century. In the 1940s, one black Miamian recalled, policing in the black community "consisted of a reign of brutality. Beatings and killings by the white police officers were common place." Other blacks reported that "these policemen liked to see blood run; they were overly aggressive," and that "there was a great deal of promiscuous killing, and they [the police] had no respect for Negro life at all." Through fear, brutality, and violence, the Miami police upheld the color line on a daily basis well past mid-century.[20]

The Ku Klux Klan also played a role in upholding white supremacy. By the late 1930s, Miami had sprouted a number of separate KKK klaverns, complete with women's auxiliaries, that periodically demonstrated and burned their trademark crosses in the city. When Miami's Negro Voters League organized black voters to participate in local nonpartisan elections in 1939, the Klan turned out in force to exclude blacks from politics. On election eve, the Klan organized a massive downtown rally, followed by a Klan motorcade through black neighborhoods. Some of the seventy-five cars and trucks in the motorcade had thick hangman's nooses "dangling menacingly" from their windows. The Klansmen burned twenty-five crosses at one-block intervals in the black district and hung black effigies from lampposts, labeled with signs announcing that "This Nigger Voted." Leaflets were distributed with an ominous KKK warning: "Respectable negro citizens are not voting tomorrow. Niggers stay away from the polls." The police were nowhere in sight. Miami police chief H. Leslie Quigg had earlier refused to deny rumors about his own Klan membership. Despite the apparent Klan-police alliance, Miami blacks voted in unprecedented numbers in the 1939 municipal primary election.[21]

Reflecting national patterns, the Klan adopted a low profile in Miami during World War II, but roared back to life after 1945. As *Life* magazine put it in a 1946 article, the Klan came "out of wartime hiding" in the postwar period. The Klan's national imperial wizard, James A. Colescott, an Atlanta veterinarian, retired to Miami in 1945. Interviewed at his Miami home by an undercover journalist, Colescott conceded that he was looking for "something to do" in his retirement years. It was no coincidence that the KKK in Miami resurfaced at about the same time. By 1946, Miami's John B. Gordon Klan No. 5 was welcoming automobile travelers to the city with several huge highway billboards at the city limits. Dozens of cross burnings, and even a few house burnings, lit up Miami's night skies over the next few years, as the Klan sought to prevent African Americans from moving out of overcrowded central-city areas into nearby white residential neighborhoods. A year after his interview with Colescott, John Roy Carlson wrote in his book, *The Plotters* (1946): "I thought of Colescott when the fiery cross was burned in a Miami Negro neighborhood.... I thought of Colescott when a road sign brazenly appeared on the outskirts of Miami inviting the bigoted to join the ranks of the postwar hate klan. I thought of Colescott when the *Miami Herald*... unwittingly ran an advertisement: 'The KKK welcomes you. Write Glenwood Heights. P.O. Box 337, Miami.'" After numerous cross burnings in racially changing neighborhoods, the Miami correspondent for the *Pittsburgh Courier* reported in 1947 that these cross burnings "signalled the beginning of a concerted Ku Klux Klan drive" to keep blacks out of white areas. As was true in Atlanta, Tampa, and other southern cities, the Klan drew membership from the local police department, which helps to explain the absence of police during cross burnings and the vigorous police enforcement of the color line.[22]

The Ku Klux Klan remained dangerously active in Florida throughout the 1950s, as segregation came under attack from blacks, progressive whites, and the federal courts. Two explosive events in the 1950s—a wave of dynamite bombings in 1951 and another bombing in 1958—symbolized the ways in which racial and religious bigots violently targeted Miami's blacks and Jews. The 1951 bombings grew out of a controversy at a white-occupied apartment complex named Knight Manor located in the Edison Center section on the fringes of Miami's black Liberty City neighborhood. When the owners—two real estate developers profiting from the racial turnover of Miami neighborhoods—began renting part of the complex to blacks, white homeowners' groups became outraged. The Klan interjected itself into the controversy, distributing hate literature and participating in protest motorcades through the area. Leaving little to the imagination, the Klan torched giant wooden Ks around the black apartment section of Knight Manor (cross-burning violated a 1951 Florida law, thus the resort to burning Ks).[23]

Nevertheless, blacks continued moving into Knight Manor, now renamed Carver Village. The failure of Klan intimidation eventually led to a series of bombings—massive dynamite blasts on September 22, November 30, and December 2, 1951, that left portions of Carver Village virtually unlivable. Bombers also targeted Jewish institutions on several occasions in 1951, as dynamite explosions damaged several Miami area Jewish synagogues and a Hebrew school. The bombed-out Carver Village buildings, one Jewish leader noted, had been desecrated with "offensive signs in German, praising Hitler and the Ku Klux Klan." One of the synagogue bombings came simultaneously with the December 2 explosion at Carver Village.[24] Miami's December 1951 bombings also roughly coincided with the Christmas Day murder-by-bombing of statewide NAACP leader Harry T. Moore in the small, central Florida town of Mims.[25]

The *Southern Patriot*, a liberal magazine published by the Southern Conference Educational Fund, labeled the Florida bombings a "reign of racist terror." Most observers linked the bombings to the coordinated work of white hate groups, especially the Ku Klux Klan. Bill Hendrix, grand dragon of the Florida Klan, denied involvement. "It wasn't us. Maybe it was the Commies," Hendrix told the *Miami Daily News*. Miami police chief Walter Headley also portrayed the bombings as "part of a Communist plot to incite racial hatred." Ira D. Hawthorne, president of the Dade County Property Owners Association, and later linked to the Klan, offered a similar analysis: "As these colored groups don't have enough support, they will do their utmost to drag our Jewish brother in to help them support their own cause. And it looks to me personally, like they are falling right in line with a Communistic group." A year later, a federal grand jury indicted several members of the John B. Gordon Klavern for perjury in connection with the Miami bombing investigation. The indictments charged that they lied to FBI agents in denying any association with the Klan or the Hialeah "sports club" that served as a front for Klan activities. One of the alleged perjurers was Helen Russell, a former vice president of the Edison Center Civic Association, who had denied meeting with Klansmen to discuss ways of keeping blacks out of Knight Manor apartments. Russell had earlier organized the white-protest motorcade through Edison Center. The grand jury interviewed one hundred witnesses and took thirty-two hundred pages of testimony, but no arrests were ever made for the Miami bombings. As if to explain the lack of progress in the investigation, in 1953 the grand jury reported that "Dynamite leaves no traces. . . . It destroys clues along with life and property." Eventually, the perjury charges against Russell and three Klansmen were dismissed. Nevertheless, the Moore killing and the Miami bombings demonstrated as late as the 1950s the willingness of some of Florida's racial and religious bigots to use bombs and violence to intimidate Jewish newcomers and enforce white supremacy.[26]

Even more insidiously, segregationists and race-hate groups such as the Klan charged that blacks and Jews engaged in a dangerous, un-American communist conspiracy. Florida Klan leader Hendrix set the tone. Soon after the Miami bombings, Hendrix launched a campaign for the Florida governorship. His political rallies seemed more like Klan meetings, Stetson Kennedy wrote, "with plain clothed kleagles filtering through the crowd to hand out klan application blanks and collect klectoken (initiation) fees." Not surprisingly, Hendrix had ties to law enforcement officials. In March 1952, he spoke at a meeting of Florida sheriffs and outlined the following program: "No Negroes in white schools; protect all Florida peace officers against attacks by Communist Negro organizations like the NAACP, and return the beaches stolen by the Jews at Miami Beach." Hendrix campaigned against Miami Jews as much as against any political opponent. If elected, he promised that he would dispatch "every bulldozer in the state road department down to Miami Beach to rip out the sea walls and give the beaches back to the Gentiles." The message was clear: blacks, Jews, and the left represented a threat.[27]

RACE RELATIONS AND SCHOOL INTEGRATION IN THE 1950S

Race relations in South Florida changed only imperceptibly during the 1950s, despite shifting population patterns. The population of metropolitan Miami grew by 89 percent to 935,000 during the 1950s, mostly as the result of an early Sunbelt migration. Jewish migration from the Northeast made up a substantial portion of that increase: the Miami area's Jewish population rose dramatically from 16,000 in 1945 to about 140,000 in 1960. The black population kept pace, more than doubling between 1950 and 1960 to 137,000, mostly as a result of migration from Georgia and other southern states. Blacks and Jews each made up about 15 percent of metropolitan Miami's total population in 1960.[28]

Despite population growth and diversity, racial segregation, religious bigotry, and right-wing paranoia persisted. As Ed Cony of the *Wall Street Journal* reported in 1958 in a long article on Miami race relations, "Miami is deep in Dixie geographically and many of its roots are Southern." Most transplanted northerners seemingly adapted to southern racial practices, and few spoke out against segregation. Cony quoted one Miamian on this subject: "The Yankees who come down here are often more prejudiced against Negroes than the natives." Racial issues heated up quickly after the 1954 U.S. Supreme Court decision outlawing segregated public schools. Building on the intensity of the school issue, the white citizens' council movement flourished in Miami, claiming more than fifteen thousand members. Something of a new Ku Klux Klan in disguise, these white citizens' councils distributed segregationist and anti-Semitic literature, resisted school integration, and generally stirred race hatred throughout the 1950s and after.[29]

As the white citizens' councils began organizing grassroots opposition to school desegregation, the Florida legislature was launching a McCarthyite witch-hunting campaign, looking especially for communists in the Miami NAACP. Established in 1956, the Florida Legislative Investigation Committee (FLIC) targeted the Miami NAACP because its legal challenge to continued school segregation in Dade County threatened to unravel Florida's deliberate efforts to keep blacks and whites out of the same schools and classrooms. Miami NAACP vice president Ruth W. Perry explained the issue in a 1958 letter to Roy Wilkins, executive secretary of the national NAACP: The FLIC, Perry wrote, "centered their activity mostly in the Miami area because of our school suit, and later our bus and golf suits. Again there is no doubt in my mind that this committee was set up for the express purpose of putting the NAACP out of business in Florida, and to try to seriously cripple the Miami branch because we have an integrated membership." The Miami NAACP fought back in the courts, frustrating the legislative red-hunters who sought its membership lists, but the organization remained a consistent target of Florida's white supremacists. Segregationists and integrationists both assumed the centrality of Miami to Florida's resistance to civil rights.[30]

Right-wingers and racists continued to target Miami Jews during the civil rights and school integration wars of the 1950s. In 1954 a Dade County anti-communist grand jury investigation headed by state's attorney George Brautigam subpoenaed 138 witnesses, all but 3 Jewish. As Deborah Dash Moore noted in her study of Jews in Miami and Los Angeles, *To the Golden Cities* (1994), "Jews increasingly recognized that in Miami anti-communist investigations were designed to thwart desegregation." The red-hunters targeted left-wing Jews who always seemed to be at the forefront of the tiny minority of white Miamians pushing for racial change. For example, a small number of Miami-area Jews involved in progressive groups such as the American Veterans Committee and the American Civil Liberties Union, along with a few local rabbis, publicly supported school integration. In 1960, local businessman Jack D. Gordon, one of those Jewish activists, ran for election to the Dade County school board.[31]

The 1960 school board campaign polarized Miami. Gordon's opponent, Republican businessman Arthur A. Atkinson, conducted a "Christian Crusade" supporting the continuation of Bible-reading in the Dade County schools. This issue had come to a head because the Florida ACLU, of which Gordon was a founding member, had just filed a law suit on behalf of several Jewish parents (including Gordon's sister-in-law, Thalia Stern) challenging the constitutionality of prayer and Bible-reading in the schools. The American Jewish Congress in Miami had joined the litigation as well, a decision that divided the Miami Jewish community. The political fallout from the Bible-reading litigation came quickly. Gordon, who advocated school integration, was accused by opponents of "paving the way for atheism and then Communist teachings by first destroying all vestige of faith in the Almighty." One of the Christian crusaders later admitted to a Miami rabbi that they really didn't think that Gordon was a communist, but that they did not "want another Jew on the School Board." However, most Miamians recognized the interlocking nature of the Christian crusade and the battle over school integration. That Gordon was an active member of the local branch of the Congress of Racial Equality, which had been conducting lunch counter sit-ins for more than a year, also played into the calculations of the conservative anti-integrationists supporting Atkinson. Gordon fought back effectively, keeping the focus on integration and even urging local rabbis to discuss school issues in their synagogues before the election. Despite the vicious McCarthyite smear campaign unleashed by Gordon's opponents, voters sent him to a four-year term on the Dade County School Board and then elected him again in 1964. During the fifties and sixties, Gordon put a public face on Miami's Jewish activism, but he also absorbed a considerable degree of right-wing anger and hostility, including bomb threats.[32]

Many of Miami's progressive Jews also worked in the political campaigns of a young Democratic state legislator from Dade County, John B. "Jack" Orr, the only state-level politician who spoke out forcefully in favor of school integration in the mid-1950s. Orr was triply damned by Miami right-wingers: he was a member of the Miami NAACP, the Florida ACLU, and the Florida Council on Human Relations, an affiliate of the racially progressive Southern Regional Council. As an attorney, and at some risk to his legal career in the city, Orr had challenged Miami's anticommunist ordinance on behalf of a Miami Beach Jewish activist, Al Rosenberg. Subsequently, Orr represented local Jewish communists jailed in the Brautigam investigation. Throughout the fifties, Orr provided legal representation to such left-liberal groups as the Civil Rights Congress and the Women's International League for Peace and Freedom. Orr was white, Christian, and a member of a well-connected Miami family—his father had been mayor of Miami and he himself would later win election as mayor of Dade County. His stand on school integration drew vicious attacks in legislative campaigns in 1956 and 1958. In an openly political letter to all Dade County rabbis in September 1958, Jack Gordon reported on the right-wing vilification of Orr: "John Orr placards have been defaced with the Jewish star scrawled on his face and the hammer and sickle on his name. A note sheet has been distributed throughout South Miami Beach accusing John B. Orr and several members of the rabbinate as being radicals who are allied in an effort to bring Negroes to Miami Beach."[33]

Orr's links to the Miami NAACP were especially damaging to his 1958 legislative campaign. The FLIC investigation of the NAACP was in full swing at the time. The Miami NAACP's legal challenge to school segregation stirred up angry white parents who supported the racial status quo. David Eldridge, Orr's conservative opponent in the Democratic primary election, played the race card effectively. The NAACP's Ruth Perry, who analyzed the election campaign for the national office, reported that "Eldridge used all the tricks of the trade, and pulled out all the old red herrings and played all the southern bourbon music he could find. . . . Both Orr and the NAACP were dragged through the political mud, with the usual red tinge, the extremist slant, and the 'would you want your daughter' theme developed to the utmost." Given the racially charged atmosphere in Miami at the time, Orr's stand in support of school integration and his connections to Miami's black and Jewish activists dictated his political defeat in 1958.[34]

Not surprisingly, given the time and place, the perceived left-wing Jewish connection with the school integration campaign led to still another Miami bombing. In March 1958 a powerful dynamite blast damaged the religious school at Miami's Temple Beth-El, revealing once again the links between white supremacy and anti-Semitism. Moments after the 2:30 a.m. bomb explosion, the rabbi of another Miami synagogue was awakened by a phone call and warned that his temple would suffer the same fate if he did not stop preaching integration. The Miami police department also received a telephone message, promising more bombings if Miami's school integration plans were implemented. According to a police report on the bombing, the caller threatened that "if this integration doesn't stop, we will kill all the Jews." Police agencies suspected "activist extremists in the segregation movement," but no arrests were ever made. Similar bombings and attempted bombings occurred in 1958 in Atlanta, Jacksonville, Nashville, Birmingham, and Charlotte, suggesting that throughout the South violent segregationists identified Jews with school integration. A "Confederate Underground," later linked by investigators to the Florida Ku Klux Klan, claimed responsibility for some of these attacks; its leaflets promised "Regular bombings . . . Negroes and Jews our Specialty."[35]

In a 1958 *Commentary* article on the Miami bombing, Nathan Perlmutter of the Florida Anti-Defamation League interpreted the incident within the larger context of southern "massive resistance" to desegregation. The school integration issue had energized the Klan and the anti-Semites, who held large rallies throughout Florida, supported segregationist political candidates, and distributed masses of hate literature attacking "Jewish Kommunist Kremlin Kikes." As Perlmutter suggested, this hate campaign emphasized "that it is the Jew and not the Negro who threatens Southern ways." The *Miami News* charged that the temple bombings in Miami and elsewhere were not coincidental, but part of an organized "reign of terror planned for the South by the White Citizens Councils." Journalists had already demonstrated that the leadership of the Florida Klan and the white citizens' councils were one and the same. Telephoned bomb threats against Dade County synagogues continued into 1959. Massive resistance to civil rights and school integration in the 1950s underlay the intensification of anti-Semitism and racial conflict in Miami and elsewhere.[36]

The Miami bombings of 1951 and 1958 represented the work of dangerous extremists who jointly targeted blacks and Jews. However, the mid-century racist and anti-Semitic thinking that underlay the bombings extended deeply into Florida's still heavily white, Protestant, southern, and segregationist culture. These attitudes can be traced in extensive files of letters from ordinary citizens in the archived papers of Florida's governors during the 1950s. After the Miami and Mims bombings of 1951, for instance, Governor Fuller Warren received dozens of letters attacking the NAACP as a dangerous communist, anti-American organization. Race-haters also targeted Jewish groups such as the Anti-Defamation League. The ADL, one correspondent charged in a 1951 letter to Warren, was "a trouble maker, a race and hate breeder of the first rank, pro-communist and anti-Christian." As for the Carver Village and synagogue bombings in Miami, "A Lover of the South" wrote: "Dear Governor don't let that annoy you, whoever was behind that, had some reason. It keeps unruly niggers and scheeneys in place." The Miami bombings prompted similar expressions from a third correspondent: "The Jew has already ruined the northern cities and wishes to invade the South.... They are teaching Communism to the colored people, and inciting rioting through them.... They think if the colored riot and get the upper hand in the South they can move in." Typically, the bigotry expressed in these letters linked white racism, anti-Semitism, and anticommunism—a powerful combination in the South and in the United States generally in the 1950s.[37]

These attitudes persisted even at the end of the 1950s. Governor LeRoy Collins had been twice elected as a moderate segregationist in the mid-1950s, but in a televised speech in 1960 he came out in support of lunch counter integration—a political turnabout that unleashed a torrent of racial hatred.

One Miamian bitterly complained that "the South is now on the cross, being crucified by the northern political mobs, by the NAACP, by the subversive Supreme Court and Eisenhower administration, and by the Red sponsored and financed sit-downs at lunch counters." Florida, this writer disapprovingly predicted, would soon "become the haven of equality for all peoples." "The Communists, NAACP and the Jews," a Miami woman charged, were promoting "the mongrelization of the White race." Still another Miami woman, who claimed to be a "former moderate" on race relations, wrote that "K.K.K. has begun to develop a strange appeal." Jews were attacked with particular relish—they created and financed the NAACP, sympathized with the Soviet Union, participated in a communist plot for "stirring up the negro," and promoted "race-mixing." Moreover, everyone knew that "every Jew organization in the country is behind the integration of the races." Others who wrote Governor Collins blasted the NAACP as a communist agency and called Thurgood Marshall and Martin Luther King, Jr., "disciples of the Kremlin." The "left-wingers," "one-worlders," and "Zionist-Jews" sought to "destroy America . . . and the white race everywhere." Another wrote: "In my opinion Florida is on the way out as a pleasure resort due to the heavy influx of Jews, Niggers, Cubans and Porto Ricans [sic]."[38]

In retrospect, the degree of racial hatred and religious bigotry in Miami as late as 1960 seems shocking. As the nation's leading vacation playground and tourist destination at the time, Miami was supposedly more northern and less southern, more progressive in its politics and social relations. On matters of intergroup relations, however, the reality rarely matched the image. Indeed, as Bella Fisher, a Jewish civil rights activist, noted with careful understatement as early as 1948, "Though on the surface Miami seems to have a more cosmopolitan population than most of the South, . . . progressives here are more prudent about activities which are accepted in other areas." A decade later, local librarian Ruth Perry, a white integrationist and NAACP officer, offered a similar and succinct analysis in a newspaper column: Miami had "an appearance of more liberality and freedom than actually exists." Miami, Perry wrote to the NAACP's Roy Wilkins in 1958, "isn't as liberal as we thought."[39]

JEWISH RESPONSES: FEAR, APATHY, AND ACTIVISM

Given the hostile racial climate of postwar Miami, in which Jews and blacks were targeted and victimized, and in which both groups were jointly smeared with the same allegations about anti-Americanism and communist conspiracies, one might expect to find a strong collaborative response. Indeed, an activist civil rights alliance among some Jews and some blacks did emerge in Miami in response to patterns of postwar bigotry and racism. However, this activism remained very much a minority movement among both groups. Most in both communities no doubt sympathized with civil rights goals and supported curbing racist and bigoted thought and behavior, but sympathy did not always lead to action. In fact, the atmosphere of repression and fear substantially curbed civil rights activism. The oppressive spirit of the postwar red scare in Miami and in Florida generally meant that relatively few Jews or blacks spoke out, stood up, or took action against discrimination or segregation in those years. Those who did so in the Miami Jewish community tended to be newcomers from northern cities, most on the political left. Among the blacks, church leaders and northern migrants, along with a few on the militant left, played similar roles in challenging segregation.

Miami's early civil rights alliance found expression in the work of some Jewish defense organizations and in the actions of individual Jews. For instance, Miami chapters of the Anti-Defamation League and the American Jewish Congress, both in place by the end of the 1930s but not yet professionally staffed, mirrored the positions of their national organizations. Members of both groups spoke out against anti-Semitism and the Ku Klux Klan throughout the 1940s. Burnett Roth, an ADL activist, attorney, and Miami Beach city councilman, helped outlaw discriminatory signs in his community aimed primarily at Jews. In 1951, Roth successfully pushed anti-Klan legislation in the Florida legislature that banned masks and cross-burning. The Miami branch of the National Conference of Christians and Jews denounced Klan cross burnings in black neighborhoods and fought racial bigotry as early as 1946.[40]

Further to the left, the Jewish-dominated Miami chapter of the American Veterans Committee (AVC), a progressive alternative to the conservative and racially exclusive American Legion and Veterans of Foreign Wars, welcomed black veterans as members in the late 1940s, held interracial meetings and dinners, and actively challenged segregation in mid-century South Florida. Jewish AVC members subsequently took leading roles in numerous activist Miami organizations, including the Civil Rights Congress and the Congress of Racial Equality. In the early 1950s, Jewish women in the Miami branch of the Emma Lazarus Federation, an ultra-leftist group linked to the communist-dominated International Workers Order, worked on civil rights issues and held rallies challenging the Brautigam red-hunting investigations. Liberal and leftist Jews dominated the activist work of the Miami branches of the American Civil Liberties Union (ACLU), the Women's International League for Peace and Freedom (WILPF), and the National Council of Jewish Women during the 1950s.

The Miami ACLU (later renamed the Florida Civil Liberties Union) had been founded in 1955 in response to the attack on left-wing Jews by the Brautigam investigators. In 1960, women from the Greater Miami section of the National Council of Jewish Women organized a local affiliate of the National Organization of Women for Equality in Education, an anti-segregationist group. Miami NOW, as it was called (not to be confused with the feminist National Organization for Women founded in 1966), worked energetically across racial lines to keep the Dade County schools open at a time when local segregationists and many in the state legislature threatened to shut them down.[41]

Jews predominated among the few white people in Miami advocating racial justice in the repressive postwar era. A few leftist Jewish lawyers worked with the NAACP on police brutality cases in the late 1940s. Some Jewish women and a few rabbis joined the NAACP in the early 1950s and worked on voter registration projects. A few Miami rabbis advocated civil rights and school integration in sermons, workshops, and synagogue study groups, although congregations usually divided on such issues. Black physicians integrated the medical staff at Mount Sinai Hospital on Miami Beach in 1952. Several Jewish-owned Miami Beach hotels and restaurants desegregated in the mid-1950s, although some others maintained discriminatory policies.[42]

By 1960 leaders of Miami's mainstream Jewish organizations were working closely with racially moderate political leaders such as Mayor Robert King High of Miami and Governor LeRoy Collins on matters concerning race relations. In particular, the Governor's Commission on Race Relations sought the expertise and advice of Miami's Jewish agency leaders in achieving the peaceful desegregation of restaurants and public accommodations in the city in 1960. On other more controversial issues, such as schooling and housing, little was done and segregated patterns persisted. Jews dominated among Miami's small group of white civil rights activists all through the postwar era.[43]

Yet the record remains mixed. Despite the power and persistence of bigotry and racism, most Miami Jews with mainstream political allegiances rarely involved themselves in civil rights activities. Despite the large size of Miami's Jewish community by the 1950s, only a relative handful of Jews worked actively for black civil rights. According to a critical 1951 report by a national AJCommittee official, Miami Jews generally "share[d] the feelings of other Southern whites" and could not be counted on to "support programs on behalf of Negroes which Jews in Northern cities heartily endorse." As historian Cheryl Greenberg has written, "As part of their struggle to avoid marginalization and discrimination, southern Jews adopted as much as possible their region's social mores." Postwar Miami experienced a huge migration of northern Jews, but the repressive politics of the time and legitimate fears of anti-Semitic backlash, such as the synagogue bombings of 1951 and 1958, seemingly dampened for most the traditional Jewish patterns of political activism and social involvement.[44]

The reluctance to get involved in civil rights activism extended to most Miami synagogues, which remained silent on the issue for most of the 1950s. In 1955 the *Miami Herald* conducted a survey of the city's religious institutions, seeking to determine what churches and synagogues were "doing about integration." Only one Miami rabbi responded to the survey, and his response suggested little in the way of a Jewish-black civil rights coalition or even much understanding of the southern integration dilemma. As the *Herald* noted, the rabbi "pointed out that integration is no problem in the synagogues since there are very few Negro Jews."[45] A few rabbis did speak out, but the fear of bombs and violence helped to enforce a voluntary silence on issues regarding racial justice before 1960.

On the national scene, Jews were active at high levels of the NAACP, and Jewish fund-raising helped support the organization, but there were few parallels at the local level in South Florida. Miami's black leaders of the NAACP and the National Urban League kept their distance from counterparts in the American Jewish Congress and the Anti-Defamation League. With the exception of the Civil Rights Congress and the Congress of Racial Equality, two cases to be discussed shortly, Jewish activists and black activists rarely engaged each other, and they mostly conducted their civil rights activities in separate white and black public spheres.

Jews in the Miami area, as in the rest of the American South, often disagreed about how far and how fast to push on civil rights, and even whether they should push at all. Many southern Jews believed that supporting racial integration would disturb Jewish-Gentile relations, produce an economic backlash against Jewish merchants, and stimulate anti-Semitism. Others asserted the line of national mainstream organizations such as the ADL and the AJ-Committee that an attack on any group was an attack on all. These issues were hotly debated at a 1955 meeting of Miami-area Jews sponsored by the socialist Jewish labor group, the Workmen's Circle. Speakers denounced segregation, but most also adopted a "super-cautious, super-gradual approach" to racial change. Miami Beach was "the most Jewish city in U.S.," a speaker from the Jewish Labor Committee in New York noted, but on civil rights matters he recommended "Don't be first, don't act alone, but join with other groups moving in the right direction." A Miami ADL speaker urged caution, warning the Miami Jewish community against "running too far ahead of the rest of the state and thus nullifying its influence." But a few years later, in June 1958, when the AJCongress held its national convention in Miami Beach, keynoter Sidney Holland of Baltimore delivered an ominous message: Southern Jews, Holland warned, should have "learned by this time that the strategy of silence, of being neutral while the fight for desegregation rages, simply does not buy protection from bombs." Holland's views were endorsed by another AJCongress convention speaker, Martin Luther King Jr., who urged Jews to stand up against the "Hitlers loose in America," segregationists who "make no fine distinctions between the Negro and the Jew."[46]

Even as late as 1959, the Florida ADL still was debating what it called "The Segregation Issue: Its Effects on Southern Jews." By that time, Miami and Miami Beach ADL leaders supported the idea of integration, but they still had not gotten beyond talking about the issue. They never directly pursued activist strategies to confront segregation within their own community. Discussing the same issue, the Miami branch of the AJCongress took a similar verbal stand: "We have no Mason-Dixon line morality in the American Jewish Congress." But at a 1959 meeting of the Greater Miami Jewish Federation, a Jewish federation leader urged Miami Jews to "go slow on integration" to stave off rising anti-Semitism. According to a *Miami Herald* survey, Miami Jews in the mid-1950s believed that school integration should not be "pushed through hot-headedly," because it would create "ill will between the races."[47]

Most southern Jews, perhaps reluctantly, held back from civil rights involvement. As Greenberg noted, "The vast majority of southern Jews, regardless of their personal political beliefs, avoided any involvement in civil rights despite the emergence and intensification of the struggle in the South." Other historians of the American Jewish experience such as Leonard Dinnerstein and Marc Dollinger have also emphasized the distinct differences between northern and southern Jewish positions on black civil rights. Dollinger contended, for instance, that "Southern Jews had been acculturated into an American culture foreign to their northern coreligionists." Civil rights agitation in the South by northern Jews threatened southern Jews' fragile niche in southern society, and even their physical safety. "Southern Jewish survival demanded acceptance of the status quo," Dollinger concluded. Clive Webb's book, *Fight against Fear: Southern Jews and Black Civil Rights* (2001), tempers these arguments somewhat, suggesting a more complex response to the struggle for racial justice. Webb agreed that most southern Jews had been "intimidated into silence by anti-Semitic extremists" during the civil rights era, but that a "conspicuous minority," especially religious leaders in larger southern cities, did speak out and take action.[48]

The Jewish experience in Miami mirrored that of the rest of the South in numerous ways. In a hostile environment where violence was not unknown, civil rights issues posed difficult choices for Miami Jews. Many chose inaction and silence. But Miami was also different from the rest of the South. The enormous postwar Jewish migration from the North brought to Miami a sizable contingent of Jews on the left—liberals and radicals, socialists and communists, retired labor union activists, social workers, teachers, and journalists. Newcomers to the South, they were invariably shocked by the racial practices they encountered in Miami. Unwilling to accept racial segregation quietly, a minority of Jews on the left worked openly for civil rights and racial justice.

However, the anticommunist hysteria of the late 1940s and 1950s injected a new and unsettling element into the Miami civil rights struggle. Red-baiting and race-baiting converged in postwar Miami. The new red scare in Florida, and in the South generally, persisted into the early 1960s, long after the national anticommunist surge had subsided, partially because of the furor over school integration. Reporting on the South in 1959, *The Progressive* magazine noted: "McCarthy never caught on down here back in his heyday, but as the last ditch fight for segregation grows more desperate, all his ugly techniques are revived." In the mid-1950s, both Dade County and the Florida legislature set up witch-hunting, anticommunist investigations that slowed civil rights and progressive reform generally. These investigations targeted especially Miami's small, left-liberal Jewish community and the Miami NAACP.[49]

As on the national level, mainstream black and Jewish organizations in Miami went on the defensive during that period, seeking more to demonstrate their patriotism and anticommunism than to push for civil rights and civil liberties. The NAACP and the Urban League appeared cautious and conservative, hoping to avoid the broad-brush communist smear. Similarly, Miami's major Jewish defense organizations sought to distance themselves from the Jewish left and the so-called "civil rights Jews," thus evading the red-baiting that had already weakened the NAACP. Under the circumstances, the civil rights efforts in Miami of two other organizations, both led by young, activist Jewish women, seem all the more remarkable. The work of these two women—Bobbi Graff of the Civil Rights Congress and Shirley Zoloth of the Congress of Racial Equality—suggests that in Miami the most persistent and the most forceful black-Jewish civil rights alliance involving interracial activism was the one on the political left.

THE CIVIL RIGHTS CONGRESS IN MIAMI

In 1946, Matilda "Bobbi" Graff and her husband Emanuel arrived in Miami. Originally from the Brownsville section of Brooklyn, they had moved to Detroit by 1941. Both came from left-wing, immigrant Jewish families, active in socialist, Zionist, and trade union circles. Bobbi Soller's parents were socialists and Zionists. Her father, a strong unionist and a member of the socialist Workmen's Circle, worked in New York City's needle trades and became active in the Amalgamated Clothing Workers Union. Her mother, a house cleaner, participated in the depression-era rent strikes conducted by New York's unemployed councils. Bobbi's socialist training began early in an "after school" Yiddish school in Brownsville. As a high school student in Brooklyn, she took a leading role in the left-wing American Student Union and her school's peace council. Emanuel Graff's parents were also labor Zionists, his father an organizer in the New York City Waiters Union in the 1930s. A painter by trade, Emanuel became a war-production worker in the Detroit auto plants during World War II. He also worked for interracialism as a shop steward in the auto workers union. In Detroit, the Graffs joined the Young Progressives, as well as other left-wing groups such as the Michigan Civil Rights Congress. By this time, they had both come to the attention of the FBI, which periodically tracked their political activities.[50]

Soon after the war, because of their child's health problems, the Graffs moved to Miami, where Bobbi's parents had recently settled. As she later wrote, South Florida at the time seemed to be a tourist "fantasy land," but she quickly discovered the reality of Miami—"a growing metropolis where segregation, discrimination, and blatant racist terror [were] the law." The Graffs soon developed an interracial circle of friends, mostly left-wing Jews and blacks, most of whom were involved in some form of activism: progressive politics, civil liberties and civil rights, world peace, and labor organizing. The Graffs went back to Detroit for a time in 1947, but returned to Miami in 1948. By this time, they had joined the Communist Party and become active in the Miami branch of the Civil Rights Congress, a left-wing group that appeared on every official list of subversive and communist-front organizations.[51]

The Communist Party since the 1920s had advocated racial equality in the United States, targeting African Americans for their revolutionary potential and denouncing segregation, in part for propaganda purposes. However, communists in the labor movement and in civil liberties groups demonstrated a commitment to civil rights that most Americans at the time did not share. As historian Harvard Sitkoff has suggested, the communists "publicized the evils of racism and the benefits of integration to a far greater extent than any other white organization." They also "sparked and financed civil rights groups whose radicalism made the established Negro organizations more militant in their tactics and yet more respectable to the American mainstream." Mark Naison, a historian who has written about blacks and communists in New York City, made a similar point: "No racial organization in twentieth century America had greater success in uniting black and white working people around common ends or in mobilizing white workers to fight racial discrimination." Gerald Horne, another scholar who has explored the links between blacks and the left, concluded that the Communist Party played "a major role in disintegrating the stolid walls of Jim Crow." American Jews were overly represented in the Communist Party and in communist-front organizations, suggesting an important component of the early civil rights alliance between blacks and Jews.[52]

Organized in Detroit in 1946, the Civil Rights Congress (CRC) reflected the racial justice positions of the Communist Party. The CRC grew from a merger of three separate left-wing groups that had focused on racial equality, civil liberties, and labor rights: the National Negro Congress, the International Labor Defense, and the National Federation for Constitutional Liberties. William L. Patterson of the International Labor Defense, a black labor lawyer and civil rights activist, as well as one of the nation's leading communists, emerged as the national executive secretary of the CRC in 1948. Building on the already established structure of the National Negro Congress, the CRC eventually established local and regional branches in thirty-three cities to pursue its advocacy of civil rights and civil liberties. Although Patterson never hid his membership in the Communist Party, he always denied that the CRC was a communist-front group. Rather, he focused on its devotion to racial equality and human rights.[53]

Around the country, branches of the CRC fought housing and employment discrimination, exposed police brutality, and forged alliances with progressive labor unions and black neighborhood groups. In a recent study of the CRC in postwar Los Angeles, historian Josh Sides noted that "the CRC pursued a bold strategy for African-American civil rights." In Detroit, historian Edward Pintzuk wrote, the Michigan CRC challenged police brutality against blacks, organized mass demonstrations for black economic opportunity, and defended the civil liberties of activists. In his book on the CRC, *Communist Front?* (1988), Gerald Horne contended that in pursuing both mass action and legal action

Patterson and the CRC fought for racial justice and confronted the anticommunist hysteria of the postwar period more forcefully than any other group.[54]

In Miami and Miami Beach, a vibrant political left had developed by the late 1940s among secular Jews. The huge migration of Jews to postwar Miami included socialists, communists, and assorted left-wingers as well as mainstream liberals. They belonged to such groups as the socialist Workmen's Circle, the communist International Workers Order, and the Jewish People's Fraternal Order, also communist. Jewish radicals often gathered at the secular Jewish Cultural Center, established on Miami Beach by the latter organization, for concerts, lectures, political discussion groups, Jewish cultural activities, Yiddish language and literature classes, and a children's secular Sunday school. At its peak, the center had more than six hundred members. Mainstream Jews had their own Jewish Community Center, also on Miami Beach, but its programs lacked the heavy political orientation of the Jewish Cultural Center. Not surprisingly, given the political climate in Cold War Florida, left-wing programs at the Jewish Cultural Center came under attack in the Miami press as early as 1948—a form of red-baiting that led to the formation of the Miami branch of the Civil Rights Congress.[55]

Jewish activists established the Miami Civil Rights Congress in April 1948. Its organization stemmed from left-wing Jewish involvement in a local civil liberties case—an illegal search and seizure at the home of Leah Adler Benemovsky, who had been targeted by the FBI as a suspected communist. Benemovsky had earlier arranged a highly publicized visit to Miami by Elizabeth Gurley Flynn, one of the leading communists in the United States. Hauled before a grand jury, Benemovsky asserted her constitutional rights and refused to answer questions about her political beliefs or activities. For her silence, Benemovsky was sentenced to ninety days in jail for contempt. She was brilliantly defended by the progressive Pensacola attorney John M. Coe, who got her out of jail on $500 bail and then successfully appealed Benemovsky's conviction to the Florida Supreme Court. This early witch-hunt outraged and mobilized the Jewish left in the Miami area, one outcome being the organization of the CRC. Most white CRC members, including the Graffs, were Miami and Miami Beach Jews with leftist backgrounds, almost all of whom were recent migrants to Miami from the Northeast and Midwest.[56]

The Graffs were joined in the Miami CRC by several CIO labor organizers and black radicals. These included Charles Smolikoff and James Nimmo, who had been organizing shipyard and laundry workers, respectively, during the war years. Nimmo was a black Bahamian immigrant to Miami who served in the U.S. Army during World War I. Angered by the racism he confronted on his return to Miami from military service in France, where black soldiers were treated with respect, Nimmo joined Marcus Garvey's black nationalist organization, the Universal Negro Improvement Association (UNIA). In the 1920s, Nimmo rose to a leadership position in the Miami chapter of the UNIA, which had a large following among the city's black immigrants from the West Indies. By the 1940s, Nimmo had joined the Communist Party, begun organizing black and white laundry and dry cleaning workers, and participated in numerous local civil rights efforts.[57]

Smolikoff, too, was a communist labor organizer. Like Graff, Smolikoff was born in Brooklyn, moving to Miami for health reasons in 1937. His early political involvements in Florida included working in support of Republican Spain and the communist-linked American Peace Movement. By the late 1930s, according to a subsequent state investigation of subversive activities in Florida, Smolikoff was said to be "the leading Communist in the Miami area." During the war years, Smolikoff wrote for a radical labor paper in Birmingham and engaged in CIO organizing among black and white shipyard workers in Miami. Eventually, he helped the Miami local of the CIO's Industrial Union of Marine and Shipbuilding Workers of America win a union election in 1943 and then a contract with the Miami Shipbuilding Corporation. By that time, Smolikoff had been appointed the CIO's regional director for Florida. In the postwar years, Smolikoff and Nimmo organized airline industry workers in Miami, first at Pan-American Airways and then at Eastern Airlines, as racially integrated units of the CIO's Transport Workers Union (TWU). Because of their leftist connections and their interracial organizing, both Smolikoff and Nimmo had been harassed regularly by the FBI, the Miami police, and the Ku Klux Klan.[58]

The formation of Miami's CRC branch coincided with the 1948 national election, when civil rights issues surged to the surface in the Democratic party. The Democratic platform for the first time contained a strong civil rights plank. More congenial to the Miami radicals, however, was the Progressive Party campaign of Henry A. Wallace, which advocated civil rights, world peace, and a variety of progressive social programs. During the 1948 presidential campaign, CRC people in Miami joined with political activists in the Florida Progressive Party, headed by Pensacola attorney John M. Coe. In Miami, the two groups had nearly identical membership, and they shared a Miami office for several years. Bobbi Graff, James Nimmo, and CRC activist Gail Gropper, among others, became energetic campaign speakers for the Progressive Party in Miami, meeting with black and white church groups, organizing political rallies, and canvassing voters. The Florida Progressive Party hoped to appeal to black voters and took strong stands on anti-lynching and anti-Klan legislation. Miami's Progressive Party members had a lot of enthusiasm, even getting out some twelve thousand people for a major campaign speech by Wallace in Miami's downtown Bayfront Park. However, in Florida and nationally, the communists had virtually taken over the Progressive Party by the time of the election, dampening its appeal to those on the noncommunist left. The Florida Progressive Party ultimately failed to produce much support for Henry Wallace in the presidential election, especially among black voters.[59]

Wallace lost decisively, but Miami's Progressive Party activists persisted into the early 1950s, working on civil rights issues, housing reform for blacks, and civil liberties for leftists. Nimmo chaired a Progressive Party club in the downtown black community. In 1949, the Progressive Party put up a black trade unionist, O. L. Nickerson, for a seat on the five-member Miami City Commission. Nickerson garnered some twenty-two hundred votes, ranking twelfth among twenty-five commission candidates. Meanwhile, a Jewish progressive, Alfred P. Rosenberg, mounted a losing campaign for a seat on the Miami Beach City Council. Represented by Jack Orr, Rosenberg later filed a law suit challenging Miami's communist registration ordinance. For a time, the Progressive Party put out a newsletter, *Miami Progressive,* and a newspaper, *The Florida Progressive,* both contesting the red hunt in South Florida. The Progressive Party's stand on racial justice posed a challenge to segregation and white power in Miami. Not surprisingly, the party's interracial political meetings and campaigns led to harassment by the Miami police and threats from the Ku Klux Klan.[60]

As the Miami Progressive Party gradually faded away in the early 1950s, local radicals increasingly focused on the CRC. Although an active member of the Miami CRC from the beginning, the energetic Bobbi Graff had become the unofficial coordinator of the group by 1949. It was not an easy assignment in conservative and segregationist Miami in the late 1940s, when the Klan was riding high and civil liberties had little meaning to the Miami police. A handful of local communists and progressives, mostly Jews and a few black radicals, formed the core of Miami CRC. The basic strategy of the CRC, building on the labor defense experience of William L. Patterson, was "mass action" such as public meetings, rallies, and picketing to draw public attention to a cause, combined with legal action to defend civil liberties. The essential goal, as Patterson asserted in 1949, was "to expose the policy of jim-crowism and segregation which dominated the policy of government to the Negro people, which the government enforces through terror and violence."[61]

Miami CRC initially kept busy dealing with several police brutality cases in the black community, providing bail and attorneys, and exposing the police department to the glare of publicity. With CIO allies in the labor movement, Miami CRC helped organize a Greater Miami Right to Work Committee that fought Jim Crow policies in local labor unions, especially the building trades. Bobbi Graff's husband, Emanuel Graff, a painting contractor at the time, played a major role in the labor organizing campaign. At the same time, CRC members Smolikoff and Nimmo were engaged in interracial organizing among Miami's airline and airport workers—workers in a new postwar industry that seemed open to interracial unionism. Miami CRC also defended the right of Miamians to hold interracial demonstrations, meetings, and parties. When the CRC's youth group, the Paul Robeson Club, held such an interracial affair in 1948, the Miami police quickly arrived, broke up the party, divided those in attendance by race, arrested some for inciting a riot, and sent the others packing. Miami CRC continued to push this issue, publicly announcing such affairs to the press and noisily demanding an end to police harassment.[62]

Graff and Miami CRC also worked hard between 1949 and 1951 in publicizing the racial injustice of the infamous Groveland case. In this case, despite flimsy evidence against them, four young black men had been accused of raping a white woman in rural central Florida in 1949. One of the blacks was killed by a sheriff's posse during a manhunt, while white mobs terrorized the Groveland black community and burned several black homes. Two years later, another of the accused blacks was shot and killed by the notorious Lake County Sheriff Willis McCall while being transported to a legal hearing. A third young man, only sixteen years old at the time of the original incident, was given a life prison term. The fourth man received a death sentence, later commuted to life in prison. The national offices of both the NAACP and the CRC quickly entered the case, which was widely publicized as a form of legalized lynching. The two groups, in fact, were competing with one another to provide legal defense for the accused, with the NAACP ultimately winning that battle. Nevertheless, Miami CRC responded quickly to the original Groveland incident, holding mass meetings, lobbying public officials, and communicating with the wider public through leaflets, newspaper articles, and radio programs. Graff wrote a hard-hitting, front-page article for the left-wing *National Guardian* that placed the Groveland case in the larger context of race and labor relations in the central Florida logging and paper-mill industry.[63]

The Groveland case dragged out over several years. The same racial tensions in central Florida that produced Groveland also contributed to the bombing death of statewide NAACP leader Harry T. Moore and his wife in December 1951. In both instances, the Ku Klux Klan in the Orlando area had stirred up racial animosity and unleashed racial violence. In response, Graff and Miami CRC brought the struggle against the Klan into the local churches and into the black community. When a federal agent from the U.S. Attorney General's office arrived in Miami in 1949 to investigate left-wingers in the local labor movement, Miami CRC pressed him on Klan violence and intimidation. To drive home its point, the CRC delegation arrived at its meeting with the Justice Department official carrying "the cross that was burned last week before the home of a Negro minister." Miami CRC encouraged the Florida legislature to outlaw the Klan, lobbied Governor Fuller Warren (a former Klansman himself), and held several interracial rallies against the Klan at the very time the racist group seemed at the peak of its influence. At the height of the Groveland battle, Graff proposed that Miami CRC picket the Klan offices in Orlando, widely believed to be the center of much of Florida's racial violence. That anti-Klan demonstration never took place, but by mid-century Miami CRC had become the Klan's most vigorous and outspoken opponent in South Florida.[64]

When focused on a cause or a case, such as the Klan or the Groveland killings, Miami CRC was effective in publicizing civil liberties and civil rights issues. But in the midst of the postwar anticommunist hysteria, Miami's CRC chapter had its problems. Pressured by FBI and police interrogators, one active member, Victor Emanuel, resigned, recanted, and exposed the CRC in 1949 as a communist-front group in the local press. The *Miami Daily News* subsequently launched a vicious red-baiting crusade—a witch-hunt that lasted for several years and targeted especially the civil rights and interracial activities of Miami CRC. Federal agents investigated and newspaper reporters publicly hounded activist CRC members such as Graff, Smolikoff, and Nimmo. Identified by the press as a communist agent, Graff was followed around town by FBI agents and her telephone was tapped for several years. Late in 1948, the TWU fired Smolikoff, as the national union cleaned out communists and distanced itself from the left. Miami witch-hunters later jailed Smolikoff after he invoked the Fifth Amendment during a local grand jury investigation of communist subversion. When the Florida Supreme Court ordered his release, Smolikoff sought refuge in Mexico. Threatened and harassed by the FBI, James Nimmo eventually became an informer and then left Miami for much of the 1950s.[65]

The attacks on Smolikoff and Nimmo were part of a larger anticommunist crusade that shaped the political culture of the postwar era. National anticommunist legislation provided the red hunters with the legal tools they needed to neutralize the left. For instance, the Alien Registration Act of 1940, also known as the Smith Act, required the registration and fingerprinting of aliens (on the theory that most communists and radicals were dangerous immigrant non-citizens), and it also outlawed seditious speech. Rarely applied until the late 1940s, the Smith Act was supplemented by the Internal Security Act of 1950, also called the McCarran Act, which required the registration of communists and communist or communist-front organizations. It also established the Subversive Activities Control Board, a federal agency designed to harass and expose suspected communists. Finally, the Communist Control Act of 1954 placed further curbs on communist activity, especially in labor unions. Similar laws were passed at the state and local level. Miami, for example, enacted a communist registration ordinance in 1950. All of these laws were subject to protracted litigation and court review. Their chief consequence was a dampening of leftist activity, which seems to have been their primary purpose in the first place. In addition to anticommunist legislation, the House Un-American Activities Committee (HUAC) and the Senate Internal Security Subcommittee were extremely active throughout the period. Jeff Broadwater, author of *Eisenhower and the Anti-Communist Crusade* (1992), noted that "the main purpose of the congressional witch-hunting committees had long been the exposure of Communists, not legislation." Taken together, these anticommunist measures made the work of left-wing civil rights advocates such as those in Miami CRC difficult and dangerous.[66]

Not surprisingly, the anticommunist crusade of the McCarthy era seriously undermined the effectiveness of Miami CRC. As Graff noted, "The red-baiting has had a very bad effect on the progressive community." Several CRC members were "frightened off" and resigned from the group. Internal divisions among the small CRC membership over issues of strategy and direction were common, and the group often became "dormant" for months at a time. Graff had difficulty in getting Miami CRC as a group to link the labor-organizing work with "the political struggle for civil rights." The Groveland case produced, as Graff wrote to Patterson, "a terrific [internal] fight on whether CRC should initiate a fight." Internal conflicts took their toll, but the attack from the right was even more damaging. Florida in the McCarthy era did not offer fertile ground for civil rights workers, particularly those on the far left. By mid-1950, Graff noted that local witch-hunters had intimidated "progressive forces" in the city and that Miami CRC was "practically non-existent. . . . Our numbers are decreasing and very few replacements."[67]

Internal divisions within Miami CRC and consequent diminishing activism caused some alarm at CRC's national office. The problem, Patterson assistant Milton Wolff wrote to James Nimmo, was that Miami CRC had emphasized "the so-called intellectual middle class crowd" and failed sufficiently to enlist

Miami's black and white working classes in the civil rights cause. The fact that both Graff and Nimmo were simultaneously engaged in other "progressive" work—Nimmo in CIO labor organizing and Graff with the Progressive Party—diminished CRC's focus and energy. It "has watered down your effectiveness in the CRC considerably," Wolff contended to Nimmo in March 1950. Wolff urged Miami CRC to conduct a "block-to-block and house-to-house" organizational and educational campaign. Lacking membership and suffering anticommunist intimidation, Miami CRC failed to follow through on Wolff's suggestions. Patterson soon was urging Graff to "do everything possible to get some activities developing there under leadership of CRC."[68]

Miami's white, Jewish CRC activists also had problems working with some leaders in the black community. At the national level, from its inception in 1946 the CRC had been engaged in an increasingly bitter rivalry with the NAACP. While William Patterson was willing to cooperate with the NAACP on various issues, national leaders of the NAACP wanted nothing to do with the leftist CRC. (Ironically, Patterson and NAACP president Roy Wilkins lived on the same floor of the same Harlem apartment building at the time.) Sometimes these rivalries filtered down to the local level. As the Groveland case unfolded in 1949, for instance, the local branch of the NAACP resisted open cooperation with CRC people, fearing press, police, and Klan repression. The Miami NAACP, a discouraged Graff wrote in 1949, was "in very bad condition . . . [with an] 'Uncle Tom' leadership which wants no participation in any kind of struggle." Graff described some of Miami's black leaders, including a few with the NAACP, as "vicious red-baiters" opposed to all forms of interracial activity. What Graff did not know was that NAACP officials in New York had warned the Miami branch to avoid cooperation with the CRC on the Groveland case.[69]

Lack of a concerted interracial push on civil rights partially stemmed from the weakness of the Miami NAACP during those mid-century years. The organization had a small membership in the late 1940s and early 1950s. Internal divisions and frequent leadership turnover diverted energy from the civil rights struggle. Moreover, the local NAACP was very much a top-down organization run by a few prominent leaders, with little in the way of a mass-action tradition. By contrast, the CRC was committed to public action but lacked clearly defined leadership roles. On issues such as the Groveland case, Miami CRC responded quickly and instinctively, whereas the Miami NAACP seemed cautious, even plodding, in response. Only in 1954, when activist black preacher Theodore R. Gibson assumed a leadership role, did the Miami NAACP begin to develop into a consistently forceful agency for civil rights advocacy. By that time, the CRC was gone from the South Florida scene.⁷⁰

Before Gibson took control of the Miami NAACP, Graff and CRC people worked much more effectively with the statewide Florida NAACP office, headed by Harry T. Moore, a relentless civil rights advocate who often had to be reined in by his superiors in New York City. Indeed, until his murder by Klan bombing in 1951, Moore was considered a troublesome activist by NAACP headquarters. At the same time, white segregationists considered him "the most hated black man in the state of Florida." Under statewide NAACP auspices, Moore founded the Progressive Voters League of Florida in 1944 to register and organize black voters throughout the state. The national office worried that Moore's effectiveness was undermined by his joint activities as a NAACP representative and as a political activist who often endorsed liberal candidates in state and local elections. In 1948, Moore encouraged black support for Henry Wallace's Progressive Party campaign, a position that the national organization found troubling. A former school teacher, Moore was also ahead of the NAACP national office in the 1940s in pushing several teacher salary equity cases in the Florida courts. Shortly before his assassination, as a consequence of NAACP concerns about Moore's political activities and his fund-raising practices (he raised more money for the Florida branch than for the national office), NAACP leaders orchestrated his removal from his paid position as executive secretary of the Florida office. Within weeks of his death, embarrassed by their treatment of Moore, the NAACP launched a public campaign lionizing him and praising his civil rights activism.⁷¹

Lack of cooperation with the Miami NAACP was not Miami CRC's only problem. The repressive political climate of Cold War Florida had even more significant consequences, and by the end of 1950, Miami CRC seemed on the verge of extinction. As Graff put it in a letter to Patterson, "The progressive movement in Miami is very slowly recovering from a bad case of the hysteria jitters." The jitters continued and intensified. Fear spread on the Miami left as a result of the Rosenberg spy case, the arrest and prosecution of many other left-wingers, and the powerful surge of domestic anticommunism, partially spurred by the Korean War. William Patterson of the national CRC was indicted on trumped-up charges of failing to file papers for himself and the national CRC under the McCarran Act. By mid-1951, after continuous red-baiting in the press and harassment by the FBI, Miami CRC had been driven underground. "Even the few progressive forces we have won't come near us," Graff wrote to Patterson in May 1951, "for fear that anything touched by us will only mean a smear and all that goes with it by the local press." By that time, Miami had a communist registration act and a form of "grass-roots McCarthyism" had emerged in South Florida.[72]

Fear, harassment, and repression led to the demise of Miami CRC. By mid-1951, Graff and her remaining colleagues disbanded the group. Subsequently, Graff and a few others joined the Miami NAACP, hoping to work from within to move the organization to a more activist role. For a time in the early 1950s, Graff chaired several NAACP committees and headed a voter registration campaign, while also continuing her efforts on the Groveland case, this time from a new base in the NAACP. But the NAACP itself soon came under increasing attack as a procommunist group, partially undermining its emerging sense of activism and militancy.[73]

A campaign against the Miami leftists paralleled the attack on the Miami NAACP. In March 1954, the Senate Internal Security Subcommittee held anticommunist hearings in New Orleans, searching out southern radicals, especially those associated with the Southern Conference Educational Fund (SCEF). The Senate committee grilled attorney Leo Sheiner and building contractor Max Schlafrock, two of Miami's Jewish CRC activists, tarred them as communists, and ruined their careers in Miami. As the House Un-American Activities Committee prepared for hearings in Miami in the fall of 1954, a local grand jury investigation simultaneously targeted Miami's former CRC activists and others on the political left, almost all of them Jewish. The national left-wing press, including *The Nation*, the *National Guardian*, and the *Daily Worker*, came to the defense of Miami's radical Jews, but Jewish mainstream organizations in Florida and elsewhere remained intimidated and silent.[74]

The attack from the anticommunist and segregationist right substantially slowed the early civil rights struggle in Miami. Along with several dozen other Jewish activists, Emanuel Graff went to jail for contempt of court after invoking the Fifth Amendment at a local grand jury hearing. Bobbi Graff was next on the witch-hunters' list of suspected communists. Subpoenaed in a hospital maternity ward after delivering a child, she soon left Miami under an assumed name to escape a jail term. When the Florida Supreme Court later ruled the jailing of the Miami CRC leftists unconstitutional, Emanuel Graff rejoined his wife in Canada, where they sought refuge from the McCarthyism of Cold War Florida. Many other CRC activists found quiet exile in Mexico, some remaining for decades. Attorney John M. Coe, who successfully defended the jailed Miamians, noted at the time that local McCarthyites in Miami had embarked on a "reign of terror"—a vicious smear campaign that destroyed an early interracial civil rights alliance between Jews and blacks on the left. Reflecting on these events nearly fifty years later, Graff noted in an interview that "our biggest crime was bringing blacks and whites together."[75]

THE CONGRESS OF RACIAL EQUALITY IN MIAMI

About the same time the Graffs were being driven out of Miami, Shirley and Milton Zoloth arrived in Miami from Philadelphia. Like the Graffs, the Zoloths came from socialist-labor and left-liberal family backgrounds. Milton's parents immigrated to the United States from Russia toward the end of the nineteenth century. His father was a stonecutter in the tombstone business and a member of the socialist Workmen's Circle. A photograph of Karl Marx hung on the wall in their home. Milton had been a member of the Young People's Socialist League and remembered as a young man voting for socialist presidential candidate Norman Thomas. Shirley's parents were more liberal than radical, members of mainstream Jewish groups including the American Jewish Congress. Shirley moved somewhat to the left of her parents, joining the Women's International League for Peace and Freedom (WILPF) in Philadelphia and getting active in other groups. Like the Graffs, the Zoloths worked in Henry Wallace's Progressive Party presidential campaign in 1948. They supported civil rights causes and participated in interracial activities. Both Zoloths had been outraged by a 1953 HUAC hearing in Philadelphia and a subsequent anticommunist investigation of the city's school system, which led to the firing of several dozen teachers, mostly Jewish. By the time they moved to Miami in September 1954, the Zoloths had staked out political positions firmly on the progressive, noncommunist left.[76]

While the Graffs discovered a community of interest among communists and labor organizers, the Zoloths found a circle of noncommunist but still very progressive Jewish friends in Miami and Miami Beach. Within a week of moving to South Florida, Shirley Zoloth connected with progressives in the Miami WILPF. Headed by Bernice Ullrich, wife of a Unitarian minister, Miami WILPF had many Jewish members, including Bobbi Graff's mother, Fannie Soller, and many others previously involved in Miami CRC. In the early 1950s, the WILPF focused on peace issues, such as supporting the United Nations, promoting world disarmament, and working to end the Korean War. In fact, the WILPF branch in Miami emerged in 1952 from an earlier, loosely organized group called Southern Women for Peace. By 1954, when the Zoloths moved to Miami, WILPF was beginning to work on civil liberties, civil rights, and school desegregation issues. The civil liberties issue seemed especially pressing at the time, as Miami was in the throes of the local witch-hunt that had just driven Bobbi Graff and other radicals out of Miami. The FBI had already infiltrated Miami WILPF, and some of its members were being investigated and subpoenaed by the Brautigam grand jury probe. Zoloth was familiar with such matters, since Philadelphia had been through similar political inquiries. She impressed her new friends as highly knowledgeable and socially committed. After meeting Zoloth for the first time, Ullrich reported: "She entered into the discussion, having been thru the Phila. situation of the Velde [HUAC] attacks and was so helpful.... She seems well informed on the Civil Rights issue and is willing to dig in and work with us on it. She paid her dues for the coming year and seems like one of us already." Within a month, HUAC brought its road show to Miami for public hearings on communist activity in South Florida, and Zoloth was getting pulled into leadership roles with Miami WILPF, eventually serving as vice president of the organization.[77]

Miami WILPF absorbed some of Zoloth's activist energy during the mid-1950s. She also got involved with several other liberal and reformist organizations, including the Florida ACLU, the National Council of Jewish Women, the Women's Division of the American Jewish Congress, and the National Committee for a Sane Nuclear Policy (SANE), among others. However, most of her activism in the middle to late 1950s focused on school desegregation, the major social issue of the day in Miami and many other southern cities and states. As noted earlier, Miami's small left-liberal community coalesced behind John B. Orr's 1958 legislative reelection campaign. Orr had spoken out in the Florida legislature against school segregation, and he made this the primary issue in his campaign. Itching to help, Shirley Zoloth walked into the Orr campaign headquarters in Miami Beach one day and volunteered her services. It was a fateful decision, as the Zoloths met a number of like-minded Jewish liberals interested in desegregating Dade County schools, including Jack Gordon, Barbara Gordon, Thalia Stern, Leonard Turkel, Marilynn Bloom, Selma Rabinowitz, and a number of others, all principals in subsequent civil rights activity. The 1958 Orr campaign turned out to be a losing battle. Nevertheless, it had the effect of pulling together a formerly disparate group of Jewish activists into a small but cohesive group (one participant described it as a sort of "extended family") that took up many other social issues and political causes, including that of the Congress of Racial Equality (CORE).[78]

Issues of race relations dominated public affairs in Miami in the late 1950s. Florida had completely ignored the Supreme Court's 1954 school desegregation decision. Elected governor in 1956 on a segregationist platform, LeRoy Collins inched toward a more moderate position in the late 1950s. The Florida legislature, however, overwhelmingly supported segregation. White people were aroused over the prospects of school integration, and there was talk of closing the schools to prevent it. The legislature actually passed a "last resort" bill in 1957, permitting school closings if integration seemed imminent, but Governor Collins vetoed the measure. The school closing threat persisted into 1959, when Collins blocked more than thirty anti-integration bills considered or passed by the legislature. This was also the period during which a new rash of synagogue, church, and school bombings took place in Miami, attacks brought on by fears of school integration and accompanying residential transitions.[79]

Pushing hard for school desegregation in the late 1950s was the now more activist Miami branch of the NAACP, still under attack by the legislature as a communist-front group. Refusing to give up membership lists to the witch-hunting Florida Legislative Investigation Committee, Theodore R. Gibson of the Miami NAACP fought the issue through the courts and was finally vindicated in a 1963 U.S. Supreme Court decision. After the successful bus boycotts in Montgomery (1955–56) and Tallahassee (1956), the Miami NAACP threatened similar action. As it turned out, the NAACP eventually used legal challenges to end the Miami Transit Company's segregated bus system in 1957. Miami's NAACP and black community leaders also challenged school segregation, especially Florida's pupil assignment law, which had been designed to maintain the color line in public schools. Gibson and another NAACP leader, Dr. John O. Brown, requested that the school board assign their children to nearby white schools, and then sued the board when they were refused. When Roy Wilkins of the NAACP headquarters visited Miami in November 1958, he spoke to a large audience at the Bethel AME Church and urged black Miamians to "do more suing" to speed up desegregation. By the late 1950s, the NAACP represented the hopes and articulated the grievances of Miami's black community, but the organization still preferred the courts and negotiations to mass action or civil disobedience.[80]

Some on the left found the legalistic approach of the NAACP irksome and overly cautious. Advocating more direct methods of challenging segregation, the activists turned to other local organizations, such as the Florida Council on Human Relations (FCHR) and the Dade County Council on Community Relations (DCCCR). A state affiliate of the racially liberal Southern Regional Council, in 1957 the FCHR had moved its offices from Daytona Beach to Miami the better to pursue its goals of improved race relations and school integration. The DCCCR was a semi-official body established by the Dade County Commission after the 1951 Miami bombings. It was a large and unwieldy group that moved very slowly and also suffered from internal divisions. Miami WILPF had already tried to work with DCCCR in the mid-1950s, seeking action on school desegregation, but without result. As the school issue intensified in the late 1950s, DCCCR and FCHR worked together to calm the atmosphere and get people talking to one another in community discussion groups and neighborhood "coffees." These community meetings coincided with the 1958 Orr campaign, and some of the Orr people, including Shirley Zoloth, jumped into the DCCCR action. Orr's defeat and the imperceptible pace of racial change frustrated Zoloth and her activist colleagues. In October 1958, an intern at the FCHR met with Zoloth and later reported the outcome: "Met with Mrs. Milton Zoloth, member of DCCCR. Spent three hours with her attempting to convince her that violent action was not the Council's mode of operation. Unfortunately, I was unsuccessful in my attempt." Zoloth never advocated violence, but she was interested in direct, nonviolent action to confront racial segregation.[81]

Pursuing still another avenue of direct action on school desegregation led Zoloth, Thalia Stern, and Barbara Gordon to the Congress of Racial Equality. Within ten days of Orr's primary election defeat in September 1958, they contacted the national office of CORE. During the previous months of study and discussion with FCHR and DCCCR, they had read a CORE pamphlet about the school desegregation crisis in Nashville, where interracial teams of local CORE people escorted black students attending white schools integrated under federal court order. At about the same time, the Dade County school board ordered a study of the consequences of assigning a few black students to the all-white Orchard Villa Elementary School as a pilot project, "a possible place to start some form of integration." Subsequently, in February 1959, the school board decided to assign four black students to Orchard Villa, beginning the following September. The Orchard Villa neighborhood was in the process of racial transition at the time, and many thought the board's action represented a phony integration plan. But in September 1958, Zoloth and her friends anticipated that the school board would make a serious effort at school integration. They believed that if interracial teams of adults accompanied children to newly integrated schools, as CORE workers had done in Nashville, this might ease integration tensions, prevent white flight from transition neighborhoods, and maintain integrated enrollments. Thus, the Miami group sought CORE literature and requested that a CORE field worker be sent to Miami to help them organize.[82]

The Congress of Racial Equality was aggressively developing new local chapters in the late 1950s, especially in the South. Its executive secretary, James

R. Robinson, recognized the possibilities presented by the Miami women. As he wrote in response, "For several years I have been interested in Miami because it is strategic and yet basically not so intolerant as most cities of the Deep South; it is south of the South and could play an important role from that side." Given postwar Miami's deep racial conflicts, Robinson may have overestimated the degree of social amity and tolerance in South Florida. Robinson also contacted some of Miami's black leaders, trying to enlist their cooperation in a "grass-roots" Miami CORE and avoid any sense of competition with the local NAACP.[83]

The Congress of Racial Equality had been founded by activist students at the University of Chicago in 1942 as an outgrowth of a Christian pacifist group, the Fellowship of Reconciliation (FOR). Its organizers included James Farmer, James Robinson, Bernice Fisher, and others who subsequently played major roles in the civil rights movement with CORE and other groups. An interracial organization, CORE pursued racial equality through nonviolent, direct-action methods. Borrowing from the sit-down strike technique used by CIO unions in the 1930s, CORE challenged segregation through sit-ins and picketing of restaurants, theaters, and public accommodations in Chicago and other northern cities in the 1940s. It conducted an early "freedom ride" through the South in 1947, when sixteen CORE and FOR members boarded Greyhound and Trailways buses to test southern compliance with a 1946 Supreme Court decision that banned segregation in interstate bus and train travel. Several of the freedom riders were arrested and jailed in North Carolina. The "Journey of Reconciliation," as the activists called the bus trip, brought nonviolent civil rights tactics into the South for the first time, setting a precedent for subsequent challenges to southern Jim Crow legislation. The Congress of Racial Equality appealed to an intellectual, secular elite of both races, but failed to gain mass support from African Americans in the 1940s. The organization maintained a low profile during the McCarthy era, but surfaced again by the mid-1950s, when FOR and CORE activist Bayard Rustin played an advisory role in the early months of the Montgomery bus boycott. As the attack on segregation heated up in the late 1950s, Martin Luther King Jr. helped mobilize the black religious community through the use of nonviolent resistance, giving it a mass appeal. As a pioneer in Gandhian nonviolent resistance, CORE and its direct-action methods had a growing appeal to black and white civil rights activists in the North and South. Thus, the initiative to CORE from Zoloth and her friends came at a decisive moment, just as civil rights issues and mass-action, nonviolent methods were emerging in local communities around the nation.[84]

The field secretaries for CORE—Gordon R. Carey and James T. McCain—

found fertile ground in Miami when they arrived for organizational work in February 1959. "Thalia Stern and Shirley Zoloth are a couple of fireballs," Carey wrote Robinson after a week in Miami. "Never have I ever seen so much energy and enthusiasm." Although the local NAACP leadership seemed "a little cagy and wary," the CORE field agents believed that they had made good contacts with a broad range of white and black organizations. But there were some potential problems: CORE-type direct action seemed more popular among Miami's left-liberal Jews than among blacks or white Christians. One NAACP leader, John O. Brown, claimed he could turn out at least twenty blacks for a picket line. Carey seemed doubtful, but went on to say:

> However, we can get 20 Jews. There are a couple of older Jewish groups which are willing to do most anything. One of them, the Emma Lazarus Club, has about 50 elderly Russian Jewish women who are anxious to work. The trouble is, of course, that the club has a reputation of being a communist front and actually was, I believe. The members are old Socialists, Communists, Wobblies, etc. Undoubtedly, most of the members are OK now, but the group would need to be very careful in working with members of this group. Some of the members, individually *might* be useful at times, however.

A more serious problem, it seemed, was that anti-Semitism in the Miami area might undermine the effectiveness of a CORE unit led by activist Jews. It would be necessary, Carey contended, to recruit white Protestants to work in the white community, while the Jewish activists—at least those "not of the Emma Lazarus variety"—could work in interracial teams with the black community. Miami's ethnic, religious, and racial mosaic presented both opportunities and problems for direct-action groups like CORE.[85]

During its early phase, Miami CORE people identified two major action projects. The first, stemming from their previous involvement in Dade County school desegregation, was a long-term community-organization effort to stem the exodus of whites from the Orchard Villa neighborhood and ease integration of its elementary school. The second project was a more immediate plan to test segregation in Miami's public accommodations—lunch counters, restaurants, bus and train terminals, movie theaters, and the like. This new focus came out of discussions with Miami blacks who attended CORE organizational meetings. Aside from the school issue, Miami blacks resented the daily indignities imposed on them by Jim Crow and they wanted to do something about it. While the school issue dragged on through the courts and interminable school board meetings, CORE's public accommodations thrust could be started quickly. Direct action such as sit-ins and picket lines would have an immediate impact, attract press attention, get blacks and whites working together, and help get CORE off the ground in Miami. In addition, as Robinson noted, "with fireballs like Mrs. Stern and Mrs. Zoloth, you have got to give them action in a hurry." From the CORE perspective, there was no substitute for direct action in the fight against racial segregation.[86]

Miami's civil rights activists went into action quickly. The Miami branch of CORE was officially established in March 1959 with fifteen active members. It was an interracial group, consisting of mostly Jews and blacks. Shirley Zoloth became "temporary" chairman, while NAACP vice president John Brown, the black physician who had earlier sued the school board to admit his son to the Orchard Villa School, served as vice chairman. Brown was already known to the Jewish activists. Zoloth had attended the trial of Brown's civil case against the school board, taking detailed notes of witness testimony. She knew it was important to recruit black members if Miami CORE was to be successful. As it happened, Thalia Stern and Barbara Gordon knew Brown's wife from their college days at the University of Wisconsin. Originally from Oklahoma and a newcomer to Miami, Brown had already made a mark locally as an uncompromising civil rights advocate in the Miami NAACP. Thus, Brown enthusiastically joined with the Jewish activists and soon became public spokesman for CORE. Zoloth remained in the background, ran the meetings, wrote the reports, and organized the sit-ins. Almost immediately, the group decided to test Miami's segregated lunch counters at three downtown "dime" stores—Grant's, McCrory's, and Woolworth's. These stores had sit-down counters where blacks traditionally had been refused service, but they had stand-up counters where blacks and whites were served together. Merchants welcomed black patronage throughout other sections of the stores. Such were the idiosyncrasies of the Jim Crow system.[87]

In March, April, May, and June 1959, Miami CORE conducted dozens of lunch counter sit-ins at the three dime stores, as well as at department stores, drug stores, and restaurants. Some of the early sit-ins involved small two- or four-person interracial testing teams, but by June the sit-ins were being carried out by as many as fifty or more black and white activists. Some sit-ins lasted only a few minutes, but others continued for six hours or more. Local television and the press covered many of the protests. Miami newspapers reported John Brown's public statements about the purposes of the CORE sit-ins. "Our aim," Brown stated during one sit-in, "is the end of racial discrimination in anything and everything." On another occasion, Brown told the reporters: "We'll keep coming again and again—and staying longer and longer.

Someone's going to have to give." Many passersby seemed surprised to learn that Miami lunch counters still enforced segregation. No violence occurred. However, these early sit-ins had unsatisfactory results—blacks did not get served, and store managers stonewalled CORE leaders. One store manager complained to a black CORE member that "it was the Jews who were stirring up all the trouble." Despite the failure to crack the color line and the absence of any formal support from mainstream Jewish or black organizations, Zoloth and her colleagues felt that these initial sit-ins brought positive results. Not only had they confronted store management on segregation, but they had demonstrated interracial cooperation in a nonviolent, direct-action campaign.[88]

The Miami sit-ins initiated by CORE reflected something new in late fifties South Florida: an interracial and cross-class attack on segregation and white power. Sit-in participants included Miami's Jewish activists, such as the Zoloths and the Gordons, a few University of Miami students, and a cross section of the Miami black community, ranging from professionals like Dr. Brown to working-class blacks. Black insurance man Albert D. Moore, later president of Miami CORE, in a 2001 interview recalled his first encounter with CORE. Walking along an Overtown street one evening in 1959, he noticed an interracial crowd spilling out of a meeting room and went in to see what it was all about. He found Barbara Gordon delivering a passionate speech about civil rights and CORE. He was impressed, he said, because he "had never met white people, some of whom were more interested in rights for Negroes than many Negroes." Moore joined up immediately. Later, when CORE needed more people for a downtown sit-in, Barbara Gordon recruited black men from bars, poolrooms, barber shops, and street corners in Miami's nearby Overtown district. Another participant in several of the early sit-ins was Barbara Zoloth, the teenage daughter of Shirley Zoloth. Her memory of one such sit-in is enlightening:

> I specifically remember going to Woolworth's in downtown Miami for a sit-in at the lunch counter. It was scary. Some of the onlookers were angry and called us names (nigger lover, dirty kikes). I wasn't afraid of the name-calling, but the anger was frightening, and I didn't know what else they might be capable of. However there was no physical violence that I recall. I do, however, remember getting very hungry! We sat there for what felt like hours (and probably was) on the stools, not talking even to each other much, just waiting to be served, which, of course, didn't happen.

Barbara Zoloth was not the only teenage activist. Robert Kunst, a Miami Beach high school student, joined CORE sit-ins despite the fears of his parents. Motivated by knowledge of the Holocaust and Jewish concerns about social justice, Kunst became an important Miami peace activist in the sixties and early seventies. Patricia and Priscilla Stephens, college students at Florida A&M University and back home in Miami during the summer of 1959, attended a CORE training workshop, participated in several weeks of intense sit-in activity on Flagler Street, and then helped establish a CORE branch in Tallahassee on their return to school for the fall semester. Interracial direct action in the 1959 sit-ins represented a new phase in Miami's civil rights movement.[89]

Miami CORE was an upstart organization that hoped to speed up the pace of racial change. However, CORE's nonviolent but confrontational tactics did not appeal to most residents at the time. For instance, none of Miami's black clergymen participated in these early sit-ins, although they did not oppose them. Almost all of the white CORE activists were Jewish, but no rabbis sat down with them at the Miami lunch counters. The more conservative, mainstream Jewish organizations such as the AJCommittee and ADL had no involvement with CORE. Even the more liberal AJCongress, to which many of CORE's Jewish activists belonged, remained hesitant. At one point in early 1959 the AJCongress asked CORE to "hold off" on further sit-ins until the Florida legislature ended its session, fearing right-wing, anti-Semitic backlash in Miami. A year later Miami CORE developed a wider base of support, but only after the student sit-ins of early 1960 dramatically altered the national race relations picture.[90]

After the energetic burst of sit-in activity in spring 1959, Miami CORE's direct-action campaign slowed during the summer. However, the pace of civil rights activity picked up quickly in September, when the national CORE organization held an Interracial Action Institute in Miami. The Action Institute brought field agents Carey and McCain back to Miami, along with a dozen or so CORE activists from other cities. The idea was to work with Miami CORE on local direct-action projects such as voter registration and sit-ins, while training CORE activists who could then bring their enthusiasm, commitment, and experience back to their home communities. After considering movie theaters, bus and train terminals, and more than twenty restaurants, the Action Institute took on as its major project the desegregation of the lunch counter at the Jackson-Byron's department store in downtown Miami.[91]

Miami's sit-in movement intensified with the Interracial Action Institute. Interracial CORE teams sat-in at Jackson-Byron's for six continuous days, eventually prompting the lunch counter concessionaire "to close temporarily while considering a change of policy." The Congress of Racial Equality then moved on to a nearby W. T. Grant lunch counter, where several days of continuous sit-ins disrupted the dime store's business. Toward the end of the two-week campaign, Jackson-Byron's agreed to integrate its lunch counters, but when local CORE people returned to test the new policy, they found that the store management had reneged on the deal. By that time, most institute activists had left town. Subsequently, Miami CORE had forty to eighty people a day sitting-in at Jackson-Byron's and Grant's for a week. Tensions boiled over, with store management calling in the police. Gordon Carey of national CORE was "roughed up" by the police and warned to "get out of Miami." Several CORE people were attacked by white segregationists and then arrested. Plainclothes policemen whispered threats to black demonstrators, some of whom immediately left the sit-in, while other black CORE members received threatening phone calls. The violent confrontations prompted Jackson-Byron's to close its lunch counter permanently. As one CORE member noted: "Well, at least we're all equal now in Jackson-Byron's; now nobody eats."[92]

The Action Institute had other consequences as well. Violence and arrests at the September sit-ins caused some local CORE activists to back off from further direct action. More significantly, there were internal disputes between local and national CORE people. National CORE officials believed that advance planning had been insufficient. A later CORE evaluation of the institute noted that "members of Miami CORE were not themselves in complete agreement on projects or on the tactics to be used in projects." Because Miami CORE was still operating with an unofficial, "temporary" leadership group, it had "not yet developed a definite organizational framework for handling disagreements within its own group." Shirley Zoloth, in particular, became "disenchanted" with CORE after the decision to target Jackson-Byron's, a small local store, rather than one of the larger department stores such as Burdine's, whose executives had wide influence in the Miami business community. Zoloth believed that cracking the color line at Burdine's was the key to desegregating downtown Miami. If Burdine's integrated its lunch counter, all the other stores would follow more easily. But some of CORE's black activists disagreed with this analysis, preferring to focus first on Jackson-Byron's because its owner had a second store in the black Overtown district that, they said, was gouging black customers. The fact that Jackson-Byron's owner was a local Jewish businessman, and that some blacks wanted to "get the Jew first," created tensions in Miami CORE.[93]

This internal dissension, with its undercurrent of anti-Semitism, troubled Zoloth and a few other Jewish activists. By this time, Zoloth had also come to believe that as CORE became more militant it should be headed by a black man rather than a white Jewish woman. In addition, her educational activism, especially the Orchard Villa battle and planning for Jack Gordon's school board campaign, began absorbing more of her time and energy. Consequently, in the fall of 1959 Shirley Zoloth withdrew from her leadership role in Miami CORE, although she remained a rank-and-file member. Official CORE leadership passed on temporarily to John O. Brown and then to A. D. Moore. National CORE's Robinson put the best face on events, suggesting to Moore that "sometimes it is necessary to have revision of membership if the organization is to progress."[94]

Internal conflicts and the leadership shakeup seemed to undercut the activist edge that Miami CORE had developed during the spring and early fall of 1959. The group continued with a few lunch counter sit-ins, and worked with black churches and the local NAACP to challenge segregated parks and recreation facilities in Miami. National CORE urged the Miami group to work with local labor unions in promoting interracial hiring, especially in Miami's increasingly important airline industry. But things moved slowly, and for several months reports from the local chapter ceased completely (Robinson had gotten used to Shirley Zoloth's regular and detailed reports). By January 1960, Moore was requesting help from the national office to reorganize and energize Miami CORE. Even the wave of activism generated by the student sit-ins in Greensboro, North Carolina, in February 1960 initially brought a slow response in Miami. "We certainly wish the Miami CORE group would again become actively engaged in the sit-ins," Gordon Carey wrote a Miami friend in March 1960.[95]

Carey did not have long to wait. In March and April 1960, belatedly inspired by the student sit-ins and with the city's leading black preachers now involved, Miami CORE went back to the lunch counters with a renewed determination. The new sit-ins were accompanied by demonstrations, pickets, and economic boycotts of offending stores. Interviewed by the *Miami News*, the NAACP's Gibson told the white establishment what to expect: "We are going to eat at those lunch counters if we have to fill up the whole of the Dade County jail." Local business and political leaders worried that negative publicity would affect Miami's national reputation, and especially its tourist business.[96]

The sit-in issue heated up considerably in late March 1960. Governor Collins wanted to prevent potential civil rights violence in Miami and elsewhere in Florida. Collins had national political ambitions and was interested in sprucing up his own image as a southern moderate. At the end of March, when Collins made a televised address to Floridians supporting the desegregation of lunch counters, he hoped to achieve those two goals. Also concerned about Miami's national image, Mayor Robert King High appointed a biracial commission to negotiate the integration of lunch counters and other public accommodations with Miami merchants. Black leaders were suspicious of Mayor High's motivations. The biracial commission seemed to be a delaying tactic and was "not worth a dime," A. D. Moore initially contended. Governor Collins also had his state-level Commission on Race Relations working on the Miami sit-in controversy. Adding to the public relations pressure, national CORE conducted a second Miami Action Institute during the summer of 1960, with new sit-ins again bringing nonviolent civil rights confrontation to downtown streets and stores. Facing potentially damaging threats to Miami's national image and lucrative tourist industry, local civic leaders opted for a more moderate position on race relations. By August 1960, the sit-ins and the backroom negotiations involving the governor, the mayor, Miami businessmen, and Miami's leading black preachers resulted in the official desegregation of lunch counters in twenty-three department stores and variety stores in downtown Miami. However, segregation continued in many restaurants in other sections of metropolitan Miami, as well as in most hotels and theaters, until further CORE sit-ins, stand-ins, and boycotts over the next few years eventually broke the race barrier.[97]

The cracking of the color line in downtown Miami began with CORE's determined lunch counter sit-in campaign in 1959. A handful of black and Jewish activists initially supplied the driving energy. In the late 1950s, as the Florida legislature pursued communists in the Miami NAACP and considered school closings, integration and the political left still stirred irrational fears in the Miami area. With its interracial activities and direct-action techniques, CORE seemed to be a dangerous and radical threat to the southern status quo that underlay Miami's subtropical tourist industry. Activist Jews such as Shirley Zoloth, Barbara Gordon, Thalia Stern, and others provided the impetus for Miami CORE's early sit-ins, but Miami's larger Jewish community kept the "civil rights Jews" at a distance. Most Miami Jews undoubtedly sympathized with civil rights objectives, but relatively few joined sit-ins or picket lines. As Zoloth noted in a 1991 interview, "No one [in the Miami Jewish community] argued against the morality of what we were doing," but few Jews were willing to confront segregation actively or directly for fear of "instigating trouble."[98] As with the Civil Rights Congress a decade earlier, the experience of Miami CORE suggests the strengths but also the limits of the black-Jewish relationship in the era of white supremacy and anti-Semitism. At a time when most were silenced by fear, Jewish activists built working relationships with counterparts in the black community and successfully challenged Jim Crow in the Sunshine State.

CONCLUSION

Taken together, these case studies of Miami CRC and Miami CORE suggest several significant conclusions about the civil rights movement. The early history of the movement in Miami, for instance, supports the interpretation that the freedom campaign for African Americans grew up around local issues with indigenous local leadership, especially that of women. Both CRC and CORE sprouted from local conditions in the Miami area. Local Jewish women with progressive or radical political inclinations supplied the drive, commitment, enthusiasm, and organizational skills for these grassroots social movements. Both groups developed important connections to national civil rights organizations, but local leadership and decision making determined the ebb and flow of civil rights activity in Miami.[99]

Moreover, the political activism of Graff and Zoloth matches new interpretations of "postwar women progressives." Earlier views asserted that the powerful postwar ideology of domesticity "pushed women back into the domestic sphere," where life focused on marriage and children. However, recent research questions "the stereotype of postwar women as quiescent, docile, and domestic," and posits the 1940s and 1950s as "a watershed in women's social activism," a period in which politically active women "employed newer strategies and styles of organizing" in, among other things, an attack on racial segregation. Miami's civil rights women not only pushed progressive social and political agendas, but they demonstrated through their actions a rejection of the postwar ideology of domesticity.[100]

The fact that Graff, Zoloth, and most of their white colleagues in CRC and CORE were Jewish emphasizes the point that Jews made up a high percentage of white activists in the Miami civil rights movement. But for the most part, the activists worked outside the framework of mainstream Jewish organizations, which distanced themselves from militant and confrontational civil rights action. Indeed, as in the rest of the South, Miami Jews generally took a less than assertive stand on civil rights during the desegregation crisis of the 1950s. Nevertheless, activist Jews and blacks developed working relationships in the struggle against segregation and racial hatred. On the left, politically progressive Jews created new organizations such as CRC and CORE and played a leading part in Miami's civil rights movement before 1960. The strength of commitment to civil rights demonstrated by these activist Jews highlights the weakness of that commitment in the larger Miami Jewish community.[101]

The expectation that Jews naturally supported African-American civil rights stems from the perception that Jews as a group traditionally stood well to the left on the American political spectrum. An extensive literature suggests that left-wing Jews dominated a few trade unions (such as in the garment industry) in early twentieth-century America; that Jews made up a substantial portion of those active in the American socialist and communist movements, although most Jews were involved in neither; and that Jews were overly represented among white financial supporters and activists in the civil rights movement. American Jews, historian Stephen J. Whitfield has written, "often have pumped visions of social justice into a polity that long has been condemned or celebrated for its evasion of ideology."[102]

Varied explanations have been advanced to explain the left-wing proclivities among some Jews. In his classic history of Jews in New York City, *The Promised City* (1962), Moses Rischin explained that "for most Jewish socialists, although often unaware of it, socialism was Judaism secularized." In his book, *American Space, Jewish Time* (1988), Whitfield offered the insightful suggestion that young Jews disproportionally gravitated to the civil rights movement in postwar America because they had grown up in left-wing or radical families where they learned a culture of opposition firsthand, where dissident traditions had already been nurtured, and where issues of social justice were discussed and debated. Vivian Gornick in *The Romance of American Communism* (1977), similarly reported on the passionate family discussions of socialist ideology and humanistic aims that typified the early twentieth-century Jewish left in New York City. Obviously, not all Jews experienced this sort of familial socialization, but those who did often participated in various movements for social change. Indeed, as historian Maurice Isserman has suggested, many from the old left, including ex-communists, ended up playing important roles in subsequent civil rights and peace movements. Regarding the Miami story, the Graffs and the Zoloths grew up in families where the adult generation had been active in trade unionism and radical or progressive politics. They carried on those traditions in the mid-century years themselves, first in socialist youth groups and later in their civil rights work in CRC and CORE in Miami. But not all Miami Jews had such backgrounds, and only a tiny handful of Miami Jews became civil rights activists in the decade and a half after World War II.[103]

Finally, the Miami experience offers insight into the impact of the Cold War on the civil rights movement. Civil rights advocates and black activists often emphasized the contradiction between the principles of American democracy and the reality of racial injustice. These contradictions resonated abroad. William L. Patterson's book *We Charge Genocide: The Crime of the Government against the Negro People* (1951), for instance, began as a lengthy petition to the United Nations hoping to bring international pressure on the U.S. government to move more forcefully on civil rights. As third world countries wavered between two superpowers, political scientist Azza Salama Layton has recently written, "domestic discrimination was a liability to American objectives abroad." With the federal government tarnished by the Jim Crow image overseas, another scholar, Mary L. Dudziak, noted, "civil rights reform came to be seen as crucial to U.S. foreign relations." These writers have argued that international pressure during the Cold War did force the U.S. government to move more expeditiously on civil rights than it otherwise might have done. But until the 1960s, many of these advances, such as the creation of civil rights commissions, seemed merely delaying tactics that did not fully embrace the concept of racial justice.[104]

Against the minimal advances described above, one must measure the impact of the domestic Cold War on the civil rights movement. In Florida and elsewhere, McCarthyism in all its guises had a damaging impact on civil rights activism. Anticommunist legislation, congressional hearings, FBI harassment, state and local anticommunist investigations, attacks by hate groups such as the Ku Klux Klan, and red-baiting by the right-wing press all weakened Miami's postwar civil rights movement. In the South, especially, the powerful combination of anticommunism, white supremacy, and anti-Semitism set back the movement for racial equality by a decade or more. Linked both to communism and racial equality, Miami's civil rights Jews faced an uphill battle against McCarthyite politicians, hostile law enforcement agencies, violent segregationists, and red-baiters in the press. They faced fear and apathy within their own community, but they did not abandon their social justice idealism. Varied Cold War pressures destroyed CRC, hampered CORE, and undermined black and Jewish activism. Nevertheless, for old leftists and progressives from northern cities, the aggressive right-wing defense of white supremacy may have galvanized their commitment to civil rights and other progressive causes. Miami's early civil rights movement did involve cooperation among *some* blacks and *some* Jews on the left, but it was not an alliance that had wide support or appeal in Cold War Florida.

PART II

* * *

Matilda "Bobbi" Graff and the Civil Rights Congress

Matilda "Bobbi" Graff, with husband Emanuel and children (from left), baby Maxine Hope, June Marian, and Lois Pauline, Miami 1954. (Photo courtesy of Bobbi Graff.)

* * *

IN THIS SECTION of the book, Bobbi Graff's autobiographical memoir of her civil rights activism in Miami between 1946 and 1954 is published for the first time. Graff was born in 1921 and spent her childhood in the heavily Jewish Brownsville section of Brooklyn. As noted earlier, she grew up in an immigrant Jewish family where labor Zionism, trade unionism, and leftist politics were the order of the day. Her father, Max Soller, worked as a sewing machine operator in a New York City garment factory. Graff became politically active in the 1930s at Thomas Jefferson High School and later at Brooklyn College. She studied Marxism, worked to build socialism in Palestine, actively supported the Loyalist side in the Spanish Civil War, demonstrated against militaristic Japan, and headed the Peace Council and the American Student Union branch at her high school. Five days a week, she attended an "after-school" Yiddish folk school, where a socialist teacher introduced her to Marxism and nurtured her political evolution. Her political beliefs stemmed from the socialist culture of family, school, and community, as well as from the economic and social conditions of the Great Depression. Like many working-class families, the Sollers suffered hard times in the 1930s, and they depended for a time on "home relief" and New Deal job programs.[1]

After graduating from high school in 1938, Bobbi Soller held a variety of part-time jobs while attending Brooklyn College at night. When she moved to Detroit in 1941 after marrying Emanuel Graff, her political and social activism evolved still further. While Emanuel worked at Detroit Diesel, a General Motors subsidiary, Bobbi engaged in political work with the Michigan Civil Rights Federation, American Youth for Democracy, Young Progressive Citizens of America, the Civil Rights Congress, and other progressive groups. Before moving to Miami in 1946, she took part in demonstrations for rent control and against universal military training, worked in local political campaigns for progressive candidates, supported striking maritime workers, distributed leaflets opposing racial discrimination in Michigan hotels and restaurants, and picketed politicians on anti-lynching, anti–poll tax, and FEPC legislation. By now she had become a member of the Communist Party and the FBI was tracking her political activities. Nevertheless, in late 1945 the FBI's chief Detroit agent reported to J. Edgar Hoover that his ongoing investigation of Graff failed to "reflect that her activities are such that they might be considered dangerous to the internal security of the United States at this time."[2]

By the time the Graffs moved to Miami, Bobbi had been a political activist for a decade or more. Living in Miami, a Deep-South city where racial segregation prevailed, provided new opportunities and new challenges for an activist interested in peace, social change, and racial justice. South Florida's mid-century political culture was much more conservative and much less accepting of activism than in the industrial cities of the Northeast and Midwest—conditions that made the work of left-wing activists more difficult and more dangerous. The Graffs and their friends enthusiastically supported Henry A. Wallace's campaign for the presidency in 1948 under the Progressive Party banner. Wallace, Graff stated in a 1992 interview, "talked the language of the people."[3]

Bobbi Graff's work with the Miami Civil Rights Congress coincided with the advent of McCarthyism and associated patterns of political repression at the national and local levels. Consequently, communist-front groups such as the CRC faced official and unofficial harassment and red-baiting. The Graffs and other activists were targeted for FBI investigation and surveillance. As the CRC eventually faded from the Miami scene in the early 1950s, and as Bobbi Graff moved on to voter registration and educational work with the Miami NAACP, that organization too came under increasing suspicion of harboring dangerous political radicals. In various forums in the early and mid-1950s, she spoke out against the Korean War, advocated admission of Communist China to the United Nations, helped raise money for the defense of the Rosenbergs, and protested the 1955 racist murder in Mississippi of Emmett Till. By 1955, now back in Detroit, Graff had been tabbed by the FBI for DETCOM, the list of "dangerous" communists, "key figures" slated to be detained in any national emergency. Consequently, Detroit FBI agents maintained their periodic surveillance of Graff through the late 1950s. In 1960 the Detroit FBI office recommended that she be removed from the agency's Security Index, but J. Edgar Hoover himself rejected that recommendation and ordered the Detroit office to continue its surveillance of Graff.[4]

Graff left the Communist Party in 1957, primarily because of anti-Semitism in the Soviet Union, but also because of pressures within the party to curb freedom of discussion. Her association with the party had always been rather loose in any event. She had never completely followed shifting party lines, and she often independently pursued issues or problems if it made sense to her to do so. She was deeply concerned about war, discrimination, civil rights, civil liberties, and labor organizing—"not things," she said in an interview, "you had to be a communist to do."[5]

In the 1960s and after, Graff's activism and engagement with social and political issues persisted. She never finished her college education at Brooklyn

College, and raising a family and pursuing political activism kept her busy through the 1940s and 1950s. However, in the 1960s she enrolled at Detroit's Wayne State University, working part-time and studying part-time, eventually completing a B.A. degree in philosophy in 1971. Along the way she became caught up in the movements of the decade. For example, she joined the Detroit branch of the Congress of Racial Equality, continuing to work for racial justice with this organization until the rise of black power ideology forced whites out of CORE in the mid-1960s. Similarly, she was active in the National Organization for Women and the American Civil Liberties Union. Not surprisingly, she gravitated very early toward the movement against the Vietnam War. She supported antiwar protests at Wayne State University and lobbied Michigan congressmen and senators against the war. Locally, she helped organize Concerned Parents for Peace, which among other things met with Wayne State administrators to develop guidelines for peaceful protest activities by students. In 1972, representing Concerned Parents, she traveled to Paris to attend the World Assembly for Peace, sponsored by the People's Coalition for Peace and Justice. While in Paris, she participated in an emotional meeting with a delegation of Vietnamese and Cambodian parents who had lost children in the war. This meeting simply confirmed her lifelong commitment to peaceful resolution of international problems, a position Graff had held as far back as her leadership role in her high school's peace council.[6]

Meanwhile, Bobbi Graff was working at the Wayne State University Medical School in the office of scholarships and financial aid. When she completed a master's degree in guidance and counseling in 1978, she was promoted to director of that office, where she remained until retiring in 1991. At the medical school, she helped to organize a unit of the Physicians for Social Responsibility, which held antiwar rallies on the campus, promoted the anti-nuclear movement, supported gay rights and environmental protection, and engaged in clinical work in the Detroit ghetto.[7]

Graff's retirement in Florida since the early 1990s has been anything but retiring. For several years, she worked as an office volunteer in the Palm Beach County Health Department and served on a foster care citizens review board that evaluated cases before they went to a juvenile court judge. She has participated actively in a local discussion group, the Delray Beach Citizens for Social Responsibility, which has taken strong stands against nuclear weapons and for environmental protection. In addition to keeping up with family and friends, she remains involved in local Democratic Party affairs, as well as in such groups as Floridians for Universal Health Care and the Society for Humanistic Judaism. Over a long life charged with political activism, Bobbi Graff noted in interviews, she has tried to "do the right thing" and "build a better world" based on peace and justice. The FBI in the McCarthy era and after considered her a dangerous subversive, but she thought of herself as a patriot doing good work and has never had any regrets about her political action or civil rights work.[8]

Graff's memoir of her activism in Miami in the immediate postwar era provides a rare first-person account of civil rights work and left-wing activism in the mid-century South. As she relates at the beginning, she wrote this memoir in 1971 as part of a class assignment at Wayne State University. She was concerned that younger students at the university seemed to have little knowledge of any civil rights activity before the 1960s. To a certain extent, then, she wrote this memoir to link the movement of the 1960s with its predecessors in the 1940s and 1950s: thus the title, "The Historic Continuity of the Civil Rights Movement."[9]

But there is more to it than that. Graff's civil rights memoir offers a powerful indictment of mid-century American society and its governing institutions. The early postwar movement for social reform and racial justice, she wrote in the memoir, was "eliminated by a society afraid of change." Official and unofficial repression—in the form of McCarthyite investigative hearings, local red-hunting grand juries, FBI harassment, police obstruction, Ku Klux Klan intimidation, vicious and biased newspaper reporting—all these inspired terror and fear among advocates of change. The year 1950 was not a good time to be an American communist crusading for racial justice and social change in Miami, or anywhere else in the United States for that matter. Graff's experience with McCarthyism in all its various guises demonstrates how anticommunism, anti-Semitism, and the defense of racial segregation converged to set back the movement for civil rights in the 1940s and 1950s.

Graff's civil rights memoir was first written in longhand and later prepared by a professional typist. She wrote from her memory and from the few materials she had retained. These included a scrapbook of Miami newspaper clippings, a few magazine articles about the Miami witch-hunt, some CRC and NAACP materials, and scattered correspondence. She corresponded with a number of former Miami activists requesting information and copies of documents. Some responded with information drawn from memory, but few had any written materials to send. She did not have access at the time to the now archived Civil Rights Congress records, which had extensive Graff correspondence and which provided an important source for the Miami civil rights story outlined in part I of this book.

After Graff completed her memoir, she sent a copy to her friend Anne Braden, another 1950s southern civil rights and Civil Rights Congress activist who in the early 1970s was editor of *The Southern Patriot*, a publication of the left-liberal Southern Conference Education Fund (SCEF). Braden liked the memoir, especially because it dealt with a "forgotten" era when "a great deal was happening, but most people today don't know about it." Braden hoped that SCEF could publish a shortened version of the Graff memoir as a pamphlet, or that it could find its way into print through some other means.[10]

Now, more than thirty years later, Bobbi Graff's civil rights autobiography appears in print for the first time. With the exception of some minor copy-editing and the identification of people left unnamed in Graff's original text, the memoir appears exactly as written in 1971. In many ways, it was a product of its times, an era when the meaning of "civil rights" was still emerging and highly contested. Appended to the memoir are two newspaper articles Graff wrote for the *National Guardian* in the early 1950s—one on the Groveland killings and one on the Miami witch-hunt—that explore more fully some of the issues discussed in the memoir. Taken together, these materials provide an exceptionally moving and informative first-person account of the Miami civil rights movement in an era of fear and danger for blacks, Jews, and anyone else advocating racial justice.

The Historic Continuity of the Civil Rights Movement

Matilda "Bobbi" Graff

INTRODUCTION

Social change in the 1960s, both in Michigan and in the U.S. generally, led to important changes in the curriculum of Monteith College, an experimental college at Wayne State University. Among other things, these changes included the development of an Afro-American Studies course. Herb Boyd, the instructor, delivered a scholarly presentation of the subject matter that evoked a flow of healthy discussion. As an active participant in the class, I became uncomfortably aware of a tendency on the part of the students to think of the struggle for civil rights as beginning during the 1960s. Their assumption that it had no predecessors and that it came on the scene full-grown was evidence of not only an unscientific approach but an immature one as well.

This lack of perspective caused me to consider the necessity of presenting in some manner the theory of historical continuity in the civil rights struggle. In this work, my B.A. thesis at Monteith College, I hoped to give concrete evidence showing that the movements of the '60s were in fact the orphaned children of the struggles of the '40s and '50s. I use the term orphaned because I can think of no better corollary. I might also add that the parents were murdered. They did not die a normal death. They were eliminated by a society afraid of change.

There were many bitter civil rights struggles before 1960, and important advances were being won. Many of the participants were literally and/or figuratively killed. These battles, even though incomplete, were the parents of the movements of the '60s. Without the seeds they planted, no new offspring could be born. In the course of telling this story, I hope to show the various ugly forms of repression, the methods employed by the local, state, and federal governments, to kill off the movement for a democratic society. I cannot stress too strongly the importance of understanding the historical continuity of the movement and at the same time underscoring why it appeared as though there were none.

There were several options open to me once I decided to make this my major project. I decided to set the time and place in that area of the South where I lived and was actively involved in the movement for civil rights—the vicinity of greater Miami, Florida, during the years 1946–1954. In my attempt to obtain as much information as possible, I sent letters to approximately twenty persons involved in the movement in Florida, as well as magazines and newspapers, advising them of my intent. I received replies from approximately half of these. In spite of the fair response, however, very little actual material was forwarded to me for various reasons. I realize, of course, that much time has elapsed and much has happened since. Files can be cleared out and memories dimmed. For many the pain of reopening the past was too great and so they preferred to keep it a closed chapter in their lives. For some others, the possible threat of renewed repression in this present period of time may have accounted for their reluctance to assist in this project. To those who did respond with valuable background material and reminiscences of struggle, I can only express my gratitude and say that America has much to thank you and others like you for your participation in that struggle. To the Southern Conference Educational Fund, which has assisted with research on some of the material and has offered to publish my story when completed, I sincerely hope that it will be worthy of the offer.

Due to lack of sufficient material from outside sources, it was necessary to re-examine my original plan for presenting this work. I shall present the events as best I am able through my personal experience, contacts, and knowledge. I am only using those incidents that can provide a sense of what transpired at that time in our nation's history. Miami was not the only area in the South where civil rights action was taking place. However, it was selected by the government for special attention, for reasons discussed in the following pages.

If at times the sequence seems to be out of order, please be patient. Some of the events are being told for the first time here, and trying to recall and authenticate the exact dates after so much time has passed is very difficult. I should add that if you think of this paper as separate parts of a puzzle, you will find that eventually all these parts will fit together to present a rather complete picture of the events leading up to and including the story of the Miami Formula—U.S.A., 1954. This is but a microcosm of the struggles taking place in the U.S. at that time. Happenings similar to these, if told from other sources and other areas, can help fill the gaps and demonstrate the historical continuity of the civil rights struggle. If, in some way, this paper imparts to the students and youth of today some of the very worthwhile efforts made in the past and some of the valuable lessons learned for the future, I will be satisfied that it will have served a purpose.

TRAUMA

Visiting hours were almost over in the maternity section of Mercy Hospital, Miami, Florida. It was August 24, 1954, and only four days earlier I had given birth to a beautiful seven pound, three ounce baby girl. That day had been exciting. I was feeling good and was anxious to take my baby home. Rabbi Morris A. Skop of the Coral Gables Jewish Center had come to visit that afternoon and we had a pleasant talk, which included plans for naming the baby at services on Saturday. Her middle name is Hope. It expressed our feelings of hope for the future. My hospital roommates had never met a Rabbi before and were very impressed by the fact that he was a young, handsome man and did not have a long beard, a long black coat, and a foreign accent. They were surprised that we were able to communicate so well and on such a friendly basis.

My other two children, aged seven and eleven, had made news only two days earlier. There was a polio epidemic and a shortage of funds to combat it, so they had organized a successful fund-raising affair for children that was an inspiration in brotherhood and humanity, sadly lacking in the adult community. The story of their accomplishments was being broadcast on the news programs and in the press. This was indeed good training in citizenship and commitment. We were still receiving congratulations on their efforts.

The doctor had prescribed beer for me to assist with nursing the baby. My husband and I were musing about what the Sisters would say if they came in and found me guzzling beer. We had just made our plans for bringing the baby home and completed the lists of what to bring to the hospital and what to have ready at home when it happened.

Two men passed the door, paused, and then looked in. My husband went to the door to see whom they wanted to see. In a few seconds there was a scuffle, as they broke into the room and came to my bed. Fred Jones, from the State's Attorney's Office, with the face and the voice of a devil, said, "Congratulations,

Mrs. Graff, I love little children," and immediately began reading a subpoena ordering me to appear before the grand jury. At the same time he served my husband his subpoena.

It was as though the world had gone mad. One minute joy and plans for the future, the next minute total despair and the feeling of being crushed. My husband had tried to bar them from entering the room, but they had said that it was "with the knowledge and consent of the doctor and the hospital" that they were there, and they forced their way in.

Can you imagine what happens when one goes into shock? It is very difficult to explain. It was as though my head had expanded ten times its original size and a piston was shooting through the middle. All my body functions stopped as though completely paralyzed. The pain was unbearable. I opened my mouth to scream but nothing happened. All of these events took about two or three minutes. It hadn't seemed real, but there were the pieces of paper in our hands.

What to do first? I needed help urgently. The Sisters were not aware that anything had happened. They wouldn't do anything without the doctor's orders. Call the doctor? But if he knew of this visit and had consented to it, what confidence could I now have in him? We called. He said he didn't know what we were talking about and called the hospital to check. The State's Attorney's Office had lied. They had never contacted him or the hospital.

What did it matter now, the damage was already done. Due to my condition new plans had to be made. It was now necessary to make arrangements for someone to care for the children, the new-born infant, and me. The doctor absolutely forbid my appearing at court or anywhere else for fear of permanent damage to my health. After three weeks of treatment for shock, he advised that I leave the area even though I was still under subpoena.

We agonized over what to do. We had always faced any adversities together, had worked hard, and after seven years had built a business that was making a comfortable living for our young family. We had bought a modest house, which we had carpeted and draped only two weeks before. There was no option left to us. My husband would remain to face whatever would be coming. I would follow the doctor's orders and leave, becoming a fugitive from "justice."

We left surreptitiously in the middle of the night. My poor widowed mother was heartbroken and unable to comprehend, like us, what horrible crime we had committed. What kind of people were we—really?

WHO ARE WE?

We were married only three months when the bombing of Pearl Harbor, December 7, 1941, transformed our lives as it had millions of others. Along with his brother and several friends, my husband Emanuel sought to enlist in the fight for freedom and against tyranny. To his dismay he was rejected due to a punctured eardrum. It seemed the only course now open to him was to seek work in war production and leave his field of work, which was nonessential. He was a good painter, having learned the trade from an old master craftsman. We knew it would mean a drastic cut in his earnings since his wages then were $137 weekly. So, voluntarily we took a cut to $57.33 weekly for five weeks and $40 every sixth week.

Manny was hired by Kelsey-Hayes in Detroit and told to report for a physical. While reviewing his application the employment manager stopped suddenly and said, "You're a Jew, aren't you? Well, the doctor won't be in tomorrow. We'll call you as soon as an appointment is set up." That was the end of the job at Kelsey-Hayes. Anti-Semitism had reared its ugly head. This time in our defense plants and in spite of the President's Fair Employment Proclamation.

General Motors, Diesel Division, was next. The line-up for employment was long since many hands were being sought. While waiting in line Manny befriended a young Negro who stood just ahead of him. Joe held in his hand a diploma from a government training school stating he had completed three hundred hours of training which qualified him as a lathe operator. Joe was given a job as a sweeper. Manny, who had no previous training, became a drill press operator on the production line. Racism, like anti-Semitism, was eating at the vitals of our nation while we were supposedly united as a people—fighting to destroy its counterparts in Europe and Asia.

What transpired in the war plants of Detroit was also frightening. It seemed more than mere coincidence when each time the Russians, our allies, went on the offensive, the production line broke down and the diesel engines, so desperately needed, were taken off the line. GM Diesel seemed to have more manpower available than was necessary. If you were concerned and conscientious and asked for more work when you had none, the foreman told you to "go to the john and kill some time." If you asked for a release so you could get work in a plant that needed more men, you were refused because your job was frozen. Is it possible they operated on a cost plus basis as so many of the workers believed? The unions endorsed a no-strike pledge during the war. Management used every provocation to irritate the workers and force them to strike in order to discredit the unions.

Manny was union shop steward. Some of his responsibilities included collecting dues, selling tickets to union functions, and keeping the morale of the men high to win the battle for production to win the war. The local sponsored a dance and told shop stewards to sell tickets to everyone but the blacks. Manny refused. They offered to hold a separate dance for the blacks, but he still refused to cooperate because he could not support the theory of separate but equal. The local union leadership then attempted to have him removed from his job as steward but failed to win sufficient support. The majority of the rank and file felt that if a man pays his dues he has the right to participate in all the union functions, even though they themselves might not attend an integrated dance.

During this time Manny helped organize a Red Cross blood donor drive at the plant. He was called to the office by management, where he was confronted by the FBI and interrogated as to his motives. It was then that he realized that there was a government within the government working hard to destroy our freedoms here. It was then, too, that "patriotism" as espoused by the great corporations of our country was revealed to him. Profit, not patriotism, was their primary concern. During this time, Anaconda Copper was selling faulty material to the government, resulting in the murder of our own men. We sometimes wonder what it is that makes people change their pattern of thought. Experiences like those described can often be a catalyst for change.

After the end of the war, after the atomic bombing of Hiroshima and Nagasaki, we hoped we could settle down to normal living in a peaceful world. Our first child was born in 1943. We had high hopes that the United Nations would be the avenue for settling international disputes. These were our dreams for a beautiful world in which our children could grow up unafraid of the future. We were young and idealistic and we were of the working class. But unfortunately, the Cold War was already in progress and the Marshall Plan, the Truman Doctrine, the Warsaw Pact, and NATO were the order of the day. These took precedence over the United Nations and our hopes for the future.

Those were bitter war years. Six million Jews were destroyed in the Nazi attempt to commit genocide against a people. The casualties suffered in loss of life and in permanent damage to survivors is inestimable. For us, like so many others, the personal loss of family and friends can never be forgotten. Time can only dull the pain and the memories.

Our baby, Lois, had suffered several bad attacks of bronchitis and pneumonia. So in 1946 we decided to leave for Miami, Florida, where my parents had just recently settled for health reasons. Manny took a leave of absence from the

Detroit Housing Commission. We sub-rented our small apartment located over some stores on Linwood and Hazelwood, and we went down South for the long winter.

MIAMI BACKGROUND

Miami in 1946 was a strange world to us. Climatically and health-wise it was a Garden of Eden. To the tourist, it was a fantasy land. But it was also a growing metropolis where segregation, discrimination, and blatant racist terror were the law. To a concerned human being it was a challenge.

Negroes working on Miami Beach were still required to carry "health" cards for identification and were prohibited to be there after six P.M. unless they were still working. They were not permitted to use the public beaches or recreation facilities. Water fountains and toilet facilities were labeled "colored" and "white." I recall my three-year-old child looking at the two lines at the drinking fountains and taking her place on the very short line, saying, "But Mommy don't they know that the water really isn't colored. It tastes just the same." It was impossible to distinguish between the police and the KKK. Only by the uniform worn at any particular occasion could one tell which role was being played. All the poverty and ignorance which persisted throughout the southland existed in Miami, but here the elements of change were already present.

In the course of familiarizing ourselves with the community, its people, and the forces at work there, we learned of the attempts made as far back as 1939 to organize the Miami area's laundry workers. Even then this was a very big industry, totally unorganized and gangster controlled. The effort was undertaken by two men, one black, Jim Nimmo, and one white, Chuck Smolikoff. They were said to be communists and may well have been. It was the communists who were then trying to organize some of the most exploited workers in the South. Jim and Chuck were the targets of both the Klan and the gangster elements. Fortunately, the bullets often intended for them did not find their targets. They succeeded in getting the support of some workers, black and white; but, because of the terror which was so prevalent, unionization did not come to the southland that easily. There was, however, minimum organization in the building trades and elsewhere on a segregated basis.

Eventually, Jim became the organizer for the Laundry Workers Union. Chuck became organizer for the IUMSWA-CIO, the Shipbuilders Union, in 1941. For the first time in the South, black, white, and Seminole Indians, some four thousand workers, were organized into one union. It spread from Miami to

Hialeah to Ojus, and in 1942 to Jacksonville. The meetings were held on an integrated basis, although frequently the workers separated themselves in the meeting hall. There were black and white shop stewards and local union officers. Union contracts covering all workers contained a nondiscrimination clause, but there were frequent attempts made by management to circumvent them.

In 1943, for the first time in the history of Florida, a public meeting in Bayfront Park, Miami, broke the segregation barrier. Eight thousand people, black and white, including many of the newly organized workers from the shipyards, laundry services, and the black ghettos as far away as Ft. Lauderdale, jammed the park. They came to hear speakers, including their union organizers, in support of the war against the Rome-Tokyo-Berlin Axis.

In 1944, Pan-American World Airways in Miami was organized on a completely integrated basis. From Miami, black and white organizers spread out to bring other bases into the new Air Transport Division of the Transport Workers Union-CIO. San Juan, Puerto Rico, had about five hundred members, including 25 percent white and a black local union president. The organizing continued, and Chuck became the official TWU Regional Director and national organizer for airlines. During this time, American Airlines, the largest domestic airline, was also brought into the TWU and the drive was on to organize Eastern Airlines.

Organization of the workers in various trades was well under way. Included among those organized were the Borden Milk Company, twelve ice plants, supermarkets, and the Amalgamated Butchers Union. The CIO, however, was organizing on a nondiscriminatory basis and this was more than the southern aristocracy could appreciate. In addition, blacks were beginning to participate in political areas. In 1946, an FDR Memorial Rally in Bayfront Park brought out a large integrated crowd to hear Senator Claude Pepper of Florida and local leaders of labor and liberal groups, including the Southern Conference for Human Welfare.

While actively organizing laundry workers, Jim Nimmo helped organize the first "sit and swim-in" on Miami Beach in 1945. As a result, Virginia Beach and Haulover Beach were opened to nonsegregated parties. The KKK did not sit idly by during this period. Harassment, cross-burnings, and unveiled threats were a constant reminder of the ever present danger. It is a matter of record that the Klan burned a cross at the home of Chuck Smolikoff and terrorized his pregnant wife who was home alone, causing her to lose the child she was bearing. The Florida State CIO Council minced no words in condemning and exposing the Klan terror.

It is also interesting to note that there were two trade schools in Miami, one for "colored" and one for "white." The "colored" school trained blacks only in hotel services, laundry work, and associated jobs. They operated on the theory that blacks couldn't get placed in any other kind of work so why waste time and money training them for something better. On the other hand, since Miami had opened up as a major base for national and international airlines and shipyards, there was a great demand for mechanics and other technicians. So the "white" trade school, Lindsey Hopkins, trained whites for these jobs as well as for all other types of employment. This was the Florida scene in 1946 when we came down for a temporary reprieve from illness and Detroit's winter wonderland.

We developed friendships with people who had interests in common with ours. We were members of the Young Progressives in Detroit and naturally gravitated in that direction for the short time we were in Miami. My activity was limited due to my pregnancy, so Manny again carried the major share of the work. He was involved in educational work in the Negro ghetto, distributing leaflets and talking to people about conditions. One Sunday he had taken Lois to visit some people he had befriended there. As he was leaving for home, he was stopped by the police and warned to "get the hell out of here and stay out if you want to keep healthy." Lois, terrified, turned to him and said, "Yeah, Daddy, let's get the hell out of here." He made it a point not to bring the child into the ghetto again.

Shortly after that experience, Manny and several others were again stopped in the ghetto by the police for a so-called traffic violation. They decided to go to court and fight the ticket. With a large group of friends in his support, they filed into Judge Louis Bandell's courtroom where the case was scheduled for a hearing. A young law student, Jerry Gordon, later with the National Peace Action Coalition, introduced him to the conservative judge who heard the case. The case was dismissed because the police officer, upon seeing the courtroom filled with unfriendly people, disappeared. Later, in the judge's chambers, Judge Bandell clued us in on the state of the police force. Prior to 1940, qualification for joining the force was membership in the Klan or just a Klan mentality. Now, in 1947, they must be able to read and write as well. An indication of police sentiment was expressed in the following statement made by William Lindley, president of the Florida Public Officers Association, at a statewide meeting in St. Augustine, Florida, January 1946: "Negro veterans must be 'kept in their place.' These boys are coming back pretending to be heroes without even having seen a gun unless they stole one and smuggled it in. We've got to keep them in their places." We had learned that entry into the Negro community was reason enough for police harassment. To know or visit anyone there was equivalent to conspiracy or subversion in their eyes. Under these conditions, we were not anxious to make this place our home.

Several days after our court experience, we left for Detroit, unaware that we would soon be returning to Miami as permanent residents. In June 1947 our second daughter, June, was born. She, too, was a beautiful baby but was asthmatic. In the spring of 1948, after a second severe attack, we moved South again.

SOUTHERN CONFERENCE FOR HUMAN WELFARE

The Southern Conference for Human Welfare was alive on the Miami scene, although by no means as active as in other southern cities such as New Orleans, Louisiana, and Birmingham, Alabama, the centers of heavy industry. Here, the CIO provided the core for the organization, which then branched out to include many of the liberal intellectuals and professionals, but it never did reach the "common" people. It was primarily a top-level group and never became a grassroots mass organization. In Miami it was more like a statement-issuing organization with a paper membership.

Since 1938, the Southern Conference for Human Welfare had given leadership to the fight to abolish the poll tax and reform the South's undemocratic electoral system. It united all shades of liberal, progressive, and radical opinions in the South, including the Socialist and Communist Parties, in an effort to extend democracy to the southland. It was a reform movement that gave almost unqualified support to FDR and the New Deal. Its policies were based on domestic issues primarily.

Tarleton Collier, chairman of SCHW in 1943, said, "I have become confirmed in the conviction that we are not going to do anything in the South without organization of the little people, and this is not going to be accomplished except through a widespread, democratic and universal labor movement that will prevail against the red herring of race, communism, CIO, etc. There flatly isn't any other way than through power."

The SCHW had been under attack by the racist bigots since its inception, but the Cold War brought another kind of attack. The mere fact that it refused to expel the communists from the organization at a time when it was politically expedient to do so made it suspect. It had never denied that there were communists in the membership. They were an active part of movements in the South, including "Operation Dixie" and all other movements for reform and change. By the end of the war and with the advent of the Cold War, the various entities that made up SCHW began scurrying for safety in an attempt to escape the "red" label. This epithet was already being flaunted at any organization genuinely working for change.

In 1945 Senator Theodore A. Bilbo expressed a wish to filibuster both the Fair Employment Practices Committee and the Southern Conference out of existence. He labeled the SCHW the South's Number One Enemy. The report on the Southern Conference for Human Welfare, given by the House Committee on Un-American Activities during the first session of the Eightieth Congress in 1947, included the following passage: "The Southern Conference for Human Welfare was not a communist front but a popular front, a conglomeration of individuals from organizations as diverse as the Baptist Church and the Communist Party, united about a minimum program on which all the constituent factions could agree. That minimum program was aimed at repairing the defects of American capitalism, bringing the South up to the economic and social standards of the rest of the country, and finally in obtaining elementary justice for American Negroes."

This in no way stopped the vicious attacks on the organization and the individuals leading it. It was finally destroyed by the red-baiting from within and without. The only remaining vestige of this tremendous effort is the Southern Conference Educational Fund and *The Southern Patriot,* its publication. They are doing what the parent organization failed to accomplish. They are organizing black and white workers throughout industrial areas of the South, as well as the poor in Appalachia. They are educating the people as to the nature of the real enemy. They work in conjunction and cooperation with the Southern Christian Leadership Conference and similar organizations. Like their predecessor, the Southern Conference for Human Welfare, they too are under severe attack by the guardians of a racist society and are targets of bombing, harassment, and arrests.

PROGRESSIVE PARTY

When we settled in Miami we were faced with the need to make a decision that we knew would affect us for many years to come. We were aware of the undemocratic racist structure of society there and the limited number of people working to change the existing conditions. We were also aware of the activity of the KKK and the mentality of the law enforcement agencies. Yet we were never sophisticated enough to think that we might be victims of it.

In Detroit we were small fish in a big ocean as compared to the Miami scene. Now we would be big fish in a small pool. We had to truly search our souls and decide now just how deeply our sincerity and our convictions went. And so it was not without much torment and it was not accidental when we reached our decision. We believed we owed it to our children and to our country to work for a better America. We had confidence in the future.

We would continue the activities in which we participated in Detroit. In 1948 we were working with the Young Progressives on the forthcoming election campaign and in a limited way supporting the civil rights movement. It was really very difficult to find a fine line dividing the political arena from the problems of civil rights, electoral reform, and the right to vote.

Once we were settled in Miami, I directed my time and energies to the Progressives' campaign and became a public spokesman for the program it endorsed. At the same time, there was a Progressive Citizens group functioning on Miami Beach among the professionals and intellectuals. I lectured at the University of Miami, debated and spoke at local churches, organizations, and homes of individuals. My views were a matter of public record and subject to question at any time.

There was support in the Negro community for Henry Wallace, but not much enthusiasm for the voting process. We worked in mixed groups there, which brought increased harassment by the police. Typical of their frequent comments was, "Get these women out of here cause they're liable to be raped." We learned by experience that the black police, allowed to patrol the black areas only, were merely an extension of the white power system. They were equally cruel, if not more so, to the blacks. They were not permitted to carry guns or arrest white persons. For this they had to call white officers. This was the advanced state of the black police force at that time in Miami.

About the middle of August 1949, we held a party to bid farewell to my brother, who was leaving for medical school. It was good to relax from the pressures around us. That Saturday night was warm. The backyard was decorated with lights as we danced to the music of the Hora and other folk dances. The food was good and the drinks were cold. This was just what we all needed. The music and our voices carried beyond the confines of our lot. About 11:30 P.M. the doorbell rang and there at the front door stood two policemen. Also, sitting so that he was facing the open door was a Negro friend. Even though we had prepared our neighbors for the party, we expected the policemen to caution us that we were making too much noise. Instead, in a deep southern drawl, they tried to make us understand that this was a friendly warning. "You'd better get them damn niggers outta here." We let them know that this was our home and that these were our friends, that no one can tell us whom we can have here. We quoted the law but knew it was a waste of breath. They did not have the faintest notion as to what we were talking about. All they could say was that they would let the chief know "so he can set you right, cause we're new on the force, only two years," and besides they were from Georgia and didn't know too much about Florida law. They said someone else had once done something bad like this and neighbors came out with baseball bats to chase the niggers away. We replied that if we ran into difficulty we would call them. They replied that they would be too busy doing other things, so we'd better get rid of them niggers now.

The next morning, our five-year-old who had been playing outside came in to tell us that there was a paper on the door. It was a crude note consisting of different-sized words and letters from the headlines of the newspapers. It read "STOP BEING UNAMERICAN—KKK." Our daughter commented how glad she was that we moved there because the police really watch and protect children here. They had been around about every fifteen minutes, watching while she played. Intuitively, we knew this was the beginning of Klan harassment in either uniform. It was only the beginning.

In spite of the poor showing the Progressive Party made nationally, Henry Wallace carried two districts in Tampa, Florida. The party was organized around a good program, so after the elections we continued as a political force around this program.

The housing problem in the ghetto was deplorable. Many people lived in little shacks, lined up row after row. A city lot that normally would hold one or two houses was jammed with twenty-five to thirty shacks. Most of these were without electricity or sanitation facilities. The need for expansion of housing facilities was desperate. All this existed in the shadow of the wealth and opulence that Miami Beach personified.

In 1951 Negroes began to occupy a portion of a housing development called Knight Manor. It was a sixty-seven unit apartment only a block away from Carver Village in the ghetto. It stood at the great wall separating the black from the white community. Throughout Florida these walls existed for that purpose. The owner of the apartment building, a racist for many years, was unable to rent to whites due to its location and thus converted it to Negro occupancy. His desire for the almighty dollar threw him into company of those against whom he had fought for many years. He was maligned by the press, threatened by the Building Department for so-called violations, and the Klan responded with bombings in September, November, and December. Needless to say, no one ever was prosecuted for those acts. The economics of segregation created strange bedfellows.

A saturation of building in the white areas developed. Economics dictated that if the building contractors were to survive and continue building and making profits, it would have to be done in the black area. The white workers, faced with unemployment, decided that since union contractors were building there, they could demand jobs as union tradesmen. The blacks were not in the unions due to the union policy of segregation. However, for some thirty or forty years a so-called gentleman's agreement had existed. Its stated purpose was that whites would do the work in white areas and blacks in their areas. Its real purpose was to keep the blacks out of the white areas, since there was rarely any sizeable amount of work in the ghetto. These agreements were fairly common throughout the South. The new situation with white jobs opening up in the black area created the basis for tensions.

My husband, Manny, was now a painting contractor and had been a union member since 1938. He was deeply involved in the proceedings, since he also had contracts with builders in black areas. These same owners had been building rental apartments in the white areas. These were fully equipped with all the modern conveniences such as hard wood floors, range, refrigerator, venetian blinds, and included water. They were rented on a monthly basis for eighty dollars and maintained by management in excellent condition. The houses being built in the black area were one-third smaller, had no hard wood floors, no appliances, and had separate water meters for each apartment. Maintenance was nil. These rented on a weekly basis at a much higher rental than their supposed counterparts in the white areas.

Manny had black painters working in this area. He paid union scale and convinced them that now was the time to apply for union membership. The union rejected their applications and advised Manny that it was not necessary for them to be union members, nor was it required that he pay them scale. This infuriated the black workers, who were now beginning to understand just how the system was using them. They talked to their fellow workers in the various trades and soon the message was spread around. A meeting was arranged by the Progressive Party. Black building trades workers met with some progressive white building tradesmen and agreed on a plan of action.

The grand opening of the Gaines Housing Development in the black section of Opa Locka was set for Mother's Day. A record crowd was anticipated. A committee visited the builder with their list of grievances. The builder agreed that they were justified in their complaints. He said that he would like to cooperate but that his hands were tied. It was the construction trades unions and not he who controlled the hiring practices. The committee then put its ace card on the table. Either the builder negotiated with them or a picket line would be thrown around the development coinciding with the grand opening to the public on Mother's Day. Unquestionably, the public would side with their black brothers on this issue. The Gaines Corporation was not anxious for this kind of action to take place and immediately called the building trades unions to discuss the new turn of events.

In the meantime, Manny, as a union contractor, had written to the International Headquarters of the Painter's Union requesting clarification of the union position on membership requirements. When the reply came, by wire, it fortified his position about blacks being eligible for membership in the same local union. The local union leadership, however, was not ready to admit defeat. They sought out the nominal head of the black community, Edward Graham, a Baptist minister who was also the president of the local National Association for the Advancement of Colored People, and made a back-door agreement with him. They would arrange to meet with him and the black workers and discuss their demands, provided the picket line was called off. The major purpose was to exclude the Progressive Party and white people like Manny from the negotiations because they [the union] could negotiate from a position of united strength with no white forces on the side of the enemy, the blacks.

Once the picket line for Mother's Day was eliminated and white allies barred from the meeting, black enthusiasm for the cause suffered. Thus, without consulting the original committee, the minister accepted a settlement that the men later termed a "sell-out." The agreement specified that the Gaines project work would be divided 25 percent to the black tradesmen and 75 percent to white, all the contractors being white union contractors. In violation of all union policy and international and local agreements, union labor worked side by side with non-union labor because they refused to admit black workers into the unions. The NAACP president was not happy with the role he played. He had accepted at face value the offer of the bigoted union leadership at the expense of his own people. He had thought that by assuming a more conciliatory posture he could win more in negotiations. The union issued the black workers temporary work permits for this job, with a promise of union membership and full union benefits sometime in the future. That future was a long time away.

Many of us in the Young Progressives were just beginning to raise families. For some, like myself, who had come from mixed communities in the North, it was very difficult to see our children growing up in a sterile atmosphere. So when my child came to me at the tender age of four and announced that she now understood why some people are dark skinned and others light, I stopped immediately to listen to her explanation. "They are dark, Mommy, because they always do dirty work. They are garbage collectors and the cleaning ladies so they get all the dirt on them and it colors their skin." We had been so engrossed in saving society that we were unaware of the impact it was having on our own children. We determined that we must do something to correct this unfortunate situation.

We organized an interracial nursery and play school in the basement of Rev. Graham's church, which was used frequently for liberal causes. There were not too many who participated, probably about fifteen to twenty, and a majority of the children were white, but it did serve to introduce black and white children to one another. They learned that they all like to play the same games, fight about the same things, and enjoyed their Saturday morning experiences. For the mothers, it was a catharsis since it eased our conscience somewhat and helped also to develop a closer relationship between the mothers by discussing mutual problems.

In the fall of 1949, when a rash of repressive legislation began to threaten even those mildly liberal, a coalition of Progressives and the unions organized a huge protest meeting in Flamingo Park on Miami Beach. It was already becoming ominously obvious that in this area the attacks were beginning to take on anti-Semitic overtones. The speakers roster included dignitaries like the mayor and members of the city council, leaders of the religious community, and ordinary people like myself. I spoke on behalf of the Progressive Party and cautioned that unless we defended the basic constitutional rights of those we may not agree with, we might soon find our own rights disappearing. That if we succumbed to the paranoia of red-herring psychology, we would be strengthening the hand of those intent on destroying even the small gains made at great sacrifice. The mayor and others quoted legal phraseology to show that these were illegal bills; at the same time they proclaimed their anti-communism. They never understood the purpose of the repressive legislation. Divide and conquer. That it did. Once the McCarran Act became law, many of them joined with the pack in helping destroy their one-time friends.

Feeling stronger as the liberal forces weakened, the Klan planned a motorcade through downtown Miami, complete with ceremonial robes, banners, crosses, and whatever paraphernalia they employed. Police Chief Walter Headley had agreed to provide an "honor guard" of police to escort the motorcade. We initiated a phone-a-protest directed at Chief Headley and his police department. For several days prior to the great extravaganza, people called to protest the use of the police department for such purposes. We demanded that the only role of the police was to prevent the Klan from committing unlawful acts and from intimidating people. I called about two hours before the motorcade was to start and the chief yelled, "God damn you and the other million calls that have been coming in day and night. We're not giving them any escort but we can't stop their motorcade." The Klan performed like clowns to a low-pitched audience. The glamour of their extravaganza had been dulled and their great show of strength had fizzled. We were delighted with the results of our campaign. That was the last open showing of the Klan that I can remember there. An ordinance was subsequently passed requiring the elimination of hoods and masks.

Of course, the Klan did not fade into oblivion. They remained very active, indeed, but not necessarily in the garb of the bedsheet. As long as their program was being carried out by officialdom in the form of repressive legislation and press intimidation, and in the guise of the Federal Bureau of Investigation and local police agents, there was no need for their bedsheet operations.

CIVIL RIGHTS CONGRESS

I don't recall exactly how we became involved in Civil Rights Congress activity in Miami. We had been active in the organization in Detroit. It just seemed to come naturally; many people we knew were active in the Miami CRC. I do recall that there had been an illegal search and seizure at the home of a suspected communist early in 1948, just prior to our return to Miami. There was no search warrant, no legal process, but records and mailing lists were seized. John Coe, former Florida state senator from Pensacola and an active and moving force in the state's Progressive Party, volunteered his services as an attorney. During the course of Progressive Party activity, I learned to love and admire this man whose family had once fought for the Confederacy. He was now involved in the battle for a democratic South and the defeat of Cold War repression. We developed a friendship that continued over many years. Each birthday the Coes received from the Graffs a five-pound kosher salami, one of the delicacies he came to enjoy in the course of his contact with Miami's progressive Jewish community.

The need existed to educate the citizenry to understand that if the rights of one individual, regardless of personal politics, were destroyed, the rights of all were in jeopardy. Since there was no other organization that would accept this challenge, the Civil Rights Congress took on the responsibility to do so. Automatically, this made the organization a target of various red-baiting groups, the press, and government agencies.

The Civil Right Congress was an active organization, based not only among the white liberal establishment but among the Negro people as well. Its concern was discussing the issues, educating the people, and acting on the issues. On July 16, 1949, Groveland, Florida, witnessed a familiar southern-style frame-up that eventually became known as the little Scottsboro case of Florida. Shortly after the Groveland terror occurred, I wrote an article that was carried as a front page story in *The National Guardian* and became the basis for articles in other publications as well [See appendix 1].

As a result of my investigation into the Groveland case, I became deeply committed to helping people there to seek justice. We contacted the Miami NAACP to co-sponsor a protest meeting. They could not do so officially since this would be contrary to national policy, but individually the leadership gave their full support to the action. We scheduled a meeting at the Community Center and then organized a campaign exposing the frame-ups. We demanded government action to properly punish those guilty of murder and the willful destruction of the homes and property of the black residents by burning and shooting. We asked for contributions of food, clothing, and money for the victims in Groveland. We covered all sections of the city, black and white, including the downtown area.

I volunteered to leaflet the downtown area and did so, albeit with much apprehension. Then the police intervened. I was properly attired and looked like an average middle-class youth. If I had been circulating Klan material, there would have been only friendly comments from the law-and-order men. But I was asking people to join in condemning the Klan and the lawless vigilantes. Two officers came by and one grabbed my arm and threw me up against the wall. I was terrified. I had heard stories about this kind of police action but thought that these were exaggerated. I was alone and did not know what to expect. The other officer took my leaflets and ripped them up. I tried to force a brave exterior and protested my rights. I demanded that they take me to the station and book me. Their response was a laugh. This was only a warning and I'd better not try the same thing again. My arm was black and blue for several days, and my shoulders were sore and stiff from the roughing up I had been given. I was really shaken and very angry. This was the accepted norm if you were caught in "subversive" activity like this. Imagine if I were black. It was enough to frighten the staunchest rights advocate. But I guess I was too stubborn, too mad to be frightened off. Yet others were arrested and beaten in the course of exercising these simple democratic rights.

The response by the Ku Klux Klan was as expected. They threatened to burn crosses at the homes and churches of the scheduled speakers, and they threatened to bomb the center where the meeting was to be held. When the time for the meeting came, we wondered how many people would respond to the call despite the Klan challenge. Gradually the hall filled to capacity. Last minute changes were necessary to replace speakers who feared appearing or who were prevented from coming by their church boards.

I was one of the speakers. As I walked to face the audience to make my presentation, I experienced a sensation that was new to me. It was fear. My stomach felt as though butterflies were flitting around. My mouth was dry and my heart was pounding. I tried to regain my composure before beginning. I anticipated that at any moment a bomb might be exploded or fire break out or KKK hoodlums would burst in. I looked straight ahead at the multitude of strong, beautiful, serious faces, mostly black, but with a good healthy sprinkling of white, and felt the tensions leave me. All these people were aware of the threats and the dangers and they still came. They came and brought food and clothing and they contributed funds to help their victimized brothers. They came and showed the Klan that threats could not stop them. All these black people were the brave ones. In spite of all the problems, the meeting was a success. The people learned the truth about Groveland and responded. A truckload of supplies went to Groveland the following day.

We then called on the nominal leaders of the black community for help. These were three persons—a dentist, an attorney, and a minister—who owned much real estate. They represented the "Uncle Toms" of the black churches and the professions. They were referred to as the "unholy alliance." They listened with closed hearts, minds, and pocketbooks. The NAACP eventually came into the case and became the legal representative for the Groveland victims.

In November 1949, in the midst of the spiraling Cold War repression, it was reported that an official of the Justice Department had announced he was coming to Miami. There was reason to believe that the purpose of his visit was a "fishing" expedition, such as those taking place in other areas of the country. The Civil Rights Congress called a mass meeting to protest attacks on the democratic rights of people while at the same time authorities were taking no action on cases like Groveland. The meeting was a tremendous success. Representatives of all sections of the community spoke out for freedom and justice, but we were totally unprepared for the reception we received upon leaving the hall. As the doors were opened, the flash bulbs told the story of a conspiracy by the federal and local government agencies, the press, and the Klan. The pictures of all participants were splashed across the pages of the *Miami Daily News* under headlines depicting them as subversives, reds, and foreign agents. Those labeled as subversive included the president of the Baptist Ministers Conference who was also president of the NAACP, organizers of local unions, businessmen, clergy, professionals, and others.

At the same time, the Klan engaged in a series of cross-burnings and threats. With the hysterical red-baiting of the press, in addition to the Klan threats, many CRC people sought to protect their jobs and their loved ones by denying support and denouncing the organization, stating they were duped by the communists. The press was drunk with joy at the unexpected recantations and continued to give full coverage to this delectable item. It published license plate numbers, sought out the owners at their places of business or employment, and if this pressure was not sufficient to produce the desired results, the Klan took up the cudgel.

The Klan sent a "love note" to Victor Emanuel, an electrical contractor who was chairman of the Civil Rights Congress, giving him forty-eight hours in which to "save his soul" and his wife and children. Within that period of time he sent letters to both major newspapers stating in the exact words of the Klan his denunciation of the organization he had chaired. He also sent a letter to the Klan advising them of his action, but it did not reach them in time. Shortly before the forty-eight hour deadline, he called an emergency Civil Rights Congress meeting and advised the group of what he had done. This completed, he left with fearful misgivings about the entire situation. He and his family went into temporary hiding.

A friend and I immediately drove to the home of Harold Tannen, an attorney who lived across the street from the now ex-chairman. As we drove down the dark street we were aware of a strange sensation in the air. It was after 11:00 P.M. A bright light was burning next door to the chairman's house. An arrow on a sign pointed next door. It was his brother-in-law who wanted to be sure that no mistake was made!

As we drove closer, the lights of our small truck picked up the eeriest sight I can ever remember. Walking silently on the sidewalk, in pairs, were about a dozen klansmen in their working habits, black robes with black hoods covering their faces. They carried a large cross and chains that rattled. From the holes in the hoods, the lights picked up the gleam of their eyes, shining bright like burning candles. It was as though a procession of the dead rising from their graves was coming at us. We were petrified with fright. We could have driven right into them, but didn't. We sounded the horn loudly, turned the truck around, and sped off to the nearest public phone to call for help. Foolishly and without thinking, we called the police. Hysterically, I yelled, "The Klan, the Klan. . . ." All they asked was what was my name and where did I live. They would not accept my report about this Klan activity and indicated their lack of interest by stating that the report was not necessary. I hung up. Evidently, they knew in advance what the plans were. I have never forgotten the horror of that night. Many were the nights I awoke in a cold sweat as I relived the terror of that experience. Until then I only had heard of the Klan in white dress robes, but this was no ceremony, this was reality.

Shortly after this terrifying experience, in the absence of anyone willing to assume the responsibility, I became acting chairman of the Civil Rights Congress. I was in frequent communication with William L. Patterson, militant Negro leader and national chairman of the CRC. He was then accumulating evidence for the petition to the United Nations called "We Charge Genocide," accusing the United States of the attempted genocide of the Negro people. Occasionally, he would call and ask that we investigate complaints of frame-ups, intimidation, and harassment in South Florida. We followed through on the requests and helped provide legal advice and services where needed. Often it meant several trips before getting to see the family. This was due to surveillance by the "law enforcement" agencies. It was most important to be as cautious as possible. If a "tail" was on you and inadvertently you led them to the family seeking assistance, it could mean the difference between life and death for the victim and endanger the livelihood of the family.

I vividly recall one particular case of a teenager, about sixteen or seventeen years old, who was already serving on the chain gang. The charge was the usual: "Raping a white woman." We drove to his family's home, a two-room shack papered with newsprint, wall to wall, to keep out the cold and the drafts. Kerosene lamps were used for lighting and there were no windows or sanitary facilities. It was reminiscent of the slave cabins and may have been just that.

We spoke to the victim's older sister. She was the only one at home at the time because their mother was a sleep-in domestic who came home only on Sundays. She told us that he was a good boy and that his only crime was that he refused to step off the sidewalk when a white woman was passing. Accidentally, his hand or arm had brushed her. This was rape! It was nothing new to the community, since it had happened many times before. There was road work to be done and the chain gang was a ready source of free labor. His mother was becoming ill with concern because the boy was considered "uppity" and she feared for his life. So a cousin, one of America's great black artists of today, but not yet too well known outside the black community at that time, was coming to give a concert in the church to raise funds for an attorney who could "pay off" to get him freed.

Due to the reputation we had earned for being leaders in the civil rights arena, which meant "subversion" to the government and the press, fewer public places were made available to us. Therefore, the image given us appeared to become almost the reality, not in the sense of committing any subversive acts, but in acting the role. It was difficult to hold a meeting of more than six persons to discuss and plan activity. The danger to a black in the white area at night, we assumed, was greater than to whites in the black areas. One night we met in a funeral parlor. The body had been prepared for viewing the following day and the mortician said that since there was no harm that could come to the corpse and little chance the police would want to go into that room, it would be the best place for us to meet. Little did we know that one of our group was a police informer. He had been notified of the meeting but no one knew in which room we would be. The police came and questioned the mortician, who responded that the family was in there with their departed. They were satisfied and left. But there were many of us besides the corpse who had stopped breathing for a brief period that night.

It took more courage than most people could muster for the mortician to do what he had done. We thanked him deeply and told him that we appreciated so very much the dangerous position we had placed him in, and that we would not allow a recurrence. He replied that he was not unaware of the risk at the time he offered his place and knew we were working in his best interests as well. I, who was always deathly afraid of even viewing a corpse, had sat with one for an entire evening. I guess that experience cured me of my old fears. We had more real fears to face.

Time passed, and in spite of the increased harassment we came forward more frequently to defend the constitutional rights of persons regardless of color, political beliefs, or association. We opened a small office in the downtown area jointly with the Progressive Party. It was the object of frequent break-ins and other types of harassment. We knew the telephone was tapped and we were certain the place was wired for sound. We felt we had nothing to hide and could not endanger the lives and livelihood of community people who offered us their facilities.

The Groveland frame-up still haunted us. We had all the necessary proof to convict those guilty of tearing up the black community. The newspapers had published photographs of their cars with the license plate numbers clearly showing, mostly from Alabama, which showed the occupants shooting into the Negroes' homes. There were photographs of fires being set. The bravado of the lynchers was exposed and was available. All this evidence and still the government did nothing to apprehend the criminals. At the same time, the government was busy harassing people who had committed no crimes. It was preoccupied with arresting alleged communists under the Smith Act. This was justice?

We decided that a committee should go to Washington to present this evidence and demand federal intervention in Groveland. Our problem was finances. We had volunteers who offered to take time off from work and family chores, but we had no car available to make the trip. The cost of traveling any other way was prohibitive. An answer to our dilemma came in the form of a young white attorney who had only recently joined the Congress and had become very active around the Groveland case. (Later we learned that he was an FBI agent who had infiltrated our organization.) He said he had discussed the case with his law firm and they thought it could be considered a public service for him to go as part of the delegation. Since he also had a car available and offered to drive, there was no reason to procrastinate.

We arranged an appointment with Mr. James M. McInerney, assistant attorney general. Five of us soon left for the capital armed with our evidence. We were shown into the office of the attorney general, and shortly thereafter Mr. McInerney entered. He was irritated because of the pickets and protests against the Smith Act convictions directed at the Justice Department. We spent approximately fifteen minutes with him, giving him the background of the Groveland case and presented him with the evidence we carried. We contended that the conspiracy was on the part of those denying the basic rights of life, liberty, and the pursuit of happiness to the black citizens in our country, as demonstrated by what happened in Groveland, and not by the communists who were being hounded by the Justice Department.

Mr. McInerney's response was hostile. He stated that justice would take its course and he would not allow us to "intimidate" him. We assured him this was not our purpose. He said that even if we thought we were not communists, as far as he was concerned we were no different since our organization was helping with their legal defense. On Groveland, the federal government would not interfere in matters that were the states' domain. His final warning to me was, "You, I'll remember you." He evidently did.

Our trip home was rather depressing and silent. The attorney, whom we had assumed would be rather vocal as part of the delegation, never uttered a word once we were inside the Justice Department. On the way to Washington, he had been giving us all the reasons for assuming the posture we did. He gave us the impression that he was extremely sympathetic to the Smith Act victims and he even compared them with the Groveland victims. His personal behavior was less than exemplary. When reminded he had a wife and child at home, he replied that we needed some relaxation. All work and no play was not for him.

We knew we had accomplished nothing in Washington. I felt that we had been had. The FBI had provided us with transportation to Washington in exchange for what it hoped would be useful information to them. The attorney disappeared immediately after our return. Although we were conscious of the police state atmosphere we worked in, we were still naive enough not to suspect that there were informers in our ranks. Some of us were guilty of a form of chauvinism in reverse. We refused to think of blacks as being amongst the informers. We continued to pay dearly for this error in political judgement in the future course of our work.

One day an important looking document was delivered to my home. The return address was U.S. Government, Department of Justice, Washington, D.C. My curiosity was aroused. It was a thank you letter in the form of a certificate complete with seal. They thanked me for registering my organization as a subversive communist front as required by the McCarran Act! The audacity! I immediately wired Washington that they had committed a grievous error. My organization was neither subversive nor a communist front. I demanded a copy of the letter supposedly sent by me and its removal from their files. Several days later I received the copy. It was a letter typed on our Civil Rights Congress letterhead and signed with my name. The signature was obviously a forgery. It was a very poor imitation. The letterhead had been taken from the office, and that could mean by almost anyone. One small section had been cut out. From what I could piece together it contained a file number. This really shook me up. I did not want to believe that our government would stoop to such depths as forgery and then use it to serve whatever purpose they desired.

We had received brochures from the national office of the Civil Rights Congress explaining in detail "Your Rights." With all the investigative committees taking junkets for "fishing expeditions," it seemed that Miami would be an ideal place for them to visit, especially in the winter. So as a precaution we had several persons visit various members of the community who had participated in some way in one of the various liberal or left of center groups. Manny and I visited with several people and advised them of their rights as described in the brochure. We left copies for them to pass on to their friends. To the chagrin of some who never thought of themselves as constituting any kind of a ripple, let alone a threat, these little booklets were put to good use in a very short period of time.

Shortly thereafter, due to the intimidation and harassment by the press, we decided to disband the Civil Rights Congress as an active force. We felt that the work we were doing was more important than the nomenclature. So with the knowledge and consent of the local NAACP leadership, the active members of the Civil Rights Congress merged their activity with the local branch. The leaders of the group were happy to have our support on civil rights issues.

NAACP

We joined the National Association for the Advancement of Colored People in the hope that it could become a leader and an organizer for the people. The NAACP had always been a "rights" organization but worked exclusively at the top level without reaching the people below. There was no ladder of evolution, no communication with the "common" man. Action was generally between the legal defense committee and the courts. The organization rarely served as an educator or organizer, except for *The Crisis* magazine and fund-raising affairs that reached intellectuals and professionals primarily.

Leadership of the Miami branch consisted of well-educated and influential professional people. Many of them were also supporters of the Southern Conference for Human Welfare. We had worked together on many campaigns. There was every reason to believe that they too were concerned with necessary changes in our society.

On the state level, Harry T. Moore was executive secretary. He was a former principal and school teacher and more on the militant side than what the national office preferred. His home was Mims, Florida, in the heart of central Florida's Klan country. He was fired from his job as school principal in Brevard County in 1945 as a result of his fight for equalization of the salaries of white and Negro teachers. From that time on he worked as executive secretary of the Progressive Voters League, and in 1946 he also became executive secretary of the Florida State Conference of NAACP.

Early in 1948 Harry Moore used his influence and pressured Florida A&M University to reject a gift of $237,500 from Florida's bigoted governor, Millard F. Caldwell. That money had been awarded to Caldwell as a result of a libel suit against *Collier's* magazine, which had earlier censured Caldwell for his racist statements and lack of effective action in the lynching case of Jesse James Payne [a black man, Payne had been lynched in Madison County, Florida, in 1945]. Moore felt that it was not in the interests of the Negro people to accept such gifts. Moore also contended that it was the state's responsibility to fund the university. Mr. Moore was traveling the state and stirring up some of the latent antagonisms that lay dormant beneath the surface. But he was reaching beyond the upper echelons, and the national office in New York was not particularly pleased. Nationally, the NAACP was caught on the horns of a dilemma. The Cold War hysteria had created a schism in its ranks.

There was one segment of the national NAACP leadership that had already withdrawn support from the Southern Conference for Human Welfare. This group could easily support a witch-hunt within the NAACP. At the same time, they recognized the danger they too faced from repressive legislation introduced in Congress. In May 1948, the NAACP called for the defeat of the Mundt Bill [a Congressional proposal in 1948 to require communist registration and outlaw the Communist Party, but not approved] because it defined subversive so loosely that the NAACP itself, as well as other progressive groups fighting for full citizenship rights for minorities, might be brought within its scope. Meanwhile, other sections of the leadership and membership supported endorsing the presidential candidacy of Henry A. Wallace of the Progressive Party.

In June 1949, the fortieth anniversary convention of the NAACP brought a flood of resolutions from branches all over the country to change the structure and involve the rank and file in decision making. Those branches, and there were many, acted on their own to involve the rank and file of the community in action, but frequently they were chastised by the national NAACP. In spite of the widespread demand for basic change, there was none. Cold War psychology prevailed. In Miami we were unconcerned with the dilemma of the national office. Many church leaders often became involved in local elections. Politicians fell over themselves seeking to address their campaigns to the black community. They paid the churches well for this privilege. The funds were willingly accepted from all contenders. This was one of the most painless ways to raise money for needed church repairs and programs.

After the Groveland terror and in spite of the various so-called investigations, still no action had been taken by the law and order people. Three of the four young men who had been framed in the Groveland case were still alive. They were incarcerated under conditions in which their lives were in constant danger. The NAACP provided legal counsel for them. Harry Moore traveled the state in their behalf raising funds as well as the consciousness of the people. In March 1951, Harry Moore protested to President Truman against appointment of Millard Caldwell as administrator of Civilian Defense on the grounds that he was a "racist and prejudiced white supremacist who opposed the 1944 Supreme Court decision making white primaries unconstitutional."

Membership in the NAACP was on the decline for many reasons. It became more difficult to raise money for the NAACP in Florida. The State Conference of the NAACP decided to cease financing a full-time executive secretary. Mr. Moore was then named coordinator of branches and a part-time functionary.

In April 1951, the U.S. Supreme Court by unanimous decision reversed the state court's ruling and ordered a new trial for the Groveland victims. On November 6, 1951, Samuel Shepherd and Walter Lee Irvin were being transported by Sheriff Willis McCall to a new trial site. In the middle of a lonely stretch of rural central Florida, the sheriff ordered them out of the car and commanded them to run. He killed Shepherd and critically wounded Irvin. No one anticipated that Irvin would live to tell the story of the sheriff's actions. In spite of this, Sheriff McCall retained his position. Subsequently, Irvin was found guilty a second time. Southern justice again triumphed.

Harry Moore, like so many other persons, was incensed at Florida injustice. He spared neither his tongue nor his energies in demanding federal intervention and justice. Florida NAACP branches demanded action to punish the sheriff. On Christmas night 1951, scarcely two months after the murder of Samuel Shepherd, the Moore home was bombed. Harry Moore was killed. Several days later, on January 3, 1952, Mrs. Moore also died of injuries sustained in that bombing. At the time of Harry Moore's death, relations with the national NAACP were less than cordial. His salary had not been paid for several months and policy changes were in the making that would have reduced his influence.

The murder of Mr. and Mrs. Moore shocked even the most insensitive. The funeral for Harry Moore included all the dignitaries, and very appropriate words were spoken by many national personalities. Mrs. Moore's funeral was very simple. There were few flowers and very few people. The grief had already been expressed a few days earlier. What else was there to be said? I recall sitting there in the grass after the service watching Rockwell Kent, one of the great people's artists, sketching a simple scene of the countryside and the Moore house. He caught the sadness and the serenity. I thought then how beautifully he had captured the mood of the moment with only a few strokes of his pencil.

We went home feeling very depressed. We had lost a friend who could not be replaced. We knew too that we owed it to this man to talk to the people as he had been doing and to let the air be filled with the hurt and anger we felt.

After the death of the Moores, financial arrangements were made by the national NAACP to repay his salary. *The Crisis* editorial of January 1952 asked, "What have the 'good' people of Florida done about these acts of terrorism? Nothing. Governor Fuller Warren—almost nothing. The federal government—nothing effective despite FBI investigations. Florida justice becomes a cruel farce and a mockery. For there is evidently one justice for the white man and another for the Negro."

In Miami, the branch planned a memorial service appropriate to the memory of this man who had given so much of himself for so long. We planned a silent funeral march to a local church where the services would take place. We anticipated no problems and were very surprised when the national

NAACP office requested that we cancel our plans. We proceeded over their objections only to find that not one church was available to us. The Klan had issued a warning to the entire black community. Anyone cooperating or participating in the services could anticipate a fate similar to [that of] the Moores. Our only hope was in one totally independent black minister affectionately known as the "Cornfield Preacher." We visited him at his simple, unpretentious home in the heart of his community and discussed our plans with him. We knew he was ill and had a bad heart and felt that he above all others had justification for denying use of his small wooden church in Overtown. We waited and then heard him say, "If we have people willing to stand up in the face of these threats, then I'm honored to take my place beside them. You may have my church for anything you wish."

It was this kind of bravery that turned out the largest interracial march in the history of Miami and probably the first of its kind in the South. No crosses were burned, no bombs exploded. We had organized our own defense and let it be known that we were very serious about it. The people were angry and the Klan was scared.

The NAACP often attracted more white liberals than blacks on the same intellectual level. In many periods the active leadership positions were held by a white majority. Perhaps the national office should have spent more time trying to understand why there was comparatively little support from black people. Even professional people such as school teachers, who held the key to contact with the adult community as well as the education of the young, provided tepid support.

At the time, the Miami NAACP was fighting for the right of blacks to use public golf courses, but its relevance was not exactly appreciated in a community that still lacked electricity and sanitation facilities. Can you imagine the unrestrained joy experienced there when in 1950 the U.S. Supreme Court reversed a Florida Supreme Court decision banning Negroes from playing on a city-owned golf course in Miami? It would be very difficult to find many black golf enthusiasts in the community, but this too was thought to be a momentous decision for the NAACP.

I recall [future] Supreme Court Justice Thurgood Marshall coming down and meeting with us over lunch or dinner at the local hotel in the Negro area. There was always a top level meeting with the "leaders" of the community, white and black—the clergy and professionals, plus the board of the local NAACP branch. Justice Marshall was a great conversationalist and without a doubt a brilliant man, but we never had the feeling that average people would be welcomed at such events. This was not part of organization policy.

Teachers and administrators in the black schools were reluctant to express their feelings on the school desegregation case then being argued in the Supreme Court. When we delved deeper into the question of why, we were shocked to discover that there was a great fear that if integration of the schools ever became a reality, black faculty in the school system would suffer. They worried that they would be discharged regardless of the quality of their work or their years of experience. How prophetic! Today we see how justified they were in their fears. How unfortunate that in our society the sacrifices that must be made in the course of change must always be borne by those least able to afford them.

The voter registration campaign became our number one priority. This was the Achilles heel of southern aristocracy. I was program chairman of the local branch and became chairman of the voter registration drive. We had a committee of seven, composed of two white and five black members. We organized the drive to include all sections of the community. The support of the teachers was genuine and wholehearted when we were engaged in an educational campaign for voter registration. Notices were sent home to parents. The children were taught the importance of registration so that they in turn could explain it to their elders.

This campaign won the support of the entire professional and intellectual community, unlike any other issue. *Ebony* magazine sent a staff of reporters and photographers to cover our campaign. I made sure I was not in the photographs, fearing further harassment by the powers that be. Teams of two were assigned to door to door canvassing. They discussed the urgency of registration and left material answering any questions that might arise. They then set up appointments to take people to the registration centers and later bring them home. We had earlier forced the city fathers to open the fire stations in the neighborhoods and other places as registration centers. We succeeded in keeping them open in the evenings and Saturdays for four weeks prior to election so working people could participate in the electoral process. We maintained the pressure and reduced some of the harassment that occurred during the registration process. Previously, one needed utility bills, rent receipts, and telephone bills over a one-year period to prove residency. This requirement effectively eliminated 90 percent or more of the community who rented on a weekly basis and did not receive receipts. There was much and frequent movement within the ghetto, but the racist city fathers knew there was no place else to go. When we encountered difficulty with the registration authorities, we often returned with additional forces. Usually a clergyman came with us to testify that the individual in question was a member of his church.

Our registration drive made progress, but we were moving much more slowly than we had anticipated. There were many lessons for us to learn in the course of our work, lessons for ourselves for the future. White registration workers often were visibly shaken on our trips into the ghetto. It took many discussions with our black friends to understand and be able to accept certain facts of life. Our white friends were very insensitive to the question of safety for the blacks who participated in NAACP activities. Too often the feeling expressed was one of paternalism—we're doing it for them. They could not understand that a white man was neither trusted nor welcomed in the ghetto. Little distinction was made between a do-gooder, a police agent, or a bill collector. The natural reaction is for the protection of a friend or neighbor. So when the driver would ask which apartment Mr. or Mrs. Jones rented, the reply most frequently would be that they never heard of anyone by that name living there. It often necessitated several trips to complete one registration. Eventually, it was determined that a black person must always be present on any of our registration drives. Appointments did not have the same significance in the black community as they did to those working on the campaign, so they were often forgotten. Only when personal friendships developed was there a basis for trust.

Our committee continuously maintained the educational campaign via leaflets, the Negro press, and a weekly radio program, as well as in the schools and the churches. In spite of our well-organized efforts on every level, many people had difficulty comprehending what benefits they would derive by supporting one politician over another.

Our efforts were being felt. The simplest way to determine this was not only by the numbers of additional voters added to the registration lists, but by the various forms of harassment and the quantity as well as quality of informers, provocateurs, and FBI and similar agents that were assigned to us.

During the course of the campaign, which extended over a prolonged period of time, a handsome young black man named George made himself available each time I needed transportation or a baby sitter. He was there to help with any problem that might arise. He was new to the area. He said he had recently graduated from a Negro college and was anxious to help with the campaign in any way possible. We never questioned his sincerity or his source of income. We were delighted that he had joined the "cause." He attended all meetings and participated in decision making.

It was during this period of time that I became pregnant and was subjected to the basest and vilest form of mental pressure and anguish I had ever known. In small doses George began dropping hints about his girl friend. I naturally asked why he never brought her with him and said we would like to meet the young lady. Gradually, over an extended period of time, I was almost convinced that I was his girl friend. This was a gradual process of first telling me that she was white, later describing her hair color, eyes, shoe size, dress, and so on. Then later that she was married and by this time, naive as I was, I began to doubt my own sanity. When he said she was pregnant and bearing his child, my suspicions were confirmed. Was I leading two lives? Was I suffering from a split personality? Was I the innocent dupe of a wild plot to destroy my sanity?

There was only one thing for me to do. I openly accused him of being an FBI agent or else a very sick individual who needed immediate psychiatric care. As suddenly as he had appeared from nowhere, George disappeared. We could only assume that he had outlived his usefulness and was sent elsewhere on another perverted assignment. For me personally, the torment did not end until the birth of my child. The thought that our government and its agents would stoop to such depths was an indication of how sick the society really was at the time.

During this period, attacks intensified on NAACP attorneys defending Miami civil rights cases, Leo Sheiner and Harold Tannen. One attorney in particular—Sheiner—had been nominal head of the Southern Conference for Human Welfare in Florida. We met with Bob Saunders, the new NAACP state organizer, and urged support for the attorneys. It was part of the nationwide campaign of repression. We argued that now it was the attorneys, next it would be the active leadership, and finally it would be the organization itself. Mr. Saunders was adamant. The NAACP would take no position on the attacks on the lawyers. It would be contrary to national policy.

Almost prophetically, that was exactly what occurred, and in that very order. The final blow was the Johns Committee investigation of the Miami NAACP as a communist-front organization, with the subsequent conviction of the two leading ministers, the president and former president of the NAACP, on charges of contempt.

MISCELLANEOUS ORGANIZATIONS

It would be remiss on my part to fail to deal with some of the other organizations that became part of the local scene at the time and with which I had varying degrees of contact. They, too, played an important role in the happenings of the period. My remarks will be limited to either experiences with them or information derived from some of the people in the groups.

Miami had a fairly large Jewish community divided into religious and secular groups. Beside these religious divisions, the heart of Jewish activity flourished in the Jewish Community Center and the Jewish Cultural Center. Some support for liberal causes came from the Rabbinate, but very little from the members of the orthodox and conservative synagogues. The social action committees of several of the synagogues had invited ministers and black representatives to speak. Several attempts were made, particularly during Brotherhood Week, to invite Negro Boy Scouts to meet with the troops in the various synagogues. This was only a beginning and it was a brave gesture. It was met with racist threats and even bomb explosions at some synagogues and temples. The Jewish reply was the formation of a twenty-four hour vigil around the various Jewish Centers. We felt that we could not rely on the police to secure our institutions, so we set our own defense system into operation. This became public knowledge and it was the end of the bombings.

The Jewish Community Center was a conglomeration of people from all walks of life and with all shades of political philosophy and social understanding. Members of the "Board" that determined policy represented a cross section of the community. These included attorneys involved in civil rights actions, as well as professional people interested only in the prestigious social benefits such an institution could provide. They also included people like ourselves who participated in many of the activities and whose children participated in the children's programs. In addition, several of the directors of local centers were graduate social workers who participated in social action programs.

The Jewish Cultural Center was the home of a secular Jewish organization, the Jewish People's Fraternal Order, which sponsored concerts, lectures, a Jewish folk chorus, a Jewish language school, and a secular Sunday School for children. Its facilities were frequently used for various liberal and leftist causes. The members of reading circles and cultural groups could usually be counted on for spontaneous assistance. They had supplied food and various kinds of support for the struggling new trade union movements throughout the years. Their generosity extended to individuals in need of help in many ways. They radiated a genuine feeling of warmth and understanding for those participating in movements for change. This was the one place on Miami Beach where people of all ages could come together to discuss problems. They, too, suffered their share of bomb threats and other forms of harassment. In addition to the anti-Semitism of the Cold War period, opponents continually sought to label the Center "red."

It was, therefore, natural that the Jewish Cultural Center should be the first target of an attack. It came in the guise of David Kraslow, a young Jewish reporter on the *Miami Herald* staff out to make a place for himself in the Cold War era. It was reminiscent of the Hearst style of reporting. He had seen books by Marx, Engels, Lenin, and Stalin on the shelves of the Center library. The works of Steinbeck, Hemingway, Emma Lazarus, Howard Fast, Thoreau, and many more could also be found there. In addition to the dangerous nature of this material, the Center library had copies of the U.S. Constitution, the Magna Carta, and other historic subversive documents. Primarily, the library contained a very large collection of Jewish literature by Peretz, Sholem Aleichem, Asch, and others. It was open to anyone who wished to use it. Kraslow of the *Herald*, this great defender of our freedoms, felt that since children came to the Jewish Cultural Center, they were in danger of being subverted. He attempted to have the Sunday School closed, using books in the library as an excuse. One wonders if he had ever taken the time to visit any public library and check the books on their shelves.

The Parent Teachers Association was a fair representation of the school situation—one for the white schools and one for the colored schools. As a matter of fact, it was very difficult to determine anything about the black group since there was no communication between the two. The PTA state convention included only white representation. There were two separate textbook depositories, and all items connected with education were segregated. It was, among other things, a most un-economical method of providing education in a system that was not exactly making great advances.

Our children attended the Shenandoah Elementary School, which was composed of primarily middle-class southern families with a smaller percentage, about 25 percent, of Jewish migrants from the North. One day our children brought home notices for a school carnival sponsored by the PTA for fund-raising purposes. Included on the list of activities was the "Nigger Baby Game." I could not believe what I read. How dare a public educational institution allow this to be sent home with the children. How dare they discuss this as a game with our children.

A PTA meeting was scheduled within a few days. I had planned to attend to hear speakers discuss the question of religion and the schools—the separation of church and state issue. I was confident that someone would raise the other question. As the meeting progressed, I became more agitated. The Catholic representative took a strong position that religion, as a necessary part of our children's education, was the school's responsibility. The rabbi took a middle of the road—"yes, but"—position. A Methodist minister was the only one on the panel who supported the constitutional concept of separation of church and state.

No one had even raised the question of the carnival and the games to be played. By the gnawing at my stomach, I knew that much as I had promised myself to keep my mouth shut, I could not allow this to pass. I raised my hand and proceeded to comment on the question of church and state separation. I then followed by suggesting a historical presentation of the Christmas-Chanukah concept to replace the religious Christmas services that were then the order of the day. To top that revolutionary concept, I strongly condemned the use of the term "nigger," the entire idea of a game of knocking down black dolls, and demanded an apology for this racist impropriety. I took my seat anticipating the roof to fall in on me. The noises were loud.

Several hands shot up immediately. By the facial expressions I could see no signs of support. The comments ran from "Our darkies love to be called nigger" to "Why this is a game we learned from our maids." I was sick to my stomach, but such were the remarks until suddenly a voice came over the microphone. It was the school principal. The auditorium was quiet once again. She apologized for the remarks that preceded her. She said it was all a horrible error, that she had not seen the notice before it went out, and would never allow that to happen again. She said that the game would surely be banned from the carnival. She concluded by asking me to remain after the meeting and suggested that all those interested in discussing the suggestion of an educational Christmas-Chanukah program remain as well.

After the meeting, the minister came up to thank me for having the courage to make those comments under such adverse conditions. A group of ten women who identified themselves as Jewish parents offered their thanks for suggesting the Christmas-Chanukah program and were among those who remained. In addition to them, the principal, about two faculty members, and a few other parents also remained behind. A committee was formed to pursue the idea and plan for its implementation. Shortly thereafter I was invited to join the executive committee and was selected as one of three delegates to attend the state PTA convention.

I shared a room with the other two delegates. One was the PTA president and the other the wife of the chief of police, Mrs. Walter C. Headley. We were given instructions that included the "do's" and "don'ts." Among the "don'ts" was the prohibition of intoxicating beverages, but my two roommates found it impossible to go very long without imbibing. They carried thermos bottles with enough liquor to last until they could get refills. This also relaxed them to the point of being less than cautious in their discussions. While drying myself after a shower, I unexpectedly heard the tail end of a discussion that included, "and we had to get stuck with that nigger-loving Jew bastard who raised all that hell at school." I was really amused because they went out of their way to try to be "so sweet" to me.

The convention provided more excitement than I anticipated. With several other delegates and a few teachers, we raised the question of having a single state PTA organization, with both black and white representatives. We were unsuccessful, of course, but this was a first and it was a beginning. The committee in charge had invited guest clergymen for the invocation and convocation for each session every day. To the chagrin of the Jewish representatives, no rabbi was invited. Even more irritating was the nature of the prayers, which were anything but nondenominational in content, as was the announced intent. Personally, I felt that here especially the separation of church and state ought to be maintained. There was more need for the important work in education than making this a major issue. However, since the feeling about the prayers ran so strong, I supported the position for nondenominational blessings.

Among the delegates was a rabbi from Palm Beach. He was a refugee from Nazi Germany and uncomfortably aware of the anti-Semitic overtones to his queries on this question. He called a meeting of the Jewish delegates from Miami Beach and the very few others from Miami and elsewhere. He proposed a petition to the arrangements committee on this matter. To his dismay the Miami Beach delegates refused to cooperate. They did not want a finger pointed at them, and they feared being on any special list. He tried to explain that this is exactly the way it began in Germany and appealed to them, in vain, not to let it happen here. Some Christians supported the effort, which resulted in the committee inviting a local rabbi to close the convention with a nondenominational prayer. However, the rabbi from Palm Beach was visibly shaken by the attitude of the Jews at the meeting. He took my name and address as well as that of some other delegates and said he would like to maintain contact with us.

Meetings and lectures were frequently held at several Miami churches. Among them were the Unitarian and Methodist (white) and the Baptist and Episcopalian (Negro), in addition to several others. Many of the religious leaders from these churches were leading and active members of various liberal-progressive groups. They, too, became targets of attack.

Other liberal organizations in the area functioning alongside the civil rights and civil libertarian groups included the Women's International League for Peace and Freedom, one of the oldest peace groups in the nation, and the American Veterans Committee, a progressive veterans group. There was a frequent interplay of persons from one group with the other, depending on the issues at a given time.

I have discussed in greater or lesser degree some of the organizations that in some way influenced the course of events in the South and in Miami in particular. The actions we engaged in were educational, but they were also based on a knowledge of the history of the area and existing conditions. The actions I have discussed laid the basis for the events that followed. Prior to discussing those events, it is necessary to have some knowledge of the role of the communists and the Communist Party on the local scene. As you no doubt have noted, I have chosen to make a distinction between the two. Some may disagree, saying they are one and the same. For me, personally, I must deal with each individual on the basis of his own behavior.

The communists were a natural part of the environment of the South. They were native-born, black and white, educated by their life experiences in a racist, semi-feudal society. In spite of, or because of, the southern school system, they looked for other answers to the problems of the South. With the gradual migration of people from all sections of the North, the number of communists increased proportionately. According to their records, however, at no time were there more than two hundred communists in the entire state of Florida. They were an integral part of the South and of the organizations there, but they had neither the numbers nor the desire to "take over" these organizations. They were representative of all types of people. Many were very warm and dedicated workers for humanity, some became leaders in local organizations and others rank and file members. Each contributed to the welfare of the group based on his personal ability and not by orders from elsewhere. But there were some who were so dogmatic in their thinking as to make it impossible for them to work with liberal groups.

As an organization, the Communist Party maintained its own program. Although this program dealt with current local events and conditions, it was based in foreign policy as well. The bureaucracy at the top was typical of the dogmatism that afflicted so much of the leadership. Their theory of democratic centralism generally omitted the "democratic" part in practice. As an example, while communist groups in the South were still in the process of debating and rewriting a program for the South based on discussions with various community people and leaders, the national office published a southern program and sent it down South for distribution. In a sense, I viewed them very much like the National Association for the Advancement of Colored People, where decisions were not made on a local basis but rather handed down from above. Here, too, many of the Communist Party members responded independently and in spite of the national organization.

The communists had a strong feeling of camaraderie. The younger and student element had deep sense of respect for the older communists, although by no means was there complete understanding or agreement. These communists were not teaching overthrow of the system. They were in reality another reform movement with radical sounding phraseology and even occasionally some revolutionary clichés. The communists were no greater threat to the South than any other group seeking to reform its racist system. To that extent, they constituted a danger to the southern oligarchy.

Time Out

There was time for relaxation in spite of the pressures under which we worked. We enjoyed our family and friends and were able to laugh together at some of the situations that developed during periods of intense surveillance. If we had no sense of humor, we would not have survived as sane human beings.

Manny was a painting contractor, licensed by the state. As such, he was entitled to bid on all jobs, including city, state, and federal work. He also subcontracted under a general contractor. He was working at an army recruiting station during the time we were being investigated. Of course we had no way of knowing we were in demand. We maintained our normal routines. One Friday I came to one of Manny's jobs to deliver the payroll. An army photographer approached me to ask if I would consent to posing for pictures for recruiting posters. He thought I had just what the army was looking for. I declined the offer. We laughed later and both agreed in retrospect that I had made an error by declining. I would really have been the right person for army recruitment.

The Opa Locka Naval Training Station was the location of another of Manny's jobs. He would enter and exit each day, using all the proper identification. On weekends we would do our shopping at the P-X. We were greeted cordially each time we came and went. This really tickled us some time later because this matter was blown up and the general contractor was accused of trying to take over the Opa Locka Base.

One of our Cuban friends, José Carbonell, a communist, was one of the best carpenters in the area. At a time when the FBI had agents with a high-powered lens observing his home from a distance of two blocks, he was working in FBI and immigration offices repairing furniture and other jobs. So he worked on one floor while on the next floor the FBI dispatched agents to look for him. In the meantime, all the parties involved rode up and down the elevators together.

During the time an FBI agent was supposedly keeping a close watch on us, he was unable to locate us. We lived on Twenty-first Street and he went to Twenty-first Terrace and kept reporting that we were nowhere to be found.

Another humorous incident occurred around the same time. An entire family was being served subpoenas, but the servers had trouble finding one family member. It was Tippy, their dog. The FBI had picked up names they had heard discussed during surveillance and issued the subpoenas accordingly.

These incidents are but a few of many. They serve to remind us that we are all only human. The great FBI that had the power to destroy so many families and lives were not supermen, no great heroes. They were men who took these jobs for various reasons. Some for ego, others for money, and still others thought it made them patriots, but they were no more able or competent than their individual selves.

The FBI Assortment

The Federal Bureau of Investigation possessed no magical powers. The only necessary ingredients for success in this almighty bureaucratic empire were a very suspicious nature, a fantasy-type imagination, the ability to take orders without thinking, and the ability to lie and convince oneself of the veracity of self-conceived lies. Most important, of course, was the conviction that by belonging to this knightly order one achieved the highest degree of patriotism.

I am by no means making light of the terror and heartache, of the destruction of lives and families caused by these agents, since that was indeed very real and very catastrophic. It is necessary, however, to understand the kinds of individuals they were so as not to become either their victims or their informers. In their sick society, there was no other alternative.

When we first became suspicious about surveillance, we laughed and said we were developing a paranoia on the subject. After all, there must be more important things for the government to do. We were not involved in any activity that we did not want as many people as possible to know about. We knew the Klan or local police would want to harass us and we could understand why, but not the FBI. Then gradually the pattern evolved. There was cooperation between the local, state, and federal agencies.

The easiest method was the phone tap, but it had not been perfected and having a bug became very annoying. So even though we knew of the tap, we complained to the phone company and requested that the beep be removed. They explained that it was a bad connection and they would repair it. The beep was removed. What we did not suspect was that the house itself was bugged. This is very difficult to find except when the installer gets sloppy in his work.

One day while I was at work and Lois was home with the woman who cared for the children, two men came supposedly to repair some telephone wiring.

The one in street clothes asked Lois where her daddy was. She replied that he was working. He then proceeded to tell the child that her daddy was a bad man doing bad things. This upset her so that the woman, Mrs. Fuller, ran in to see why she was screaming hysterically, "My daddy is a good man, I love my daddy, he's a good daddy. Go way from here." Mrs. Fuller ordered them out of the house and in their hasty retreat they left the soldering bar, which was imprinted "Southern Bell Tel. Co." in the closet. From that day on we knew that we could not even discuss personal questions in the house. We made it a practice to go into our backyard to enjoy the beautiful foliage and talk with our friends.

We had only one car for a long period of time. During the day when I had errands to take care of, I used public transportation. During the hours I traveled, there was no rush hour traffic and no great throngs of people on the bus. Eventually, I became aware of certain familiar faces, but not always the same. The type of individual and his attire, however, were similar. Usually he wore a striped seersucker-type summer suit. After a more or less scientific method of deduction, I discovered that one would either get on the bus with me or a stop after me and get off the bus after I left. Invariably, I would notice one of a group of about three or four of this type following me through my chores. When this happened, if I had planned to visit someone, I would call to cancel the visit whenever possible. It seemed incredible that this amount of effort and expense would be expended.

We discovered that it was like playing a game of cat and mouse. We began to experience a peculiar feeling of excitement, a challenge of wits, and at the same time a revulsion at the entire proceedings. We had no idea as to the purpose of it all. We were given a role to play and in spite of ourselves we were in a sense playing that role.

The game played with automobiles was more complicated. We learned that license plates with the numbers 68X plus other numbers were assigned to agents and other state employees. We made a listing of all the 68X cars found near our homes or meeting places. We generally found three cars would crisscross in the course of following one of our cars. As soon as we would spot one with the plate number on our list we would change plans. It sometimes took three attempted visits before seeing someone in connection with a civil rights complaint. No one person was followed continuously, but the pattern was the same for all.

As a basis for harassment and intimidation on the local level, the state decided to dust off the statute books and use a sedition law reminiscent of the 1800s. In addition, Miami passed its own communist registration act, which gave so-called communists and front organizations a specified period of time in which to register. Then came a new series of harassment tactics. This was in the form of cards addressed for the benefit of the postmen to "COMRADE So and So." The other side would merely say, "Only 30 more days to register," and [would be] signed by "The Gremlin from the Kremlin." In addition, letters were being sent to the wives or husbands of persons active in civil rights, saying that while they thought their husband (wife) was away at a meeting on (date), he (she) was actually shacking up with his (her) girlfriend (boyfriend) in (some motel or town). In families where both husband and wife did not share the same ideals, there was much cause for alarm. We also received letters from persons requesting information about the Civil Rights Congress and its activities, asking that they too be considered for conspiratorial work. These letters also began with the "Dear Comrade" salutation.

In the course of our detective work, and we were becoming almost expert at it, we began to match the type on the typewritten material and compare the handwriting as well. Most often a post office box number was given, so we staked out a watch at the postal box and discovered when the mail was picked up. One day we confronted the man who picked up the mail. According to his letter to me, his name was Mr. Gilman. We called him by that name and received no response. We tapped him on the shoulder and when we asked why he was carrying Mr. Gilman's mail he said, "Oh yes, he's my roommate and works for the railroad. I just forgot his name for the moment." We left a message that we were on to him and it wouldn't be necessary to send any more poison pen letters or cards. We were correct. All the junk mail ceased as of that day. We realized that even though this was a change for the better, it had taken much of our time and effort from the work that should be done. Perhaps this was also part of the master plan.

By far the most damaging of all the FBI antics was the role of the informer within our ranks. Here was an individual who not only was considered a trusted friend but one who was also responsible for making decisions. It was he who alerted the other agents as to the weaknesses of individuals, the health of persons, organizational problems, and so on, so that the agents could make the most mileage. White persons in the movement were very insensitive to the problem of Negro stool pigeons. They had the peculiar notion that to question the sincerity of a black man was showing one's racism. So even when blacks questioned the legitimacy of another black, we were the ones to try to explain away the questions.

The black man who sat in front of the open door at my home when we encountered our first visit from the police was in fact an informer. He even may have called them from our house that night. He was probably the one who had access and had taken the stationery from the Civil Rights Congress office to send to the Justice Department. It took almost six years to identify the informer. His excuse for the various phone calls was that he was a reporter on the local Negro paper and had to call in to check if there were any stories he needed to run down. Whenever we were stopped by the police, we assumed he was showing his newsman's credentials and that was what got us off the hook. In reality it was his I.D. His undoing was effected thanks to one of the black painters who worked for Manny. He confronted him with the evidence and then came to Manny and warned us about him. We should have listened sooner. If only we had taken the time to think about what had been happening, but we were "color" blind.

A Cuban was introduced to us as a friend of José. He was newly married and had no job. His wife was the daughter of an army sergeant in Key West and couldn't bring a Cuban home to her father. They were literally starving and without a roof over their heads. We found a room in a friend's house temporarily and bought a supply of groceries. In addition we collected clothing to tide them over until he or she found a job. He found a job, or it found him. He became an informer for the FBI. When his new wife became aware of what he was doing to all their friends who had helped them, she became furious. She had no political astuteness but she knew it was so very wrong. She came to his friend José and both came to us and told us all she had learned from her husband. We gave her fare back to Key West and after a while, in the process of seeking a divorce, [she] discovered that her husband was a bigamist as well. He had a wife in Tampa, too. This was the reason used by the FBI to entice him into becoming an informer.

Early in my story I mentioned Jim Nimmo, the black man who organized the Laundry Workers Union. Jim was an honest and sincere organizer, but many attempts were made to force him to become an informer. Several times the authorities tried to convict him of participating in various acts of violence in the laundry and dry cleaning industry. They were always unsuccessful. One day we received a visit from a mutual friend who said Jim was in jail and the charge was murder. No one wanted to risk going to see him. Manny was the sole person among his many friends who went to speak to Jim. He was convinced that it was another frame-up. Further, he was told that some one could buy off the proper parties for around nine hundred dollars. In a few days Manny got the money to Jim and he was freed. He disappeared shortly after. He had been thoroughly frightened. It was too close for comfort.

Many attempts were made by the FBI to make informers and stool pigeons out of various active people. There was no limit to the extremes to which they went. One afternoon after work I approached my car, which was parked on the lot opposite the DuPont Building, where I worked as a bookkeeper for an insurance brokerage. I became aware of two men in summer seersucker suits standing near my car. It could only mean the "boys," as we called them, were here. They identified themselves without my asking and offered me a card. Then one—the other did no talking—said they would appreciate it if I would come to their office to talk to them. My reply was simply that there was nothing to talk to them about, and so I refused their invitation. His tone became harsher, and he said something about revolution. I laughed and asked if he had been doing his homework lately, and then added that the American history books were filled with all the revolutionary ideas for which he might be searching. I suggested the Bill of Rights and the Constitution as a primer for him. He turned red with rage and said, "This is no laughing matter. Would you like the same to happen to your children as what happened to the Rosenberg children?" I was shocked, absolutely dumbfounded. Would they dare?

These incidents can be multiplied many times over. They are only an indication of the various methods used by our "law enforcement agencies" in "defense" of our freedoms.

The Miami Formula

In spite of all the harassment, the intimidation, the fears, and the threats, the movement had not died. The U.S. Supreme Court's historic decision on school desegregation set off a new wave of resistance by the white supremacists, who viewed the Court decision as "red inspired." Senator James O. Eastland of Mississippi stated, "The South will not abide by nor obey this legislative decision by a political court. Integrated schools are not desired by either race in the South. Any attempt to desegregate our schools would cause great strife and turmoil. We will take whatever steps necessary to retain segregation in education."

We, on the other hand, were pressing for the implementation of the law. To them this was an invasion of states' rights unlike anything that had taken place since the Civil War. It was war, and the battle lines were being drawn. The battle of resistance took many forms. The witch-hunt was one of them, sedition and anarchy the charge. Miami and Dade County became a testing ground for a new formula—McCarthyism at the grassroots level. It is a story of how vigilantism can flourish behind the facade of legality. The Miami campaign became a dangerous pattern for similar campaigns of repression elsewhere in the

United States, under local auspices and away from the spotlight of Washington.

The target was not just the communist. It was anyone who might have at some time in his life participated in liberal action or who in any sense contributed to the movement for reform and change. The first phase of the attack came immediately following the school desegregation ruling. The opening shot was Senator Eastland's Subcommittee on Internal Security and its notorious investigation of the Southern Conference Educational Fund [successor organization of the Southern Conference on Human Welfare, dissolved in 1948] in June 1954.

Two Miamians were called. One was a building contractor, Max Schlafrock, the soft-spoken vice-president of the Jewish Cultural Center. The other was attorney Leo Sheiner, vice-president of the Jewish Community Center, NAACP attorney, and a respected leader of the community. He later stated, "I chose not to speak in a forum when falsehoods are taken for the truth and oppression substituted for liberty." Both were uncooperative witnesses, but they were not cited by the Senate subcommittee. Other plans were being prepared for them. The stage had been set, and now the Dade County authorities were ready for the next phase of the attack. From its inception, it was obvious that a strong thread of anti-Semitism ran through the entire proceedings. Ninety percent of the people victimized in Dade County were Jewish.

Following the attacks on Leo Sheiner, those of us who were members of the board of the Jewish Community Center prepared to raise the question of his defense with that body. He refused to allow any issue to be made of his case. He did not want the question of anti-Semitism raised. There was no doubt in his mind that this was all a mistake. After all, he had never done anything that could in any way be interpreted as illegal. The Constitution was on his side. He isolated himself from any individual he considered left of center. Unfortunately, he was smeared unmercifully in the press. Perjured testimony by FBI informers, later discredited, made this man out to be the "Red Czar" of Florida. He eventually was disbarred in what was described as the first action of its kind in the country.

Then followed the attack on the trade union leadership, the educational institutions, and the business and professional communities. Then came the civil rights activists, leaders of the Jewish Community Center, and religious leaders. Each was an outspoken foe of Jim Crow. Those who had refused to cooperate with the FBI previously were given another opportunity to cleanse themselves by turning informer at the Dade County grand jury inquisitions. For the thirty-one brave souls who took the path of the Fifth Amendment, there was a contempt of court and contempt of grand jury citation, and they were summarily jailed for one year. The court refused to grant any bail, and some of these people spent as much as six weeks in prison until the Florida Supreme Court finally did order bail in each one of the cases. Chuck Smolikoff, the union organizer who suffered with a severe cardiac ailment, sat in jail for a month under the most inhuman conditions. When he left Miami, he was hospitalized for two months due to the conditions under which he had suffered.

On September 22, 1954, Judge Holt signed orders requiring seventeen witnesses to show cause why they should not be cited for contempt. This was rather unusual since they were not scheduled to appear before the grand jury until September 23. Mimeographed opinions, identical in text, stating the judge's reasons for convicting the seventeen were filed in advance of the hearings, so reminiscent of the "lettres de Cachet" of the French Revolution.

What is interesting and frightening were the methods employed. Each uncooperative witness was tried and condemned in the local press first. The *Miami Daily News* helped create the policy, provoked the harassment, and utilized the columns of its newspaper to smear and destroy individuals and deprive them of a livelihood. The liberal Knight newspaper, the *Miami Herald*, was guilty of silence in the face of these attacks.

The State's Attorney's office worked with dissident elements in the painters union to enact a grandfather clause in union bylaws requiring all members to register whether they are, ever were, or intend to be communists or members of any organization that had appeared on the attorney general's list. At the time, a battle for power was being fought in the union. The dissident group thought it could strengthen its position by taking this approach, even though it was in direct violation of the International Union's bylaws. Being anti-red was a most popular pastime during this period. This was the only union to impose such a requirement on the rank and file and the only one to cooperate with the State's Attorney's office. We knew why.

They came in the middle of the night to serve the subpoenas. They came into a house where a man lay in an oxygen tent and served a subpoena to his daughter. A doctor, eaten away by cancer and struggling for survival, was forced into the courtroom for the inquisition. Many people we had never met, some only visitors to Miami, were called.

Doctors were ordered to appear without giving them the opportunity to complete appointments with patients. Parents of adopted children and foster children were threatened with having their children taken from them. Professors were smeared and dismissed even though they were not questioned about their activities in Miami; instead, they were questioned about activities in other states at earlier times. Manny was not questioned about Florida but about his activities at Detroit Diesel Engine and the Michigan painters' union. Two women were called because records showed that they had signed a Communist Party nominating petition, one in 1942 and one in 1949. Others were called because they had signed petitions or written letters expressing their opposition to the Smith Act or the McCarran Act. My husband and I were both served subpoenas in the hospital immediately after I had given birth. There was no humanity, no feeling [See appendix 2].

How did the media—the press, television, and radio—affect people's lives? They used mass psychology to rouse latent antagonisms and spur them to action. I'll speak of our own experiences. The crank calls came day and night. Calls threatening that our house would be bombed, the children would be kidnapped, or we would be killed. The profanity was unbelievable. These had to be sick people. Then the insurance companies canceled our insurance on the house, claiming they could not cover us for fire and theft due to the danger of hostile acts. At the same time, workmen's compensation and liability insurance were canceled, forcing Manny out of business immediately. The children were harassed at school, and then it became too dangerous to allow them to walk the streets to school.

During this time, although I was undergoing treatment for shock, many interesting things were happening at home. We had all kinds of unexpected visitors. A Negro man, someone we considered a good friend, came to tell us that blacks had been subpoenaed separately. They had been told that their white friends had implicated them and had not cared about what happened to the black man. He cried like a baby while telling us that they threatened that he would never get a job unless he corroborated whatever they asked for. He had reluctantly agreed, he said, because he had a wife and seven children and could not allow this to happen to them. He begged us to leave town before it was too late. He was ashamed that he had done their bidding, asked for forgiveness and left. We never saw him again.

The rabbi came with his wife. They brought a gift for the baby as a token of their feelings. They offered any kind of assistance that might be needed. Their friendship was sufficient. The president of the NAACP came with a greeting card that indicated that the baby had been made an honorary member of the chapter. He stated he was sorry to say that he was here not in any official capacity, but as an individual, a friend, offering any kind of help we might ask. He too felt this was only one phase of the struggle and there was more ahead. So prophetic were his words. It was not very long after that the NAACP came under attack and both he and his co-leader were cited for contempt for refusing to turn over membership lists to the Johns Committee.

We issued a statement and sent it to people we though might respond. To my surprise, I received a call from the rabbi I met at the PTA convention. He offered the services of an attorney gratis. The attorney came. He was an FBI trainee. He said he knew I had nothing to hide so why not just cooperate and everything would be O.K. We could not make him understand that there was a principle involved, that people who exercised their constitutional rights and refused to cooperate in a witch-hunt were not automatically guilty. We also maintained that one did not have to be a communist to be principled, that it would be wrong to permit communists to be isolated from other victims in this manner. It was actually the Constitution that was under attack, not any particular group of people. There was no conspiracy except on the part of the government agencies and the vigilantes to suppress democracy.

When the Florida Supreme Court finally ruled that bail must be set, the problem of funds became very serious. Very few people had five thousand dollars, the set amount for bail. People who had money left the area since they did not want to get caught up in the grand sweep. Some sold their homes, cars, and small businesses to help raise money for the thirty-one people jailed. Meanwhile, the press continued a barrage of lies stating that Moscow gold was financing the victims, whom they labeled Soviet agents.

During this time, Jim Nimmo, the laundry workers union organizer, was nowhere to be seen, but another Negro friend came to tell Manny that Jim had sold out to the FBI. At the time of the big frame-up, when Manny had given the nine hundred dollars for Jim's release, Jim had agreed to become an informer as part of the deal. This friend had tried in vain to make Jim understand that he was really destroying himself by turning on the people who had loved him and been his friends. The fear and terror he had experienced were the only things Jim could understand. Manny confronted Jim with the accusation, which he then denied. The testimony before the Velde Committee [the U.S. House Un-American Activities Committee, which held hearings in Miami in 1954], however, confirmed the report.

Scores of people were called by the FBI. Many went to the FBI offices out of curiosity. They claimed they wanted to find out what the FBI knew and what it was after. Some excused their cooperation on the flimsy basis that there had to be someone on the outside to take care of raising funds and alerting the citizens to the dangers. Others argued that since they were not communists, they had nothing to hide and could not hurt anyone. Some others, out of fear and for business reasons, cooperated. This category comprised primarily those in the upper-income levels. The most dangerous philosophy was the expressed feeling that "they" know everything anyway. "What difference will it make if I go down?" It did make a difference, since the FBI was not interested in knowing the truth but rather in using small pieces of personal information to help weave fantasy plots out of whole cloth and make them appear to be fact. Whatever the reasoning behind the cooperation of some, it did not serve the interests of a more democratic South or advance the battle against repression. Once they had succumbed to the pressures, they forfeited the right of trust, so necessary in the work to end racism in the South.

Affectionately, our infant was given the dubious distinction of being named "Miss Subpoena of 1954," the only baby born with a subpoena in her mouth. Surreptitiously, in the middle of the night, we left. My eleven-year-old remained behind with her daddy and grandmother. She could not bring herself to leave her daddy. The flight to Detroit was a nightmare. Arrangements had to be made to care for the children. We were fugitives but could not comprehend why. After meeting with civil liberties attorneys in Detroit, it was decided that temporarily, in the absence of a Supreme Court decision in Florida, it would be advisable to take the children and go to Canada. After two days Lois joined us, convinced that her grandma would take good care of her daddy. Then the four of us made the long trip by train to Toronto.

We were greeted by our devoted Canadian friends, who made room for us in their small home. The children were enrolled in school, I was placed under a doctor's care, and arrangements were completed for caring for the children should the need arise. Burdened by the pressures of existing conditions, my recovery was very slow. We had no winter clothing and little other than the barest necessities with us. The only money we had was either tied up in our house or used as bail money to keep Manny out of jail pending the court's decision. Friends contributed clothing and understanding and love. The doctor graciously provided his professional skills as well as his friendship for us. His efforts and those of our dear friends were the most precious memories of that time.

During this most difficult period of adjustment, the "boys" in collaboration with the press, were preoccupied with spewing out columns condemning me as an international spy who traveled between the United States and Canada. In November, some three months later, the Florida Supreme Court ruled in our favor. We were advised not to attempt to return to Florida, that this was only the end of one phase of attack and additional action would be forthcoming. Manny sold our home and furnishings and packed his truck with all the essentials he could carry and came north to join us. It was a wonderful feeling to be free and together again. We decided to visit Detroit. Some of our family were pleased to have us, while others were fearful that a stigma might be attached to them. Our friends were concerned, responsive, and thoughtful.

We were gone but a few days when we received a call from our friends in Canada advising us that the Royal Canadian Mounted Police had been around and inquiring about us. This was not the red-coated Mounty affectionately known for his exploits in the Canadian Northwest. This was the Canadian counterpart of the FBI working in conjunction with American agents. It seemed unbelievable that a great country like ours would allow its public servants to wallow in the depth of such filth and lies. The orders had to come from some bureaucrat who, no doubt, was suffering deep paranoia. We wonder how many more spy stories are conceived in this manner.

Conclusion

The relationship between the Federal Bureau of Investigation, the grand jury, the press, and the State's Attorney's Office was too close to be coincidental. On the heels of the local witch-hunt came the Velde Committee [HUAC], which after its much heralded hearings was forced to acknowledge that "the situation is not as bad in Florida as in other parts of the country." The press then condemned the committee's performance as inept.

Many questions remain unanswered by those who participated in perpetrating the Miami formula and by those who silently sat by and accepted it. These questions include:

1. Who instigated the witch-hunt and why?
2. Was there any relationship between it and the growth of the Christian-anti-Jewish Party whose slogans were "Free America from the Jews" and "Defend the white race"?
3. What was the relationship between the witch-hunt and the Miami anti-desegregation groups?
4. Why were witnesses questioned so intensely about their activities in the FDR Club, the American Veterans Committee, the Southern Conference for Human Welfare, the National Association for the Advancement of Colored People, unions, and other activities, including those prior to coming to Miami?
5. What purpose did the witch-hunt serve?

There are lessons to be learned from these experiences. Briefly they include the following:

1. It is essential that blacks and whites work together for change in the South and elsewhere.

2. The rejection of red-baiting, one of the most lethal weapons for the immobilization of movements and organizations.
3. Constant vigilance against agents sent to disrupt constructive programs.
4. Never underestimate the danger of wiretapping and political surveillance by federal, state, and local agents intent on denying your constitutional rights.
5. Never permit the age-old philosophy of divide and rule to paralyze you.

Despite the fears and terrors and the destruction of lives and families caused by the inquisition, the movement did not die. As long as the causes that gave rise to the movement for change exist, so will that movement. It may suffer temporary setbacks and necessitate new tactics and organization, but its historical continuity cannot be denied. It did suffer for a period of approximately ten years, but the seeds planted grew and the struggles took on a new life. The movement will live until those causes that gave it birth are eradicated from our society and a new and healthy America is born.

Appendix 1

Matilda Graff, "What's Behind the Anti-Negro Terror: Groveland Murder Bares Drive to Keep Negroes in Economic Shackles," *The National Guardian* **(August 29, 1949), 1.**

Not far from Groveland, Florida, is a cluster of paper mills. They are fed by the scrub pine that grows in the region. Negroes do the logging and perform the evilest jobs in the mills. Their wages are less than $3 a day average. Some in the woods get as little as $1.50 a day.

The mills are owned by vast companies controlled by northern bankers. For 11 years these firms have fought federal wages and hours legislation under which a 40¢-an-hour minimum pay was set. For 11 years Dixiecrat congressmen like Rep. Frank W. Boykin of Alabama have sided with the big paper companies in their evasion of the law.

This year their 11-year campaign paid off—in profits and in blood. The 75¢-an-hour minimum wage law adopted by the House exempted pulp loggers and sawmill workers from its benefits—under this bill they are no longer covered even by the old 40¢ minimum.

"Too Damned Fancy": Groveland is a small community of 600 whites, 400 Negroes. Nearby are the smaller towns of Mascotte and Stuckey. For more than a year trouble had been brewing in the region. Negroes were refusing to work for the prevailing low wage. Relations became more strained when Negro women refused to work as servants for a prominent white family after one of them had been taken advantage of by a man of the house. And there were "trouble-makers" in the region: a Negro named Shepherd built himself a substantial house that was, by white standards for Negroes, too fancy. His son drove a late model Mercury with one white-walled tire. Shepherd's next door neighbor was even better off: he owned two substantial houses. The talk in the region was that these people were getting "too damned uppity."

The Hunt Is On: The lesson came late in July. A young white man reported that he had been beaten and robbed and his 17–year-old wife raped by four Negroes. That was all that was needed. The word spread quickly that the "attackers" had fled in a Mercury with one white-walled tire. Everybody knew that car. Young Shepherd and two other teen-aged Negroes were arrested. An NAACP investigator found later that the three were not even friends; one of them had never even seen the other two before being jailed.

There had been four "attackers" and only three were arrested. The man-hunt was on. From Mascotte, from Stuckey, from all the cross-roads for miles around the whites came running. And then strange cars turned up in Groveland: they bore license plates from Miami, from Georgia, from Alabama.

Death in the Woods: The posses knew their targets. Shepherd's house and his neighbor's two fancy houses were burned to the ground. Then they ranged over the countryside. Negro shacks were peppered with shotgun blasts; crosses were burned where they would do the most good. After a time a mob of 100 armed men, including four sheriffs, found the fourth "suspect" in the woods. He was shot dead before he could move.

In Tavares, 25 miles away, an 18–man jury, including one Negro, was hastily convened. It took no notice of the lynching in the woods of Ernest Thomas. It took no notice of the mob violence that had terrorized the region for days. Circuit Judge Truman Futch promised a quick trial and said: "I don't see that there is any likelihood of transferring the case to another county. I have no fear of violence or attempted violence in the event of a trial in Lake County."

Boys Will Be Boys: To State's Attorney J. W. Hunter the entire affair was just one of those things. It was only a matter of "a few hotheads, scalawags and drunkards" cutting loose.

In Groveland 200 members of the 116th Field Artillery Battalion of the state National Guard were stationed. But they were guarding empty huts: nearly every one of Groveland's 400 Negro residents had left the town. A Miami reporter wrote: "Groveland misses its Negroes, not only because of a loss of their business, but because ... their exodus has left it with a labor shortage."

Through the state there was not much reaction to the Groveland events. In nearby Leesburg, State Representative Tim Sellers demanded a thorough investigation and prosecution of the mobsters. (Everybody in the region knew who they were.) But his was a lone voice in that part of Florida.

The Bleating Press: Down in Miami the Civil Rights Congress called a mass meeting. Girls circulating leaflets announcing the rally were told by plainclothes detectives that they had better leave town or they would be raped or beaten. Two men, Alfred Rosenberg, chairman of the Progressive Party of Dade County, and Joseph Cohen, a student at the University of Miami, were arrested. The local press bayed against the meeting, set off a witch-hunt on the University campus that forced Cohen to quit the school and leave the state. But more than 200 persons, 70% of them Negroes, attended the meeting and contributed a carload of clothing to the victims of terror in the Groveland area.

Beaten to a Pulp: The *Miami News* had some editorial comment to make. It deplored the whole thing because, it said, "there will always be the suspicion of vigilantism in this affair." And such suspicion "gives rise to just such clamor as that which has been raised by the local Civil Rights Congress which does a good job in stirring up controversy." Up in Raiford, Florida, NAACP investigator Franklin H. Williams reported that the three arrested Negroes had been horribly beaten in an effort to get "confessions."

Trial for the three has been set for Aug. 29.

Wages in the Groveland woods and sawmills have not been raised.

Appendix 2

Matilda Graff, "A Child Is Born in Fear," *National Guardian* (September 27, 1954), 6.

Most parents who read this will remember their feelings of deep pride, satisfaction, happiness and serious responsibility at the birth of their children. Such were our thoughts as my husband and I made plans to bring our third child home from the hospital.

We had for the moment forgotten the McCarthy-Brownell madness that is sweeping our country, and the Brautigam witch-hunt in Miami. But on Aug. 24, at 8 P.M., a process-server from State Atty. Brautigam's office walked into my room at Mercy Hospital, falsely stating he had my doctor's knowledge and consent to do so, and served a subpoena upon me and my husband. My child had been born four days earlier. My husband was ordered to appear before Brautigam at 11 A.M. the next morning, although he had been scheduled to bring me home from the hospital at noon that day. I was ordered to appear Sept. 1.

This invasion of the privacy of a hospital room; this severe shock to me just after childbirth; this persecution of us both, parents of three young children, aged 11 years, 7 years, and 4 days—all constitute a brutal attack upon human life and family that reeks of Hitlerism.

We assume that we are being summoned as part of Mr. Brautigam's hunt for "subversives." I inherited a sense of civic responsibility and patriotism from my parents. I was taught to be proud of my heritage as an American Jew. My father, a shop worker, was always a devoted trade unionist until the day of his death two years ago. My mother showed her keen sense of responsibility to her family and the community. From my student days I was imbued with the ideal of world peace, and in later years my interest in peace drew me into activity for the Wallace candidacy. Coming to live in Miami, and moved by the sharper forms of discrimination prevalent here, I joined with others, in the face of Klan terror, to defend the Groveland victims. I was also among the hundreds here who, shocked by the bombings that culminated in the dynamite murder of Mr. and Mrs. Harry T. Moore, raised their voices for punishment of the criminals.

I have devoted time and energy to parent-teachers work at the school my children attend. Young as our children are, they have already begun to develop civic consciousness. Just last week, they organized on their own initiative a fund-raising effort for the emergency polio fund which netted $25.

If my life and conduct can be labeled "subversive," that label fits the majority of decent, thinking, civic-minded Americans. If my principles and community service record make me fair game for Mr. Brautigam's persecution, then none but the minority of bootlicking conformists are safe.

Let my bitter experience at the birth of my child be a warning to all who value their individual rights and their self-respect.

PART III

* * *

Shirley M. Zoloth and the Congress of Racial Equality

Shirley M. Zoloth in the mid-1960s, at work at Equal Opportunity Program, Inc., Miami's anti-poverty agency. (Photo courtesy of Barbara Zoloth.)

* * *

THIS SECTION OF THE BOOK documents the civil rights activism of Shirley Zoloth in the late 1950s. As noted earlier, Shirley and Milton Zoloth moved to Miami in late 1954, actually within a few weeks of Bobbie Graff's departure for Canada to escape the consequences of the Brautigam grand jury subpoena. Shirley's parents had already moved to Miami, where her father was in the real estate business. Although Milton's training at Drexel University was in chemical engineering, he moved his family to Miami to join his father-in-law's real estate firm. Like many other Jewish migrants to South Florida, the Zoloths had been engaged in social activism in postwar Philadelphia, worked in the Progressive Party presidential campaign of Henry A. Wallace in 1948, and supported various progressive, left-wing, and civil rights causes. In interviews Shirley Zoloth remembered involvement in Philadelphia with an interracial nursery school and a cultural group that sponsored interracial concerts, recitals, plays, and parties. In addition, she was deeply involved in Hadassah, the Women's Zionist Organization of America. Generally, Hadassah focused on Zionist issues and remained aloof from domestic politics. However, Zoloth recalled attending a national Hadassah meeting in 1950 where the delegates hotly debated and then approved a public statement supporting Senator Claude Pepper, who was being race-baited and red-baited by George Smathers in a nasty campaign in Florida for the Democratic nomination for Pepper's Senate seat. Although Florida remained in her future, Zoloth was already learning about the state's race-based political culture.[1]

Within days of her arrival in Miami, Zoloth plunged into South Florida's activist arena. She had joined the Philadelphia branch of the Women's International League for Peace and Freedom in 1953 when that city's school teachers came under attack from HUAC and local right-wingers, a witch-hunting investigation she labeled "a sickeningly cruel circus." Newly arrived in Miami, Zoloth quickly gravitated toward the WILPF and began attending its meetings. Bernice Ullrich, president of the Miami WILPF, sent Zoloth some information about the group, whose next meeting dealt with "the local problem of Civil Rights" and which featured a presentation on the issue by leaders of the Dade County Council on Community Relations (DCCCR), a group that Zoloth soon joined as well. Ullrich also sent Zoloth a copy of Leslie Bain's August 1954 article from *The Nation* magazine, "Red Hunt in Miami," which attacked the Brautigam investigation and condemned the sensationalist anti-red reporting of the *Miami Daily News* in the early 1950s. Zoloth had been distressed about the investigation and termination of leftists in the Philadelphia school system, but Bain's article suggested that the political and racial climate in Miami in the mid-1950s posed far greater threats to civil liberties and civil rights.[2]

In interviews, the Zoloths recalled their deep concerns about the Jim Crow racial practices they found in Miami, especially school segregation. They were outraged that the local school board was doing nothing to implement the 1954 U.S. Supreme Court decision on school desegregation. Racial liberals in the North applauded the Court's move, but state and local officials in the South avoided or delayed school integration by various means. Shirley Zoloth's activist work in the mid-to-late 1950s focused primarily on confronting the school issue and promoting desegregation. By 1957, now vice president of the Miami WILPF, Zoloth was writing the Dade County school board on behalf of that organization, challenging the board's delaying tactics and urging a public statement on its plans for desegregation. Simultaneously, she was involved in the community relations work of the DCCCR, an effort to prepare Miami area parents for peaceful school integration. She began attending and taking notes at school board meetings and keeping a scrapbook of newspaper clippings on the school issue.[3]

Zoloth's intense involvement in school desegregation issues led her into local politics in 1958. State representative Jack Orr's campaign for re-election that year attracted Miami's racial liberals. Orr's 1956 speech in the state legislature advocating gradual school integration had created a big stir. Florida's integrationists praised Orr, but Democratic party loyalists and anti-integrationists turned against him. In 1958 the party ran a well-known Miamian with no political experience, former college football star David C. Eldridge, against Orr in the Democratic primary, calculating that Eldridge's name recognition and support of the racial status quo would be sufficient to win the election. Eldridge won by a comfortable margin. Nevertheless, the 1958 Orr campaign served as a catalyst for Miami's left-liberal Jewish activists.[4]

In interviews, Miami activists recalled the significance of the Orr campaign in forming a coherent group of racially liberal, mostly Jewish activists. Jack Gordon's wife, Barbara, was managing Orr's campaign with another Jewish activist, Selma Rabinowitz. At the same time, Gordon was managing Claude Pepper's Dade County campaign for the U.S. Senate against the incumbent, former Florida governor Spessard L. Holland. The Orr and Pepper campaigns were linked, as were all the principals involved. Gordon was close to Pepper, who sat on the board of Gordon's Miami Beach bank, Washington Federal Savings and Loan. Orr, another Gordon friend, had managed Pepper's losing

1950 Senate campaign in Dade County and then become a partner in Pepper's Miami law firm in the early 1950s.[5]

In any case, Jack Gordon remembered that Shirley Zoloth walked into the Orr campaign office one day and offered to help. They gave her a batch of mailing lists, and asked her to type the names, addresses, and phone numbers on index cards. To everyone's surprise, Zoloth returned the next day with the assignment completed, even typing a duplicate set of index cards. Orr campaign people quickly recognized Zoloth's organizational and typing talents and assigned her to work with Selma Rabinowitz on a series of neighborhood political meetings and coffees, a community education campaign to explain Orr's positions to the voting public. This work paralleled Zoloth's engagement with the Florida Council on Human Relations (FCHR) and the Dade County Council on Community Relations (DCCCR), which had now merged their community outreach efforts as the Dade County Council on Human Relations. Jack Orr had a committed group of political activists in his corner, as well as most of Dade County's black vote, but he lost the election because of his stand on school integration. In retrospect, many of those involved have suggested, the chief outcome of the Orr campaign was its role in forging a powerful sense of community among Miami's Jewish activists.[6]

During the Orr campaign, Zoloth connected quickly with Jack and Barbara Gordon, and with Barbara's sister, Thalia Stern. They shared a progressive political stance, as well as a passionate commitment to social action. When the Orr campaign ended, they moved on to other issues and other organizations, often simultaneously. As Jack Gordon recalled in an interview, "The three women, Barbara, Thalia, and Shirley, generally acted as one. It was hard to tell who was the leader. They simply divided up the work and got things done collectively." After Jack Orr's defeat, they mulled over what to do next about school integration, then decided to contact the national CORE office about initiating a CORE branch in Miami, with results that have already been described. Initially, they thought their work with CORE would be focused on school integration rather than the public accommodations thrust that CORE quickly embraced. During this period in the late 1950s, Zoloth continued her involvement in the DCCCR, which had organized a "Save Our Schools" campaign to prevent the closing of Dade County schools by anti-integrationists. This effort led to still another ad hoc organization, the Dade County Citizens Committee for Better Schools, also focused on keeping the schools open. As an officer of the Miami chapters of the Women's International League of Peace and Freedom and the National Council of Jewish Women, she pushed those organizations to get involved in the school integration battle. Zoloth's progressive politics and relentless activism also found expression in her participation to one degree or another in the work of the Florida ACLU, the American Jewish Congress, the National Committee for a Sane Nuclear Policy (SANE), and the Southern Conference Education Fund (SCEF). After the Zoloths and the Gordons attended a 1960 SCEF meeting in Orlando, they were investigated by the Florida Legislative Investigation Commission (FLIC), which portrayed SCEF's efforts for school integration as part of "the subversive thrust of the Communist Party in Florida."[7]

Zoloth continued her political activism into the 1960s. School integration continued to be a volatile political issue, typified by Jack Gordon's 1960 campaign for election to the Dade County school board. Gordon and his activist colleagues, weary of fighting the educational bureaucracy from the outside, believed they might have better success from inside the system. Shirley Zoloth successfully managed Gordon's school board campaign, drawing on her organizational skills and many community connections. The campaign was clouded because the Florida ACLU and the American Jewish Congress had simultaneously sued the school board over mandatory prayer and Bible reading in the Dade County schools. The plaintiffs included two couples from the AJCongress, Thalia and Philip Stern and Phyllis and Ed Resnick, as well as Cindy and Robert Thorner from the ACLU. They were labeled communists and atheists during the subsequent Dade County school wars. Gordon supported the suit, drawing the wrath of the Christian right, but in his public statements he emphasized his commitment to quality education and his business acumen. Gordon won election to the school board in 1960 and again in 1964, and he used his influence on the board to promote integration on many fronts. Zoloth, meanwhile, had developed into a highly effective political campaign manager. She worked in still another Orr legislative campaign in the early 1960s, and later managed Gordon's successful campaign for a Florida Senate seat in 1972. She also found time to head up the pamphlet and group-letter committee of George McGovern's presidential campaign in Dade County in 1972.[8]

In the late 1950s and the 1960s, the anti-nuclear, antiwar, and peace movements also attracted Zoloth's interest and talents. Jewish activists provided the nucleus of the Miami chapter of SANE, which held meetings and rallies in Miami in the late 1950s. The National Committee for a Sane Nuclear Policy began in mid-1957 over concerns about radioactive fallout from nuclear weapons testing. Within a year anti-nuclear and peace activists had set up some 130 SANE chapters around the nation with about twenty-five thousand members. Thalia Stern and Leonard Turkel, a Korean War veteran from New York City who had recently moved to Miami, were the major organizers of Miami SANE, but most of the core group of Jewish activists, including the Zoloths, were involved. For several years, the *Miami Herald* reported in 1963, the Sterns' home in Miami Beach served as the chief "gathering place for people intensely interested in the peace movement."[9]

The National Committee for a Sane Nuclear Policy and two other groups promoting disarmament—Women Strike for Peace (WSP) and the Committee for Nonviolent Action (CNVA)—remained active in South Florida into the mid-1960s, when peace activists began gravitating toward the movement against the Vietnam War. Reflecting this new dimension of Miami activism, in 1969 Jack Gordon chaired the Florida Mobilization Committee to End the War in Vietnam, or Florida MOBE, which held marches, demonstrations, and peace vigils in October and November 1969. Hundreds of antiwar Miamians traveled to Washington, D.C., by plane, train, and bus for a National MOBE "March against Death" on November 15, 1969. Along with Gordon, Shirley Zoloth played a key role as an organizer and publicity person for Florida MOBE.[10]

Opposition to the Vietnam War simmered through the middle and late 1960s. At the same time, President Lyndon Johnson's Great Society programs also created new breakthroughs on the domestic front, especially in dealing with race, poverty, and economic development. Zoloth and other CORE activists found in one new program, the War on Poverty, a way of carrying on their earlier civil rights work. Soon after passage of the Economic Opportunity Act in August 1964, Dade County political, educational, and welfare leaders brainstormed on ways to tap into federal funding for economic development and a local war on poverty. The result was the creation of a new federally funded nonprofit agency, Economic Opportunity Program, Inc. (EOPI), which developed and coordinated Dade County antipoverty programs such as job training, dropout prevention, preschool training, small business development, community centers, medical and dental clinics, and VISTA (Volunteers in Service to America), a sort of domestic Peace Corps. Jack Gordon was appointed to the EOPI board of directors as a representative of the school board. Subsequently, he played a role in the hiring of Shirley Zoloth as administrative assistant to EOPI director Richard Weatherley, a social welfare administrator who had been hired away from the Dade County United Fund.[11]

Weatherley was relatively new to the Miami area, but Zoloth knew everybody, especially in the black community where few white people had access. Moreover, she had great organizational skills. As Zoloth later recalled in an interview, she quickly rose up the EOPI job ladder to educational director, Head Start director, and then program and planning director. Although she never held the title, Zoloth essentially had become EOPI deputy director by the late 1960s. By that time, EOPI was running a dozen different programs and had a weekly payroll of more than $100,000. It had hired more than 850 people, staffed nine community centers, and regularly served, according to one newspaper report, some 85,000 Dade citizens. Through the community action program, thousands of low-income Miamians became involved in their own communities. However, shrinking federal antipoverty funding, partisan politics, public criticism, and internal squabbling over programs and spending—typical of antipoverty agencies nationwide—eventually undermined EOPI's effectiveness and forced a shutdown of many programs. In 1970, the Metro-Dade County government took over EOPI's remaining functions and the agency went out of existence.[12]

Reflecting on her five-year EOPI experience, Zoloth subsequently noted that the agency did a lot of good work for poor people in Miami, but that most of its programs addressed only the symptoms and not the root causes of poverty. She also recalled her growing disenchantment with a program that had grown too fast, suffered from numerous personality conflicts, and gotten out of control. The EOPI also clashed with federal antipoverty officials, who later reported that the agency "had reeled from one crisis to another in its dealing with a variety of federal agencies." Zoloth felt strongly about many of these issues and began writing, but never finished, a book analyzing the War on Poverty and its problems. The main impact of EOPI, she came to believe, was that it provided training and leadership skills to dozens of African-American professionals, who later pursued careers in Dade County government agencies.[13]

In retrospect, it is also significant that many CORE activists assumed important positions in EOPI. In addition to Shirley Zoloth and Jack Gordon, CORE and ACLU attorney Howard Dixon became director of EOPI legal services. Barbara Gordon, who held a doctorate in education from Columbia University, served for a time as an EOPI consultant running a Head Start training program at the University of Miami. Thalia Stern, a certified teacher, spent three years as a Head Start teacher in a Liberty City elementary school, while her mother, Doris Yaffey, worked as a school librarian. Marilynn Bloom, a CORE activist and teacher, worked in EOPI's early childhood program. Another CORE activist, Lillian Kaplan, became EOPI assistant research director. Still others who had worked with CORE took community-level positions in neighborhood centers in the black community. According to Zoloth, Stern, Bloom, and Gordon, these activists believed that working with EOPI in the late 1960s was a way of continuing the civil rights work they had started with CORE in the late 1950s.[14]

Zoloth cut back on her social activism in the 1970s. Nevertheless, she still found time in 1972 to manage Jack Gordon's campaign for a seat in the Florida Senate, as well as play a role in George McGovern's presidential campaign. During this period, Zoloth fulfilled her dream of completing a college degree. Sidetracked from college in the 1930s because of the Great Depression, she worked for many years as a legal secretary until moving to Miami in 1954. During the late 1950s, while busy with WILPF, CORE, and political campaigns, she squeezed in part-time college courses at the University of Miami. Full-time work, primarily with EOPI, absorbed her attention in the 1960s, but in the mid-1970s she went back to college and finished her B.A. degree in Liberal Studies at Florida International University. Also in the 1970s, Zoloth ran a consulting and grant-writing firm with Frances Henderson, an African-American colleague from EOPI. Among other things, she recalled in an interview, they wrote a grant proposal for the Miami Beach Chamber of Commerce on ways of attracting more black tourism, using the untapped resources of black travel agencies. She remained active in many organizations and wrote a lot of letters to newspapers on political and social issues. When she died in October 1999, Shirley Zoloth's obituary in the *Miami Herald* recounted her relentless activism on behalf of racial justice and other progressive causes. As Jack Gordon noted at the time, Zoloth "always retained her commitment to racial equality and an open society. Her contributions really pushed desegregation in Miami. If there [was] any kind of progressive [action] in Miami, she was there—it was a given."[15]

In the pages that follow, the reader can trace the evolution of Zoloth's early civil rights activism through some of her letters, discovered in the Jack Gordon Papers at Florida International University. More significantly perhaps, this section reprints the many CORE reports and meeting minutes Zoloth wrote in 1959, when Miami CORE began its downtown lunch counter sit-ins. Few in CORE knew it at the time, but after each sit-in or meeting Zoloth typed up an account of what happened and sent it to the national CORE office. These CORE sit-in reports, along with associated correspondence and a few of Zoloth's published articles, provide detailed discussion of a local civil rights movement in action. These materials have not been edited in any way and, with the exception of some minor punctuation and paragraphing changes, they appear exactly as they were written at the time. Unless otherwise noted, all of these Zoloth writings are from the archived CORE Papers at the Wisconsin State Historical Society in Madison.

Civil Rights Correspondence and Miami CORE Reports and Minutes, 1957–1960

Shirley M. Zoloth

Letter, Zoloth to [Dade County] Board of Public Instruction, September 18, 1957

Gentlemen:

In a telephone call to the office of the Superintendent this morning I learned that a letter addressed by us to the Board of Public Instruction on September 12, 1957, had not been received at that office. For this reason, I am below repeating the text of that letter:

In view of the newspaper report to the effect that the Board will be discussing the recent statement by the Dade County Council on Community Relations, we take the liberty of calling your attention to a resolution sent to you in April of this year by the Miami Branch of the Women's International League for Peace and Freedom. This resolution opposed the pupil assignment cards then being distributed in the schools as a delaying action and urged that the Board proceed with steps for complying with the Supreme Court decision on desegregation.

We would like at this time to state that our organization stands squarely for elimination of segregation in all areas of community life. Desegregation of the schools, because of the Court's genuine effort to give local communities an opportunity to achieve this end in their own manner, has become a local job for understanding and responsible citizens working in good faith with all deliberate speed. Our organization urges that the Board express its intentions of complying with the Supreme Court directive. We not only support the position taken by the Dade County Council on Community Relations, but further would respectfully suggest that much would be gained for the entire community if the School Board and this Council could continue their efforts to proceed in the wisest manner toward early desegregation.

We repeat here our willingness expressed in our letter of September 12, to present our position to the Board whenever its agenda permits the time. Advance notice on the time and date would be greatly appreciated.
Respectfully,
Shirley M. Zoloth
Vice President, Miami Branch, WILPF
[*Source:* Jack Gordon Papers, Box 10, Folder: Desegregation]

* * *

Shirley M. Zoloth, Observations Made at Meeting of Board of Public Instruction, October 2, 1957

Mr. Angus MacGregor read a paper and made some remarks on the subject of Segregation.
—Referred to the statement made by the Dade County Council at the Sept. 18 meeting.
—Called attention to the fact that there was not one "nigger" in the auditorium when people came there to ask for desegregation.
—Used the word "nigger" several times, once very pointedly correcting it by saying an exaggerated "Neeeeeeeeee-gro."
—Referred to Supreme Court as "hand-picked left-wing justices."
—Referred to the only people pushing for integration as being from somewhere else, came from foreign countries, many of them. If they didn't like the way "we" ran things here they should have gone somewhere else. They knew what they were getting into here. They have no business trying to change "our ways."
—If some of these whites want integration so bad why don't they put their kids into the "nigger" schools. Better that, why don't they move into the "nigger" sections so they can live right there. That way they can join the PTAS and DADDIES Clubs.
—God created separate races. We have to be on guard against mongrelization.

Mr. P. D. Armstrong spoke on Religious Instruction. This is a Christian nation. Law says we should have the Bible in school. Much implication against minority groups. No reaction or statement from Board on either speech. Much hard applause from group of about 12 or 15 men and women in audience.

Anna Brenner Meyers [member of school board] made a series of motions, each of which died for want of a second:

—To rescind action of Board in approving distribution of Bibles and to oppose religious instruction in school.

—Asking Dade Board to set up a committee which would study and clarify the Board's position on just how much they want to go beyond what the law actually requires. (Florida Law Annotated, Chapter 231.09 on Bible Reading: "Have once every school day reading in presence of pupils from Holy Bible without sectarian comment.")

—To write to Tallahassee to find out legal status of contemplated plans.

During this discussion by members of Board, a woman in the audience who had been sitting alone rose and walked to the floor mike. Chairman Van Dusen recognized her and she made a statement to the following effect: I am Jewish just like Anna Brenner Meyers is Jewish. I am just as religious as she is. I have a child in school and she has not. I am not afraid of my child hearing the Bible. I want the Board to know that not everybody in Anna Brenner Meyers' district agrees with her. I live in her district. Chairman Van Dusen here suggested that this woman should talk to Mrs. Meyers after the meeting, since Mrs. Meyers was her "representative." She said: I can't talk to Mrs. Meyers because we don't see eye to eye on some things.

When she sat down another woman rose (Mrs. Sherrer?) and made a statement: I am Protestant and the majority of people in this country are Protestant. The Jews are a minority and have to accept what the majority want. The majority want religious (Christian) instruction and the schools should have it. The minority will have to go along with it.

Another woman (Dot Mitchell) stood up and very firmly announced that she was an Episcopalian and that she was in full accord with Anna Brenner Meyers, that she believed in separation of church and state and that there are a great number of people in the community that feel that way.

[*Source:* Jack Gordon Papers, Box 10, Folder: Desegregation]

* * *

Shirley M. Zoloth, Notes Taken at School Board Trial: John Brown, August 29, 1958

Mrs. Ratcliffe, a Negro, was called as witness. Principal of Northwestern High School. Stated that students coming to her school have to pass in the general area of 5 or 6 white schools.

Then, Question: If you received an application from a white student who lived in an area reasonable to your school, what would you do?

Answer: This has never happened. I don't know.

Question: If it happened tomorrow, what would you do?

Answer: I guess I would refer it to the administration.
Question: Why would you do that?
Answer: Because I couldn't handle this myself (or something similar).
Question: Why not?
Answer: I couldn't (wouldn't?) handle this problem—I mean, this situation—myself (stumbling here, but smiling, said something about customs in the area). School system's position has been that since 1956 the schools have not been operated on a segregated basis.

Dr. Brown, a Negro, called as a witness. Moved here in 1956, child apparently enrolled in Negro school in area in Sept. 1956. Later (January), father tried to enroll child in white school in area which was both closer and also less crowded and also had better facilities. Filled out application. Letter came shortly to his home from Board denying application. This would have been application for re-assignment. In letter statement appeared that a hearing could be requested. Dr. Brown requested a hearing, but then a few days later he canceled the request and there was no hearing.

On stand today in answer to a question, Brown stated: let's not talk about leading questions. Let me state plainly that my child has no choice. He was denied admission to a white school nearer him than the Negro school. Brown's remarks were ruled out of order because he went beyond answering question, but everyone heard it. Dr. Brown also stated that he himself had never seen a pupil assignment card. Plaintiffs claim that in Negro schools teachers fill it out and put in name of school of "choice" and that in white schools, parents get them. (Note from S.Z.–I have filled these out.)

Brown child called as witness and confirmed what father had stated about pupil assignment card, said he had never himself filled one out. The teacher had always done it. Negro principals yesterday had stated that only in younger classes did teachers do it, and only for helping legibility.

Joe Hall [Superintendent of Dade County Schools] called as witness. Attorney for plaintiffs reminded him that in previous testimony he had stated that the school board had changed the operation of schools in 1956 to a non-segregated basis. In answer to questions today Hall stated that he had never instructed the public, the parents or the teachers or pupils that they could now attend any school they chose. He said it was in all the papers and he "assumed" people knew.

Question: How do you explain, Dr. Hall, that the schools are still either all Negro or all white? Answer: 90% because of where they live, housing determines school area; 10% because of assignment *requested*. But Hall emphasized that final assignment and placement is up to the Board.

[*Editor's Note:* In June 1956, several black parents, including Dr. John Brown, all members of the NAACP, filed suit in federal court to end segregation in Dade County schools. The 1959 court decision upheld the black parents and forced the school board to begin planning for desegregation.
Source: Jack Gordon Papers, Box 10, Folder: Desegregation]

* * *

Dade County Council on Human Relations, Report of the Committee on Public Accommodations, n.d. (ca. fall 1958)

The purpose of the survey on Public Accommodations was to determine current practices and attitudes in the Greater Miami area toward minority groups and to ascertain how much these attitudes are regulated by law and how much they are dictated by custom. We wished to find out whether practices are the same in different areas of the community and whether they are changing; if they are changing, is it in the direction of easier association and greater mutual respect.

The fields in which this committee observed were: public transportation, including buses, taxis, jitneys, depots, movies, theaters, restaurants, public restrooms and drinking fountains; public libraries; retail shops. We checked on the laws of the state of Florida, Dade County, and the municipalities of Miami, Coral Gables and Miami Beach to find out what separation of the races the laws demand.

To ascertain the facts we made phone calls, spoke to people and investigated as individuals and by going out in teams of Negro and white women. It should be noted that where possible all information was obtained either by personal contact or from persons in authority.

The Laws

The laws of the State of Florida requiring racial segregation according to Richard W. Ervin, Attorney General of the State of Florida, are as follows:

> Article XII, Section 12, of the Florida State Constitution and Section 228.09, Florida Statutes, both require that white and colored children shall be taught in separate schools. These provisions, however, have been declared unconstitutional by U.S. Supreme Court in its 1954 decision in the case of Brown vs. Board of Education of Topeka. Other provisions of Florida law relating to racial segregation are found in Section 955.12 (Florida School for Boys); intermarriage between white and colored

prohibited, Article 16, Section 24, Florida Constitution; Chapter 352, Florida Statutes, relating to railroad transportation.

In addition to these sections of the Florida State Constitution and Statutes, the Florida State Sanitary Code, Chapter 7, entitled *Drinking Water and Washing Facilities in Buildings Serving Public and in Places of Employment,* provides in Section 4, Paragraph A that if members of white and colored races are employed, separate toilet facilities shall be provided for each race and shall be labeled "White Men," "White Women," "Colored Men," "Colored Women." Paragraph B states that if members of the white and colored races are to be served, separate facilities shall be provided on the basis of seating capacity for each race. Violating, disobeying, refusing, omitting or neglecting to comply is a misdemeanor punishable by fines of $6,000 or 6 months.

This same section of the Sanitary Code provides for the furnishing of a water supply in public places and in places of employment. There is no provision for separate drinking fountains or for marking them in any way.

Dade County laws do not mention separation of the races in any particular, the county being covered by the laws of the State of Florida. The City of Miami (the office of Mr. William L. Pallot, City Attorney, unverified by a written statement) says that the ordinance or statute of the city that mentions segregation [requires] that seating in buses shall be from the rear for colored, and this provision is now unconstitutional. The City of Coral Gables (office of the city Attorney, Mr. Semple) says that it has no regulations requiring separation of the races. As regards the Venetian Pool, operated by the city, there is a gentlemen's agreement that Negroes will not use it. In both cities, in reference to real estate zoning, there is also a gentlemen's agreement that the present arrangement and neighborhoods will not be changed. There is no zoning law prohibiting or restricting Negro housing. Miami Beach has no statutes or ordinances that would effect a separation of the races. However, no Negroes live on Miami Beach.

In 1957, the Florida Legislature passed the law known as Section 509.092, providing that purveyors of public lodging and public food services shall have the right to refuse service to any person, etc., objectionable to the manager. Section 509.141 deals with "Ejection of undesirable guests." This gives managers of places of public accommodation [the authority] to choose their customers and vary their services.

Public Transportation

In the field of transportation, we found that the Supreme Court decision forbidding segregation on buses is observed by the bus lines, the policy being compliance with the law. Individual bus drivers may observe the letter of the law, but may be unpleasant and may suggest to customers that they go to the back. One of the members of our committee, when she seated herself in the forward part of the bus, was asked to move to the back. She refused, whereupon the bus driver stopped the bus at a public telephone and called his office. After the phone conversation he returned to the bus, got in and drove off, without another word to the passenger. At another time, one of our teams of a white woman and a Negro woman entered a bus together. The white woman paid the bus driver for both, then both sat down side by side on a double seat. The bus driver eyed them, then made a remark about "this business of integration." The remark was taken up by another passenger, but that was the end as the team left the bus shortly after. This team had made a previous trip with no incident or remarks. The members of our committee reported that in observing passengers on various buses throughout the city, they noticed that it seemed to be habit on part of the Negroes, more especially the older ones, to go to the back of the bus, and that, too, may help explain the lack of incidents. Trips on buses to Coral Gables, South Miami, Opa Locka, and Liberty City were without incident, although Negro passengers sat anywhere. On buses to and from Miami Beach Negroes sit anywhere, but there is a special bus labeled "COLORED," which originates in Miami in the morning and at the Beach in the late afternoon. Its purpose is to bring and take back to their own neighborhoods Negroes who work on the beach. Why this bus will not accept white passengers or why a sign giving its destination will not suffice, we do not know.

Taxis and jitneys are in a different situation. Companies are chartered as public carriers and pay heavily for their licenses. In Miami Beach and Coral Gables, where there are no Negro-owned taxi companies, the white-owned and driven taxis will transport them. In Miami, where there are Negro-owned companies, the white companies will not take Negroes and the Negroes have promised not to give whites a ride. This is a business understanding not to poach on each other's preserves. The same applies to the jitneys.

The law forbidding segregation does not apply to intra-state waiting room facilities. Waiting rooms at the two railroad stations are segregated, and while, possibly because it is newer, the waiting room marked "Colored" is cleaner at the Seaboard Airline R.R. and the similar waiting room at the Florida East Coast R.R. is dingy and shabby, neither is as pleasant as the ones marked "White," although there has been no reduction in fares for the lesser service.

A member of our committee reports that signs indicate separate facilities in the Miami Bus Station. This includes the waiting room itself, restroom facilities and lunch room. At the depot there are two waiting rooms, one with a sign which reads "Colored-Intrastate" and the other with no signs. The restrooms in the unmarked waiting room have signs which say "Men—Reservados Para Hombres Blancos." The women's restroom is similarly marked, although one Negro woman was observed going in. She apparently did not speak Spanish and therefore could not know that this room was "reserved." In the restrooms adjacent to the other waiting room, one was marked simply "Women" and the other "Men-Colored Intrastate." An *interstate* ticket would gain admission to the reserved room.

There are separate eating facilities. In both the bus station and the depot, the Negro people seem to use the separate facilities almost without exception. The airlines do *not* have separate facilities.

Movies and Theaters

Except for movie theaters in the Negro neighborhoods, which are patronized exclusively by Negroes, this community makes no provision for permitting them admission to other and first run movies since "White" movie houses do not have segregated sections. The only legitimate theater in the community does not accept them because "their presence would keep other customers away." The local auditoriums—the Dade County, Miami Beach and Dinner Key Auditoriums rent to leasees who make their own rules of admission and their own seating arrangements. A leasee like the University of Miami permits a scattering of Negroes; the Opera Guild has a separate section in the balcony for Negro seating so that it "does not deprive the Negroes of the pleasure of hearing good music." Negroes are permitted in the end zone at football games, but when the yearly game between two Negro teams is played, one half of the stadium is for Negroes, the other for whites.

Movies in white neighborhoods do not permit Negroes to be admitted because of the Sanitary Code requirement of separate marked washrooms for the races, which none of them have. Members of our committee have been turned away by movie house cashiers, or if they obtained tickets, found themselves refused entrance at the door by the ticket-taker, manager, head usher, or other management representative. This was true throughout the Greater Miami area, from South Dixie Highway to Lincoln Road. In two instances, a team was admitted; one, when a theater on Flagler Street admitted the team whose Negro member was so light as to arouse no recognition of the fact that she was a Negro. The manager of this theater was later called on the phone and asked whether the caller would be admitted with Negro friends. He answered that the law prohibited the admission of Negroes and that they would be refused entree. At a Lincoln Road movie, the team on the Beach was accepted and permitted to enter by the manager himself at a time in the afternoon when there were few patrons. Having been refused at other movie houses on Lincoln Road, the team went back later in the week to attend an evening showing. The manager who had himself sold them tickets at the afternoon performance categorically refused them admission in the evening. It was "against the policy of the management." Drive-in movies admit Negroes in cars but show them to a special section away from white cars.

Restaurants

Restaurants turned out to be quite interesting, as much in the difference of reaction among the waitresses and other help as in the variety of responses. The stores are not "set up to accommodate colored customers," one department store restaurant hostess told the team. In one department store our team was served at a table, but only because the Negro member was not recognized as such. One member of the Committee had been served coffee at a national chain 5 and 10 cent store. When the waitress realized she was a Negro, the waitress poured the coffee into a paper cup, telling her she could not sit at the counter.

One team made the round of all the national chain 5 and 10 cent stores on Flagler Street, as well as one of the smaller department stores. They sat at the lunch counter in each store and each time were approached by an upset, angry, or distressed waitress. Some waitresses were apologetic and tried to explain "This is the South, you know." Others were defiant; none addressed themselves to the Negro member of the team but to the white member, explaining that they were not allowed to serve Negroes seated at the counter, but that the Negro could go to the stand-up counter and be served hot dogs. One waitress was quite unhappy. She explained "I am from the North. I am not accustomed to this. I am terribly sorry but I have orders." Requests for the store manager only served to bring reiteration of the "store policy in this state." This team was not served at any lunch counter on Flagler Street. One department store in the midtown area did serve the team at a small table near the lunch counter. The waitress was pleasant and nothing was said by anyone, although the team fancied that it was observed with interest.

Our Coral Gables team made the rounds of both chain and privately owned restaurants. They were served in two branches of a nationally known, higher-class restaurant where they were not made to feel uncomfortable. In several branches of a local, low-price chain, they were turned away by the managers after their orders were taken, and once when they had already been served and had begun to eat. Refusals had also been the experience of the midtown team with this particular chain. In both branches of a Coral Gables restaurant, they were refused; in the first store when they sat at a counter to the distress of the waitress; in the other store when they sat in a booth, the waitress offered to serve them in the back. The chain drug stores on Miracle Mile refused them service at the counter. At a privately owned restaurant the manager and hostess were extremely embarrassed and after letting the team sit until they asked if they would be served, explained that "No, they would not be served, because . . ." A team on the beach had no difficulty in being served when they went into a restaurant in a group of two White and two Negro women. Since there is an agreement about serving convention delegates among the Beach restaurants, although the team did not wear delegate badges, there was no question because they were in a group. The Negro women did not attempt to go in alone.

Hotels

The hotel situation as regards the accommodation of Negroes is different as far as the two communities most involved—Miami and Miami Beach—are concerned. The Miami Beach Convention Bureau states that individual Negroes will not be housed at the Beach, but Negroes attending conventions will be accepted as part of a mixed group. In checking with various hotels, we found that acceptance means different things to different hotels. The smaller hotels below Lincoln Road do not accept a mixed group. The smaller the hotel the more definite the refusal. The larger hotels were all willing to take a mixed group, represented as being about ten to fifteen percent Negro. The two prestige hotels in the North Beach area placed no restriction on any activities, including the pool and beach, as well as dining facilities. Some of the smaller or less expensive hotels permitted [using] the dining room, but not sitting in the lobby. The pool was to be used "with discretion, such as before 9 A.M. and after 5 P.M." Some felt that they would allow only a possible ten to fifteen percent. Fifty percent would be far too many.

In Miami, the hotels varied from a downright "No, not at all," to readiness to take a mixed group if the Negroes did not sleep at the hotel but slept elsewhere. Some accept Negroes in mixed private parties such as luncheons or dinners, but the attitude is less liberal than that of the better hotels at the Beach. Only one hotel in Miami would accept a mixed group for a convention with full and free use of facilities and the same type rooms for the same rates.

Shopping and Washroom Facilities

It is in the areas of shopping, the use of washroom facilities and drinking fountains in public places, and the attitudes in the libraries that there is a lightening of restrictions and an increasing acceptance of the Negro as a co-resident and co-buyer. The Zoo, a County institution, admits Negroes. The libraries in Miami are open to all residents, with a deposit requirement for tourists, and Negroes report they are treated with consideration. Coral Gables requires residence, as does Miami Beach, which has no restrictions against Negroes but no Negroes live at the Beach.

There was a time, members of our team reported, when a Negro woman was not permitted to try on a hat, or a dress, or a pair of shoes. She could point to the article she wanted and take it, guessing as to its fit. Members of our committee, commenting on recent shopping trips made by themselves and by friends, found they tried on shoes, hats, and dresses in one of the higher-priced department stores and commented that they were treated "cordially." They tried on hats and shoes in the other department stores and felt that the saleslady in one may have been "flabbergasted" but she made no comment. In small retail shops they find that they get waited on with sales help in the purchase of shoes and that they can try on hats at the counters and dresses in the dressing rooms to a much greater extent. Members of the committee shopped in South Miami, the Flagler Street section of Miami, in Hialeah, and at the 79th Street shopping plaza, as well as on Lincoln Road at the Beach. The consensus was that shopping was not unpleasant, that salespeople were generally polite, with occasional over-politeness or haughtiness which seemed individual while the store policy seemed to be accommodating. In departments where they do not try on they were welcome as customers. This seemed to contrast with the restaurant and lunch counter situation where the management insisted on not serving Negro customers and the waitresses and counter boys were sorry and protested their own sentiments to the contrary.

Washroom and Drinking Fountains

Washrooms come under the Sanitary Code, and most of the department stores have two sets, separate but not equal. The second floor washroom at Jordan Marsh is marked "White Women," as is the washroom on Sears's main floor and the plush one on Burdine's third floor. The washroom on Richard's second floor is marked "Ladies Lounge," but there are separate washrooms in Richard's basement. Our committee members report that they and others have used the washrooms in all the Miami department stores regardless of markings, without incident or comment from other shoppers or store personnel.

Although the Sanitary Code does not require separate or marked drinking fountains, most places of public accommodation, including the supermarkets, have had two fountains standing side by side dispensing the same water. In many places, one of the fountains has been removed; in many others the signs have been painted out. There are still very many left, but the tendency on the part of more and more of our citizenry is to disregard these signs.

Conclusions

Policies in establishments serving the public do not appear to be consistent, as is shown by the difference in hotel attitudes, restaurant service, and even acceptance by movies of Negro patrons at slack hours but not during busy times. The phrase, "This is the South" seems to be used often to cover excuses for non-service and to explain the necessity of following community modes, even against personal preference. Popular confusion as to what is and what is not state and local law is used to perpetuate local custom and as a defense against change.

The aura of apologetics which seems to exist in places which refuse service portends a coming change. Many establishments in the Miami area do not conform to the discriminating attitude prevalent among the majority and their numbers are being increased. From the experience of this committee and the attitude of many of the people interviewed and spoken to, it appears that many in our community, if they were given the external backbone of legal sanction, would be willing to see their Negro neighbors accepted as the integral part of the community that they are.

[*Editor's Note:* The Dade County Council on Human Relations was created in 1958 from the merger of two organizations: the Dade County Council on Community Relations and the Florida Council on Human Relations. Both sought to improve race relations and to ease tensions over school desegregation issues. This document was intended to inform people of segregation practices in Dade County. Zoloth prepared the final report from the work of several teams of investigators.]

* * *

Dade County Council on Human Relations, Suggested Presentation for Discussion Leaders, January 29, 1959

In May, 1954, the United States Supreme Court, in the case of Brown versus the Board of Education of Topeka, Kansas, ruled that separate educational facilities for Negro students were inherently unequal and violated the equal protection of the law guaranteed by the 14th Amendment to the United States Constitution. That decision threatened the segregation pattern which had become a part of the mores of the South.

Immediately following the decision, several of the southern states called their legislatures into session to devise laws which would contravene the Court's decision. Ten of the seventeen southern states and the District of Columbia have implemented the Court's decision, but seven states, of which Florida is one, have defied the court and have not integrated any schools.

All of us are familiar with the Little Rock situation, where the President of the United States felt it necessary to order Federal troops into that city to preserve law and order when the desegregation of Little Rock High School began. We are also aware that the situation was provoked by the attitude of Governor Faubus, who expressed and urged opposition to the Court's decision. We know from Communist propaganda that Little Rock has cost the United States prestige in international affairs. The situation in Little Rock divided the community and has ultimately resulted in the deprivation of education for many of the children of that city. In passing it should be noted that other communities in Arkansas have integrated their schools with little or no difficulty. The Governor doesn't talk about that.

Another result of the Supreme Court decision is to be found in the renewed activities of extremist groups. In several communities throughout the South, the Ku Klux Klan has been rejuvenated. The White Citizens' Councils have sprung up throughout the area. In Alabama, the state legislature redistricted one of its counties in an effort to deprive the bulk of the Negroes living there an opportunity to vote. Since January 1, 1955, there have been some 72 bombings attempted or achieved in synagogues, Jewish centers, Negro homes, churches, and white and Negro schools. Hundreds of bomb threats have been made to leaders of both white and Negro communities by these same extremists.

Politicians have campaigned for office on a segregation platform and have told the voter, if elected they will guarantee segregation will be preserved. As Ralph McGill pointed out in a recent column in the *Miami News,* the politicians have failed to keep their pledges because the law on the matter of segregation is clear. In 1958 again, in a unanimous decision, the Supreme Court said, "The Constitutional right of children not to be discriminated [against] in school admissions on grounds of race or color declared by this Court in the Brown case can neither be nullified openly or directly by state legislators or state executive or judicial officers; nor nullified indirectly by them through evasive schemes for segregation whether attempted ingeniously or ingenuously."

The Court couldn't speak more clearly on any issue than they did in the above decision. When the Supreme Court of the State of Virginia was required to give a ruling on the legality of the closed public schools in Norfolk, Front Royal, Charlottesville and other communities in Virginia, it had no recourse except to declare the laws of the State of Virginia which sought to evade the Supreme Court mandate as unconstitutional.

Today, the State Legislature of Virginia is frantically seeking other means of avoiding school integration. Legislatures in Georgia and Alabama are doing likewise. In Florida, several proposals to avoid integration of the schools will be proposed when the State Legislature convenes in April 1959. Florida Attorney General Ervin has called publicly for the strengthening of the State Pupil Assignment Law, which the Supreme Court has not yet held unconstitutional, but only because the case involving that law did not allege discrimination on account of race by application of the Pupil Assignment Law. The latter case was heard in connection with the Alabama law. From the decisions of the Court, it is obvious that no matter what the law, if in the enactment of it there is the intent to continue segregation, that law will be held unconstitutional.

Hundreds of thousands of dollars have been spent trying to evade the Supreme Court decision. In the Miami area, our economy has suffered because of racial strife in the South. As Governor Collins pointed out, it is his opinion that the Democratic National Convention did not choose Miami Beach for its 1960 site because of racial tensions here. The money which that convention would have brought to our area would have amounted to a sum of many millions. Miami is the center of inter-American trade. We are trying to develop industry in our area. Tourism is the life blood of our economy, yet all of these have suffered because of the race issue. Industry will not open new plants where there is any possibility that their employees will have difficulty in sending their children to public schools. Many winter tourists bring their children to attend schools. They will not come if their children cannot attend a school.

What are the possibilities of schools in Florida being closed and what can be done to prevent it? There have been several proposals made for continuing segregation in our schools. The most popular of these is the one to strengthen the Pupil Assignment Law. As noted above, the Pupil Assignment Law has not been tested on the grounds of discrimination. Another proposal is to do away with our public school system as we know it and provide parents with funds to enable their children to attend private schools. In effect, the proposal would make the public schools private. Whatever the scheme, however, in light of the 1958 Supreme Court decision, so long as there is discrimination or separate facilities, the courts will eventually hold these schemes unconstitutional. More and more, thinking people have realized that they are fighting a losing battle in opposing desegregation. The very most they can gain is time to desegregate. Now, knowing this, what do we do as a group of interested citizens to be sure that our public schools are not closed?

Perhaps it would be better before posing that question to take an informal poll of this group to see how you feel about closing the schools. Does anyone here favor closing the schools instead of having desegregation? If so, how do we provide an education for our children? In the event that none of us favor closing the schools, how can we make our wishes known in the community? [*Editor's Note:* Zoloth prepared this document for use in small-group community meetings designed to encourage support for school desegregation.]

* * *

Miami CORE Minutes, March 12, 1959

The meeting was held at the Mt. Zion Baptist Church and called to order at 8:00 P.M. Mr. Gordon Carey, field secretary, served as temporary chairman for the evening.

After questions and answers concerning CORE, it was unanimously agreed that membership be open for acceptance. After which seventeen persons were accepted, and: The Greater Miami CORE was accepted as the name of the Miami Group. Due to uncertainties of prior commitments, two of the aforementioned seventeen members had to withdraw their names, leaving a total of fifteen.

Dr. John Brown was nominated for temporary chairman, which he declined in favor of First Vice Project Chairman.
Temporary officers were installed as follows:
Chairman: Mrs. Shirley Zoloth
First Vice Project Chairman: Dr. J. Brown
Treasurer: Mrs. Alice Barr
Constitution Committee: Dr. E. A. Ward, Mrs. Rose Sipser, Mr. Charles Williams, Mr. Sumner Hutcheson, Jr.
Secretary of Minutes: Mrs. Rose Sipser
Secretary of Correspondence: Mr. Jack Ivory, II

Public Accommodations Coordinator: Mrs. Thalia Stern
Meeting Notification: Mrs. Gert Leiner

A project for active members was suggested. Dr. Brown, First Vice Project Chairman, recommended thought on the matter. It was finally decided there be no projects until after the next meeting, which would be held at 8:00 P.M. Wednesday March 18th at the branch office of the NAACP. The question arose concerning dues, and a committee for dues was recommended.

The meeting closed with a farewell message from Mr. McCain and Mr. Carey, Field Secretaries, both of whom will have left the city by our next meeting. Both members and spectators wished them a safe trip and a speedy return to our city.

Respectfully submitted,
Jack Ivory, II
Corresponding Secretary
Acting Secretary of Minutes

* * *

Letter, Zoloth to Rep. W. C. Herrell, Florida House of Representatives, April 3, 1959

Dear Rep. Herrell:

I was one of those present at the Conference you spoke to at the Dupont Hotel on March 25, and I would like to express my thanks to you for taking the time to come and also praise you for having the courage to come. Many of your remarks have been the basis for a great deal of concern on my part.

Let me first say that my husband and I are both opposed to any legislation which attempts to delay or circumvent or evade compliance with the letter and the spirit of the desegregation decision of the Supreme Court. We are opposed to the already existing Pupil Assignment Law, and are hoping for the defeat of the "last resort" bill which threatens to close the schools, or the "parent-option" bill which promises a financial reward to people for evading the law.

Aside from the poor economics of the matter—the cost of extra litigation since even the most virulent of the segregationists admit that they know they are only "buying time," the burden on school budgets that are inadequate at best, the adverse effects on businesses in tension areas—we find it increasingly difficult to explain to our children the lack of morality in the matter. They have an embarrassing way of sometimes taking seriously the words they say in the Pledge of Allegiance, or the Preamble to the Constitution, or in their history books, or in their religious teachings.

As you well know, the existing Assignment Law requires principals of

schools, teachers and school staff individuals to lie—or more politely to equivocate. It is admittedly based on keeping racial segregation as long as possible, and it legally denies this. Would you care to explain the morality of this to my children for me?
Shirley M. Zoloth
[*Editor's Note:* W. C. Herrell was a state legislator from Dade County.
Source: Jack Gordon Papers, Box 10, Folder: Desegregation]

* * *

Letter, Zoloth to James Dombrowski, Southern Conference Educational Fund, April 13, 1959

Dear Mr. Dombrowski:

Let me first of all assure you that I have not "done most of the work that has been done in the area." Without pretending to a false modesty, however, I admit to having participated in most of it. Most of my energy in this period has gone into the mechanics of setting up discussion groups: persuading "hostesses," enlisting and briefing leaders, getting material, and the actual setting up of dates, etc. I might add that Haskell Lazere, who is the Executive Director of the American Jewish Congress, was officially the coordinator of this project for the Dade County Council on Community Relations. The AJCongress has consistently taken a position more forthright than others in the community, but in the "unified" agency effort (through the DCCCR) it of necessity became somewhat watered down.

The AJCongress has taken the initiative now, partially because of impatience of its members and [its] own Council, and partially because of the lack in the community of a positive declaration of a moral and/or ethical position urging desegregation and compliance with the law. The AJCongress sent out to all other agencies and organizations who might likely commit themselves (limiting itself to Dade County, I think) [to] a Resolution asking not merely for "keeping the schools open at all costs," [but] for desegregation. More specifically, I believe it asks for peaceful and orderly compliance. These other organizations have been invited to join with the AJCongress in taking this stand.

Another correction—on the working of CORE in this area. True, it is a very small group—about 10 active and 40 more or less committed in interest—and it is timid and unsophisticated. But it is doing a little bit. I have been a part of this. The man really who is the moving light is Dr. John Brown, a young Negro ophthalmologist, relatively new in the community. I think it will continue to grow. Gordon Carey and Jim McCain, field workers for CORE, spent 10 days or so here last month and managed to see a great many people in the community who are sympathetic to its aims. But this has proceeded independently of any other activities in the community.

There were indications that NAACP and the Negro Young Democrat Club were going to start a bang-up registration campaign, but so far to my knowledge this has not begun.

This would be more complete if more time were allowed for some checking and research. However, I do feel with Barbara Gordon that time is of the essence. In particular, I am anxious that we learn as soon as possible just who in Florida is in favor of desegregation. No one seems to know how many people we can count on if a need for social action should arise quickly. A March on Tallahassee on a state-wide basis might have an impact on some issue. From Dade County alone it would probably be a farce.

Sincerely,
Shirley M. Zoloth
[*Source:* John M. Coe Papers, Box 3, Folder 92]

*   *   *

Miami CORE Sit-in Report, April 15, 1959

Mr. and Mrs. Zoloth (white)
Mrs. Alice Barr (Negro)
Mr. Ishmael Howard (Negro)

All four met in front of Woolworth's on Flagler Street. We went inside and waited near the lunch counter in the hope that we would get four seats together. This seemed difficult, so Mrs. Barr and I sat down together; and a few minutes later Mr. Zoloth and Mr. Howard sat down about two seats away from us. We were not any of us served. We noticed that the woman who was apparently in charge there left the counter. We were left sitting there. Shortly, a young man came over to us and said that they did not "serve colored here." We asked if he was the manager and he told us he was the assistant manager. We asked to see the manager and he told us he was out. We told him we would like to speak to him (the assistant manager—Mr. Pole or Paul) and asked if we might go to the office. He indicated that we might just as well stay where we were. We told him about CORE and gave him a *This Is CORE* pamphlet. He reluctantly told us the name of the manager, Mr. Harrington, only after we pressed him, saying that we would gladly give him our names. He said he would give Mr. Harrington the pamphlet and that we would find Mr. Harrington there in the store most days. When I asked a salesgirl earlier where the ladies room was located, she told me that they had none and that I would have to go to Burdine's or Kress's. I was alone at that time.

We then went over to McCrory's and were able to get four seats together at the lunch counter toward the middle of the store. The waitress served us quickly and graciously and was equally interested and conversational with all four of us. She seemed completely unaware that she might be doing something that wasn't ordinary.
Submitted by Shirley M. Zoloth

* * *

Miami CORE Sit-in Report, April 17, 1959

Mr. and Mrs. Zoloth
Mr. Howard

We had made an appointment with Mr. Harrington, manager of Woolworth's. We found him at a counter in the back of the store and Mr. Z. introduced himself, Mr. Howard and Mrs. Z. He did not shake hands with Mr. Howard. After telling him who we represented and what our goal was, Mr. Harrington told us it was custom not to serve Negroes sitting at counter. After further discussion he said it was the law of the State, but on questioning could not state that he knew this to be a definite fact. He would not respond to questions as to whether it was his policy or Woolworth's policy and refused to discuss his personal attitude. We all felt that his attitude was hostile.

We then went back to McCrory's to re-test, sitting at different parts of the counter—toward the front this time. The three of us sensed this time that it was not as friendly a spot. A waitress walked by with a significant "uh-uh," as if to say "here's trouble." We were kept waiting and then a young Negro girl who had been washing dishes came over and told Mr. Howard that "Negroes aren't served at this counter." She said it was the policy of the store. Mr. Howard asked if we could see the manager and she told us he was in the back of the store. In reply to Mr. Howard's question she also told us his name: Mr. Edwards.

We walked to the back of the store immediately and found Mr. Edwards. We all had the feeling that he was friendly. He shook hands easily with both men and was quick to "bless" us for the work we were doing. He was full of agreement with us that Negroes should have the same service and have the same seating accessible to them, but said it wasn't up to him. We told him about CORE and gave him a pamphlet and he promised to read it. Even though we all felt his friendship to be sincere, he was firm about refusing to do any "opening up" or even permit any deliberate testing. We did mention that we had been served (the four of us) earlier in the week at the same counter. He indicated that the day before they had served four Puerto Ricans and had had some

repercussions about it. We asked how the waitresses knew whom they were permitted to serve. He answered "We use our instinct."
Submitted by Shirley M. Zoloth

* * *

Miami CORE Sit-in Report, April 22, 1959

Several weeks ago a test was made at Grant's sit-down lunch counter in downtown Miami. Grant's has, as have the other 5 and 10 stores in the downtown section, a sit-down lunch counter for whites only and a stand-up counter where both Negroes and whites are served.

A mixed group had gone in and the Negroes had been refused service at the sit-down counter. Dr. John Brown and Miss Lillian Kaplan were part of that group. They had tried to see the manager then, but he was out. Repeated efforts were made to telephone him for an appointment, but they were not able to get to talk to him, even on the phone. Two young women who had been part of this initial testing went on their own (both were white) and managed to stop in and see the manager. Dr. Brown had gone there several times and the manager had always been "out" to him, even though a porter had told the group that he was there most of the time. The two women, Mrs. Reynolds and Mrs. Crawford, both white, represented themselves as interested bystanders and students and the manager spent time talking to them. They did not say anything about CORE but spoke only in terms of civil rights and prejudice. After they reported this to our CORE group, we all agreed that while they had been able to get some angles on the man's personal opinions, it still had not been a CORE negotiation in any sense. The question was how to get an appointment with the manager. This was worked finally by Mrs. Reynolds calling him, telling him that she had talked to CORE people about the conversation with him and that we were very interested in getting him to tell us his views, too. He reluctantly agreed to see us and made an appointment.

This interview took place in his office. Present from CORE were Dr. John Brown, Jack Ivory, Alice Barr, Lillian Kaplan, Shirley Zoloth, and Mrs. Reynolds. The manager also had with him a young man whom he introduced as his "personnel" man. We suspected that he was either a lawyer or public relations man, for in the course of the conversation it could be seen that the manager was very ill at ease and apprehensive, that he had apparently spoken to the Merchant's Association, and that he was not at all sure of himself. We gave the manager the *This Is CORE* pamphlet after we had spoken to him for almost an hour. He had been rather non-committal with us, but Dr. Brown did most of the talking with him, with the others injecting a few comments occasionally.

Dr. Brown had one of the Grant's pamphlets put out by CORE—and the so-called personnel man reached over and was very agitated by this. He handed it to the manager. We left them with the understanding that they would be in touch with both their national office and the Merchant's Association. We told them we would be glad to take his suggestion that we, too, approach the Merchant's Association—plus the other 5 and 10 cent stores. He was in the meantime going to take our suggestion (so he said) of getting figures from his national organization to find out if business was adversely affected in Baltimore after the counter was opened up for Negroes.

Submitted by Shirley M. Zoloth

* * *

Letter, Shirley Zoloth to James R. Robinson, Executive Secretary, National CORE, April 22, 1959

Dear Mr. Robinson:

I am writing to you on behalf of Miami CORE both to bring you up to date on our activities and also to ask help of you.

We have tentatively decided to have a quick demonstration next Wednesday, April 29. This will probably take place at Grant's and perhaps also at McCrory's. We are meeting Tuesday night to set up the details. What we are hoping to do is have a show of strength, rather than a real sit-in, and we are trying to get press and TV coverage.

Enclosed are reports on our testing and interviews with the managers of Grant's, McCrory's and Woolworth's. Grant's seems to be the store that gets most of the Negro patronage. McCrory's which is next door to Grant's also gets many Negro shoppers. Woolworth's is across the street and just from a superficial observation does not get as many Negro shoppers. They all have sit-down lunch counters for whites only, and stand-up counters where both Negroes and whites are served and eat together. There is a sanitation code here which requires a place serving Negroes to have separate bathroom facilities. Grant's does not have those. Woolworth's has no bathrooms at all, which might in itself be a violation of the code, and McCrory's has not been checked on this yet. However, they all do serve Negroes at stand-up counters and the law does not specify "position," so that it will probably be a feeble support for them to use. They seem to want the Negro customers to do their shopping there!

What we thought you could do from New York, if you agree that it might be useful, is to write to the national offices of these three firms, informing them of our efforts to have Negroes served where they may sit down, informing them that we mean to persist in these attempts, and asking them what their national policy is. I might add here that Grant's manager had indicated that he was his own boss, but would consult with the Merchant's Association of the Chamber of Commerce and abide by their policy. Woolworth's and McCrory's managers would not say whether they had autonomy in this matter or whether it was established by the organization. They were asked this question directly and answered that they did not want to make a reply to this—that is, as to whether the manager had autonomy or whether it was company policy.

If you decide to do this, we would like copies of letters you send them—or reports on conversations you might have with the firms. In any event, we would like some word from you on your reaction to our suggestions here made. Your letter explaining the Grant's Baltimore project threw a great deal of light on the subject for us. For one thing, we had not realized that Grant's had been the last to open up its counter. We thought it had "led" the others.

You may reply to either Dr. John Brown or to me in this matter.
Sincerely,
Shirley M. Zoloth

* * *

Letter, Zoloth to Robinson, April 30, 1959

Dear Mr. Robinson:

The enclosed clipping is the only write-up we received in either of the two large newspapers here. We had excellent TV coverage, and some radio coverage. The UP had a representative with us, and the whole story was on this morning's "Today" show, films and all, I understand. Each of the three TV stations devoted a good portion of the early evening and late evening news reports on film and interview reporting on this small demonstration. The photographers and press were there when we arrived and started taking pictures immediately. The time spent in Grant's, which we went to first, was probably about 25 or 30 minutes, during which most of the picture-taking and interviewing occurred. Police officers were there, onlookers gathered, but there was no hostile exchange or action that we know of. It was all quite amicable. We had about 18 or 20 people, about half Negro. From Grant's we went next door to McCrory's and sat for about 10 or 15 minutes.

In Grant's, the waitresses disappeared—a half-made sandwich was on the board facing us. In McCrory's, the waitresses stayed there but did not "see" us. They did not answer when spoken to. The managers did not appear in either case.

The newspaper people and TV men were quite friendly and tried to be helpful. The questions asked were not intended to be difficult to answer. Dr.

John Brown was the spokesman and did admirably. He was cool, calm, reasonable—and not at all uncomfortable-looking—in view of the barrage of lights and cameras and mikes. The reporting was all either neutral or slanted a little in our favor, we felt. None of it that has come to our attention so far was really hostile.

Re: Florida Council for Racial Cooperation: This is a bi-racial group. Honorary chairmen are Rt. Rev. Henry L. Loutit, Episcopal Bishop of South Florida; Dr. R. W. Puryear, President of Florida N.&I.M. College; Dr. Richard V. Moore, president of Bethune-Cookman; and Dr. W. B. Stewart, president of Edward Waters College. *The Southern Patriot,* publication of the Southern Conference Educational Fund, Inc., had a short story on this group on page 4 of its March 1959 issue (Vol. 17, No. 3). In the event that you aren't familiar with this, let me mention that it has an eight-point program which includes voting and economic rights of Negroes, recreation, education and cultural facilities, and "the elimination of all segregation and second-class citizenship in our way of life." It has two specific projects now, I think mostly in St. Petersburg, which is home base. One is to obtain integration of ambulance services and the other to mobilize public opinion for correction of sub-standard housing conditions in Negro communities. The Rev. Ben F. Wyland, former executive secretary of the United Churches of St. Petersburg, is president and executive secretary. Address: 3028 Ninth Avenue North, St. Petersburg, Fla.

Gordon Carey's and Jim McCain's reports on their Miami work may have indicated the general concern several of us have felt over the lack of some structured medium in the State, as well as in Dade County, through which action could be taken. The session of the Florida legislature now going on has pointed out this need even more glaringly. On several issues where state-wide pressure should have been exerted on legislators, the lack of community structure throughout the State defeated liberal forces, which are weak to begin with.

Barbara Gordon (who was in Europe when Gordon Carey and Jim McCain were here) and Thalia Stern and I were the three who originally wrote to CORE, Thalia Stern doing the actual writing. Thalia and Barbara Gordon are sisters. We had also some time ago gotten in touch with Jim Dombrowski, of the Southern Conference, to see if some effort was being made in this State—or could be. The organization mentioned above is apparently getting moving—and I am enclosing a letter from Jim that I received today, plus a carbon of the letter he addressed to Barbara Gordon. Please return the carbon of his letter to Barbara Gordon to me after you have read it, as he requests it back and I want to answer him.

As you can gather from his letter, I had told him about the visit of Gordon Carey and Jim McCain and that I was sure that your office had a good report in

its files which would save a lot of energy for us here—in that we wouldn't have to go through the whole thing again. Would it be possible for you to send him a copy of Gordon's report? I would like one myself. If there is [an] office hold-up because of extra typing loads, I'll be glad to make copies if you mail me the material. Barbara Gordon is going to be in New York this weekend and thought she would try to call—in the hope that someone is there.
Sincerely,
Shirley M. Zoloth
PS: We still want—more than ever—the results of anything you may have pursued on Grant's and McCrory's.

* * *

Shirley Zoloth, Unsigned Editorial, *Miami Times,* May 2, 1959

CORE

These four letters—CORE—signify the name of a recently formed integrated organization known as the Congress of Racial Equality.

On Tuesday 25 of its members visited the well known W. T. Grant Store on West Flagler Street. They sat at the counter awaiting service for more than 20 minutes. No waitress appeared, so the group left.

They tried another nationally known store, McCrory's, and sat for luncheon. The waitresses remained on their jobs, but paid no attention to these customers. After sitting for 20 minutes they left, but were not at all discouraged.

Dr. John Brown, who was spokesman for the group, said they will make other visits.

This was just a peaceful attempt to get service at places where Negroes spend thousands of dollars. The police had been notified of their coming and were on hand to see what would happen.

Negroes now are served at McCrory's and Woolworth's lunch counters, but they must stand, not sit. Some day they will be sitting to enjoy their luncheon the same as White customers.

There's an old saying about the power of the dollar, and there is really some truth in it.

* * *

Miami CORE Minutes, May 5, 1959

Dr. John Brown presided. At his suggestion, all present gave their reactions and comments they had heard as a result of the protest demonstration held by the group on Wednesday, April 29, at Grant's and McCrory's 5 and 10 stores. No one had received comments from anyone showing lack of sympathy for our goals. Many reported words of praise that had come from different sources.

Dr. Brown mentioned that Bill Bayer, the local TV commentator, had canvassed about 100 people in the area while we were sitting at the counters. He said only two of these were not in sympathy. Most whites did not even know that Negroes could not be served at the sit-down counters. Everyone felt that the TV news reports and the radio reports had been favorable.

There was discussion on what our next moves should be. Several people at the meeting had been spoken to by people from different organizations in the community, specifically the American Civil Liberties Union and the American Jewish Congress. Strong requests that we hold off on any further actions that would bring publicity were made. The primary reason for the request was that it was extremely unwise to do anything that would provoke the Legislature into passing some of the anti-Negro and anti-liberal bills now in Committees and perhaps they might even pass an act that would make demonstrations like we had just had illegal. Since it was a matter of holding off on a publicity-getting operation for the 30 day period it was felt that if we could pursue other activities without jeopardizing our goals we ought to try to do so.

A motion was made, seconded, and passed unanimously that we delay our next major sit-in until the week after the Legislature has adjourned. The entire group present felt strongly that we should continue with some activities, however, and that it was important that we keep on rather than just sit back and wait.

Dr. Brown reported that he had called the managers of Grant's and McCrory's the morning after the demonstration. The manager of McCrory's said he did not want to negotiate or meet with us, that his opinion was unchanged, and that he had nothing more to tell us. Mr. Wark, manager of Grant's, would not come to the phone. Dr. Brown heard his voice ask "Who is it?" and when told that it was Dr. Brown, Mr. Wark said "Tell him I'm not in." It was agreed that we send a letter to each of these two managers formally requesting a meeting with them.

It was also decided that more testing should be done, in Grant's and McCrory's again, and also in Woolworth's and Kress's. Six teams, two in each team, were set up: Rose Sipser, Alice Barr; Lillian Kaplan, Mrs. Tomlin; Mr.

Moore, Mr. Zoloth; Mr. Stander, Mr. Tomlin; Miss Simpson, Mrs. Barkley; Mr. Howard, Mr. Williams.

Submitted by Shirley Zoloth

* * *

Miami CORE Minutes, May 12, 1959

Present: Dr. Brown, Harry Wheatley, Mr. and Mrs. Tomlin, Alice Barr, Mildred Simpson, Lillian Kaplan, Mrs. Reynolds, Ishmael Howard, Milt and Shirley Zoloth

Correspondence between our national office and Grant's and McCrory's national offices, plus our local group and the local Grant's and McCrory's stores, was read.

Dr. Brown, who was presiding, asked the various people who had done testing to make their reports.

Alice Barr reported. She was to have met Rose Sipser. They crossed signals somewhere and Alice Barr went on alone. She went to Grant's first, sat down at the counter and was ignored for about 15 minutes. A colored girl came over and told her that they didn't serve colored there at that counter. She left. She went to McCrory's next. There she was ignored altogether, and finally left. Next, Miss Barr went to Woolworth's, where she was informed by the white waitress that "We don't serve colored." At Kress's she felt a lot of tension. Waitresses finally asked her if she wanted something. She ordered a coke. Waitress asked if it was to take out. Miss Barr said that it was not. The waitress said "Sorry."

Lillian Kaplan submitted a report on her experiences in testing with Mrs. Tomlin. (See report attached).

Ishmael Howard reported that he went to Grant's and sat for 15 minutes without being served. He heard a lady customer saying "It's a shame they don't serve that man."

Mr. Tomlin reported on the testing he had done with Mr. Stander. They went to Woolworth's and sat about 20 minutes. No one paid any attention to them and they left. They went to Walgreen's. Mr. Stander ordered a slice of pie. He was not served. They waited about five minutes after that, then left.

Dr. Brown felt that the reports indicated that the managements of the 5 and 10 stores were not trying to do anything to stop our small visitations.

Mrs. Zoloth read the list of questions that have been submitted for legal opinion—covering the sanitation code, public accommodations laws, rights to picket, hand out leaflets, stage demonstrations. In the meantime, while we are waiting for the answers on these legal matters, and possible answers from Grant's and McCrory's to the letters sent to them, it was felt that we should tentatively set our sights on Saturday, June 13, for a large-scale sit-in, from 10 to 2 or 3, and try to round up participants in this. It was emphasized that this date was not for public information yet.

Testing was to be continued. The point was also made that in testing and in demonstrations it is important that participants dress and behave conventionally.

Submitted by Shirley Zoloth

* * *

Miami CORE, Report of Testing, May 9, 1959

Team: Mrs. M. Tomlin, Miss L. Kaplan
Places Tested: Grant's, McCrory's, Woolworth's, Kress's

Grant's

11:13 A.M.: Mrs. Tomlin and I took seats at the middle of the lunch counter which was approximately half filled. I was seated to the right of Mrs. Tomlin.
11:15: To the left of Mrs. Tomlin, the waitress placed a sign which stated "This section closed."
11:23: A white woman took a seat at the counter, three seats away from us, in the "closed" section. Her order was taken.
11:25: Mrs. Tomlin and I left. We were completely ignored by the people working behind the counter. As far as we could tell, none of the customers paid any attention to us.

McCrory's (Flagler Street side)

11:27 A.M.: I took a seat at the counter and ordered two cups of coffee, explaining the second cup was for a friend who was making a purchase and would be there in a moment. I asked that both coffees be served now and they were. According to our prearranged plan, Mrs. Tomlin was making a small purchase at a nearby counter; after the coffee was brought, she approached the lunch counter.
11:30: Mrs. Tomlin sat down and drank her coffee.
11:35: We left. The waitresses seemed a bit surprised when Mrs. Tomlin sat down, but nothing was said to us. No reactions from customers were noticed other than an occasional glance in our direction.

Woolworth's

11:38 A.M.: Again I sat down at the counter while Mrs. Tomlin went to make a small purchase at a nearby counter. While the waitress wrote my order for two coffees, a man in a dark blue suit who had in his hand some papers he apparently had been working with, paced back and forth in back of me. Both he and the waitress moved to the end of the counter and spoke briefly. After leaving him, the waitress walked past me to a woman behind the counter who seemed to have a supervisory position there. I could not hear what the waitress said to this woman, but I did hear the woman say, "If that's what he said, then do it."
11:45: I asked the waitress about my order. She was rather annoyed and said, "Just a minute, I'm busy."
11:50: I signaled Mrs. Tomlin to come to the counter. A moment or two after she was seated, an elderly white woman took the seat next to hers. In no way did this woman give any indication that she thought it at all unusual for Mrs. Tomlin to be sitting at the lunch counter. She was ignored as completely as we were. After waiting a while, she turned to us and said, "You could fall asleep here." Once, as the waitress darted by, the woman called out to her, "How's to get a cup of coffee?" She waited a bit longer, commented to us that they were giving better service at another part of the counter and she thought she'd go there.
12:00: The woman moved to another part of the lunch counter. Mrs. Tomlin and I left. The lunch counter was three-fourths or more filled. None of the customers seemed to pay any attention to us. As for the man in the dark blue suit, my first thought about his being there was that it was a coincidence, that he had seen me speaking with Mrs. Tomlin as I pointed out the purchase for her to make (an item I happened to need), and, because of our recent publicity, he had become suspicious. However, after our next experience, I now believe someone in McCrory's dashed to a phone and notified the other 5 and 10's that we were on our way.

Kress's

12:05 P.M.: I took a seat at the lunch counter on the first floor and gave the usual order for myself and friend who would be there in a moment. The waitress asked if I wanted cream. Since I knew Mrs. Tomlin had taken her coffee black in McCrory's, I said I'd have cream and my friend would have hers without cream. Our method of operation had preceded us. The waitress, who remained pleasant throughout, first mentioned something about being sorry, but I'd have to wait as she had to go to the other end of the counter for the coffee. She then said something that sounded like, "Oh, you wanted cream." A cup of coffee with cream in it was served to me. After this she poured the coffee from the almost full Pyrex coffee pot into a metal pot and began making fresh coffee in the Pyrex pot. A waitress who served at the tables asked for a cup of black coffee for someone at her table. She was given coffee from the metal pot. I asked that the other cup of coffee I had ordered be served so that it might cool off a bit and was told, "I'll have to get the other coffee."

12:15: I moved the coffee that had been served to me over to the place I was saving for Mrs. Tomlin and signaled her to come over. She sat down beside me, but, before she had a chance to touch the cup, a woman working behind the counter (again, someone who seemed to have a supervisory position there) snatched the cup away and moved it back toward me. She said, "We don't serve colored here. You can be served if you go to the window outside." She was most annoyed.

12:16: We left. Again, no reaction from customers was observed. The counter was almost completely filled. In all cases, whether food was served or not, a tip was left for the waitress.

Submitted by Lillian Kaplan

* * *

Miami CORE Minutes, June 2, 1959

Mr. Zoloth presided since Dr. Brown had phoned saying he would be late. The minutes of the previous meeting were read and approved.

A report was given by Mr. Zoloth and Mr. Moore and Dr. Brown on the meeting the three of them had with Mr. Patton, attorney for McCrory's. The three were in agreement that although the meeting was friendly enough on the surface, no commitments had been made. Dr. Brown saw it as a hopeful sign that the attorney had not mentioned any legal plans or legal action—but instead tried to shift responsibility to the national office, indicating that policy is made there. Dr. Brown and the rest of our committee felt that this was unrealistic. Dr. Brown also mentioned that Mr. Patton had tried to make the point that public opinion supported segregation, reminding the committee that it has existed for 80 years. The committee called Mr. Patton's attention to the poll conducted at the time of the demonstration by the TV commentator, Bill Bayer–where out of 100 people questioned only two objected to CORE's attempt to get the lunch counters open to Negroes; they also pointed out that other people not connected with CORE continued to sit down at the counter, unaware or unconcerned that an interracial group was waiting for service; also, many people who had been sitting when we came in and took seats continued to sit. Mr. Zoloth felt that perhaps letters should be sent again to the national offices of McCrory's and maybe the other chains, too. This was agreed to by the group.

Plans were discussed for the sit-in to begin June 13. It was emphasized that the date be kept as quiet as possible, but that we should all begin getting commitments from people who would participate. It was agreed that we should try to get enough people to hold the lunch counters at both Grant's and McCrory's, if possible, for Saturday, June 13 from about 10 or 10:30 A.M. to 2:30 or 3 P.M., repeating on the following Monday, Tuesday, and Wednesday. We are to meet again next Tuesday, June 9, and everyone should have a list of the names of people and the days and times they would participate. We are each to be responsible for briefing those we invite to participate to make sure they understand the principles of CORE and to make sure that they will respect the importance of keeping the date of the sit-in from being public knowledge. Another meeting will be held Friday night, June 12, which should be attended by all who will participate in the sit-in. Mrs. Sipser suggested trying to get a research firm or agency or group from the University to do a survey during the sit-in. This idea was to be explored.

Miss Alice Barr gave a Treasurer's report. A total of $36.35 has been received in weekly contributions by those attending our meetings. Disbursements have been $7.50, leaving a balance of $28.85. $2.50 was to be sent to the national office for literature.

A report was given on the search for living arrangements for the Workshop. Lillian Kaplan reported that she had checked with the Chamber of Commerce, who could not supply any hotel where a small interracial group could meet. Large [interracial] conventions are tolerated. She also checked various hotels in downtown Miami, the Alcazar, the Commodore, the Tamiami. No success.

Alice Barr checked the Carver and was quoted a rate of $3.00 per day—or $40 a week for two in a room. The Sir John gave the following rates:

Non air-conditioned: $3 per day per person. There will be two two-bedroom suites and three one-bedroom suites available. Mrs. Keel at the Sir John Motel told Miss Barr that the third floor rooms get a nice breeze and air-conditioning is not necessary. These rooms have little kitchens in them which can help make meals less expensive if it seems indicated. The food in the restaurant here reportedly is not too good and the prices relatively high. They figure on six people in the 2–bedroom suite and four people in the 1–bedroom suite. There are also studio apts. that accommodate three people.

Air-conditioned: the same kind of facilities but three people to a room and $3.50 per person per day.

The proposed Constitution was read to the group—this making the second

complete reading. The corrections made were acceptable. It was agreed that we would have one more reading before voting on its acceptance.
Submitted by Shirley M. Zoloth

* * *

Miami CORE Minutes, June 9, 1959

Mr. Zoloth acted as chairman in the absence of Dr. Brown. Minutes from the previous meeting were read and approved. Correspondence was read.

Plans were made for the sit-in to take place at Grant's on Saturday, June 13. Dr. Brown had said that he had ten people committed to participate, with a possible additional six. Alice Barr stated that she had four people for Saturday. Mrs. Barkley said she would be present Saturday and Monday, too. Mildred Simpson said that she would be there Saturday. Mrs. Ray has several women who will come. Lillian Kaplan said she would be there Saturday. Thalia Stern, Ishmael Howard, Mr. Stander, Dr. Chas. Williams, all said that they would be there. Mary Brick expected to have three participants.

It was agreed that a meeting would be held Friday night and that every effort would be made to get all participants to attend. If it was impossible for someone to attend, the person who had invited him or her would be responsible for giving the necessary background and instructions.

The Constitution was read for the third time. It was voted on and accepted as corrected. Mrs. Kaplan is to send it to the New York office for their approval.

Mrs. Zoloth was asked to order copies of the CORE *Rules for Action*.

Mr. Howell reported that he had gone to Grant's and McCrory's counters but had been refused service.

A suggestion was made by Mrs. Ray that we should in the very near future arrange a social get-together. This idea was warmly received and it was agreed that we do so as soon as possible. Meeting adjourned 10 P.M.
Submitted by Shirley M. Zoloth

* * *

Miami CORE Sit-in Report, June 13, 1959

The group assembled, as had been planned, at a parking-lot on N.W. 1st, just north of Miami Avenue. We had been scheduled to meet at 10:45 A.M. and arrive at the W.T. Grant's lunch counter at 11.

A few minutes before 11, two CORE members went in to the store to see if it had been alerted. It was immediately obvious that they expected us. There were fake packages being put in paper bags and distributed on the stools at the lunch counter, with quite a few employees sitting and standing in the vicinity. There were some customers being served and eating, but as the two walked along the counter, no vacant seats were open. A waitress called to the two, both white women, telling them that they could take off the packages and sit down if they wanted to eat something. They said they'd be back shortly and went back to report to the group. It later developed that the give-away had been when the UP [United Press] man had arrived at the store at 10 A.M. looking for action. He later told this to Dr. Brown and apologized for any extra difficulties this had caused us.

The entire group did not fully assemble until 11:20 and we then proceeded to Grant's. By the time we walked in the store there was no seat available at the lunch counter. However, since some of the stools were occupied by regular customers, by standing behind them we were able to capture seats as they left. Grant's employees were sitting in many of the seats and had a good number of the stools protected with packages. [The] CORE members and friends were passive about the packages, asking politely if the seat was taken. The answer was always affirmative. What did happen was that when regular customers came in, the packages would be quickly removed from the seats they wanted to sit on. In the confusion many of them were not waited on, and if they left we usually managed to get their seats. Within an hour or so we had more or less gotten possession of the entire lunch counter. The seating capacity is about 50 or 55, but by spreading out we kept fairly good possession, without any disorder or confusion or controversy. The action of the store in getting employees and packages to occupy stools worked to our advantage, since the cash register was not ringing up sales, and we were accomplishing our purpose.

We started out as a group of about 25 or 30, about evenly divided in color. More Negroes kept coming in, so that by afternoon we ended up with a group close to 40 or 50. If any of our white members were offered service by a waitress, their reply was that they would wait until after the waitress had taken the orders of the Negroes in the group.

The management and waitresses were hostile in attitude even though no overt threats were made. The manager himself did not make an appearance, but a man who seemed to be somewhat in charge of the "defense" was very much in evidence throughout the day. We kept our places at the counter until a little after 3 P.M. at which time the person in charge for the management roped off the front entrance and several of the front aisle entrances to the counter. There still were several aisles left open to the counter at the end away from the front entrance to the store. The row of lights over the lunch counter were turned on and off several times, and then left off for a short period. Then the man in charge came to the front end of the counter, where three of our participants were sitting, and asked them to move so he could sweep. They relinquished their seats and he swept around the area. When they started to move back to their seats he started sweeping there again. Then he moved several large post-card racks into the aisle blocking the way back to the front seats. Gradually he swept the floor and moved toward the group, pushing the racks toward the group and thus pushing the group back toward the rear of the counter. He did not physically push any person. He did, however, repeatedly threaten that we move out of the way because the broomstick might just hit us. The entire group eventually was moved in this way out of the lunch counter aisle. The lunch counter was empty. We stayed there for about another hour, leaving at about 4:15 or 4:30. A group went back about twenty minutes later and saw that the counter had remained closed. We were rather certain they would not reopen because the waitresses had cleared off the mustard, ketchup, etc. and had left.

Most of the customers that came in expressed surprise that Negroes were not served at the lunch counter and thought that they certainly ought to be. There were two or three men and a few women of the "hate" variety who made the most of the situation by making the usual anti-Semitic, anti-Negro remarks and insinuations. At no time did any of our participants answer any of these or engage in any discussion. It was orderly and peaceful. We dispersed, to meet again on Monday, June 15, at 11 A.M. Saturday's TV news and radio coverage was friendly. Sunday's newspapers gave a small but friendly space to the demonstration. The *Miami News* article was a little more comprehensive than the *Herald*. However, on Monday, June 15, the *Herald* gave a good background story on CORE, under Phil Meyer's by-line. This was the reporter who had interviewed Dr. Brown and Mrs. Zoloth a few weeks ago to have a story ready to run with our next action.
Submitted by Shirley M. Zoloth

* * *

Miami CORE Sit-in Report, June 15, 1959

At about 11:15 A.M. we went into W. T. Grant's 5 & 10 store, a group of about 35 or 40, mostly Negro. No attempt was made to keep us from taking seats at the lunch counter and we promptly occupied all unused stools, and our people began taking other seats as customers finished eating and left. There were about ten stools open in scattered places after we were all seated. It was interesting to note that regular customers continued to come in off the street and take these seats, completely unconcerned that the people sitting there were not all white. In fact, most were Negro.

Mr. J. D. Wark, the manager of Grant's, was standing near the lunch counter. He and Dr. Brown spoke together there and then went up to Mr. Wark's office. Dr. Brown later came down and invited Mrs. Zoloth to join them. Mr. Wark's position was that no matter how long we kept sitting there or how often we came back, he was not going to serve Negroes at the lunch counter until the other stores did the same. He felt that we were remiss in not taking it up with the Retail Merchant's Association of the Chamber of Commerce. Dr. Brown agreed that we should do this. Mr. Wark telephoned the Chamber of Commerce people and found out that it was a Mr. Craig we should speak to on this matter. Mr. Wark tried to call Mr. Craig right then, but Mr. Craig was not in his office and not expected back until 1:30.

Dr. Brown and Mrs. Zoloth agreed that to show our good faith in this we would agree to suspend the sit-in for the time being—on the assumption that we would get a hearing within a reasonable time by the Chamber people. Mr. Wark was obviously pleased with this offer and immediately promised that he would see to it that we would get such a hearing, assuring us, of course, that we should understand that he cannot *tell* the Chamber what to do about it. But he would take it upon himself to see that we were given the courtesy of a hearing. The sit-in was then temporarily ended at about 12:35.

About 2:30 Dr. Brown called Mr. Craig and an appointment was made for a meeting for the following day, Tuesday, June 16, at 2 P.M. at Mr. Craig's office at 345 NE 2nd Avenue. Dr. Brown informed Mr. Craig that a committee of three would be present from CORE.

Channel 10 (TV) had a story with film on its 6:30 P.M. show. It showed the group emerging from Grant's and quoted Dr. Brown as having said that at the suggestion of the manager of Grant's, an appointment was being scheduled with the Chamber of Commerce to discuss this matter and that the demonstration had been suspended because we felt that lines of communication had been opened.

Submitted by Shirley M. Zoloth

* * *

Miami CORE Minutes, June 16, 1959

Mrs. Shirley Zoloth chaired the meeting; and for those new people present, the principles of CORE were reiterated and questions invited. Lillian Kaplan defined the rules of membership from our constitution. Dr. Brown felt that a brief orientation on CORE be given at the opening of each meeting. It was also suggested that those signing the attendance sheet indicate M (for member) or F (for friend) next to their names.

Mrs. Zoloth read the reports on the Grant sit-in of Saturday, June 13 and Monday, June 15, copies attached to minutes.

Dr. Brown, Mr. & Mrs. Zoloth and Mr. Jack Gordon met with Mr. Craig at the Chamber of Commerce on Tuesday, June 16. Mr. Craig indicated that this was bigger than he and that he would arrange for a meeting in the near future with the Executive Committee of the Chamber of Commerce. No definite date was set but Dr. Brown indicated that our people would be back if he, Mr. Craig, did not hasten with getting the meeting set. Dr. Brown thanked Mr. Gordon for attending the meeting with Mr. Craig.

After some discussion on the sit-in observer reports, it was noted that we had to begin compiling data on availability of people to sit or observe, car pools, etc., and above all, making sure that all involved know of our policy of non-violence. More observers are needed so that we really know what is going on throughout the store or stores.

It was agreed that efforts be made to contact organizations and church groups, asking them to write letters to the Chamber of Commerce, expressing their views, etc. A Committee consisting of Mrs. Simpson and Mrs. Zoloth will work on this project.

A report was made by a group who tested at Burdine's and Jordan Marsh's on Monday, June 15th, after leaving Grant's. They were refused service on the basis of having no reservations. In view of this, it was suggested that groups of four instead of six be used for testing—four being considered a normal group of diners, whereas six have to wait on separate lines for larger accommodations, etc.

A group of testers was set up for Wednesday and Thursday. List attached. It was decided that where possible, they would speak to management; and also that only luncheon counters would be tested. Attached also is list of persons present who would participate in testing.

Mrs. Alice Barr was nominated as Membership Chairman. Nomination was accepted and approved.

It was suggested that high school students be sought to help put "CORE Needs You" posters in windows.

Dr. Brown announced that the next meeting would be held at the Sir John Hotel at 6th St. & 3rd Ave. The meeting was adjourned.

Submitted by Rose Sipser

* * *

Miami CORE Sit-in Report, June 17, 1959

Team: Shirley Zoloth, Peg Biderman, Phyllis Resnick, Earnestine Phillips. Hattie Burnett joined us in testing Richards only.

Burdine's Lunch Counter

Four of us sat down at the counter. Two seats had become available and these were taken by Shirley Zoloth and Earnestine Phillips. Shortly after that the other two in the group were able to sit down next to them. We sat there without service for almost 15 minutes. The dirty dishes had been cleared from the counter in front of Shirley Z. and Earnestine P., but not the other two. Waitresses ignored questions asked by Shirley Z., which were: "Do you serve this counter?" And a few minutes later, "Are you planning to wait on us?" A man finally made an appearance behind the counter and said with an air of finality: "I am sorry. We cannot serve you." Shirley Z. said "May I ask why?" He answered "I am not in a position to discuss it." In answer to the question "Can you tell who would be?" he said "There's no need to discuss it." Shirley Z. asked "Are you the manager?" He did not answer, but walked away. The group left the counter and the restaurant.

It should be noted that a woman who moved over one seat at her own initiative so that the fourth member of our group could sit down, asked her (Phyllis Resnick) if she was from Puerto Rico. Also, when we walked by the cashier on the way out, we told the cashier that we had not been served. She twice said "I'm sorry."

Jackson-Byron's

The group walked into the store and was able immediately to get four seats together. There was about a five minute wait, during which there was a show of confusion by the countermen, who obviously did not know what to do. We asked one waiter if he would take our order and he pointed to another and said "He'll do it." However, it was the first one that finally came over. We had arranged for the Negro member of our group to order first. He took the orders of the group (two ordered pie, one coffee, and one a large coke) and immediately proceeded to serve us what we had ordered. After we had begun eating, he then said to one of the white members "This is very embarrassing. I have to ask. She's a Puerto Rican, isn't she?" (indicating Earnestine). We answered "No, she isn't." He asked Earnestine "What are you?" She replied "I am a Negro." He then said "I am terribly sorry. This is very embarrassing, but I am not supposed to serve Negroes." We asked if we could speak to the manager. He pointed to a man at the end of the counter who had been watching us and who apparently had made a telephone call to someone while were sitting there before we were served. The counterman who had waited on us then called the man over. He came over looking at us in an innocent manner and said "Yes?" Shirley Z. said "We've been told we cannot be served here. Can you tell me why?" "It's the policy of the store." "Is this official policy?" "It's a policy of all the stores in Miami." "An official policy?" "It's not a law, it's a policy."

We left the counter and walked to the front of the store. Shirley Z. and Earnestine P. then walked back to where this man was standing. There was a big hub-bub. They obviously thought we had left the store—and four or five men were standing at the end of the counter, all very agitated, talking about what had just occurred. We asked the man we had just been speaking to if he was the manager. He indicated a second man saying "He is." We turned to the second man, who pointed to a third man. A fourth man finally in a very firm voice spoke to the others saying "None of you here makes policy. No one. Mr. Sussman is the only one." Mr. Sussman, we were told, was the store manager. This we knew anyway, because Earnestine P. had at one time worked as a stock clerk in the store and knew the people on the staff. We asked where we could find Mr. Sussman. We were told to use the phone and call him. We asked several times which phone. The assistant manager, a Mrs. Sumner, whom Earnestine knew, was standing nearby. She spoke in a friendly way to Earnestine, but she was ill at ease when Shirley Z. asked her which phone to use to call Mr. Sussman. "You won't be able to get him," she said. We told her we wanted to try anyway. She showed us where to go.

The men in the meantime were standing off watching us. We walked over to the switchboard operator and asked her if we could see Mr. Sussman. She told us she was trying to locate him as his wife was on the phone, and she paged him over the speaker. It took a few minutes, and then Earnestine saw Mr. Sussman over on the other side of the store. We started to walk over there but the switchboard operator asked us to wait. She spoke to him and then told us that he was in an important meeting with the store department heads and would be busy for a long while. We left a *This Is* CORE pamphlet and Shirley Zoloth's name and phone number, asking that Mr. Sussman get in touch with us. It should be noted that Earnestine Phillips saw several people on the floor as we walked through the store after this conversation, such as the assistant manager, Mr. Labell, and several other floor men who all would normally have been in on one of those staff meetings. She said it was the custom there to pull them all off the floor at the same time when such a meeting was held.

Richards Lunch Counter

Group of five was able to get seats together immediately at the counter. We were ignored. Shirley Z. asked "May we have menus, please?" The waitress handed her one menu. She did not come to take our order. A man appeared behind the counter and said "I'm sorry, our accommodations are too limited to serve you." "Can you tell us why, please?" "That's all," he said, walking quickly away. He walked around the counter. Shirley Z. by getting up from her seat was able to get to him as he came past where she had been sitting, but he did not stop as she asked him "Are you the manager?" "No, I'm not," he said, walking on. "Who is?" she asked, walking out the door of the lunchroom with him. "Mr. Thouvenelle," he said, not too civilly. "There's no point in your seeing him. He'll tell you the same thing. He told me to tell you this." "Will you tell me where I can find him?" "It won't help you." "Will you tell me his name?" "Mr. Thouvenelle, 5th floor, but it won't do you any good." (Said rather uncivilly, and the name badly slurred.) "Can you spell that name?" "No, I can't." We expressed surprise. We took the elevator up to the 5th floor and found the office. We told the receptionist we would like to see Mr. Thouvenelle (B. E. Thouvenelle, we later found out) and she used the phone on her desk, immediately after which two gentlemen came walking out. We were ushered into the manager's office and seated graciously—and then spent about half an hour talking with Mr. Thouvenelle and the other gentleman, whom he introduced as Mr. Pulaski.

We introduced ourselves, told them we were a committee from CORE, and described what had just occurred in the lunchroom at the counter. We told him what the objectives of CORE are and that we preferred always to try to negotiate with the manager and see if some gradual way of ending discrimination could be introduced.

Mr. Thouvenelle referred to the "spectacle" we had created at Grant's and indicated that he thought what we had "done" downstairs was also a "spectacle." He mentioned many times during the conversation how much Richards had done for its Negro customers. He said that Negroes could use 99 percent of the facilities of the store. He seemed to think it was quite generous of Richards and said that Negroes could go into all departments and buy whatever they wanted. He mentioned that Richards had spent $20,000 not too long ago to fix up beautiful toilet facilities in the basement for Negroes. He mentioned that Richards did not have separate drinking fountains, but that single unit fountains were in the store.

In answer to questions put to him, he said that he had had many complaints, even though he admitted they might be from a small minority of his customers. When pinned down to when he had complaints, he was vague, for he had previously said that Negroes had never been served either in the tearoom or at the lunch counter. The complaints, he said, had been once when a

Negro had bought a pack of cigarettes from a vending machine in the tearoom, and also sometimes a Negro might come in and try to be served, as we had done. He mentioned that the whole matter of lunch facilities was a losing proposition to Richards. A primary reason for maintaining it is that they had closed up their employee cafeteria and the employees now used the other eating facilities. We asked if he had Negro employees. This question embarrassed him, but then he said that they had a few. We asked if they were permitted to eat at the lunch counter. "Oh, no," he said. But then quickly he told us of the lovely quarters they had for employees who brought their lunch; and Negroes even had their own room so they could relax, play cards, etc. The attitude of Mr. Thouvenelle and Mr. Pulaski was that Richards does more for Negroes than any of the other stores downtown. Mr. Pulaski wanted to know if we had spoken to Burdine's manager yet. We told him that we had not as yet seen him. He wanted to know if we had tried to eat there, for he said Burdine's resists serving Negroes in the store. They both said that Richards has more liberal try-on privileges and return privileges than others.

We assured them that we knew that discrimination against Negroes occurred in all of the downtown Miami stores, but that our project now was in terms of finding places where Negroes could sit down at lunch counters and be served on an unsegregated basis. Mr. Pulaski indicated he suspected we wanted more than just opening up of lunch counters for Negroes. We agreed that we wanted to break down racial segregation barriers wherever they existed in the community. Mr. Pulaski made the statement that there is no agreed policy on this matter between the stores. He said that there are no agreements between the stores on any matter other than on closing times.

We asked if Richards would go along with opening up its lunch counters if the others did. Mr. Thouvenelle assured us that Richards would. We asked if he would say so to the Chamber of Commerce. He said he would be glad to if he was asked. We asked if it came to a vote as to whether all stores should desegregate their lunch counters would he vote in favor of this. He said that he would. We asked if he would give us this statement in writing. He balked at this, saying that the whole lunch counter business was insignificant to Richards and they had no reason to do anything that might result in disturbance or trouble. He stated that what we were doing could be inflaming under the present circumstances. We asked him what he meant by "the present circumstances." He didn't quite know and said "at the present time," but couldn't explain that, or wouldn't. He did repeat, however, in answer to another question, that he definitely would go along with the others in opening the lunch counter.

Mr. Pulaski wanted to know if we knew a Rev. Jackson, of Mt. Zion Church, who had worked with them, he said, in giving Negroes better service in the store.

Submitted by Shirley Zoloth

* * *

Miami CORE Sit-in Report, June 22, 1959

Two teams tested lunch counters. Alice Barr, Mrs. Seymour, and Barbara Gordon went to Kress's, Royal Castle, and Walgreen's. They were not served. Shirley Zoloth, Earnestine Phillips, and Raymond Ray went to Woolworth's and Walgreen's, at Flagler and S.E. 2nd, and were not served—although in one place a cup of coffee was given to Shirley Zoloth, who passed it immediately with the waitress's knowledge to Earnestine Phillips. Another cup was ordered, but not served.

At 4 P.M. all of these people, except Mr. Ray, met with Mr. Reichenbach, who has the lunch counter concession at Byron-Jackson's. Mr. Sussman, manager of this store, had told Shirley Zoloth on the telephone that Byron-Jackson's had nothing to do with the lunch counter concession, but that either Sid Schwartz or Jack Reichenbach would be the ones to talk to about policy in this matter. He suggested calling Mr. Reichenbach immediately, which is what we did. Mr. Reichenbach quickly agreed to see us the same afternoon.

The meeting with him was no more productive than our other meetings have been. He was persistent in his belief that his business would suffer if he opened the counter to Negroes. He further stated that he had doubts if his employees would wait on Negroes. He also expressed the belief that he would be put out of business if he did this. He admitted the justice of our cause but stated that he had to protect his own interests. He was doing good business and would not risk doing anything that might jeopardize that. He was quick to agree to opening his lunch counter to Negroes when all the others did—but would not be the first—and would not commit himself in writing to say that he would do it. Generally, he was sympathetic but quite firm in his refusal to change his policy.

Submitted by Shirley Zoloth

* * *

Letter, Zoloth to Robinson, June 23, 1959

This is off the record, and you can dispose of it, if you like.

The Supreme Court decision last week (or two weeks [ago]?), which gave a sort of carte blanche to State witch-hunts to proceed, has been followed—as we here expected—with the announcement [of] the return of Florida's "Charley Johns" Committee to smoke out reds in the NAACP. Charley Johns will not be chairman this session, but a local legislator named Cliff Herrell—also a jerk, although perhaps more subtle.

Since John Brown is a V.P. of the NAACP and some of our active people (not many, but some) are also active in the NAACP, and since we know that there will be a heavy smear job attempted, we are expecting to be worked over a bit.

We never had elections in the group, but have been operating on temporary officers. We have given no officers' names to the press other than Dr. Brown as our "spokesman," which was picked up as "Chairman," which we sort of accepted by not challenging.

In our affiliation form sent to you, we put in the names of the temporary officers, figuring that in another month or so, as our membership got more stable, we would get people to take these jobs who had time and ability, etc. Our membership has a tremendous potential. Many, at least 30, are kind of probate members, but we haven't had proper time to do the mechanical work of really setting up a membership list, etc., which is probably just as well in the light of coming events. We have for this reason been devoting at least ten minutes (and sometimes more, if questions come up) on *This Is CORE* and *Rules for Action* at each meeting. Last night's meeting (you'll get minutes in a few days) had forty attending, about half white and half Negro.

We are going ahead with sit-in plans—no reply yet from [the] Chamber of Commerce—and will have another "do" of some kind this Saturday, depending on how many show to join us. Also have a meeting today with the CAIRO [County Association of Intergroup Relations Officials, Dade County affiliate of the National Association of Intergroup Relations Officials] boys who are willing to help some. We had really hoped to have elections by another few weeks. Do you think it wiser to wait? This would mean a real "listing" of members in order to establish democratic procedures properly. Shall we hold off?

We have been saying to newspaper people that we will disclose neither names of members nor their numbers. So far the questions had always been asked in a friendly spirit and the answer accepted in the same way. Under heat, this may not be so. The community does think we have a great deal more than we have, which we think is good.

Shirley Zoloth

[*Editor's Note:* The U.S. Supreme Court issued two decisions on June 8, 1959 that enhanced the authority of legislative committees to compel witness testimony: *Barenblatt v. United States*, 360 US 109 (1959), and *Uphaus v. Wyman*, 360 US 72 (1959).]

* * *

Miami CORE Minutes, June 30, 1959

Dr. Brown presided and reviewed the Grant's and McCrory's lunch counter project and the entire Flagler Street lunch counter situation.

The sit-in demonstration on Saturday, June 27, was briefly described. The group, about 25 in all, had gone to Burdine's lunch counter at about 11:30, had been permitted to sit for 10 or 15 minutes, and then a representative of the store (later determined to be the store detective) told each Negro member of the group quietly that he or she would not be served and should please leave. There was an officer present. The spokesman spoke to the store representative. He would not say whether he was the manager, he would not meet with us to talk, he would not tell us his name, he would not tell us the manager's name, he would not tell us what he would do if we did not leave. He did say that he had asked each of our colored participants to leave. The spokesman asked if this was because they were colored. He would not say. Due to a misunderstanding, some of the group had left, and it seemed wise for the rest to leave, too.

The group went to Woolworth's lunch counter next, getting seats easily. The group was permitted to stay there. At 2:15 or 2:30, the manager went along the counter, asking each of the Negroes to leave and telling them they would not be served. The group stayed about 20 minutes or half hour after that, and then left. No one was asked to leave again.

Dr. Brown reported on a follow-up conversation he had with Mr. Craig of the Better Business Division of the Chamber of Commerce, in which Mr. Craig denied that he had agreed to arrange a hearing before the Chamber of Commerce for us. He said he had agreed to call it to the attention of the Board. He said he did that, and it was as much as he felt he had to do.

Mr. Zoloth reported that he had called Mr. Patton, attorney for McCrory's, who had previously met with a CORE committee. Mr. Patton had nothing more to say. He had received no word or instructions from McCrory's.

The reports from legal counsel have still not been completed. Because of this an evaluation of our next step would be difficult, it was felt by Dr. Brown. It was felt that we are now at the organization stage where a Board or Steering Committee should be set up, which could take care of some of the details and do some of the planning between membership meetings. The group gave Dr. Brown the authority to appoint such a Board. Those suggested by Dr. Brown and the group were A. D. Moore, Alice Barr, Shirley Zoloth, Milt Zoloth, Barbara Gordon, Lillian Kaplan, Eddie Resnick, James Otis, Peg Biderman, Hirsh Howard, Thalia Stern, Marjorie Martin, B. Givens.

A question was raised on the principle of tipping: should a sit-in group tip?

This was discussed, but no ruling made. It was felt that the individual situation should be dealt with since many factors were involved.

It was felt that a committee should go back to see that manager of Grant's again, since the Chamber of Commerce meeting he had suggested had not come off.

It was agreed that we had to seriously go about getting a larger membership and build up a good reserve of friends of CORE, so that in future sit-ins we can have enough people to sustain a long-period sit-in if it seems indicated.

A proposed letter to organization representatives in the Negro community was read, in which support was asked for, both as individuals and organizations. This letter was to go out as soon as possible.

The draft of the brochure on the September 5–20 Workshop was read, telling some of the plans for the Miami project. A tentative committee was appointed by Dr. Brown to prepare for the workshop: Thalia Stern, Leonard Turkel, Marjorie Martin, Milton Zoloth.

It was agreed that there should be no membership meeting the following week, and that the next meeting would be July 14. In the meantime, Dr. Brown was to get the Board appointed and it would meet the following week.
Submitted by Shirley M. Zoloth

* * *

Letter, Zoloth to Robinson, n.d. (ca. early July 1959)

Dear Mr. Robinson:

Sorry for leaving so many of your letters unanswered. Somehow with very many details to be taken care of here, there is little time left for writing to you.

The momentum created by our sit-ins has been stepped up, and what happened here is that we seem to have gotten more members and potential members and friends than we had anticipated. Our meeting time and activities between meetings were on projects rather than mechanics of organization, so that we have to now concentrate on our structure. Miami obviously is ready for a CORE group. The support has been excellent. The local newspapers have not given us a great deal of space, but on the whole the notices have been favorable. After the first few times of nothing happening, the sit-ins are less newsworthy, really.

The Chamber of Commerce hearing did not materialize, which did not really amaze us. Mr. Craig, of the Better Business Division of the Miami Chamber of Commerce, met with us and agreed to recommend that the Chamber itself or some "higher echelon" hear our story. He subsequently denied this to a *Herald* reporter, but last week told John Brown that he had so recommended and felt that that was as much as he should or would do. We will try other ways of getting the Chamber of Commerce to listen to us, but think it not too likely that they will do so.

An interesting development is that we got some widespread publicity because of the fact that the Better Business *Bureau* does not like to have its name confused with any other agency or organization. In particular, the local Better Business *Division*, connected with the Chamber of Commerce, is in poor repute here because of some of its activities. There is a Better Business *Bureau* on Miami Beach, but not in Miami. Jack Gordon is a member of the Bureau and also, I think, a member of the national board of the B. B. *Bureau*. In any event, the B. B. Bureau circularized its members all over the country telling them about this CORE thing. The newspaper clipping they quoted was favorable to CORE, even though the letter accompanying it apparently was non-committal. I'll get a copy to send to you from Jack Gordon, who received it.

Our last Saturday's sit-in [June 27, 1959] was not too successful. We went to Burdine's luncheonette and Woolworth's lunch counter. Burdine's is the prestige department store in downtown Miami. They have a tea-room in the store itself, and across the street in a different building they have a luncheonette—all counter seats. In the last week [or] so a sign had been tacked on the wall near the entrance reserving their right to refuse service. About 25 of us (about 2/3 Negro) walked in and took stools without difficulty. We were permitted to just sit for about ten minutes. Then a man (a reporter later told us that he was the store detective) came to each Negro person separately saying something like "We cannot serve you here. Will you please leave?" While the spokesman was talking to the manager, one or two of our members thought they were supposed to leave and told others. Some had gone out, some were standing, and there was uncertainty. I was spokesman and quickly decided that we should, under the circumstances, all go out together.

In the conversation with the "manager" (the store detective), I asked him if he was the manager. He wouldn't tell me. When he said he had asked each of these colored people to leave, I asked if he had asked them to leave because they were colored. No answer. He would not agree to a meeting. He would not tell us his name, nor the name of the manager. He also said that if we did not leave he would take the "next action." He did not threaten us with arrest, but did have an officer standing with him. The policeman left the premises, however, before the CORE group. It really was an error to leave, for no doubt the man was bluffing. This is speculation, of course.

We went into Woolworth's about 12 noon and stayed until 2:30 before the manager did the same as the man at Burdine's had done. He went down the counter telling each Negro quietly that he would not be served and asking him to leave. This time the group stayed put quietly. We waited 20 minutes or so. The manager made no attempt to evict any of the group. A good many of our people had to leave, so we decided to go all at once in a group. The manager was approached several times to sit down and talk to us. His reply was that he had nothing to say to us.

We have spoken to several local attorneys. We want to get a really clear idea of the legal situation. As you may remember, the law is not good protection against discrimination. In fact, it supports it rather strongly. If we do get involved in a court case, we feel it ought to be in the best possible area, not in some peripheral aspect that might not succeed in knocking out the heart of the law. I am assuming we would win, as you can see. We have several attorneys analyzing this for us.

In the meantime, John Brown left yesterday for several weeks vacation, and I may shortly be doing the same. We have set up a tentative "Board" which will meet next week in an attempt to strengthen the mechanics of the group and implement our by-laws as far as membership and other matters are concerned.

We will also probably continue with more testing, and perhaps, if we can get people interested, work on voter registration. We are fearful of not doing anything, for we want to keep our momentum. At the same time, we are stymied temporarily on the lunch counters—waiting for legal opinions, putting more pressure on the Chamber of Commerce, waiting for results from pressure which is supposed to be put on presidents and vice-presidents of several of the department stores. We will probably try to stage another sit-in toward the end of July, hoping that we will have enough people to maintain it at least for a full day and hopefully longer.

I assume by now that you did receive at least the second TV film clip. They swear they sent one out the day they were supposed to, and I suppose we will never know if this is so. The second one was mailed out by registered mail the day after I got your June 24 letter. I hope you can get photographs out of this. The only other still you might be able to get quickly is the one that appeared in *Jet* magazine after the April 29 sit-in. This is a little paperback weekly.

Re: Workshop: I hardly know quite what to say about your brochure. It seems rather long, yet I would not dare suggest what might be eliminated! I was a little startled at the title you gave me—Co-ordinator of Greater Miami CORE. I suppose I have been serving in this capacity, but am getting concerned at how inextricably I have become involved. I am most hopeful that the setting up of a board will mean that some of the detail work and arranging can be spread wider. I think I would prefer not to be identified as the co-ordinator. I seem to have both the authority and the responsibility for this as far as our group is concerned and have permitted this while the group is in the formative stage. Thalia Stern has sort of backed away from real activity, even though her heart is still with us and she has participated in most of the sit-ins. She and I and John Brown were the three whose baby it was. John is a busy man. That left me for most of the detail work. With all the energy we had all invested in the setting up of an effective CORE group, I simply could not back away until I felt it was stronger. I think it is certainly approaching that point. I do want to continue as an active part of the CORE group. I'll be among the faithful few, and so will my husband, but I do not want it as a total way of life, excluding all other things. This it has become because of my involvement. All of which is to say, please do not list me as co-ordinator. Another reason for this is that I will probably be out of town almost until the Workshop begins, which means I can do little of the preparatory work that might be required.

Your sentence "(1)" under "Why Miami?" on the first page is rather strong in describing the CORE group here. In fact, a few of us are a little concerned at the looseness of including people in the CORE group who have simply professed interest or support. It is a problem. Certainly, we want as strong and as large a group as we can get, but we have attracted many people who have "just turned up." This is one of the reasons we feel it is important to implement the membership rules we have adopted. The experience at Burdine's luncheonette showed that we need better discipline, even though the so-called newcomers were not at fault. As far as the rest of the community is concerned, I think we can safely say that we have at least the moral support of the so-called liberal organizations.

I have a great deal more to write, but little time to sit down and organize my thoughts, so please forgive me for incoherence and/or omissions.
Sincerely,
Shirley M. Zoloth

* * *

Letter, Zoloth to Robinson, July 14, 1959

Dear Mr. Robinson:

Glad you finally received the film strip. I will report it to Jack Gordon.

We have a few people lined up to assume responsibility for things that have to be done here prior to the Workshop. I have a feeling that we ought to be starting soon with advance publicity work if we are planning a large public meeting. If we are getting Martin Luther King, this would be good to know because the local press would no doubt be willing to start using publicity releases as soon as we are ready to feed them. It would be helpful if Gordon Carey would send us his schedule, even though it may be tentative, so that we will have some kind of idea on how to plan. None of us has an inkling of what ought to be done here, such as setting up meetings, publicity, transportation, etc., depending on the scheduling. September 5 to 20 is long, and we want to know how many people will have to be involved in a big way. Not many of our local people can give all their time to this for that period. As far as projects for the Workshop, it would seem to have to rest on how many people we will have and how much time they can give. Will we know this as far as out-of-towners are concerned soon?

We are having a meeting tonight which we hope will be a good sound organization meeting—long overdue. We are gearing it toward the meeting July 21 (see letter enclosed) [an open letter to Miami community leaders] and the Workshop. The letter, incidentally, was sent out to some 75 people who are nominal heads or representatives of Negro organizations in Miami. There is a small book called the *Miami Register* that is a compilation of Negro organizations, professions, [and] businesses. Dan Lang, Executive Director of the Urban League, spent two full days with Barbara Gordon and me working on this thing. We also had a "board" meeting last week. I have the word in quotes because it was rather informally chosen by John Brown before he left. A. D. Moore, manager of Central Life, is an excellent man, and the only one present who wasn't just a little disgusted with what seems some time like unwillingness of people to take responsibility. He is awfully busy himself, but he took on a load of work and has accepted responsibility for membership in general, and getting more people in who have both the time and ability to play an active part in leadership matters.

We need more people who can be and are willing to be articulate on CORE principles and its history. With only a few exceptions, our membership is timid about being in a position where they might have to act as spokesman or public relations or contact. I fully realize that the development of this kind of leadership is a slow and painful process, but if CORE is to survive here this is going to have to be done. Each of the people in a leadership position is deeply and compellingly involved in other affairs. We are therefore trying to get in as many people as we can, not losing sight of CORE methods, so that there can be both wider distribution of work and wider selection of leaders.

By the direct mailing to the organization and community leaders in the Negro community, we are answering a question often put to us: how do people know we need them to help? We have assumed up to now that (1) the liberal community knows what CORE is and also what CORE is trying to do here, and (2) those who believe we are right will come to us uninvited. Both of these assumptions seem to be invalid, so we are setting about to remedy the situation the best way we know how. Barbara [Gordon] and I have, and will continue to, spend time in seeing people and soliciting community support and individual commitments of interest, both with Negroes and whites. We both of us are very pressed with non-CORE matters but feel too strongly about CORE to be able to lessen our own activities in it when it is still so unsound, even though externally this does not appear so.

Also, are you sending notices of this Workshop to people in Florida? Jim Dombrowski would probably be glad to put publicity about it in *The Southern Patriot,* and perhaps send out notices to the people in Florida that he knows. He has a mailing list that ought to know about the Workshop (Southern Conference Educational Fund, Inc.).

I will let you know the results of our meeting tonight. We are counting a great deal on the next few weeks in getting a more solid group.
Sincerely,
Shirley M. Zoloth

* * *

Miami CORE Minutes, July 14, 1959

Shirley Zoloth presided over the meeting due to the absence of Dr. John Brown. The minutes of the meeting on June 30 were read and approved.

It had previously been decided that Dr. Brown would be responsible for selecting a Board of Directors. The results of his selection were read: John O. Brown, Otis James, Alice Barr, A. D. Moore, Peg Biderman, Rose Sipser, Barbara Gordon, Thalia Stern, Lillian Kaplan, Shirley Zoloth, Milton Zoloth.

A letter, which was read at the last meeting, had been sent out to 75 organizations and individuals, inviting representatives from these various organizations to attend the CORE meeting of July 21, 1959 at the Sir John's at 8:30. The letter also introduced them to CORE and some of its activities.

Mrs. Zoloth then suggested following-up these letters by telephoning and/or letters. Another suggestion was made that personal contact would be better than telephone calls. A list of these names was then passed around in order that people could take as many names as they wanted to call or visit, preferably the latter. Other lists were also distributed, containing names of friends and members of CORE, to those who volunteered.

Phyllis Resnick gave a report on the legality of the sit-ins which had been compiled by her husband. A certain Florida statute says that proprietors have the right to eject people who are undesirable to them. It described those "undesirables" as those who are intoxicated, immoral, profane, detrimental or injurious to the reputation, dignity, or standing of the enterprise. [The] CORE immediately eliminates intoxication, immorality, and profanity. A manager must call a policeman to make an arrest, but who may not arrest people on the basis of color. However, if the policeman insists on arrest, it is wise to co-operate so as not to be accused of resisting arrest. A court cannot rule that people are undesirable because of color. Also, the officer has to request the party to leave or they are not subjected to arrest. Refusing the manager's request to leave is not an action subject to arrest.

Mr. Earl Edge then gave an account of a group of several Negro couples who attended a ball game in Miami Stadium on Sunday, July 12, 1959. He and his friends purchased tickets for reserved seats at $1.25 a ticket. It was a doubleheader and they sat through the first game completely undisturbed. However, at that time, someone who appeared to be an usher came over to them and asked them to move. They wanted to know why, and he merely replied that he had orders to make them move. Then some other white people came to occupy those seats, but the Negroes refused to move. A policeman came over and he asked them to move, but they again asked why and weren't told so they stayed. Next the ticket salesman told them that they had the $.75 tickets and would have vacate these seats. They again refused and it turned out that they stayed there for the rest of the game. At one point during this incident, Mr. Edge asked "Where does Valentine (a Negro player on the Miami Marlins) sit when he isn't playing, on top of the dug-out or inside of it with the other players?" At this point, it had become an embarrassing situation for the whites, so they just left.

Shirley Zoloth gave a report on the board meeting held July 10. It was decided that the immediate objective of the organization should be to build it up into a stronger one by recruiting more people. Certain committees were set up at the Board meeting:

The *Workshop* committee is to be in charge of the Workshop, which will be from Sept. 5 to 20. The members are Peg Biderman, Marjorie Martin, Hirsh Howard, and Leonard Turkel. It was mentioned that Gordon Carey, a CORE field worker, might come to Miami for the workshop.

The *Membership* committee consists of Alice Barr, A. D. Moore, and Lillian Kaplan. Block signs had been printed which said "CORE NEEDS YOU" and gave two phone numbers. These are to be posted in merchants' windows in the downtown area. The signs were printed by Leonard Turkel, and Mr. Moore was placed in charge of seeing that they get distributed. Mr. Howell and Mr. Williams both volunteered to help distribute them.

It was decided that a *Speaker's Bureau* is necessary, both to provide speakers and people to find organizations to accept the speakers.

An *Intercommunity Relations* [committee] was also set up. Mildred Simpson was put in charge of the churches, and Barbara Gordon and Shirley Zoloth were put in charge of organizations and agencies.

A *Project* committee was set up consisting of John Brown and Shirley Zoloth. This is for the purpose of arranging sit-ins, testing groups, and negotiations with managers, attorneys, etc. Mrs. Zoloth then emphasized the importance of the July 21 meeting. It will be an opportunity to bring any new prospects, and all were urged to bring as many people as possible. She spoke of the need for more people to participate in sit-ins.

Mr. Zoloth then told of the possibility of a meeting with Martin Luther King in Miami. Dr. Brown contacted him and he said that he might fly down for a meeting, possibly in September. James Robinson, said Mrs. Zoloth, is fairly sure of King's visit.

Shirley Zoloth then invited everyone to her house for a bar-b-q during the Workshop in September.

Groups were then set up for testing during the following week: Peg Biderman, Charles Kaman, Hirsch Howell, Ishmael Howard, Wednesday, July 22, 11:30, at Sir John's; Ruby Curry, Rozalind Seymour, Earl Edge, Milton Zoloth, Lillian Kaplan, Saturday, July 18, 1:30, in front of McCrory's.

* * *

Shirley M. Zoloth, Report on Greater Miami CORE, July 21, 1959

Several factors combined in the early part of January to motivate a few Miamians to send out a call for CORE field workers. It was apparent that a decision allowing "token desegregation" in a Miami school had not been preceded by any real social work in the community to be affected—nor was there any reason to believe that any of the existing agencies or organizations in the area were planning to undertake the project. When four Negro children were approved for assignment to the previously all-white Orchard Villa elementary school in a so-called transition area, CORE's work in the Nashville situation as described in *A First Step* [Anna Holden's CORE pamphlet *A First Step Toward School Integration* (1959)] was remembered—and it was this that served as the imperative for calling on CORE to come to Miami.

Jim McCain and Gordon Carey arrived on February 28, and by March 12 the Greater Miami CORE had its first official meeting with some fifteen members. Dr. John O. Brown, an ophthalmologist, became temporary Chairman of the group and has been the major spokesman. The group's decision for its first project was to work in the public accommodations field to begin with, rather than school desegregation.

Miami, despite its geographical positions, is far from a "deep South" city. Its population has increased in the last few years at a phenomenal rate—largely with Northerners who have moved here. Segregation is firmly entrenched in Miami proper in practically all areas of life, but across the Bay in Miami Beach, where tourism is the number one industry and conventions are part of the economy, public accommodations are in many places open to Negroes, especially if they are not Miamians.

There is no set pattern in public accommodations in Miami itself. Some places serve Negroes and some do not. The Latin American tourists complicate things still more by virtue of the fact that many of them are quite dark-skinned. It is generally the policy in the area to serve Spanish-speaking people of color. In fact, several of the public schools have pupils whose inability to speak English permits them to be in schools that their color would otherwise keep them from.

So it was felt by the Greater Miami CORE group that its immediate object should be the knocking down of one of the most outrageous and illogical barriers of all. There is no place in the downtown Miami shopping section where Negroes may *sit down* and have a cup of coffee or sandwich or dish of ice cream. This, despite the fact that only a few blocks away is Miami's largest Negro residential area. It was felt that all of the lunch counters, including the 5 and 10 stores and department stores, should be the first point of attack. Grant's was the first choice and McCrory's the second, mostly on the basis of an educated guess as to the proportion of Negro customers who shopped in these two stores in preference to Woolworth's and Kress's.

[The] CORE's first method of testing was scrupulously followed. The first testing team went to Grant's on March 19, was refused service, and made several attempts to see the manager both that day and during the next few days. A meeting was finally arranged with the manager who sat and spoke with the CORE committee for an hour, but was firm in his refusal to be the first to open his lunch counter. He would not listen to suggestions on a trial serving of Negroes to see reaction of other customers. He was bitter at the fact that the group was "picking on" Grant's, when all of the other lunch counters were just as guilty. He realized that he has a large Negro patronage, and assured the committee that he wanted to keep it, but felt the committee was being unreasonable in expecting Grant's, the least wealthy and influential of all the 5 and 10's, to be the first to open its counter. He felt that it was something for all the merchants to take responsibility for, not just one store. The group requested that he take it up with the Chamber of Commerce. He refused to do this, saying it was not his problem. He did agree to write his national office to see if business had been adversely affected when the Baltimore Grant's opened its counter.

He did not deny the justice of CORE's request. Incidentally, this was the consistent reaction of all the managers of lunch counters who met with us. Always the manager agreed that certainly it was wrong for Negroes not to be served at the counter, certainly it was only a matter of time until this injustice is corrected, but positively they would not be the first to open up. Generally, they said they would also not be the second or the third, but that they would not open up the lunch counter until all the lunch counters were opened, including the department store lunch counters.

McCrory's was subsequently tested. The importance of repeated tests was demonstrated here, for the first CORE team (interracial) that took seats in McCrory's was served quickly and graciously by one of the waitresses. However, on the following day, at a different part of the counter, the team was totally ignored by the waitresses. Finally, a young Negro counter-girl came over and said "Negroes aren't served at this counter." It should be mentioned that the 5 and 10 stores have separate stand-up counters where neither segregation nor discrimination is practiced. Negroes and whites make their purchases in turn and stand next to each other eating and drinking. This "vertical integration," as usual, is permissible. The sit-down counters, however, are closed to Negroes.

McCrory's manager, in his first conversation with a CORE committee, was warm and even respectful. In fact, he said "God bless you for what you are doing. It has to be done." But he was firm in refusing to open his lunch counter to Negroes. He refused also to permit any trial service. Quoting from the committee's report: "We did mention to him that the four of us had been served earlier in the week at the same counter without any repercussions. This upset him, but he indicated that the day before they had served four Puerto Ricans and did have some repercussions about it. We asked how the waitresses knew whom they were permitted to serve. He answered, 'We use our instinct.' It might be noted at this point that in a conversation several weeks later, this same manager told one of CORE's Negro members that things were really going along fine as they were before and that it was the Jews who were stirring up trouble."

The Miami CORE decided in favor of having a protest demonstration at Grant's and McCrory's on Wednesday afternoon, April 30, 1959. About 18 or 20 people participated, about half of whom were Negro. There was excellent TV and radio coverage. The UP had a representative there and the story appeared in many places throughout the nation. It was also on [Dave] Garroway's "Today Show." Each of the local TV stations, three of them, devoted a good portion of their early evening and late evening news reports to film and interviews of this small demonstration. About 25 or 30 minutes was spent in Grant's, during which most of the picture-taking and interviewing occurred. Police officers were there, onlookers gathered, but there was no hostile exchange or action. It was all quite amicable. After Grant's the group went next door into McCrory's and sat about fifteen minutes. The management at McCrory's would not permit microphones or cameras to be brought in. In Grant's the waitresses simply disappeared. A half-made sandwich sat deserted on the sandwich board. In McCrory's, the waitresses remained behind the counter, but ignored the group. The manager did not appear in either case.

The newspaper and TV and radio people were all quite friendly and tried to be helpful. The questions asked were sympathetic in nature. The reports were generally favorable. A great deal of community interest was shown immediately after this action, and the CORE group found itself with an increased number of supporters at its initial stages. Testing continued and a series of letters were written from the Miami CORE to the local managers of stores, and from the national CORE office to the national offices of the store chains.

The other stores in downtown Miami tested were Woolworth's, Kress's, and three department store lunch counters: Burdine's, Richards, Byron-Jackson's. Two of the Walgreen's drug stores were also tested, as were several Royal Castle hamburger counters. Meetings were held during this time with any of the managers who would meet with us. The managers of Richards Department Store and Jackson-Byron's each sat down with a CORE committee, with noncommittal results, but in a friendly spirit. McCrory's turned their letter over to their attorney, who wrote Dr. Brown asking for a conference. A meeting took place, friendly but with no commitment.

During this period one of the local reporters from the *Miami Herald*, Phil Meyer, had done a long interview with Dr. Brown and Mrs. Shirley Zoloth in preparation for the next action, so that the paper would have a background story. This was well used on June 15, for on June 13 the group had a sit-in at Grant's.

The meeting with Mr. Craig of the Better Business Division of the Chamber of Commerce was held on June 16, and covered by the *Miami Times* and TV Channel 10. Mr. Craig, after about an hour's discussion, reluctantly agreed that perhaps the complaint of discrimination and misrepresentation did fall under the Better Business Division's responsibilities. The meeting ended with his statement that he would call it to the attention of the "higher echelon" of the Chamber of Commerce and ask that the CORE committee be given a hearing.

On Saturday, June 27, a sit-in demonstration was held at Burdine's lunch counter and Woolworth's. At Burdine's, a representative of the store, after about a fifteen minute wait, told each Negro member of the group that he or she would not be served and should please leave. There was no attempt at eviction. At Woolworth's, the group was permitted to sit for over two hours before the management did the same thing. The group stayed about half an hour after that and then left of its own accord.

Since that time the Greater Miami CORE group has been concentrating on strengthening its committees and membership, getting more community support, and trying to build up a reservoir of strength for future sit-ins, which may have to be sustained for long periods of time. There have been follow-up conversations with Mr. Craig, with McCrory's attorneys, and repeated testing and attempts to remind managers that CORE would like to work the whole thing out amicably. The legal situation has also been explored. Some of the committees now beginning to function are Membership, Telephone, Speakers, Intercommunity Relations, [and] Projects.

In addition, the group is pulling more strength toward the September 5–20 Workshop being planned by National CORE. There is great hope that, in addition to helping publicize CORE's object in Miami and CORE's methods, the actual opening of the lunch counters may be closer to accomplishment with the added impetus.

Various items point to the timeliness of the opening of these lunch counters. For one thing, during the sit-in on April 29, a local TV commentator conducted his own survey of opinions of passers-by. He questioned one hundred white people, 98 of whom had absolutely no objection to Negroes being served at the lunch counters. In fact, most of them were astonished to learn that this was not already the custom.

Another even more pointed indication of the readiness of the community to end this particular discrimination is that during the longer sit-ins on June 13 and 15, there were frequently vacant seats available. There was a constant stream of white customers, totally unaware that service was not being given as usual, who sat down to order something to eat or drink. In view of the high number of Negroes sitting there, this seems particularly indicative. This, incidentally, has repeatedly been pointed out to the managers.

Another interesting feature is that the group found that when a TV, radio, or newspaper man was present there was practically no overt hostility. At times when the sit-ins were not covered by one of these media, the two or three hecklers who were hanging around would get bold enough to do some name-calling and become verbally abusive. There was no physical abuse at any time. Submitted by Shirley M. Zoloth

* * *

Miami CORE, Report on Testing for Racial Discrimination, July 24, 1959

Two teams did the testing, each consisting of two Negroes and two whites.

Seaboard Terminal

1. Signs posted: Prominent sign reading "COLORED INTRASTATE" over doorway leading to separate waiting room and restrooms. This appears in two places where such a doorway leads into the separate waiting rooms. The restrooms in both waiting rooms are *not* designated for WHITE or NEGRO. The "Ladies" and "Men" Signs are in both English and Spanish. There are no signs in the terminal that say "WHITE" or "WHITE ONLY."

2. Facilities tested: The terminal was almost completely without people when the tests were made. The Negroes sat in the main waiting rooms, used the unmarked water fountain, used the restrooms. There was no objection of any kind to this. One team sat down at the lunch counter, located in a separate room at one end of the terminal. The woman in charge came over and told the group that she was sorry but "We can't serve you in here, but you can take something out." When asked the reason for it, her answer was "It's the law in Florida." "What's the law?" "They can't eat here." "Because they are colored?" "Yes, oh, yes, that's the law." The group left quietly and promptly.

One of the white members of the group went back in to buy a package of chewing gum. The woman was apologetic about "What happened." She said she did not like to have to do that, but it was the law and it made it "doubly hard" for her. No sign was posted in the lunch room and this was called to her attention. Her reply was "Oh, no. I wouldn't put a sign like that up." Five minutes later one of the Negro women went in and the woman let her browse at the magazines and made small talk. The woman in charge was reported to be "extremely friendly" and sympathetic. There were no other customers in evidence.

3. Conversation with person in authority: The group was told that there is no station master at this station, and that the ticket agent would be the one to see about policy. Spokesman for the testing team asked what the "COLORED INTRASTATE" sign meant. The ticket agent said it didn't mean anything and that the Negroes in the group could buy tickets and sit anywhere. He said they

had one ticket window for everyone, and colored and white stand in the same line. When asked why they had the sign hanging if it didn't mean anything, he answered that Florida law required it, but that no one paid any attention to it. When asked if the law did not require it, he thought it would be removed. He was quite sure it would be removed if the law didn't require it.

Florida East Coast Terminal

1. Signs posted: Sign reading "COLORED INTRASTATE" at entrance to separate waiting room. Restrooms in main waiting room are marked "WOMEN RESERVADAS PARA MUJERES BLANCAS" and "MEN RESERVADOS PARA HOMBRES BLANCOS." Single unit water fountain in main room unmarked.

2. Facilities Tested: The terminal was almost completely without people when the tests were made. The Negroes sat in the main waiting-room, drank from the unmarked water fountain, used the restrooms. No objection of any kind was made to this. There were a few scattered people who were either disinterested or unaware, or mildly curious. One team went into the coffee shop (a counter) and was served. Three Negroes went in about ten minutes later and were refused service and told to go to the colored waiting room.

3. Conversation with authority: Two of those testing (one Negro, one white) went to talk to the station master. His answer to a question on what the COLORED INTRASTATE sign means was "look it up in the dictionary." One of the team told him that we knew the dictionary meaning, but wondered how it was applied here as far as station facilities were concerned. He told us to talk to Mr. Gray, chief clerk of the terminal superintendent. When we asked this question of Mr. Gray he told us he was not in a position to answer and we should see Mr. Norwood, the terminal superintendent. Mr. Norwood was out, and it was not known when he would return.

Greyhound Bus Terminal

1. Signs posted: On the street floor, a large sign reads: "WHITE WAITING ROOM AND REST ROOMS ON MEZZANINE." Toward the back of the terminal a sign says "COLORED WAITING ROOM." Inside this separate waiting room are rest rooms. One, visible from the main corridor, is marked "COLORED MEN," another all the way inside the waiting room is marked simply "WOMEN." There is a separate door to the street from this "COLORED" waiting room and a sign outside (on the Street side) reading "COLORED WAITING AND REST ROOMS." Upstairs there is a large sign reading "WHITE WAITING ROOM" [and] "LADIES REST ROOM." Inside this waiting room the restrooms are marked "LADIES"

[and] "DAMAS" and "MEN" [and] "CABALLEROS." The drinking fountain was unmarked.

2. Facilities tested: This terminal was moderately busy when the tests were made. The Negroes sat in the main waiting room on the mezzanine, used the restroom in the so called "WHITE" waiting room, drank from the water fountain. No objection was made to this. One team went into the lunch room and sat down at a table. A waitress came over, said "Señoras," and was prepared to take the order, then apparently realized that this was not a Spanish group and refused service, saying that there was a place in back for colored. When asked what the reason for this was, she was non-committal. In answer to a question, she said that the lunch room is a part of the bus terminal.

3. Conversation with authority: A team was told that the person in charge of the terminal was Mr. Milton. He was there and talked to the team. He insists that the signs are there only because the law requires it, both state and city, and that the Greyhound people would like to do away with all of the discrimination and the signs—100%.

Comments: There was no sign of hostility, with the possible exception of the station master at FEC. Otherwise, the people we spoke to, and the on-lookers, expressed little interest. It should be emphasized that of the three places visited, only the bus terminal was even moderately crowded. In reference to the conversation with Mr. Milton, at the bus terminal, it ought to be pointed out that what they are really doing in putting up the signs is not complying with any laws so much as [they are] circumventing Supreme Court decisions and federal decisions in a legally permissible way, [through] careful use of *Intrastate*. The bus terminal did *not* have the word *Intrastate* on its signs, however.

* * *

Letter, Zoloth to Robinson, July 27, 1959

Dear Mr. Robinson:

On Thursday afternoon of this past week, I received a phone call from Phil Meyer, reporter on the *Miami Herald*. He was planning a story for Sunday's paper on the extent of segregation at the two local railroad stations and the bus terminal in Miami, and wanted to know whether we had done any investigating and/or testing there. I told him we had not. When I offered to have some of our people do this, he was delighted. We managed to get two interracial teams out the following morning (Friday). The report shows the results [see report dated July 24, 1959]. I took it up to the *Herald* office and we talked further about it. He told me he was going to make it a CORE story. The story did not appear. Meyer is the *Herald* "education writer" and he probably got involved with the story on the enclosed clipping [a Dade County School Board controversy over a new black elementary school and playground]. In any event, I'll see if I can get in touch with him tomorrow. Perhaps he will use our story next Sunday.

We had a fairly good attendance at our meeting Thursday night, and it was gratifying to see new people commit themselves to an interest in CORE work. The meeting was not a good meeting, due to many reasons. It started out wrong because the Sir John [Hotel] had a convention booked. We have been meeting there every Tuesday and had been working on the assumption that this was the arrangement Dr. Brown had made. Up to now, there has been no objection voiced nor any request for prior reservation. Since we do not pay, certainly this was an error on our part. Obviously, if they get a paying group that wants the room, such a thing would and should have priority. So at the last minute, after all the mailing and phone reminders, we had to switch to another place. This was around the corner and quite O.K. as a meeting hall, except we found out at the last minute that we had to get out before 10 P.M. By 9:30 we still had people just coming to our meeting, even though we did start a little before 9. So we had to move to another place. It had gotten a bit frantic by then. One of the new people (about 25 or 30 were there) was persistent about pursuing ideological and tactical courses. It was hard to rule someone out of order when we were trying to be sure people understood CORE and we really wanted sincere questions raised. This one woman kept speech-making. It made for disruption. With it all, it wasn't too bad, really.

The coming Institute has aroused a great deal of interest. I do hope, however, you are not counting on full-time participation by people here. The only one I know of, so far, who can do this is Alice Barr, whose boss at Afro-American [Afro-American Life Insurance Company] has made arrangements for her not to work for those two weeks, and she will be at CORE's disposal. This should be helpful.

We had a "Board" meeting yesterday afternoon. Peg Biderman, young divorcee with two children, enthusiastic but impressionable, is going to work with Alice Barr. Peg is trying to straighten out the different jobs that have to be done here for the Institute. Al Moore, manager of Central Life Insurance, and Alice Barr have taken responsibility for the *public meeting* job. They will explore ideas of who should be asked and what kind of places are available. We had all hoped Martin Luther King would be the big attraction. If you have suggestions, you might write to Al Moore (Central Life, 176 N.W. 14th St.) or Alice Barr (Afro-American, 840 N.W. 3rd Ave.).

Please note: It is all right with you if the public meeting is changed from Friday, Sept. 18 to Thursday, Sept. 17? I can call on some of the local organizations to help us in publicizing this meeting and getting people to it. American Jewish Congress has been most helpful to us, and so have some of the other Jewish groups. If we have this meeting on Friday night, I cannot ask them to do this, for they are prevented by religious leaders and their own by-laws, etc. from "pushing" anything but synagogue-going for the Sabbath.

Question: When you say on the schedule—"Sept. 6, Full meeting with Miami CORE (evening)," do you mean CORE members only? Does this include our Friends of CORE, and also probate members? Also people who say "please keep me on your mailing list?" Please answer this question to Lillian Kaplan, 13 S.W. 22nd Rd., Miami.

I am leaving for Philadelphia on August 4 and will be up North at various places until the last week of August. I will be in New York and will be in touch with you there—probably the 2nd or 3rd week in August. Lillian Kaplan is a good liaison for you with the group in addition, of course, to Dr. Brown. He comes back at the end of this coming week (August 1) and will probably be very busy at his office, so that it is probably a good idea for you to write to both. Until August 4, I can still take care of odds and ends that you might want to write about. On general instructions for the Institute, you probably ought to write to Mrs. Peg Biderman, 19715 N.W. 5th Place, North Miami. I gave her the extra copy of the schedule you sent.
Sincerely,
Shirley M. Zoloth

*   *   *

Shirley M. Zoloth, "The Miami CORE Story," CORE-*lator,* No. 77 (summer 1959), 2.

Several factors combined this past January to motivate a few Miamians to send out a call for CORE field secretaries. Main factor was that when four Negro children were approved for assignment to the previously all-white Orchard Villa elementary school, CORE's outstanding community work in the Nashville school situation was recalled and CORE's presence in Miami was felt needed.

Field secretaries James McCain and Gordon Carey arrived on February 28, and by March 12 Greater Miami CORE had its first meeting with some 15 members. Dr. John Brown, an ophthalmologist, became temporary chairman and has acted as the group's chief spokesman.

Tests

For its initial project, the group chose—not school desegregation—but what was deemed one of the most illogical areas of discrimination: the downtown dime store and department store lunch counters. Despite the fact that Miami's large Negro residential section is only a few blocks away, there is no place in the downtown Miami shopping area where Negroes can sit down and have a cup of coffee, or a sandwich or a dish of ice cream. They are confined to the stand-up counters where, paradoxically, they are allowed to make their purchases in turn with whites and stand next to them eating and drinking.

Grant's was the first objective of CORE's campaign and McCrory's the second—largely on the basis of the apparently bigger proportion of Negroes who shop in these two stores in preference to Woolworth's and Kress's. [The] CORE's method of testing was followed scrupulously. The first testing team went to Grant's on March 19, was refused service, and made several attempts to see the manager. A few days later, such a meeting was arranged. Like the other managers with whom CORE met subsequently, he didn't deny the justice of CORE's request, but refused to be the first to change policy.

McCrory's was tested next. The importance of repeated tests was demonstrated here, for the first CORE team that took seats was served quietly and graciously. However, the following day, another CORE team sitting at a different part of the counter was refused service. The attitude of McCrory's manager in conferring with CORE was similar to that of Grant's manager.

Sit-ins

So, the group decided on sit-ins at both stores April 29. Some 20 persons participated, about half of them Negroes. First, the group sat for a half-hour in Grant's, where considerable picture-taking and interviewing occurred. The waitresses simply disappeared. The manager was not in view. Police were on hand, but there was no hostility. It was all very amicable.

Afterward, the group went next door to McCrory's and sat for about 15 minutes. Here, the waitresses remained at their posts but ignored the group. The manager was not present, but a policy of prohibiting cameras and microphones was enforced.

TV and radio coverage of the sit-ins was excellent. The story was on Garroway's "Today" show. Each of the three local TV stations devoted a good portion of their early and late evening news reports to films taken at Grant's and on-the-scene interviews. Through UPI coverage, stories appeared in many newspapers throughout the country.

As a result of the community interest aroused by this first action of its type in Miami, CORE found itself with an increasing number of supporters. Tests were then conducted at Woolworth's and Kress's; at three department store lunch counters: Burdine's, Richards, Byron-Jackson's; at two of the Walgreen drugstore lunch counters and at several Royal Castle hamburger counters. Meetings with several more managers and with the Better Business Division of the Chamber of Commerce followed.

In anticipation of our next action—a sit-in June 13 at Grant's—Phil Meyer of the *Miami Herald* had an extensive interview with Dr. Brown and myself. This action got under way at 11:30 with some 30 participants, about half of them Negroes. More Negroes kept arriving so that by 4:30 we ended with a group of about 50. The attitude of the management and waitresses was hostile, though no overt threats were made. Many of the customers expressed surprise that Negroes were not served and expressed the viewpoint that they should be. Only a very few customers made anti-Negro or anti-Semitic remarks. A second sit-in, involving about 40 persons was conducted two days later. Sit-ins at Woolworth's and at Burdine's took place June 27.

Future Plans

Since then [the] group has concentrated on enlarging its committees, increasing its membership, getting more community support and building up a reservoir of strength for future sit-ins, which may have to be sustained for long periods of time.

Various factors indicate the timeliness of our lunch counter campaign. A survey of 100 white passers-by, conducted by a local TV commentator during our first sit-in, revealed that 98 not only had no objection to Negroes being served, but were surprised to learn that discrimination prevails at the lunch counters. This was borne out during our longer sit-ins, when a constant stream of white customers sat down alongside members of our group and placed their orders, completely oblivious to the fact that Negroes were sitting nearby.

* * *

Shirley M. Zoloth, "Leaders Back CORE in Fight for Equality,"
***Miami Times*, September 26, 1959**

Greater Miami Committee on Racial Equality was the object of praise and calls for support at a public meeting Sept. 17, with Rev. Fred Shuttlesworth, veteran fighter for integration in Alabama, as guest speaker.

Rev. S. A. Cousins, pastor of the Greater Bethel AME Church where the meeting took place, welcomed the audience saying he "loves CORE because it stands for the same things as his own AME Church." He expressed hope that CORE can make Miami a place where a person can call another brother, and mean it.

Daniel H. Lang, executive secretary of Miami Urban League, told the integrated audience of some 1,000 people that CORE can stand on its record of effectiveness. For he has seen a CORE group in Detroit open up the restaurants on Woodward Avenue.

Rev. Father Gibson, popular Episcopalian minister and president of Miami NAACP, quipped: "Because you have well come into Miami, you are welcome." He went on to say that CORE had awakened the consciousness of people in Dade County by confronting the man who is doing wrong. "Now is the time to choose sides," Rev. Gibson urged. He pledged the support of NAACP to CORE. "We are all interested in the same goals. There is no competition."

Rabbi Jonah Caplan, of American Jewish Congress, declared: "Democracy is indivisible. It applies to all or none. We cannot be half a democracy. All minorities suffer if all are not free." He further suggested that the work of CORE if well done could make Miami the model city for all communities.

Rev. Edward T. Graham, of Interdenominational Ministerial Alliance of Miami, warned that unless we are united we will lose the fight for equal citizenship. He pledged the Alliance to stand behind CORE, for "CORE teaches us a means of liberating the soul of man, and if we follow CORE under God, we will gain our end."

Susan Bodan, national board member of Americans for Democratic Action and a CORE institute member, gave a brief history of Miami CORE and spoke also about the institute now in Miami. She stressed the difference between CORE's method of direct non-violent action and that of other groups also doing excellent work for integration. She offered two reasons for CORE's current action in Miami downtown restaurants: 1. The humiliation to Negroes not being able to sit down to eat. 2. The necessity for shoppers, Negro shoppers, with packages and children, to have the comfort of sitting down for rest and refreshments. In conclusion, Mrs. Bodan invited all present to join in a mass sit-in demonstration at Grant's lunch counter on Saturday, Sept. 19.

* * *

Shirley Zoloth, "Miami Integration: Silence Causes Failure," *The Southern Patriot,* **17, no. 10 (December 1959), 1–3.**

This city's much publicized "experiment" in school desegregation, at the Orchard Villa Elementary School, was doomed to failure before it started.

The Dade County (Miami) School Board must have known this and, in the opinion of many people, never intended it to work. It must take the blame for the failure—along with that section of the public whose "neutral" silence is bound to have indicated to the Board that an honest effort toward workable integration would have little community support.

The 400-pupil Orchard Villa school opened in September with 18 pupils enrolled—14 white children and four Negroes. A month later the School Board replaced the all-white staff with all Negro teachers and a Negro principal and assigned 379 more Negroes to the school.

Although in November nine white children remained in the school, it was apparent that Orchard Villa was destined soon to be another all-Negro institution. One local newspaper commented that "one phase of Florida's first experience with school desegregation" was now at an end.

But actually any observer could have predicted the outcome long before school opened in September. It was forecast early in 1959 when the then all-white PTA at Orchard Villa voted to give its lovely tea service to a neighboring all-white PTA. For the Orchard Villa School is located in a 1600-block section that is rapidly "changing" from white to all-Negro. Besides Orchard Villa, there are eight elementary schools in this area, three white and five Negro.

Not quite five years ago, 5,000 children lived in the area—about half of them white and half Negro. Today there are 7,428 children, but only 1,622 are white and 5,806 are Negro. The Negro schools have all become badly overcrowded; all of the white schools have empty classrooms. Before the announcement that Orchard Villa would be a "pilot school" for integration, its enrollment had decreased from 429 in 1957 to 222 in 1958.

Under the masquerade of an "experiment," a school destined to become all-Negro anyway was called "token desegregation." And by pretending that this was an attempt in good faith to proceed with planned desegregation, the Dade County School Board was actually seeking to help preserve the constitutionality of the Florida Pupil Assignment Law.

For everyone with foresight knew that unless some Negro children were admitted to some previously white schools, this law would eventually be declared unconstitutional. The tendency of the Federal Courts has been to interpret such a move as token desegregation on its face, until such time as it is clearly shown to be mere subterfuge.

Actually, the Dade County Board delayed the decision to admit Negroes to Orchard Villa until it had made a survey of Negro-white real estate transactions in the area. Four Negro children applied for transfer to the school in September, 1958, and were refused. Their parents then requested a hearing, under the Assignment Law, and this was held. In October, 1958, the board announced it was instituting a study among white parents in the neighborhood to determine whether desegregation was practical.

The results of this survey were announced in November, but the board again delayed a decision until the real estate survey could be completed. In February, after stalling until the second school semester started, the board announced that the Negroes would be admitted in September, 1959.

The 14 white children who entered the school with them in September did so in spite of strong pressures to stay away. Representatives of the White Citizens Council and the Ku Klux Klan harangued and threatened the white parents as they went to and from the school. With the shifting of the faculty and the assignment of the additional 379 Negroes in October, the pressures became too much for most of them.

Mrs. Corinne Perrine, who had a daughter and two sons in the school, had told newsmen in September: "This is the way I want my children to learn about democracy." But after the change-over in October she said she no longer considered Orchard Villa an integrated school and would ask for transfers.

Baldomero Prieto said he was bowing to neighborhood pressure by taking his 10-year-old daughter out of the school. "All I want to do is live in peace," he said. "The neighbors keep on asking me why I don't send my daughter to a white school, and the other kids bother her and say nasty things to her. My daughter brings home the little Negro girls from school to play in her yard. She doesn't know anything about hating other people. But my neighbor who used to have his dog in my yard to play with mine keeps his dog in the house now. He doesn't want his dog in the yard because Negro children are playing with my Leonore. So what can I do? I have to transfer her."

Defenders of the School Board say it can't be held responsible for such reactions as this—that it was not called on to conduct a "social experiment," but only to uphold the law. And the law as interpreted by the Supreme Court, it is pointed out, does not call necessarily for mixing of white and Negro students but merely says that no child can be denied the right to attend the school of his choice because of race.

There is a germ of truth in this defense. If the Orchard Villa failure proves anything, it proves again that the problem of school segregation can never be truly solved until the problem of housing segregation is licked—until open occupancy policies everywhere remove the pressures that create ghettos.

Nevertheless, there were constructive things the School Board could have done. For one thing, if the Negro applicants had been admitted simultaneously with the announcement of their acceptance at Orchard Villa, there would have been greater chance for success. At the time of the announcement last February, there were still many white children in the school. If the four Negroes had been admitted at that moment, many of the white children and parents might have adjusted quickly to integration and stayed.

Or better still, the announcement and actual admission could have come back in September, 1958, when there were 222 white children enrolled. As it was, the delay from February to September, 1959, provided time for an organized exodus—many people think the School Board planned it that way.

The good faith of the Dade County School Board, even in applying the letter of the law, remains to be proved. Its only other current "integration experiment" really doesn't count. This is the Air Force Base Elementary School [at Homestead Air Force Base], where desegregation also started this year. However, all but two of its 770 pupils are children of Air Force personnel. Had it not been built with federal aid, it probably would not have been desegregated.

The Board's real test may come in North Miami Beach. Here a group of Negro children have applied for admission to the all-white Fulford Elementary School. The situation surrounding Fulford is quite different from that at Orchard Villa. Unlike the Orchard Villa area, this community is not in a stage of transition from white to Negro; the Negro population has not grown much in the past three years.

The Board turned down the original applications for transfers to Fulford. The NAACP is seeking to have this ruling reviewed. What the Board does now may indicate whether it intends real compliance with the law or a continued masquerade.

But the public has a responsibility. Many individuals who are privately committed to the concept that segregation is evil are reluctant to stand squarely on this position in a public way. Statements to the School Board, letters to public officials [and] to newspapers, are conspicuously lacking.

This fearfulness of taking a forthright position on the moral issue may well turn out to be one of the greatest deterrents to desegregation—not only in Miami, but throughout the South. For the silence does not express neutrality or moderation. Instead, it implies consent to the evils of segregation and encourages their perpetuation.

And a tiny handful of frightened bigots make loud hate noises and thus manage to sound like a large group—or give authorities a looked-for "voice of the people" to defer to. Somehow it must be made clear to people of good will that, although they perhaps believe that they are simply "minding their own business," what they are really doing is consenting to and aiding in a nightmare of injustice.

*   *   *

Letter, Zoloth to Helen Raebeck, National Council of Jewish Women, July 12, 1960

Dear Miss Raebeck:

At the suggestion of Florence Lewis, President of the Greater Miami Section of NCJW, I am writing to you for some further clarification on the degree to which our Section may participate in the local Miami NOW [National Organization of Women for Equality in Education].

We know that some months ago Jessie Gertman was in touch with the national office, and it is our understanding that NCJW policy is to participate in NOW only as observers. However, at a recent meeting of our Section's Legislative Committee (attended by the Legislative and Discussion Group Chairmen from our Divisions, as well as by Florence Lewis and Evelyn Schwartz, Vice-President in charge of Public Affairs), some pertinent questions were asked relating to Council policy toward NOW. In accordance with NCJW policy, our Section has had observers at each of the few local meetings that have been held by Miami NOW. The feeling of the women at our Legislative meeting was decidedly in favor of more active participation. It is for this reason that I am writing to you.

At our meeting we spoke of some of the problems that can arise in some of the southern sections if Council should take a more militant role in school integration. However, several of the women pointed out instances in other parts of the south (which can far more accurately be termed "deep south" than can Miami) where NCJW has assumed a real leadership role on this issue. Some of the questions to which we would like answers are these: In southern communities where Council has been forthright on this issue, have there been any adverse effects organizationally? Specifically, has membership been decreased? Has Council been made a target by anti-Semitic forces? (Apparently every Jewish organization with southern chapters finds itself on the horns of the dilemma, and it might be a good idea to see if the fears are well-founded.)

While it is true that our women, as individuals, can help in NOW's work, such a project can only be successful in Miami if it has the united *committed* strength of many women's organizations—for only then can it exert the kind of moral force so desperately needed here. The general aura of conformism, though perhaps not peculiar to Miami, has a paralyzing effect on organized groups which might otherwise be, if not more vigorous about civil rights, at least more forthright.

Miami is frequently referred to as an anomaly. On the one hand, it has the largest Jewish community in the South and caters to northerners (as tourists as well as new residents) by the hundreds of thousands. It is regarded by the rest of Florida as being "militant" and "liberal." On the other hand, it is provincial and timid about so-called controversial matters. Narrow-mindedness abounds. Although the School Board has ostensibly "integrated" four of its public schools, the significance of these actions is not clearly understood. Of these four schools, the first (Orchard Villa), as you probably are aware, is in a neighborhood that had already been changing rapidly from white to Negro, and was in any event destined in short time to become totally Negro. The original handful of Negroes admitted to it grew last year to 350, with now only 6 whites remaining.

The second "experiment" with integration was at an elementary school which serves the Homestead Air Force Base. Schools for service personnel ordinarily are integrated, and the School Board simply followed service custom in sending the 600 white children and a dozen or more Negroes there last year. This is a new school, built with federal aid, and all but 3 or 4 of its pupils are children of servicemen. In the new integration a week or two ago, two Negro girls were assigned to previously all-white schools, one to Fulford Elementary School in North Miami, and her sister to a Junior High in the same area. Their brother was denied assignment to the white school, presumably because of his low academic rating—one of the criteria set forth in Florida's Pupil Assignment Law. Other applications for Negroes were denied.

Neither the School Board nor the Superintendent of Schools has ever stated any intention of compliance with the 1954 Supreme Court decision. After the decision, the Board indicated that all pupils would continue in the schools they were then attending. After the passage of the Florida Pupil Assignment Law in 1957, the Board and administration promptly eliminated all reference to race in its records, technically maintaining that schools in this County are not segregated. The community has never been given any real policy statement on desegregation.

I tell you all of this as a preface to the statement that there has been a dismal lack of communication between the local authorities and the community, plus almost a total absence of vocal petition to the School Board to proceed with less trepidation. The school people are reluctant, at best, but have had practically no support from the so-called liberal forces in the area—organizational or religious.

People here and there are beginning to see that being neutral condemns them to silence, and that the silence implies their consent to the evil of continued segregation—indeed, reinforces it. But the organizations whose scopes embrace the achievement of human rights simply by non-commitment effectively lend aid and comfort to the staunch segregationists even though the numbers of the latter are dwindling. An indication of a favorable trend, I believe, is the fact that Jack D. Gordon, not only Jewish but also an integrationist, won the primary county-wide for a seat on the School Board.

Miami NOW, because it wants broad representation, has made for itself the problem of being a neutral force trying to stimulate activity. It sees success only with real leadership from a cross-section of responsible organizations and religious groups. [Miami] NOW is moving very slowly and deliberately here. While its opening conference in March of this year was very successful and a Continuing Committee was given power to move ahead in direct action, it has not as yet been formally organized and has actually taken no real "action," limiting itself so far to educational work in the community and attempts to interest organizations in joining forces on this issue. Its position is simple: there is no equality of education in segregated schools, according to our moral, ethical and religious codes and according to the law of the land. The hope is to get the major "respectable" groups (Jewish and non-Jewish) to affiliate, and have delegates from these groups constitute the policy-making body of Miami NOW. Tentative goals have been set up, subject to confirmation or change by such a body. These are:

1. To gather factual information regarding existing conditions in the public schools of Dade County concerning equality in education.
2. To provide information about equality in education and related areas to member groups.
3. To develop programs for member groups and others.
4. To establish and maintain better communication between organizations.
5. To develop a large organized group which can support the schools when the process of integration begins, a group which will be the nucleus of a community education program.
6. To undertake action programs which have the unanimous support of all affiliated organizations.
7. To facilitate joint action programs by member groups by providing the opportunity for them to establish better intergroup communication.

You will recognize, particularly from the sixth point, that the specific goals will remain tentative until there are enough organizations participating not only to assure strength, but to make a realistic policy-making body (even though this will undoubtedly have limiting aspects).

Just to keep the record clear, let me state that as one of the initiators of NOW in Miami, I am very much in favor of more active NCJW participation. However, my position at the Legislative Committee's meeting was that we are, and properly so, bound by National's policy. It is because of the points I have raised here, particularly on the difference between Miami NOW and national NOW, that our women felt a letter to you was in order.

Shirley M. Zoloth

[*Source:* Jack Gordon Papers, Box 10, Folder: Desegregation]

* * *

Shirley M. Zoloth, Urgent Statement, National Council of Jewish Women, Miami Section, October 1960

You all know that Council does not endorse political candidates. At the Section Board meeting on October 12th, however, it was agreed that one of our local campaigns must be brought to the attention of every Council member.

The campaign for the school board election has been carried to such ugly proportions that it has become more than a campaign against Jack Gordon—it is clearly and overtly a campaign against having another Jew on the school board. For the benefit of those who are unaware of the significance of this situation, let me review some of the facts—all of which have been carefully substantiated.

First, let me tell you the role of certain members of the Churches and Ministerial Association in this whole thing. Several influential ministers in the Greater Miami Ministerial Association, together with a similar narrow-minded group from the Council of Churches, have launched what they have chosen to call a Christian Crusade against the Democratic Candidate for the School Board—Jack D. Gordon. A letter on the letterhead of the Ministerial Association dated September 15, 1960 invited all of its members to a meeting at which "vitally important information and inspiration will be given to all ministers present, who in turn will transmit this information to the members of their congregations, all regarding the developments and significance of the Bible reading suit in our civil courts, and perhaps other matters of local interest such as the school board election and the national presidential election."

Enclosed with this letter was a scurrilous piece of literature. (Hold up literature to group and point to flag and Bible—read all of top page.) This is deceptive on its face. A School Board member has no say whatsoever about whether the Bible should be read in the public schools. Whoever is elected will take an oath of office to uphold the law. There is a state law requiring the daily reading of the Bible in the schools. Jack Gordon has said repeatedly that unless and until that law is changed Bible reading must continue. The Republican candidate Atkinson, himself, has admitted privately that it is a matter that only the courts and the legislature can decide. So this is a blatant lie. (Show front of literature. Then show inside of literature.) The entire left page is a vicious attack on Jack Gordon, full of deceitful statements; familiar Joe McCarthy attempts to establish guilt by association; distortion and half truths. Jack is accused with others of "paving the way for atheism and then Communist teachings by first destroying all vestiges of faith in the Almighty." In bold print in the center are the words "ULTRA-LIBERAL ELEMENTS ARE OUT TO SEIZE CONTROL OF THE DADE COUNTY SCHOOL BOARD." On the right hand page we read "while our forefathers wanted to separate Church and State, they never dreamed of separating our children from God—as powerful elements are now trying to do."

There is not one word about this man Atkinson's qualifications for being in a policy-making position for educational tasks. No background for it, no experience, no expression of interest in schools, no pretense of any kind of ability to participate in what is one of the most vital jobs facing us today—giving a better education to all of our children.

I quote some more from this nonsense: Mr. Atkinson claims his supporters "are acting first as AMERICANS for ATKINSON—a man who will protect the treasured principles and high morals for which both parties stand firm against all who would diminish and subvert them." They don't mean AMERICANS for ATKINSON at all. They mean Christians for Atkinson.

There is a scum sheet in this town some of you may be familiar with. It's called the *Florida Free Press*, and is the usual kind of hate sheet. In this, Jack Gordon was accused of "masterminding" all kinds of subversive plots in the community. It was full of lies of the worst kind. I am telling you this so you will know what kind of campaign this is. It is far beyond partisan politics.

Let me get back to the Ministerial Association. It was a rigged meeting. There were some ministers there who were outraged that religious leaders were permitting themselves to be used in such a dishonest maneuver. They wanted to object, but were not permitted to do so. It was at the end of this meeting that Don Swanson, Executive Director of the Council of Churches said: "Thank gosh we have a Christian Republican candidate for the School Board." This is the same man who subsequently told one of our Rabbis that they don't really think Jack is a communist or an atheist. They just don't want another Jew on the School Board. One is enough, meaning of course Anna Brenner Meyers. And at the end of this meeting, this *Christian Crusade* (these are the words of Don Swanson, not mine), Jack Gordon was refused permission to appear or even to have a statement of his read.

I repeat—this is an overt anti-Semitic attack on all of us. And we are reacting. Jewish organizations and synagogues all over Dade County are bringing this to the attention of their membership. Intelligent people, Jews and non-Jews, are outraged at this horrible kind of attack. Many ministers and Christian lay people have repudiated this religious attack.

What we must do: This attack can be defeated with dignity. And the place to do it is at the polls on election day. Alert your neighbors. This is not a Council endorsement. It is a statement of facts that every thinking individual will recognize as going far beyond partisan politics. If as *individuals* you want to help Jack Gordon, no doubt he will be glad to hear from you. It *is* more than just his battle.

[*Source:* Jack Gordon Papers, Box 17, Folder: Gordon-Personal]

Notes

Introduction

1. First-hand accounts of civil rights activism at the community level include Anne Braden, *The Wall Between*; Merrill Proudfoot, *Diary of a Sit-in*; Daisy Bates, *The Long Shadow of Little Rock*; Anne Moody, *Coming of Age in Mississippi*; Hollinger F. Barnard, ed., *Outside the Magic Circle*; Jo Ann Robinson, *The Montgomery Bus Boycott and the Women Who Started It*; Clarice T. Campbell, *Civil Rights Chronicle: Letters from the South*; Mary Kimbrough and Margaret W. Dagen, *Victory without Violence: The First Ten Years of the St. Louis Committee of Racial Equality (CORE), 1947–1957*; Constance Curry, et al., *Deep in Our Hearts: Nine White Women in the Freedom Movement*; Gilbert R. Mason, *Beaches, Blood, and Ballots: A Black Doctor's Civil Rights Struggle*; Richard D. Leonard, *Call to Selma: Eighteen Days of Witness*; Tananarive Due and Patricia Stephens Due, *Freedom in the Family: A Mother-Daughter Memoir of the Fight for Civil Rights*. Not to be overlooked are two important oral history collections: Howell Raines, *My Soul Is Rested: Movement Days in the Deep South Remembered*; Henry Hampton and Steve Fayer, eds., *Voices of Freedom: An Oral History of the Civil Rights Movement from the 1950s through the 1980s*.

2. Vicki L. Crawford, Jacqueline Anne Rouse, and Barbara Woods, eds., *Women in the Civil Rights Movement: Trailblazers and Torchbearers, 1941–1965*; Belinda Robnett, *How Long? How Long? African-American Women in the Struggle for Civil Rights*; Peter J. Ling and Sharon Monteith, eds., *Gender in the Civil Rights Movement*; Douglas Brinkley, *Rosa Parks*; Debra L. Schultz, *Going South: Jewish Women in the Civil Rights Movement*; Lynne Olson, *Freedom's Daughters: The Unsung Heroines of the Civil Rights Movement from 1830 to 1970*; Bettye Collier-Thomas and V. P. Franklin, eds., *Sisters in the Struggle: African American Women in the Civil Rights-Black Power Movement*.

3. William H. Chafe, *Civilities and Civil Rights: Greensboro, North Carolina, and the Black Struggle for Freedom*; Robert J. Norrell, *Reaping the Whirlwind: The Civil Rights Movement in Tuskegee*; David R. Colburn, *Racial Change and Community Crisis: St. Augustine, Florida, 1877–1980*.

4. Charles W. Eagles, "The Civil Rights Movement," 467. For a major interpretation of civil rights at the local level, see Aldon D. Morris, *The Origins of the Civil Rights*

Movement: Black Communities Organizing for Change, as well as Morris's restatements of the initial argument: Aldon D. Morris, "Centuries of Black Protest: Its Significance for America and the World"; Aldon D. Morris, "A Retrospective on the Civil Rights Movement: Political and Intellectual Landmarks." For historiographical treatments of the civil rights movement, many arguing the need for additional local case studies, see Armstead L. Robinson and Patricia Sullivan, eds., *New Directions in Civil Rights Studies;* Adam Fairclough, "Historians and the Civil Rights Movement"; Clayborne Carson, "Civil Rights Reform and the Black Freedom Struggle"; Steven Lawson, "Martin Luther King, Jr., and the Civil Rights Movement"; Steven Lawson, "Freedom Then, Freedom Now: The Historiography of the Civil Rights Movement"; Kim Lacy Rogers, "Oral History and the History of the Civil Rights Movement"; Richard King, "The Role of Intellectual History in the Histories of the Civil Rights Movement"; Charles M. Payne, "The Social Construction of History," in Payne, *I've Got the Light of Freedom: The Organizing Tradition and the Mississippi Freedom Struggle,* 413–41, 483–87; Charles W. Eagles, "Toward New Histories of the Civil Rights Era"; Kevin Gaines, "The Historiography of the Struggle for Black Equality Since 1945."

For a sampling of local case studies published since the mid-1980s, see Alan B. Anderson and George W. Pickering, *Confronting the Color Line: The Broken Promise of the Civil Rights Movement in Chicago;* James W. Button, *Blacks and Social Change: Impact of the Civil Rights Movement in Southern Communities;* James F. Findlay Jr., *Church People in the Struggle: The National Council of Churches and the Black Freedom Movement, 1950–1970;* Kim Lacy Rogers, *Righteous Lives: Narratives of the New Orleans Civil Rights Movement;* Charles W. Eagles, *Jon Daniels and the Civil Rights Movement in Alabama;* John Dittmer, *Local People: The Struggle for Civil Rights in Mississippi;* James R. Ralph Jr., *Northern Protest: Martin Luther King, Jr., Chicago, and the Civil Rights Movement;* Adam Fairclough, *Race and Democracy: The Civil Rights Struggle in Louisiana, 1915–1972;* Charles M. Payne, *I've Got the Light of Freedom: The Organizing Tradition and the Mississippi Freedom Struggle;* Glenn T. Eskew, *But for Birmingham: The Local and National Movements in the Civil Rights Struggle;* Ronald H. Bayor, *Race and the Shaping of Twentieth-Century Atlanta;* Glenda Alice Rabby, *The Pain and the Promise: The Struggle for Civil Rights in Tallahassee, Florida;* Stewart Burns, ed., *Daybreak of Freedom: The Montgomery Bus Boycott;* J. Mills Thornton III, *Dividing Lines: Municipal Politics and the Struggle for Civil Rights in Montgomery, Birmingham, and Selma;* Jeanne F. Theoharis and Komozi Woodard, eds., *Freedom North: Black Freedom Struggles Outside the South, 1940–1980;* and, for a debate between advocates of top-down and bottom-up approaches, Steven F. Lawson and Charles Payne, *Debating the Civil Rights Movement, 1945–1968.*

5. For examples of work on African-American agency and activism before the 1950s, see August Meier and Elliott M. Rudwick, "The Boycott Movement against Jim Crow Streetcars in the South, 1900–1906"; Andor Skotnes, "'Buy Where You Can Work': Boycotting for Jobs in African-American Baltimore, 1933–1934"; Robin D. G. Kelley, "'We Are Not What We Seem': Rethinking Black Working-Class Opposition in the Jim Crow South"; Tera W. Hunter, "Domination and Resistance: The Politics of Wage Household

Labor in New South Atlanta"; Kenneth W. Goings and Gerald L. Smith, "'Unhidden' Transcripts: Memphis and African American Agency, 1862–1920"; Robert L. Zangrando, *The NAACP Crusade against Lynching, 1909–1950;* Mark V. Tushnet, *The NAACP's Legal Strategy against Segregated Education, 1925–1950;* Herbert Shapiro, *White Violence and Black Response: From Reconstruction to Montgomery;* Michael K. Honey, *Black Workers Remember: An Oral History of Segregation, Unionism, and the Freedom Struggle;* Timothy B. Tyson, *Radio Free Dixie: Robert F. Williams and the Roots of Black Power;* Kimberley L. Phillips, *AlabamaNorth: African-American Migrants, Community, and Working-Class Activism in Cleveland, 1915–45;* Robert Cook, *Sweet Land of Liberty: The African-American Struggle for Civil Rights in the Twentieth Century.*

6. Raymond A. Mohl, "The Pattern of Race Relations in Miami since the 1920s"; Marvin Dunn, *Black Miami in the Twentieth Century.*

7. Mark K. Bauman and Berkley Kalin, eds., *The Quiet Voices: Southern Rabbis and Black Civil Rights, 1880s to 1990s,* especially Bauman's "Introduction," 1–18; Deborah Dash Moore, "Separate Paths: Blacks and Jews in the Twentieth-Century South"; Cheryl Greenberg, "The Southern Jewish Community and the Struggle for Civil Rights"; Leonard Dinnerstein, "Southern Jewry and the Desegregation Crisis, 1954–1970"; Marc Dollinger, *Quest for Inclusion: Jews and Liberalism in Modern America;* Clive Webb, *Fight against Fear: Southern Jews and Black Civil Rights.*

8. Stuart Svonkin, *Jews against Prejudice: American Jews and the Fight for Civil Liberties;* Richard M. Fried, *Nightmare in Red: The McCarthy Era in Perspective.*

9. John M. Coe to Edward Maxted, July 5, 1954, Box 3, John M. Coe Papers; Frank J. Donner, "The Miami Formula: An Expose of Grass-Roots McCarthyism"; Carol Polsgrove, *Divided Minds: Intellectuals and the Civil Rights Movement,* 75.

Part I. South of the South

1. Miami CORE, Sit-in Report, April 15, 1959, Papers of the Congress of Racial Equality (hereafter cited as CORE Papers), Reel 19. Civil rights sit-ins occurred in at least fifteen cities between 1957 and 1960, all prior to the Greensboro student sit-ins. See Aldon D. Morris, "Black Southern Student Sit-in Movement: An Analysis of Internal Organization."

2. James Farmer, "Foreword," 13; Seymour Martin Lipset and Earl Rabb, *Jews and the New American Scene,* 155; Stuart Svonkin, *Jews against Prejudice: American Jews and the Fight for Civil Liberties;* Samuel C. Heilman, *Portrait of American Jews: The Last Half of the 20th Century,* 86; Julian Bond, "Introduction," 1.

3. For discussion of the historic black-Jewish relationship, see John Bracey and August Meier, "Towards a Research Agenda on Blacks and Jews in United States History," 66; Peter I. Rose, "Blacks and Jews: The Strained Alliance," 55; Jonathan Kaufman, *Broken Alliance: The Turbulent Times between Blacks and Jews in America;* Murray Friedman, *What Went Wrong? The Creation and Collapse of the Black-Jewish Alliance;* Cheryl Greenberg, "The Black-Jewish Alliance, 1930–1955: Revisiting the 'Golden Age' Hypothesis"; Arthur Hertzberg, *The Jews in America: Four Centuries of an Uneasy Encounter;* Milton D. Morris and Gary E. Rubin, "The Turbulent Friendship: Black-

Jewish Relations in the 1990s"; David Brion Davis, "Jews and Blacks in America." An early survey of the enormous literature on the subject can be found in Lenwood G. Davis, *Black-Jewish Relations in the United States, 1752–1984*. Four recent collections of essays that demonstrate the complexity of the subject are Jack Salzman and Cornel West, eds., *Struggles in the Promised Land: Toward a History of Black-Jewish Relations in the United States;* V. P. Franklin, et al., eds., *African Americans and Jews in the Twentieth Century: Studies in Convergence and Conflict;* Maurianne Adams and John Bracey, eds., *Strangers and Neighbors: Relations between Blacks and Jews in the United State;* and Jack Salzman, ed., *Bridges and Boundaries: African Americans and American Jews*.

4. For the "south of the South" comment, see James R. Robinson to Thalia Stern, October 13, 1958, CORE Papers, Reel 19.

5. Robert Korstad and Nelson Lichtenstein, "Opportunities Found and Lost: Labor, Radicals, and the Early Civil Rights Movement," 799. On these points, see also Donald R. McCoy and Richard T. Ruetten, "The Civil Rights Movement, 1940–1954"; Richard M. Dalfiume, "The 'Forgotten Years' of the Negro Revolution"; Harvard Sitkoff, "Harry Truman and the Election of 1948: The Coming of Age of Civil Rights in American Politics"; Harvard Sitkoff, "Racial Militancy and Interracial Violence in the Second World War"; Lee Finkle, "The Conservative Aims of Militant Rhetoric: Black Protest during World War II"; Peter J. Kellogg, "Civil Rights Consciousness in the 1940s"; James A. Burran, "Urban Racial Violence in the South during World War II: A Comparative Overview"; William H. Chafe, "The Civil Rights Revolution: The Gods Bring Threads to Webs Begun"; Beth Tompkins Bates, "A New Crowd Challenges the Agenda of the Old Guard in the NAACP, 1933–1941"; Patricia Sullivan, *Days of Hope: Race and Democracy in the New Deal Era;* Nancy J. Weiss, *Farewell to the Party of Lincoln: Black Politics in the Age of FDR;* Patrick S. Washburn, *A Question of Sedition: The Federal Government's Investigation of the Black Press during World War II;* Herbert Garfinkel, *When Negroes March: The March on Washington Movement in the Organizational Politics for FEPC;* Richard M. Dalfiume, *Desegregation of the U.S. Armed Forces: Fighting on Two Fronts, 1939–1953;* Merl E. Reed, *Seedtime for the Modern Civil Rights Movement: The President's Committee on Fair Employment Practice, 1941–1946*. On Truman and civil rights, see William C. Berman, *The Politics of Civil Rights in the Truman Administration;* Barton J. Bernstein, "The Ambiguous Legacy: The Truman Administration and Civil Rights"; Donald R. McCoy and Richard T. Ruetten, *Quest and Response: Minority Rights and the Truman Administration;* Desmond King, "'The Longest Road to Equality': The Politics of Institutional Desegregation under Truman"; Michael R. Gardner, *Harry Truman and Civil Rights: Moral Courage and Political Risks*.

6. *Pittsburgh Courier*, May 18, 1946, December 6, 1947; American Jewish Committee, *American Jewish Yearbook, 1947–1948*, 189; Harold Preece, "The Klan Declares War," 4. See also Heywood Broun, "Up Pops the Wizard"; John Roy Carlson, *The Plotters;* Stetson Kennedy, *Southern Exposure;* Carey McWilliams, *A Mask for Privilege: Anti-Semitism in America;* E. A. Pillar, *Time Bomb;* Dorothy Roberts, "Feuds among the Fascists"; Stetson Kennedy, "The Ku Klux Klan: What to Do about It"; Carey McWilliams,

"The Klan: Post-War Model." In the late 1940s, J. B. Stoner headed the Stoner Anti-Jewish Party, which according to Stetson Kennedy "promoted a constitutional amendment making it illegal to be Jewish in the U.S., punishable by death." See Stetson Kennedy to Adam Clayton Powell, June 5, 1949, Stetson Kennedy Papers, Georgia State University, Box 1511, File 11.

7. James Graham Cook, *The Segregationists*; Herman E. Talmadge, *You and Segregation*, viii, 26–36; Bert C. Newton, *Uncle Tom's Cadillac: Not with Simon Legree but the NAACP*, 53–59; Florida Legislative Investigation Committee, *Communism and the NAACP*; Loren Miller, *The Petitioners: The Story of the Supreme Court of the United States and the Negro*, 375–91. For attacks on agencies and activists promoting better race relations in the South, see Thomas A. Krueger, *And Promises to Keep: The Southern Conference for Human Welfare, 1938–1948*; Linda Reed, *Simple Decency and Common Sense: The Southern Conference Movement, 1938–1963*; Frank T. Adams, *James A. Dombrowski: An American Heretic, 1897–1983*.

8. Richard M. Fried, *Nightmare in Red: The McCarthy Era in Perspective*, 164–65; Frank J. Donner, *The Age of Surveillance: The Aims and Methods of America's Political Intelligence System*, 141; Athan Theoharis, *Spying on Americans: Political Surveillance from Hoover to the Huston Plan*, 135; Tony Poveda, "The Rise and Fall of FBI Domestic Intelligence Operations," 114; Athan Theoharis, *Chasing Spies: How the FBI Failed in Counterintelligence but Promoted the Politics of McCarthyism in the Cold War Years*. The FBI pattern of linking the civil rights movement to communist subversion intensified in the 1960s. See David J. Garrow, *The FBI and Martin Luther King, Jr.: From "Solo" to Memphis*; Michael Friedly and David Gallen, *Martin Luther King, Jr.: The FBI File*; and, for a recent update, David J. Garrow, "The FBI and Martin Luther King."

9. Edward S. Shapiro, *A Time for Healing: American Jewry since World War II*, 36; Stuart Svonkin, *Jews against Prejudice: American Jews and the Fight for Civil Liberties*, 161–77; Richard M. Fried, *Nightmare in Red: The McCarthy Era in Perspective*, 165. Similar points have been made in Manning Marable, *Race, Reform, and Rebellion: The Second Reconstruction in Black America, 1945–1982*, 12–41; Adam Fairclough, "Historians and the Civil Rights Movement"; Hugh T. Murray Jr., *Civil Rights, History-Writing, and Anti-Communism: A Critique*.

10. Hasia R. Diner, *In the Almost Promised Land: American Jews and Blacks, 1915–1935*, 118–63, 185–88; David Levering Lewis, "Parallels and Divergences: Assimilationist Strategies of Afro-American and Jewish Elites from 1910 to the Early 1930s," 544, 564; David Levering Lewis, "Shortcuts to the Mainstream: Afro-American and Jewish Notables in the 1920s and 1930s"; B. Joyce Ross, *J. E. Spingarn and the Rise of the NAACP, 1911–1939*. For an overview of NAACP history, see August Meier and John Bracey, "The NAACP as a Reform Movement, 1909–1965: 'To Reach the Conscience of America.'"

11. Clayborne Carson Jr., "Blacks and Jews in the Civil Rights Movement," 117. For the work of progressive CIO unions during this period, see F. Ray Marshall, *The Negro and Organized Labor*, 34–52; Sumner M. Rosen, "The CIO Era, 1935–55"; Michael K. Honey, "Labor, the Left, and Civil Rights in the South: Memphis During the CIO Era, 1937–1955"; Donald T. Critchlow, "Communist Unions and Racism"; August Meier and Elliott

Rudwick, "Communist Unions and the Black Community: The Case of the Transport Workers Union, 1934–1944"; Allan M. Winkler, "The Philadelphia Transit Strike of 1944"; August Meier and Elliott Rudwick, *Black Detroit and the Rise of the UAW;* Maurice Isserman, *Which Side Were You On? The American Communist Party during the Second World War,* 141–43; Joshua B. Freeman, *In Transit: The Transport Workers Union in New York City, 1933–1966,* 255–56; Michael K. Honey, *Southern Labor and Black Civil Rights: Organizing Memphis Workers,* 116–44; Michael K. Honey, *Black Workers Remember: An Oral History of Segregation, Unionism, and the Freedom Struggle;* Alan Draper, *Conflict of Interest: Organized Labor and the Civil Rights Movement in the South, 1954–1968.*

12. Cheryl Greenberg, "The Black-Jewish Alliance, 1930–1955: Revisiting the 'Golden Age' Hypothesis," 1–2; American Jewish Committee, *On Three Fronts: Thirty-Ninth Annual Report, 1945,* 24–28; Sanford Goldner, *The Jewish People and the Fight for Negro Rights,* 7; Ruth G. Weintraub, *How Secure These Rights? Anti-Semitism in the United States in 1948: An Anti-Defamation League Survey; Pittsburgh Courier,* February 15, 1947; Arthur Hertzberg, *The Jews in America: Four Centuries of an Uneasy Encounter,* 334–36; Bertram Wallace Korn, ed., *Retrospect and Prospect: Essays in Commemoration of the Seventy-Fifth Anniversary of the Founding of the Central Conference of American Rabbis, 1889–1964,* 100–1; James Yaffe, *The American Jews: Portrait of a Split Personality,* 283; William M. Phillips, *An Unillustrious Alliance: The African American and Jewish American Communities,* 78–81; and, more generally, Milton R. Konvitz, "Jews and Civil Rights."

13. Morris Frommer, "The American Jewish Congress: A History, 1914–1950," 519–27; Milton R. Konvitz, ed., *Law and Social Action: Selected Essays of Alexander H. Pekelis;* Morroe Berger and Joseph B. Robinson, *Civil Rights in the United States in 1949: A Balance Sheet of Group Relations;* Joseph B. Robinson, et al., *Assault upon Freedom of Association: A Study of the Southern Attack on the National Association for the Advancement of Colored People;* Gus J. Solomon, *The Jewish Role in the American Civil Rights Movement,* 13; Meier and Bracey, "The NAACP as a Reform Movement, 1909–1965: 'To Reach the Conscience of America,'" 23–24. The American Jewish Congress bimonthly newsletter, *Law and Social Action,* 1946–1950, details the civil rights work of the American Jewish Congress.

14. Robert G. Weisbord and Arthur Stein, *Bittersweet Encounter: The Afro-American and the American Jew,* 64; Leonard Dinnerstein, *Antisemitism in America,* 197–227; Leonard Dinnerstein, *Uneasy at Home: Antisemitism and the American Jewish Experience,* 218–54; L. D. Reddick, "Anti-Semitism among Negroes"; Kenneth B. Clark, "Candor about Negro-Jewish Relations," 8, 14. The Reddick and Clark essays are reprinted in Jack Salzman, ed., *Bridges and Boundaries: African Americans and American Jews,* 79–85, 91–98. See also Gary T. Marx, *Protest and Prejudice: A Study of Belief in the Black Community.*

15. David G. Singer, "An Uneasy Alliance: Jews and Blacks in the United States, 1945–1953"; *Chicago Defender,* May 18, 25, 1946; *Amsterdam News,* June 1, 1946; *Pittsburgh Courier,* November 8, 1947, June 19, 1948, March 19, 1949.

16. Donald S. Strong, *Organized Anti-Semitism in America: The Rise of Group Preju-*

dice during the Decade 1930–40, 138–47, 162–63; Stetson Kennedy, Notes from Interview with Frank Pease, March 26, 1946, in Stetson Kennedy Papers, Schomburg Library, Reel 3; Frank Pease, *Program and Platform, American Defenders,* copy in Kennedy Papers, Schomburg Library, Reel 3; *Miami Life,* August 28, 1943, February 19, 1944, copies in Kennedy Papers, Schomburg Library, Reel 3. On wider patterns of anti-Semitic and pro-fascist activities, see Leo P. Ribuffo, *The Old Christian Right: The Protestant Far Right from the Great Depression to the Cold War;* Michael Barkun, *Religion and the Racist Right: The Origins of the Christian Identity Movement;* Neil Baldwin, *Henry Ford and the Jews: The Mass Production of Hate.*

17. *Miami Herald,* March 17, 21, 22, 24, 1939; *The White Front* (newsletter), March 10, 16, 1939, unpaginated, copies in Stetson Kennedy Papers, Schomburg Library, Reel 1; Stetson Kennedy, untitled manuscript fragment, n.d. (ca. 1941), in Stetson Kennedy Papers, Schomburg Library, Reel 1; William Blanchard, *Racial Nationalism: Principles and Purposes;* Harry Simonhoff, "The Anti-Semitic Crusade in Miami between 1935–1940." On the Khaki Shirts of America, see Francis MacDonnell, *Insidious Foes: The Axis Fifth Column and the American Home Front,* 32, 40–41; Philip Jenkins, *Hoods and Shirts: The Extreme Right in Pennsylvania, 1925–1950,* 101–4; and more generally, Johnpeter Horst Grill and Robert L. Jenkins, "The Nazis and the American South in the 1930s: A Mirror Image?"; Charles Higham, *American Swastika.* For extensive files on Blanchard and the White Front, see Stetson Kennedy Papers, Schomburg Library, Reel 1.

18. *Miami Herald,* May 3, 1939; *The Fiery Cross,* 3 (October 1941), 7; Stetson Kennedy, *The Klan Unmasked,* 220–21.

19. Stella Suberman, telephone interview with author, February 7, 2002; Deborah Dash Moore, *To the Golden Cities: Pursuing the American Jewish Dream in Miami and L.A.,* 154–55, 167–71; Arnold Foster, *A Measure of Freedom: An Anti-Defamation League Report,* 207; "Religious Discrimination in Tourist Accommodation Declines Here, Report Says," *St. Petersburg Times,* May 17, 1953; N. C. Belth, *Barriers: Patterns of Discrimination against Jews,* 37–38, 101–2; *Jewish Floridian,* April 29, 1960; Jim Heyrock, *Prejudice or Privilege?*

20. Paul S. George, "Criminal Justice in Miami, 1896–1930," 151–97; Paul S. George, "Policing Miami's Black Community, 1896–1930," 434–50; Marvin Dunn, *Black Miami in the Twentieth Century,* 131–38; "Sunny Florida," 203–4; David H. Cohn, "The Development and Efficacy of the Negro Police Precinct and Court of the City of Miami," 73, 84, 90; George Lardner Jr., "Miami Declares War: An Epidemic of 'Law and Order.'"

21. *Miami Herald,* April 26, May 18, 19, 1938, May 1, 2, 3, 12, 1939; "Miami Klan Tries to Scare Negro Vote"; Ralph J. Bunche, *The Political Status of the Negro in the Age of FDR,* 199–200, 307–309; Hugh D. Price, *The Negro and Southern Politics: A Chapter of Florida History,* 23; and, on Quigg, W. Y. Bell, "Miami Takes on Negro Policemen," typescript (1945), 8, in National Urban League Papers (hereafter cited as NUL Papers), Part I, Box A75, Folder: Miami 1945.

22. "The Ku Klux Klan Tries a Comeback," 43. On Colescott, see John Roy Carlson, *The Plotters,* 42–44; *Philadelphia Afro-American,* April 6, 1946; Harold Preece, "The Klan Declares War," 3–7; Stetson Kennedy, *Southern Exposure,* 173–74, 176–79, 203–4, 209–12.

On the KKK billboards and other Miami activities, see Stetson Kennedy, *The Klan Unmasked,* 219–57; Jessie Parkhurst Guzman, ed., *Negro Year Book, 1941–1946,* 218; *Pittsburgh Courier,* April 6, 1946. That the Klan billboard in Miami was not an uncommon sight in southern towns and cities, see Borden Deal, "The Sign on the Highway," 141–56; Lewis W. Jones, *Cold Rebellion: The South's Oligarchy in Revolt,* 76. On Klan efforts to enforce residential segregation in Miami, see Sam B. Solomon to Millard Caldwell, November 3, 1945, telegram, Millard Caldwell Papers, Box 18; Wesley E. Garrison to Millard Caldwell, May 4, 1946, ibid.; "Pattern of Violence"; George Earle Owen, "Cross-Burning in Miami"; *Atlanta Daily World,* November 11, December 1, 1945; *Pittsburgh Courier,* August 11, November 17, 1945, November 15, 22, 1947; The *Pittsburgh Courier,* which had a Florida edition, was widely read in the Miami area. The paper employed a black correspondent, John A. Diaz, as its Florida editor. Diaz regularly reported on black Miami for the *Courier* in the 1940s and 1950s.

23. Ira D. Hawthorne to Fuller Warren, August 28, 1951, Fuller Warren Papers, Box 22; *Miami Herald,* July 14, 1951; Charles Abrams, *Forbidden Neighbors: A Study of Prejudice in Housing,* 120–36; Teresa Lenox, "The Carver Village Controversy"; Raymond A. Mohl, "Making the Second Ghetto in Metropolitan Miami, 1940–1960."

24. *Miami Times,* September 29, December 1, 29, 1951; Stetson Kennedy, "Miami: Anteroom to Fascism"; William S. Fairfield, "Florida: Dynamite Law Replaces Lynch Law"; Arnold Forster and Benjamin Epstein, *The Troublemakers: An Anti-Defamation League Report,* 294–99; Teresa Lenox, "The Carver Village Controversy."

25. On the Harry T. Moore killing, see Stetson Kennedy, "Murder by Bombing"; "Bigotry and Bombs in Florida"; Gloster B. Current, "Martyr for a Cause"; "The Bomb Heard around the World"; Joe Alex Morris, "The Truth about the Florida Race Troubles"; Joseph North, *Behind the Florida Bombings;* George Breitman, *Jim Crow Murder of Mr. and Mrs. Harry T. Moore.* On Moore, see Karen Dukess and Richard Hart, "The Invisible Man"; James C. Clark, "Civil Rights Leader Harry T. Moore and the Ku Klux Klan in Florida"; Caroline Emmons Poore, "Striking the First Blow: Harry T. Moore and the Fight for Black Equality in Florida"; Caroline Emmons, "'Somebody Has Got to Do That Work': Harry T. Moore and the Struggle for African-American Voting Rights in Florida"; Ben Green, *Before His Time: The Untold Story of Harry T. Moore, America's First Civil Rights Martyr.*

26. "Jury Investigating Florida Terrorism Indicts Four," 7; *Miami Daily News,* clipping, n.d. (ca. December 1951), Clipping File, Box 16, Papers of the Florida Legislative Investigation Committee (hereafter cited as FLIC Papers); Stetson Kennedy, "Miami: Anteroom to Fascism," 546; Miami City Commission Minutes, December 5, 1951, Miami City Hall; *Miami Herald,* March 26, 1953. For the prosecution of Klansmen for the bombings, see "Florida: First Fruits"; *New York Times,* December 11, 1952, March 26, 1953; *Miami Herald,* March 26, 1953; *Miami Times,* April 4, September 19, 1953; and indictments, affidavits, and dismissals in the following cases: *United States v William Glenn Orwick,* Case No. 8363–M-Cr, November 6, 1953; and *United States v Harvey G. DeRossier,* Case No. 8760–M-Cr, December 17, 1954, both in U.S. District Court Records.

27. Stetson Kennedy, "Florida—A Kluxed State," unpublished article manuscript, n.d., ca. 1952, Stetson Kennedy Papers, Georgia State University, Box 1518, File 62; "Florida: Klan Vs. Conscience"; Charles Abrams, *Forbidden Neighbors: A Study of Prejudice in Housing*, 122–23; Michael Newton, *The Invisible Empire: The Ku Klux Klan in Florida*, 126–29. For the linkage made by southern politicians between Jews and communism, see Edward S. Shapiro, "Anti-Semitism Mississippi Style," 129–51.

28. On postwar Jewish migration to Miami, see Ira M. Sheskin, *Demographic Study of the Greater Miami Jewish Community: Summary Report*, 4; Deborah Dash Moore, "Jewish Migration in Postwar America: The Case of Miami and Los Angeles"; Deborah Dash Moore, *To the Golden Cities: Pursuing the American Jewish Dream in Miami and L.A.*, 25–52. On black population growth in Miami and Dade County during these years, see Raymond A. Mohl, "The Settlement of Blacks in South Florida," 112–19.

29. Ed Cony, "Miami Race Plan." On Florida race relations in the wake of the Supreme Court's school integration decision, see David R. Colburn, "Florida's Governors Confront the *Brown* Decision: A Case of the Constitutional Politics of School Desegregation, 1954–1970"; Neil R. McMillen, *The Citizens' Council: Organized Resistance to the Second Reconstruction, 1954–64*, 100–2. The progress of school desegregation in Miami during this period can be followed in *Southern School News*, 1954–1960, a monthly publication that tracked integration in the South.

30. Ruth W. Perry to Roy Wilkins, October 31, 1958, Papers of the National Association for the Advancement of Colored People (hereafter cited as NAACP Papers), Part III, Box C23. On the FLIC, see Steven F. Lawson, "The Florida Legislative Investigation Committee and the Constitutional Readjustment of Race Relations, 1956–1963." For similar committees in other states, see M. J. Heale, *McCarthy's Americans: Red Scare Politics in State and Nation, 1935–1965;* Yasuhiro Katagiri, *The Mississippi State Sovereignty Commission: Civil Rights and States' Rights;* Calvin Trillin, "State Secrets"; Anne Braden, *House Un-American Activities Committee: Bulwark of Segregation* (Los Angeles: National Committee to Abolish the House Un-American Activities Committee, 1964).

31. Deborah Dash Moore, *To the Golden Cities: Pursuing the American Jewish Dream in Miami and L.A.*, 173, 176; Jack Gordon, telephone interviews with author, October 25, December 6, December 14, 2001; Minutes of Board Meeting, Greater Miami Chapter, American Civil Liberties Union, July 3, 1956, Jack Gordon Papers, Box 1B, Folder: ACLU; Florence Morgenroth, "Organization and Activities of the American Civil Liberties Union in Miami, 1955–1966," 9–29.

32. Thalia [Stern] Broudy, telephone interview with author, July 30, 2002; Cindy Thorner, telephone interview with author, December 18, 2002; Shirley Zoloth, "Urgent Statement," n.d. (ca. October 1960), Miami Branch, National Council of Jewish Women, Gordon Papers, Box 17, Folder: Graham–Personal; Rabbi Leon Kronish, "Open Letter to the Greater Miami Council of Churches and to the Greater Miami Ministerial Association," October 11, 1960, Gordon Papers, Box 16, Folder: School Campaign; "Gordon Linked with Bible Suit," *Florida Free-Press* (September 1960), 1–2; *Jewish Floridian*, October 7, 1960; Florence Morgenroth, "Organization and Activities of the American Civil

Liberties Union in Miami, 1955–1966," 78–79. On the Bible suit, see "Groundless Fears," [American Jewish Congress] *Congress Bi-Weekly;* Richard Cohen, "Decision in Miami," *Congress Bi-Weekly.* For division among Miami Jews on the Bible-reading litigation, see Shad Polier (AJCongress), Open Letter to Colleagues, November 4, 1960, in NAACP Papers, Part III, Box A100, Folder: Desegregation Schools, 1959–65, Library of Congress; J. J. Goldberg, *Jewish Power: Inside the American Jewish Establishment,* 122–24.

33. *Miami News,* March 7, 1955, July 26, 1956; *Miami Herald,* July 7, 25, 1956; *Tampa Morning Tribune,* July 26, 27, 31, 1956; Hampton Dunn, "Miami's Jack Orr First Dixie Politician to Support Openly Integration Move"; Lawrence Renfroe to Claude Pepper, October 16, 1957, Claude Pepper Papers, Box 401B/15/8; Bernice Ullrich to Mildred Scott Olmsted, October 6, 27, 1954, Records of the Women's International League for Peace and Freedom (hereafter cited as WILPF Records), microfilm edition, Reel 130.88; Florida Council on Human Relations, Monthly Report, May 1958, Southern Regional Council Papers (hereafter cited as SRC Papers), microfilm edition, Reel 141; Ed Seney, "John B. Orr—The Man Who Shocked the State"; Wilma Dykeman and James Stokely, *Neither Black nor White,* 357–59; Jack Gordon to Rabbi Jonah E. Caplan, September 10, 1958, Gordon Papers, Box 17, Folder: Personal 1958.

34. Perry to Wilkins, October 31, 1958, NAACP Papers, Part III, Box C23.

35. For the synagogue bombings and the Confederate Underground, see H. V. Branch, "Report on Miami and Jacksonville Bombings," May 3, 1958, FLIC Papers, Box 1, File 20; Nathan Perlmutter, "Bombing in Miami: Anti-Semitism and the Segregationists"; "Bombings and Hate Sheets," *Congress Bi-Weekly,* 15; Melissa Fay Greene, *The Temple Bombing,* 2, 9, 225, 245, 250; Jackson Toby, "Bombing in Nashville: A Jewish Center and the Desegregation Struggle"; *Southern School News* 4 (April 1958), 9; 4 (May 1958), 5; 4 (June 1958), 13; *The Southern Patriot* 10 (November 1952), 4. Bill Hendrix of the Florida KKK also served as "Adjutant General" of the "American Confederate Army," which was dedicated to segregation and racial purity. See "Join the American Confederate Army," flyer, n.d., FLIC Papers, Box 17; Stetson Kennedy, "Inside the Confederate Army," [New York] *Sunday Compass Magazine,* copy in Kennedy Papers, Georgia State University, Box 1518, File 64.

36. Nathan Perlmutter, "Bombing in Miami: Anti-Semitism and the Segregationists," 499, 501; Harry L. Golden and Julian Scheer, "Klan without Hoods"; Elizabeth Geyer, "The 'New' Ku Klux Klan"; Florida Council on Human Relations, Monthly Report, June 1959, SRC Papers, Reel 141. See also Numan V. Bartley, *The Rise of Massive Resistance: Race and Politics in the South during the 1950s;* and Francis M. Wilhoit, *The Politics of Massive Resistance.*

37. Edward James Smythe to Fuller Warren, December 31, 1951, Warren Papers, Box 64; "A Lover of the South" to Warren, December 7, 1951, ibid., Box 22; Elizabeth Riefler to Warren, December 25, 1951, ibid., Box 64.

38. H. Bond Bliss to LeRoy Collins, March 21, 1960; Myrtle Pendrey to Collins, March 24, 1960; Dorothy C. Busey to Collins, March 22, 1960; George E. Deatherrage to Collins, March 20, 1960; J. H. McDaniel to Collins, March 22, 1960; D. Clarence McConnell to Collins, March 21, 1960; Mrs. J. H. Bondeson to Collins, March 21, 1960; Dana Wier to

Collins, March 21, 1960, all in LeRoy Collins Papers, Box 47, University of South Florida Library, Tampa.

39. Bella Fisher to Civil Rights Congress, December 16, 1948, in Papers of the Civil Rights Congress (hereafter cited as CRC Papers), microfilm edition, Part II, Reel 24; Ruth Perry, "Along Freedom's Road," *Miami Times,* in Ruth W. Perry Papers, Box 1, Folder 3; Perry to Wilkins, October 31, 1958, NAACP Papers, Part III, Box C23.

40. "Fighting the Klan," *The Southern Patriot;* Miami City Commission Minutes, December 5, 1951; Deborah Dash Moore, *To the Golden Cities Pursuing the American Jewish Dream in Miami and L.A.,* 153–55; Michael Newton, *The Invisible Empire: The Ku Klux Klan in Florida,* 129; *Pittsburgh Courier,* May 4, 1946.

41. Gordon interview, December 14, 2001; June Gordon to Lena K. Ray, January 19, 1960, April 3, 1962, in Emma Lazarus Federation Papers, Box 3, Folders 1 and 2; Joyce Antler, "Between Culture and Politics: The Emma Lazarus Federation of Jewish Women's Clubs and the Promulgation of Women's History, 1944–1989," 281; Richard K. Fink to All Members of the American Civil Liberties Union Residing in Dade County, Fla., n.d. (ca. July 1955), Box 1, File 1, Florida ACLU Papers; Shirley M. Zoloth to Bernice Ullrich, September 24, 1954, Gordon Papers, Box 10, Folder: Desegregation; Zoloth to Dade County Board of Public Instruction, September 18, 1957, ibid.; Zoloth to Helen Raebeck, July 12, 1960, ibid.

42. *Pittsburgh Courier,* November 15, 1947, May 26, 1956; Matilda "Bobbi" Graff, Voter Registration Files, 1953, Graff Scrapbook, copies in author's possession; Henry A. Green, *Gesher Vakesher, Bridges and Bonds: The Life of Leon Kronish,* 106–10; Gladys Rosen, "The Rabbi in Miami—A Case History," 33–40; Paul S. George, *Visions, Accomplishments, Challenges: Mount Sinai Medical Center of Greater Miami, 1949–1984,* 50–51; "'Miracle' Occurs at Miami Beach," *The Southern Patriot;* "Miami Welcomes Negro Baptists," *St. Petersburg Times,* September 13, 1953; Deborah Dash Moore, *To the Golden Cities: Pursuing the American Jewish Dream in Miami and L.A.,* 167–71.

43. Paul Seiderman (ADL) to LeRoy Collins, July 23, August 28, 1956, Collins Papers, Box 33, Florida State Archives; Nathan B. Rood (AJCommittee) to Collins, March 29, 1960, ibid.; Nathan Perlmutter (ADL) to William Rose, June 9, 1960, Papers of Governor's Commission on Race Relations, Box 3, Florida State Archives; Haskell L. Lazere (AJCongress) to William Rose, June 7, 1960, ibid., Box 4.

44. Cheryl Greenberg, "The Southern Jewish Community and the Struggle for Civil Rights," 128, 163.

45. *Miami Herald,* September 17, 1955; Aldon C. Taft, "Miami Spurns Integration."

46. Esther Levine, "Southern Jewish Views on Segregation," 524–27; American Jewish Congress, "Proceedings of the Convention," 1, 2; Michael E. Staub, *Torn at the Roots: The Crisis of Jewish Liberalism in Postwar America,* 19–22.

47. *Jewish Floridian,* January 9, February 6, March 20, June 3, 1959; *Miami Herald,* September 17, 1955.

48. Cheryl Greenberg, "The Southern Jewish Community and the Struggle for Civil Rights," 134; Marc Dollinger, "'Hamans' and 'Torquemadas': Southern and Northern Jewish Responses to the Civil Rights Movement, 1945–1965," 68, 71; Marc Dollinger,

Quest for Inclusion: Jews and Liberalism in Modern America; Leonard Dinnerstein, "Southern Jewry and the Desegregation Crisis, 1954–1970"; Leonard Dinnerstein, "American Jews and the Civil Rights Movement"; Clive Webb, *Fight against Fear: Southern Jews and Black Civil Rights,* xv.

On these issues, see also Charles Mantinband, "Integration and the Southern Jew"; Theodore Lowi, "Southern Jews: The Two Communities"; Will Maslow, "Negro-Jewish Relations"; Naomi W. Cohen, *Not Free to Desist: The American Jewish Committee, 1906–1966,* 390–95; Allen Krause, "Rabbis and Negro Rights in the South, 1954–1967"; Jack Nelson, *Terror in the Night: The Klan's Campaign against the Jews;* Deborah Dash Moore, "Separate Paths: Blacks and Jews in the Twentieth-Century South"; Seth Forman, "The Unbearable Whiteness of Being Jewish: Desegregation in the South and the Crisis of Jewish Liberalism"; David Goldfield, "A Sense of Place: Jews, Blacks, and White Gentiles in the American South"; Clive Webb, "Closing Ranks: Montgomery Jews and Civil Rights, 1954–1960"; Leonard Rogoff, *Homelands: Southern Jewish Identity in Durham and Chapel Hill, North Carolina,* 223–31.

49. Wilma Dykeman and James Stokely, "McCarthyism under the Magnolias," 6; Louis Harap, "Nightmare in Miami"; "Tempest in Miami," *The Nation;* Leslie B. Bain, "Red Hunt in Miami: Who Formed the Posse?"; Frank Donner, "The Miami Formula: An Exposé of Grass-Roots McCarthyism,"; Steven F. Lawson, "The Florida Legislative Investigation Committee and the Constitutional Readjustment of Race Relations, 1956–1963," 296–325; Deborah Dash Moore, *To the Golden Cities: Pursuing the American Jewish Dream in Miami and L.A.,* 172–76; Randall Kennedy, "Contrasting Fates of Repression: A Comment on Gibson v. Florida Legislative Investigation Committee." When the legislative attack on the Miami NAACP stalled, the McCarthyites in Tallahassee moved on to an easier target—gay students and professors in the universities. See James T. Sears, *Lonely Hunters: An Oral History of Lesbian and Gay Southern Life, 1948–1968,* 48–84. For the latest critical study of McCarthyism, see Ellen Schrecker, *Many Are the Crimes: McCarthyism in America.* For a revisionist study of McCarthy, see Arthur Herman, *Joseph McCarthy: Reexamining the Life and Legacy of America's Most Hated Senator.* For an analysis of the shifting historiography of Cold War McCarthyism, see Jacob Weisberg, "Cold War without End."

50. Matilda "Bobbi" Graff, interviews with author, May 18, 1992, September 30, 1992, January 29, 1993, April 26, 1994, December 19, 2000; Graff, telephone interview, March 8, 2002. Bobbi Graff also shared with me her FBI file, obtained under the Freedom of Information Act. Graff was a target of FBI investigators and informers from 1942 until 1972.

51. Graff interviews, May 18, 1992, December 19, 2000; Matilda Graff, "The Historic Continuity of the Civil Rights Movement" (manuscript, 1971), 1–14, published as part II of this book; U. S. House of Representatives, Committee on Un-American Activities, *Report on Civil Rights Congress as a Communist Front Organization,* House Report No. 1115 (Washington: U.S. Government Printing Office, 1947).

52. Harvard Sitkoff, *A New Deal for Blacks: The Emergence of Civil Rights as a National*

Issue, The Depression Decade, 140; Mark Naison, "The Communist Party in Harlem in the Early Depression Years: A Case Study in the Reinterpretation of American Communism"; Gerald Horne, "The Red and the Black: The Communist Party and African-Americans in Historical Perspective," 229. See also William A. Nolan, *Communism versus the Negro;* Wilson Record, *The Negro and the Communist Party;* Wilson Record, *Race and Radicalism: The* NAACP *and the Communist Party in Conflict;* Mark Solomon, *The Cry Was Unity: Communists and African Americans, 1917–1936;* Gerald Horne, *Black and Red: W.E.B. Du Bois and the Afro-American Response to the Cold War, 1944–1963;* Mark Naison, *Communists in Harlem during the Depression;* Robin D. G. Kelley, *Hammer and Hoe: Alabama Communists during the Great Depression.* On Jews in the Communist Party, see Nathan Glazer, *The Social Basis of American Communism,* 130–68; Arthur Liebman, *Jews and the Left,* 55–66; Paul Lyons, *Philadelphia Communists, 1936–1956,* 72–80.

53. William L. Patterson, *The Man Who Cried Genocide;* Gerald Horne, *Communist Front? The Civil Rights Congress, 1946–1956;* Charles H. Martin, "The International Labor Defense and Black America"; Lawrence S. Wittner, "The National Negro Congress: A Reassessment"; Earl Ofari Hutchinson, *Blacks and Reds: Race and Class in Conflict, 1919–1990,* 195–221.

54. Josh Sides, "'You Understand My Condition': The Civil Rights Congress in the Los Angeles African-American Community, 1946–1952," 235; Edward C. Pintzuk, *Reds, Racial Justice, and Civil Liberties: Michigan Communists during the Cold War,* 71–116; Gerald Horne, *Communist Front? The Civil Rights Congress, 1946–1956,* 13–51.

55. Graff interview, December 19, 2000; Gordon interview, December 6, 2001; Sandi Wisenberg, "Left on the Beach," *Miami Herald, Tropic Magazine,* 10–15.

56. Graff interviews, May 18, 1992, September 30, 1992, January 29, 1993; Graff, telephone interview, March 8, 2002; Bella Fisher to Civil Rights Congress, July 26, 1948, CRC Papers, Part II, Reel 24; Fisher to William L. Patterson, September 13, 1948, ibid.; Communist Party of Central Florida, "It's Happening Here," mimeo flyer, n.d. (ca. 1948), Caldwell Papers, Box 15; Coe to Max Baer, May 20, 1948, Coe Papers, Box 1; Benemovsky Case File, Coe Papers, Box 31, which includes correspondence and legal briefs; Sarah Hart Brown, *Standing against Dragons: Three Southern Lawyers in an Era of Fear,* 69–70. On Flynn's visit to Miami, see Helen C. Camp, *Iron in Her Soul: Elizabeth Gurley Flynn and the American Left,* 208.

57. "Testimony of James Nimmo," Dade County Grand Jury, Investigation into Communistic Activities in Miami, Florida, October 27–28, 1954, FLIC Papers, Box 6; "Statement of James Nimmo," in U.S. House of Representatives, Committee on Un-American Activities, *Investigation of Communist Activities in the State of Florida,* Parts I and II, November 29, 30, December 1, 1954, 7426–48; James Nimmo, videotape interview with Gregory Bush, University of Miami, 1987, copy of videotape in author's possession. On black Bahamian immigrants in Miami, see Raymond A. Mohl, "Black Immigrants: Bahamians in Early Twentieth-Century Miami." On Miami's UNIA activities, see Robert A. Hill, ed., *The Marcus Garvey and Universal Negro Improvement Association Papers,* III,

513–15; VI, 594–95; VII, 124, 133–34, 141–42, 166–71; *Negro World,* June 11, 1927, April 7, 1928; Kip Vought, "Racial Stirrings in Colored Town: The UNIA in Miami during the 1920s."

58. "Testimony of Charles Smolikoff," Dade County Grand Jury Investigation, June 25, 1954, FLIC Papers, Box 6; Ellis S. Rubin, *Report on Investigation of Subversive Activities in Florida,* 30–45, Smolikoff reference on p. 32; Alex Lichtenstein, "Exclusion, Fair Employment, or Interracial Unionism: Race Relations in Florida's Shipyards during World War II." On Smolikoff's commitment to interracialism in the Shipbuilders Union, see Charles N. Smolikoff to Thomas J. Gallagher, December 27, 1943, Archives of the Industrial Union of Marine and Shipbuilding Workers of America, Series II, Subseries 4, Box 12. On Smolikoff's interracial work in the TWU, see Charles N. Smolikoff to Douglas L. MacMahon, May 9, June 29, September 1, 1946, Papers of the Transport Workers Union of America (hereafter cited as TWU Papers), Local 500 File; Smolikoff to Art Shields, undated (ca. August 1946), ibid.; *Miami Herald,* December 26, 1944, August 6, 1946.

59. Graff interviews, May 18, 1992, January 29, 1993; *Miami Daily News,* February 28, 1948; Gail Gropper to Coe, October 8, 1948, Coe Papers, Box 1; Marjorie Haynes to Coe, December 10, 1948, ibid.; Curtis D. MacDougall, *Gideon's Army,* III, 737–39; Harvey Klehr and John Earl Haynes, *The American Communist Movement: Storming Heaven Itself,* 113–22; Sarah Hart Brown, "Pensacola Progressive: John Moreno Coe and the Campaign of 1948"; and, for a fuller discussion of John M. Coe's civil rights and civil liberties work in Florida during the postwar red scare, Sarah Hart Brown, *Standing against Dragons: Three Southern Lawyers in an Era of Fear.*

60. Haynes to Coe, March 1, 14, 1949, Coe Papers, Box 2; Gropper to Coe, April 16, 1949, ibid., Box 2; Gropper to Miriam Arons, June 22, 1949, ibid., Box 2; Al Rosenberg to Coe, August 25, 1950; ibid., Box 2; *Miami Progressive* 1 (May 1949), ibid., Box 2; Al Rosenberg, "This Thing Called 'Fear,'" *The Florida Progressive,* ibid., Box 2; Al Rosenberg, "Officials Put 'Squeeze' on Miami Y.P.A.," *The Florida Progressive,* ibid., Box 2; "Miamians Stage Anti-Mundt Rally," *The Florida Progressive,* ibid., Box 2.

61. Graff interview, September 30, 1992; Patterson to Graff, October 4, 1949, CRC Papers, Part II, Reel 24.

62. Greater Miami Right to Work Committee, "An Appeal to Reason," mimeographed flyer, n.d. (ca. 1950), CRC Papers, Part II, Reel 24; Bella Fisher to Len Goldsmith, December 16, 1948, ibid.; Graff to Leon Josephson, March 24, 1949, ibid.; Patterson to Graff, October 4, 1949, ibid.; *Pittsburgh Courier,* December 25, 1948; *National Guardian,* April 5, 1950. On left-wing labor organizing in Miami, see also Eric Tscheschlok, "'So Goes the Negro': Race and Labor in Miami, 1940–1963"; Alex Lichtenstein, "'Scientific Unionism' and the 'Negro Question': Communists and the Transport Workers Union in Miami, 1944–1949"; Alex Lichtenstein, "Putting Labor's House in Order: The Transport Workers Union and Labor Anti-Communism in Miami during the 1940s."

63. Patterson to Graff, August 13, 1949, CRC Papers, Part II, Reel 24; Graff to Patterson, August 7, December 12, 1949, ibid.; Matilda Graff, "What's Behind the Anti-Negro Terror"; Graff interview, September 30, 1992; Graff, telephone interview, March 8, 2002. In interviews, Graff related that she asked the *Guardian* to omit her by-line from the

Groveland article. She was already being tracked by the FBI and hoped to avoid further harassment. On Groveland, see also Steven F. Lawson, David R. Colburn, and Darryl Paulson, "Groveland: Florida's Little Scottsboro"; and Ben Green, *Before His Time: The Untold Story of Harry T. Moore, America's First Civil Rights Martyr,* 81–153.

64. Len Goldsmith to Patterson, n.d. (ca. March 1949), CRC Papers, Part II, Reel 24; Patterson to Graff, March 28, June 22, August 19, December 14, 1949, ibid.; Graff to Patterson, March 31, July 9, August 17, 1949, ibid.; Graff interview, September 30, 1992; "Editorial: Governor Fuller Warren," *The Crisis;* Michael Newton, *The Invisible Empire: The Ku Klux Klan in Florida,* 106–39; Ben Green, *Before His Time: The Untold Story of Harry T. Moore, America's First Civil Rights Martyr,* 154–97.

65. "Testimony of Victor Emanuel," Dade County Grand Jury Investigation, June 29, 1954, FLIC Papers, Box 6; Graff to Josephson, March 24, 1949, CRC Papers, Part II, Reel 24; Goldsmith to Patterson, n.d. (ca. March 1949), ibid.; Patterson to Graff, March 28, 1949, ibid.; Graff to Coe, Nov. 1, 1951, Coe Papers, Box 2; Coe to Graff, November 3, 1951, ibid.; Graff FBI File; Graff interviews, September 30, 1992, April 26, 1994; *Miami Daily News,* March 16, 1949; Ellis S. Rubin, *Report on Investigation of Subversive Activities in Florida,* 38–45; "Statement of James Nimmo," in U.S. House of Representatives, Committee on Un-American Activities, *Investigation of Communist Activities in the State of Florida,* Parts I and II, November 29, 30, December 1, 1954, 7426–48; Michael J. Quill, *Michael J. Quill Answers the Rantings of the Edwards-Smolikoff Open Letter,* pamphlet, in TWU Papers, Local 500 File; Frank J. Donner, *The Un-Americans,* 154–56; Cedric Belfrage, *The American Inquisition, 1945–1960,* 220–23; Horne, *Communist Front? The Civil Rights Congress, 1946–1956,* 190–95.

66. Jeff Broadwater, *Eisenhower and the Anti-Communist Crusade,* 168–75; Richard M. Fried, *Nightmare in Red: The McCarthy Era in Perspective,* 53–54, 83–84, 116–18, 171–72; Harvey Klehr and John Earl Haynes, *The American Communist Movement: Storming Heaven Itself,* 126–36; M. J. Heale, *American Anticommunism: Combating the Enemy Within, 1830–1970,* 122–66; John E. Haynes, *Red Scare or Red Menace? American Communism and Anticommunism in the Cold War Era,* 163–69; Frank J. Donner, "The Congressional Pillory"; Michal R. Belknap, *Cold War Political Justice: The Smith Act, the Communist Party, and American Civil Liberties;* Mary Sperling McAuliffe, *Crisis on the Left: Cold War Politics and American Liberals, 1947–1954,* 78–80, 132–44; Harold W. Chase, *Security and Liberty: The Problem of Native Communists, 1947–1955.*

67. Graff to Patterson, March 31, August 17, 1949, May 4, 1950, CRC Papers, Part II, Reel 24; Alfred Neufeld to Patterson, May 12, 1949, ibid.

68. Milton Wolff to James Nimmo, March 3, 1950, CRC Papers, Part II, Reel 24; Patterson to Graff, April 12, 1950, ibid.

69. Graff to Patterson, July 9, December 12, 1949, March 17, 1950, CRC Papers, Part II, Reel 24; Patterson to Graff, August 19, December 14, 1949, ibid.; Walter White to Roger Armster, telegram, March 7, 1949, NAACP Papers, Group II, Box C-33; Graff interview, September 30, 1992; Gerald Horne, "Civil Rights Congress," 134–35.

70. For evidence of internal problems in the Miami NAACP, see Harry T. Moore to Lucille Black, December 29, 1947, NAACP Papers, Group II, Box C-35; Franklin H. Wil-

liams to Gloster B. Current, December 5, 1949, ibid.; I. C. Mickens to Current, May 6, 1950, ibid., Box C-33; R. H. Bennett to Walter White, August 30, 1950, ibid.; Ramona Lowe to Roy Wilkins, September 21, 1950, ibid.; Vashti Coleman to White, June 8, 1951, ibid.; Inez Armster to Black, September 25, 1951, ibid.; Edward T. Graham to Black, October 1, 1951, ibid.

71. Williams to Current, December 5, 1949, NAACP Papers, Group II, Box C-35; Caroline Emmons Poore, "Striking the First Blow: Harry T. Moore and the Fight for Black Equality in Florida," 21–61, 78–86; Ben Green, *Before His Time: The Untold Story of Harry T. Moore, America's First Civil Rights Martyr*, 4, 109–31, 155–64, 176–79; William G. Carleton and Hugh Douglas Price, "America's Newest Voter: A Florida Case Study"; Jake C. Miller, "Harry T. Moore's Campaign for Racial Equality"; and, on the teacher salary issue, Mark V. Tushnet, *The NAACP's Legal Strategy against Segregated Education, 1925–1950*, 94–97.

72. Graff to Patterson, November 20, 1950, May 8, 1951, CRC Papers, Part II, Reel 4; Patterson to Graff, May 12, 1951, ibid.; Graff to Aubrey Grossman, May 6, 1952, CRC Papers, Part II, Reel 24; Patterson to Graff, May 19, 1952, ibid.; Graff to Patterson, June 30, 1952, ibid.; Graff to Coe, November 21, 1951, Coe Papers, Box 2; *Miami Herald*, September 1, 1954; Graff FBI File; Graff interviews, September 30, 1992, April 26, 1994; Graff, telephone interview, March 8, 2002; Gerald Horne, *Communist Front? The Civil Rights Congress, 1946–1956*, 155–63; Jeffrey M. Marker, "The Jewish Community and the Case of Julius and Ethel Rosenberg"; Deborah Dash Moore, "Reconsidering the Rosenbergs: Symbol and Substance in Second Generation American Jewish Consciousness"; and, on the Rosenberg case more generally, Ronald Radosh and Joyce Milton, *The Rosenberg File: A Search for the Truth*.

73. Graff interviews, May 18, September 30, 1992; Graff, Voter Registration Files, 1953; "Beachhead in Miami," *Ebony*.

74. On the New Orleans hearings, see John A. Salmond, "'The Great Southern Commie Hunt': Aubrey Williams, the Southern Conference Educational Fund, and the Internal Security Subcommittee"; Dorothy M. Zellner, "Red Roadshow: Eastland in New Orleans, 1954"; Sarah Hart Brown, *Standing against Dragons: Three Southern Lawyers in an Era of Fear*, 115–39. On the Miami witch-hunt, see "'Red' Terror in Dade County, Florida," *National Guardian*; "Miami's 'Red' Terror Takes on an Anti-Semitic Hue," *National Guardian*; *Daily Worker*, September 16, December 23, 30, 31, 1954; Royal W. France, "Miami Miasma"; Louis Harap, "Nightmare in Miami," 4–9; Leslie B. Bain, "Red Hunt in Miami: Who Formed the Posse?" 110–12; Frank J. Donner, "The Miami Formula: An Exposé of Grass-Roots McCarthyism," 65–71; U.S. House of Representatives, Committee on Un-American Activities, *Investigation of Communist Activities in the State of Florida*; Ellis S. Rubin, *Report on Investigation of Subversive Activities in Florida*, 46–52; Michael Linfield, *Freedom under Fire: U.S. Civil Liberties in Times of War*, 108; Milton R. Konvitz, *Expanding Liberties: Freedom's Gains in Postwar America*, 80–85.

75. Graff interview, April 26, 1994; Graff, telephone interview, March 8, 2002; Matilda Graff, "A Child Is Born in Fear"; John M. Coe to Edward Maxted, July 5, 1954, Coe Papers, Box 3. On Miami exiles in Mexico, see Diana Anhalt, "Resuscitating Corpses: Memories

of Political Exile in Mexico"; Diana Anhalt, *A Gathering of Fugitives: American Political Expatriates in Mexico, 1948–1965.*

76. Milton Zoloth, telephone interview with author, December 15, 2000; Shirley Zoloth, telephone interview, October 2, 1992; Zoloth to Ullrich, September 24, 1954, Gordon Papers, Box 10; "Fight to Defend Philly Schools Continues," [Pennsylvania Civil Rights Congress] *Let Freedom Ring,* newsletter, in CRC Papers, Part II, Reel 30; "Philadelphia Fights Back against Witch-hunters in Its Schools," *National Guardian;* David Caute, *The Great Fear: The Anti-Communist Purge under Truman and Eisenhower,* 419–20, 555; Philip Jenkins, *The Cold War at Home: The Red Scare in Pennsylvania, 1945–1960,* 118–41.

77. Graff interview, December 26, 2001; SAC, Miami to Director, FBI, August 30, 1951, July 1, 1952, March 25, 1954, FBI Investigation and Surveillance Records, Women's International League for Peace and Freedom Collection, Series 7, Box 2; Report from Miami, November 14, 1952, June 24, 1953, ibid.; Bernice Ullrich, "Civil Rights Being Violated," *Miami Herald;* Zoloth to Ullrich, September 24, 1954, Gordon Papers, Box 10; Ullrich to Mildred Scott Olmsted, October 6, 1954, WILPF Records, Reel 130.88; Catherine Rumball to Hanna Barshak, October 22, 1954, ibid., Reel 130.87; Rumball to Olmsted, November 21, 1954, ibid., Reel 130.87; Robbie Lieberman, *The Strangest Dream: Communism, Anticommunism, and the U.S. Peace Movement, 1945–1963,* 128–29. The WILPF, Program of Annual Meeting, June 1957, held in Miami Beach, listed Shirley Zoloth as vice president of Miami WILPF, in WILPF Records, Reel 130.4.

78. Zoloth, interviews with author, August 23, 1991, December 14, 1992; Broudy interview, July 30, 2002; Gordon interviews, October 25, December 4, December 6, 2001; Leonard Turkel, interview with author, Miami, April 25, 2002; Marilynn Bloom, telephone interview with author, August 6, 2002; Zoloth to [Dade County] Board of Public Instruction, September 18, 1957, Gordon Papers, Box 10; Zoloth to Raebeck, July 12, 1960, ibid.; Shirley Zoloth, Clipping Scrapbook, 1957–1959, in author's possession; *Miami Herald,* Jan. 15, 1990.

79. David R. Colburn and Richard K. Scher, *Florida's Gubernatorial Politics in the Twentieth Century,* 220–36; Helen L. Jacobstein, *The Segregation Factor in the Florida Democratic Gubernatorial Primary of 1956; Miami News,* September 18, 1957; Ed Cony, "Miami Race Plan"; Nathan Perlmutter, "Bombing in Miami: Anti-Semitism and the Segregationists."

80. For the attack on the Miami NAACP, see Steven F. Lawson, "The Florida Legislative Investigation Committee and the Constitutional Readjustment of Race Relations, 1956–1963"; Bonnie Stark, "McCarthyism in Florida: Charley Johns and the Florida Legislative Investigation Committee, July 1956 to July 1965," 21–87; Mark V. Tushnet, *Making Civil Rights Law: Thurgood Marshall and the Supreme Court, 1936–1961,* 296–300; Milton R. Konvitz, *Expanding Liberties: Freedom's Gains in Postwar America,* 80–85; *Theodore Gibson v. Florida Legislative Investigation Committee* 372 U.S. 539 (1963); "Father Theodore R. Gibson," *The Crisis;* Robert W. Saunders to Roy Wilkins, November 6, 1959, Robert W. Saunders Papers, Box 3. A good account of Florida NAACP activities in the 1950s can be found in Robert W. Saunders, *Bridging the Gap: Continuing the Florida*

NAACP *Legacy of Harry T. Moore, 1952–1966*. On the Miami and Tallahassee bus boycotts, see Saunders to Gloster B. Current, January 19, 1957, NAACP Papers, Group III, Box C-25; Ruth W. Perry to Roy Wilkins, October 31, 1958, ibid.; Charles U. Smith and Lewis M. Killian, *The Tallahassee Bus Protest;* Charles U. Smith, ed., *The Civil Rights Movement in Florida and the United States;* David L. Chappell, *Inside Agitators: White Southerners in the Civil Rights Movement*, 84–96. For the Miami NAACP fight for school integration, see *Southern School News* 5 (September 1958), 9; *Miami Herald*, August 19, September 14, 18, 26, 1958; *Miami News,* September 18, 1958. For the Wilkins comment, see *Miami News,* November 24, 1958.

81. Florida Council on Human Relations, Monthly Reports, December 1956, February 1957, Southern Regional Council Papers (hereafter cited as SRC Papers), microfilm edition, Reel 142; *Miami Times,* February 16, 1952; M.A.F. Ritchie, "The Fourth 'R' in Miami: A City Works at Human Relations"; Ullrich to Olmsted, October 6, 1954, WILPF Papers, Reel 130.88; *Miami News,* February 2, 1957, January 30, 1959; Dade County Council on Community Relations, Community Planning Committee, *Dade County Schools and Desegregation;* Zoloth, Clipping Scrapbook, 1957–1959; Florida Council on Human Relations, "Monthly Report of Intern, Jane Leeds," SRC Papers, Reel 142.

82. Thalia Stern to James R. Robinson, October 10, 1958, CORE Papers, Reel 19; Zoloth interviews, August 23, 1991, October 2, 1992; Anna Holden, *A First Step toward School Integration;* Zoloth Clipping Scrapbook, clippings from Miami press, 1958; *Miami Herald,* November 20, December 28, 1958; *Miami Times,* December 27, 1958, February 21, 1959; Martin Waldron, "Dade's Token Gesture"; Joe Hall, "Statement of Joe Hall, Superintendent of Schools, Dade County, Fla."; Ed Cony, "Miami Race Plan"; *Southern School News* 5 (October 1958), 17. On Nashville, see August Meier and Elliott Rudwick, CORE: *A Study in the Civil Rights Movement,* 81, 85–86; and, more generally, J. W. Peltason, *Fifty-Eight Lonely Men: Southern Federal Judges and School Desegregation,* 154–78; Hugh Davis Graham, *Crisis in Print: Desegregation and the Press in Tennessee,* 154–87. At the same time they were organizing Miami CORE, Shirley Zoloth and Barbara Gordon were also corresponding with James A. Dombrowski of the Southern Conference Education Fund on school desegregation issues in South Florida. See Zoloth to James A. Dombrowski, April 13, 1959, Coe Papers, Box 3; Gordon to Dombrowski, undated (ca. April 1959), ibid.

83. August Meier and Elliott Rudwick, CORE: *A Study in the Civil Rights Movement,* 83; Robinson to Stern, October 13, November 9, 18, December 2, 1958, CORE Papers, Reel 19; Robinson to Edward T. Graham, November 11, 1958, ibid.; Graham to Robinson, December 29, 1958, ibid.

84. August Meier and Elliott Rudwick, CORE: *A Study in the Civil Rights Movement,* 3–98; Mary Kimbrough and Margaret W. Dagen, *Victory without Violence: The First Ten Years of the St. Louis Committee of Racial Equality (CORE), 1947–1957,* 1–2, 11–17; Sudarshan Kapur, *Raising Up a Prophet: The African-American Encounter with Gandhi,* 118–23; Rhoda Lois Blumberg, *Civil Rights: The 1960s Freedom Struggle,* 46–47; James Farmer, *Lay Bare the Heart: An Autobiography of the Civil Rights Movement,* 101–16. On Bayard Rustin in Montgomery, see Bayard Rustin, "Montgomery Diary"; Jervis Ander-

son, *Bayard Rustin: Troubles I've Seen,* 183–96; Daniel Levine, *Bayard Rustin and the Civil Rights Movement,* 51–56, 78–87; Murray Friedman, "The Civil Rights Movement and the Reemergence of the Left." For a contemporary sociological study of CORE activists, see Inge Powell Bell, CORE *and the Strategy of Non-Violence.*

85. Gordon R. Carey to Robinson, March 3, 1959, CORE Papers, Reel 19.

86. Zoloth interview, August 23, 1991; Gordon interview, October 25, 2001; Turkel interview, April 25, 2002; John O. Brown, "Straight Talk with Audrey Finkelstein"; Robinson to Carey, March 5, 1959, CORE Papers, Reel 19; Dade County Council on Human Relations, *Community Audit of Human Rights in Greater Miami,* printed pamphlet in ibid.; "CORE's Furthest South Group," *CORE-lator,* 4.

87. Zoloth interview, August 23, 1991; Shirley M. Zoloth, "Notes Taken at Court Case: John Brown," August 19, 1958, in Gordon Papers, Box 10, Folder: Desegregation; Broudy interview, July 30, 2002; Gordon interview, October 25, 2001; John O. Brown, "Straight Talk with Audrey Finkelstein"; Turkel interview, April 25, 2002; Miami CORE, Minutes, March 12, 1959, CORE Papers, Reel 19. On Brown, see also Fletcher Knebel and Ben Kocivar, "The Negro in Florida: One Man's Progress and the Fight Ahead."

88. Zoloth interview, August 23, 1991; Turkel interview, April 25, 2002; Miami CORE, Minutes and Sit-in Reports, April 15, 22, May 5, 9, 12, June 2, 9, 13, 15, 16, 17, 22, 30, 1959, CORE Papers, Reel 19; Zoloth to Robinson, April 22, 30, 1959, ibid.; Robinson to John O. Brown and Shirley Zoloth, May 13, 1959, ibid.; Shirley Zoloth, "Report on Greater Miami CORE," July 21, 1959, ibid.; *Miami Herald,* April 30, June 14, 15, 1959; *Miami News,* June 14, 1959; *Miami Times,* May 2, 1959; Shirley Zoloth, "The Miami CORE Story," 2; Jim Peck, *Cracking the Color Line: Non-Violent Direct Action Methods of Eliminating Racial Discrimination,* 18–20; Jim Peck, *Freedom Ride,* 51–53.

89. Albert D. Moore, "Conversations with A. D. Moore"; Albert D. Moore, "Straight Talk with Audrey Finkelstein"; Zoloth interview, August 23, 1991; Gordon interview, December 6, 2001; Barbara Zoloth, e-mail message to author, August 24, 2001; Robert Kunst, telephone interview with author, February 4, 2003; Tananarive Due and Patricia Stephens Due, *Freedom in the Family: A Mother-Daughter Memoir of the Fight for Civil Rights,* 38–46.

90. Gordon interview, December 6, 2001; Turkel interview, April 25, 2002; CORE Minutes, May 5, 1959, CORE Papers, Reel 19.

91. Zoloth to Robinson, July 14, 27, 1959, CORE Papers, Reel 19; Carey to Zoloth and Brown, July 21, 1959, ibid.; Miami CORE, Minutes, May 5, June 30, July 14, 1959, ibid.; Shirley Zoloth, "Report on Testing for Racial Discrimination," July 24, 1959, ibid.; Gordon R. Carey, "Action Institute Aids Miami Campaign."

92. Gordon R. Carey, "Action Institute Aids Miami Campaign," 2–3; Susan Bodan and James R. Robinson, *1959 Miami Interracial Action Institute: Summary and Evaluation,* 1–4; Robinson to Carey, September 30, 1959, CORE Papers, Reel 19; Carey to Brown, October 16, 1959, ibid.; *Miami Times,* September 26, 1959; Gordon interview, December 6, 2001; Marvin Rich, "Miami Experiences Racial Stalemate."

93. Susan Bodan and James R. Robinson, *1959 Miami Interracial Action Institute: Summary and Evaluation,* 9–11; Zoloth to Robinson, undated (ca. June 1959), December

27, 1959, CORE Papers, Reel 19; Zoloth to Robinson, December 27, 1959, ibid.; Robinson to Carey, September 20, 1959, ibid.; Robinson to Brown, October 16, 1959, ibid.; Robinson to Lillian Kaplan, October 29, 1959, ibid.; Zoloth interviews, August 23, 1991, December 14, 1992; Broudy interview, July 30, 2002; Bloom interview, August 6, 2002; Gordon interview, December 6, 2001. Jack Gordon noted in an interview that he and other Jewish activists in CORE enclosed letters critical of segregation in the Miami store when paying their monthly Burdine's bill; still others canceled their accounts with Burdine's. Gordon also wrote to the head of the Burdine's firm, also a Jew, about the Miami store's lunch counter segregation and other discriminatory practices, saying that "he should be ashamed to be a Jew." For the larger context of black anti-Semitism, see Dinnerstein, *Antisemitism in America*, 197–227.

94. Zoloth interviews, August 23, 1991, December 14, 1992; Gordon interview, March 13, 2002; Shirley Zoloth, "Miami Integration: Silence Causes Failure," 1–3; Robinson to Carey, September 20, 1959, CORE Papers, Reel 19; Robinson to Albert D. Moore, October 29, 1959, ibid.; Zoloth to Robinson, December 27, 1959, ibid.

95. Brown to Carey, November 24, 1959, CORE Papers, Reel 19; Marvin Rich to Moore, December 4, 1959, January 27, 1960, ibid.; Moore to Rich, January 25, 1960, ibid.; Carey to Ralph Frankenberg, March 18, 1960, ibid.; *Miami Times,* October 24, November 28, 1959; *Newsweek* 54 (December 7, 1959), 36.

96. *Miami News,* April 12, 1960; Moore to Lula A. Farmer, March 17, 1960, CORE Papers, Reel 19; Moore to Rich, March 30, 1960, ibid.; Moore to Robinson, July 28, 1960, ibid.; *Miami Herald,* March 5, April 12, 13, 1960.

97. Moore to Rich, March 3, 1960, CORE Papers, Reel 19; Robinson to Moore, July 29, 1960, ibid.; *Miami Times,* July 23, August 6, 20, September 3, 1960; Edward T. Graham to Theodore Gibson, August 8, 1960, Collins Papers, Florida State Archives, Box 33; Governor's Commission on Race Relations, Minutes, April 16, May 14, 1960, ibid.; Congress of Racial Equality, *Nonviolence in Theory and in Action;* Weldon Rougeau to Rich, May 31, 1963, June 14, 1963, CORE Papers, Reel 19. On the roles of Mayor High and Governor Collins, see Faith High Barnebey, *Integrity Is the Issue: Campaign Life with Robert King High,* 49–51; Tom R. Wagy, *Governor LeRoy Collins of Florida: Spokesman of the New South,* 132–43; LeRoy Collins, "How It Looks from the South." For the 1960 Collins speech on integration, see LeRoy Collins, "But in Florida—We Cannot Wash Our Hands"; "Governor Collins and the Sit-ins," *The Reporter;* Harold C. Fleming, "The Price of a Cup of Coffee," *The Reporter.*

98. Zoloth interview, August 23, 1991.

99. Aldon D. Morris, *The Origins of the Civil Rights Movement: Black Communities Organizing for Change;* Aldon D. Morris, "A Retrospective on the Civil Rights Movement: Political and Intellectual Landmarks"; Charles Payne, "Men Led, but Women Organized: Movement Participation of Women in the Mississippi Delta." Working as activists and organizers, "Jewish women helped to build the infrastructure of the civil rights movement," according to one women's historian. See Joyce Antler, "Activists and Organizers: Jewish Women and American Politics."

100. Susan Lynn, "Gender and Post World War II Progressive Politics: A Bridge to Social Activism in the 1960s USA," 216–218; Joanne Meyerowitz, "Beyond the Feminine Mystique: A Reassessment of Postwar Mass Culture, 1946–1958," 1480. See also Kate Weigand, "The Red Menace, the Feminine Mystique, and the Ohio Un-American Activities Commission: Gender and Anti-Communism in Ohio, 1951–1954"; Sara Evans, *Personal Politics: The Roots of Women's Liberation in the Civil Rights Movement and the New Left*; Leila J. Rupp and Verta Taylor, *Survival in the Doldrums: The American Women's Rights Movement, 1945 to the 1960s*; Susan Lynn, *Progressive Women in Conservative Times: Racial Justice, Peace, and Feminism, 1945 to the 1960s*; Daniel Horowitz, *Betty Friedan and the Making of* The Feminine Mystique: *The American Left, the Cold War, and Modern Feminism*; and, for postwar activism among Communist women, Kate Weigand, *Red Feminism: American Communism and the Making of Women's Liberation*.

101. As if to emphasize this point, in an otherwise excellent and witty overview article on Jews in Miami and Miami Beach, Stephen Whitfield never mentions Miami's civil rights movement or Jewish activism on the left. Stephen J. Whitfield, "Blood and Sand: The Jewish Community of South Florida."

102. Stephen J. Whitfield, *Voices of Jacob, Hands of Esau: Jews in American Life and Thought*, 105. See also Stephen J. Whitfield, "Famished for Justice: The Jew as Radical"; Rafael Medoff, *Jewish Americans and Political Participation: A Reference Handbook*, 73–180.

103. Moses Rischin, *The Promised City: New York's Jews, 1870–1914*, 166; Stephen J. Whitfield, *American Space, Jewish Time*, 106–28; Vivian Gornick, *The Romance of American Communism*, 3–27; Maurice Isserman, *If I Had a Hammer: The Death of the Old Left and the Birth of the New Left*, 33. On oppositional cultures in early twentieth-century New York City, see Hadassa Kosak, *Cultures of Opposition: Jewish Immigrant Workers in New York City, 1881–1905*; Anita Schwartz, "Ethnic Identity among Left-wing American Jews." For other discussions of Jewish radicalism, see Lawrence H. Fuchs, *The Political Behavior of American Jews*, 171–203; Louis Ruchames, "Jewish Radicalism in the United States," 228–52; Maurice Isserman, "The 1956 Generation: An Alternative Approach to the History of American Communism"; Stanley Rothman and S. Robert Lichter, *Roots of Radicalism: Jews, Christians, and the New Left*, esp. 80–145; Stephen J. Whitfield, *Voices of Jacob, Hands of Esau: Jews in American Life and Thought*, 73–96; Gerald Sorin, *The Prophetic Minority: American Jewish Immigrant Radicals, 1880–1920*; Paul Buhle, "Themes in American Jewish Radicalism," 77–118; Paul Buhle and Robin D. G. Kelley, "Allies of a Different Sort: Jews and Blacks in the American Left"; Ben Halpern, "The Roots of American Jewish Liberalism"; Charles S. Liebman and Steven M. Cohen, "Jewish Liberalism Revisited."

104. Peniel E. Joseph, "Waiting till the Midnight Hour: Reconceptualizing the Heroic Period of the Civil Rights Movement, 1954–1965"; William L. Patterson, ed., *We Charge Genocide*; Azza Salama Layton, *International Politics and Civil Rights Policies in the United States, 1941–1960*, 151; Mary L. Dudziak, *Cold War Civil Rights: Race and the Image*

of American Democracy, 6. See also Mary L. Dudziak, "Desegregation as a Cold War Imperative"; Thomas Borstelmann, *The Cold War and the Color Line: American Race Relations in the Global Arena.*

Part II. Matilda "Bobbi" Graff and the Civil Rights Congress

1. Graff interviews, May 18, 1992, December 19, 2000; Graff, telephone interview, March 8, 2002; Graff, videotaped interview with Gregory Bush, August 19, 1992, copy in author's possession; Graff, videotaped interview, University of Miami, Focus 51 Program, December 4, 1992, copy in author's possession. On Jews in Brownsville during the early decades of the twentieth century, see Wendell Pritchett, *Brownsville, Brooklyn: Blacks, Jews, and the Changing Face of the Ghetto,* 9–49; Carole Bell Ford, *The Girls: Jewish Women of Brownsville, Brooklyn, 1940–1995.* For a wider perspective on Jews in New York City, see Irving Howe, *World of Our Fathers;* Deborah Dash Moore, *At Home in America: Second Generation New York Jews;* Beth S. Wenger, *New York Jews and the Great Depression: Uncertain Promise.*

2. Graff interviews, May 18, 1992, December 19, 2000; SAC [Special Agent in Charge], Detroit to Director [J. Edgar Hoover], FBI, November 2, 1945, Graff FBI File.

3. Graff, interview with Gregory Bush, August 19, 1992.

4. SAC, Miami to Director, FBI, February 18, 1955, Graff FBI File; SAC, Detroit to Director, FBI, November 14, 1960, ibid.; Director, FBI to SAC, Detroit, November 30, 1960, ibid. On DETCOM, see Athan Theoharis, *Spying on Americans: Political Surveillance from Hoover to the Huston Plan,* 48; Frank J. Donner, *The Age of Surveillance: The Aims and Methods of America's Political Intelligence System,* 162–66.

5. Graff interview, May 18, 1992; Graff, interview with Gregory Bush, August 19, 1992.

6. Graff interviews, December 19, 2000, December 26, 2001; Graff, interview with Gregory Bush, August 19, 1992.

7. Graff interview, December 19, 2000.

8. Graff interview, December 19, 2000; Graff, interview with Gregory Bush August 19, 1992; Graff, interview, University of Miami, Focus 51, December 4, 1992; *Delray Citizens for Social Responsibility Newsletter* 127 (November 2000).

9. For some interesting parallels to Graff's activist career, see Gerda Lerner's *Fireweed: A Political Autobiography.* A refugee from the Holocaust, Lerner lived for a time in New York City, joined the Communist Party, worked for the election of Henry Wallace, and became an activist in the Civil Rights Congress in the late 1940s and 1950s.

10. Graff interview, December 19, 2000; Anne Braden to Graff, January 6, 1973, Graff Scrapbook. On Braden, see Anne Braden, "The Civil Rights Movement and McCarthyism"; Catherine Fosl, *Subversive Southerner: Anne Braden and the Struggle for Racial Justice in the Cold War South.*

Part III. Shirley M. Zoloth and the Congress of Racial Equality

1. Zoloth interview, August 23, 1991; Milton Zoloth, telephone interview, December 15, 2000.

2. Zoloth to Bernice Ullrich, September 24, 1954, Gordon Papers, Box 10, Folder:

Desegregation; [Miami] "Women's Intern'l League for Peace and Freedom," two page information flyer, 1954, Gordon Papers, ibid.; Leslie B. Bain, "Red Hunt in Miami: Who Formed the Posse?" For the Philadelphia teacher purge, see Philip Jenkins, *The Cold War at Home: The Red Scare in Pennsylvania, 1945–1960*, 118–41; David Caute, *The Great Fear: The Anti-Communist Purge under Truman and Eisenhower*, 419–20, 555.

3. Zoloth interview, August 23, 1991; Shirley Zoloth to [Dade County] Board of Public Instruction, September 18, 1957, Gordon Papers, Box 10, Folder: Desegregation; Zoloth, "Observations Made at Meeting of Board of Public Instruction," typescript, October 2, 1957, Gordon Papers, ibid.; Zoloth, Clipping Scrapbook, 1957–1959, in author's possession.

4. John B. Orr Jr., "Explanation of the Vote of Honorable John B. Orr, Jr.," typescript, July 1956, Gordon Papers, Box 29, Folder: John B. Orr; *Miami News*, September 18, 1958; *Miami Herald*, October 1, 1958.

5. Gordon interviews, October 25, December 6, 2001; Claude Pepper to Abe Aronovitz, November 21, 1949, Claude Pepper Papers, Box 204A/7/1; Pepper to Gordon, November 18, 1952, Gordon Papers, Box 16, Folder: Miscellaneous, School Campaign.

6. Zoloth interviews, August 23, 1991, December 14, 1992; Gordon interviews, October 25, December 6, 2001; Thalia [Stern] Broudy, telephone interviews with author, July 30, 2002, February 11, 2003; Leonard Turkel, interview with author, April 25, 2002; Marilynn Bloom, telephone interview with author, August 6, 2002.

7. Gordon interviews, October 25, 2001, March 13, 2002; Dade County Citizens Committee for Better Schools, Open Letter, March 16, 1959, Gordon Papers, Box 6, Folder: Dade County Committee for Better Schools; Zoloth to [Dade County] Board of Public Instruction, September 18, 1957, Gordon Papers, Box 10, Folder: Desegregation; Zoloth to Helen Raebeck, July 12, 1960, ibid.; Zoloth to James Dombrowski, April 13, 1959, Coe Papers, Box 3. For the legislative investigation of SCEF, see FLIC, "Report of the Florida Legislative Investigation Committee to the 1961 Session of the Legislature," 1961, typescript, pp. 10–18, FLIC Papers, Box 1, Folder 21; FLIC, "Report of Organizations, Publications and Findings Pertaining to Communists and Racial Agitation in the State of Florida," 1961, typescript, pp. 1–2, ibid.

8. Zoloth interviews, August 23, 1991, December 14, 1992; Gordon interviews, October 25, December 4, 2001; Broudy interview, July 30, 2002; Cindy Thorner, telephone interview with author, December 18, 2002; Libby Strauss, telephone interview with author, December 23, 2002; Jack D. Gordon, "Public Education in Dade County: A Businessman's Report," March 27, 1964, typescript, Ross Beiler Papers, Box 7, Folder 142; Neisa DeWitt to Sandy D'Alemberte and Libby Strauss, "Dade County Working Organization Personnel," n.d., ca. 1972, Gordon Papers, Box 24, Folder: George McGovern.

9. Turkel interview, April 25, 2002; Broudy interviews, July 30, 2002, February 11, 2003; Gordon interview, December 14, 2001; Leonard Turkel, "Horror of Hydrogen War," letter to editor, *Miami News*, May 8, 1960; Lee Winfrey, "What Miami's Peaceseekers Try to Do"; David Lawrence, "Home-taught Values and the Homeless" [on Leonard Turkel]. On SANE, see Milton S. Katz, *Ban the Bomb: A History of SANE, the Committee for a Sane Nuclear Policy, 1957–1985*; Lawrence S. Wittner, *Rebels against War:*

The American Peace Movement, 1941–1960, 240–46; W. J. Rorabaugh, *Kennedy and the Promise of the Sixties,* 52–57.

10. Lee Winfrey, "What Miami's Peaceseekers Try to Do"; Broudy interview, July 30, 2002; Gordon interview, December 14, 2001; Robert Kunst, telephone interview with author, February 4, 2003; Gordon to Pepper, April 29, 1963, Pepper Papers, Box 401B/166/11; Florida MOBE, Press Releases, October 17, 31, 1969, Gordon Papers, Box 26, Folder: Florida Mobilization; Florida MOBE, Television and Newspaper Contact List, n.d., ca. October 1969, ibid.; *Miami Herald,* November 14, 15, 1969. On Women Strike for Peace, see Amy Swerdlow, *Women Strike for Peace: Traditional Motherhood and Radical Politics in the 1960s.*

11. *Miami Herald,* August 14, September 4, 9, October 13, 1964, February 20, 1966; *Miami News,* October 13, 1964, January 22, 1965; Zoloth interview, August 23, 1991; Gordon interviews, December 6, 2001, March 13, 2002.

12. Zoloth interview, August 23, 1991; Strauss interview, December 23, 2002; *Miami Herald,* February 20, 1966, November 27, 28, 29, 1967; Office of Economic Opportunity (OEO), Anti-Poverty Program Evaluation Records, "Report of the Inter-Agency Close-Out Review of Economic Opportunity Program, Inc., Dade County, Florida," December 10, 1970, typescript, Box 18, U.S. Community Service Administration Records, Record Group 381.

13. Shirley Zoloth, Letter to the Editor, *Miami News,* April 9, 1968; Zoloth interview, August 23, 1991; Barbara Zoloth, e-mail message to author, August 24, 2001; OEO, "Report of the Inter-Agency Close-Out Review," 31, Box 18, U.S. Community Service Administration Records, Record Group 381.

14. Zoloth interview, August 23, 1991; Broudy interviews, July 30, 2002, February 11, 2003; Bloom interview, August 6, 2002; Gordon interviews, December 6, 2001, March 13, 2002; *Miami Herald,* April 27, June 2, 1966, November 27, 1967, April 11, 1968.

15. Barbara Zoloth, email message to author, June 9, 2003; Zoloth interview, August 23, 1991; Shirley Zoloth, Letter to Editor, *Miami New Times,* December 3, 1998; Anabelle deGale, "Shirley Zoloth, Played Key Role in Desegregation."

Bibliography

Manuscript Collections

Ross Beiler Papers, Archives and Special Collections Department, Richter Library, University of Miami, Coral Gables, Florida.
Millard Caldwell Papers, Florida State Archives, Tallahassee, Florida.
Civil Rights Congress Papers, Schomburg Library, New York City, New York, microfilm edition.
John M. Coe Papers, Special Collections, Robert W. Woodruff Library, Emory University, Atlanta, Georgia.
LeRoy Collins Papers, Florida State Archives, Tallahassee, Florida.
LeRoy Collins Papers, Special Collections Department, University of South Florida, Tampa, Florida.
Congress of Racial Equality Papers, Wisconsin State Historical Society, Madison, Wisconsin, microfilm edition.
FBI Investigation and Surveillance Records, Archives, Marquette University Library, Milwaukee, Wisconsin.
Florida ACLU Papers, P. K. Yonge Library, University of Florida, Gainesville, Florida.
Florida Legislative Investigation Committee Papers, Florida State Archives, Tallahassee, Florida.
Jack D. Gordon Papers, University Archives, Florida International University, Miami, Florida.
Governor's Commission on Race Relations Papers, Florida State Archives, Tallahassee, Florida.
Matilda "Bobbi" Graff, Clipping Scrapbook, copy in author's possession.
Matilda "Bobbi" Graff FBI File, in Graff's possession.
Matilda "Bobbi" Graff, Voter Registration File, in Graff's possession.
Industrial Union of Marine and Shipbuilding Workers of America Archives, Archives and Manuscripts Department, University of Maryland Library, College Park, Maryland.
Stetson Kennedy Papers, Schomburg Library, New York City, New York, microfilm edition.

Stetson Kennedy Papers, Southern Labor Archives, Special Collections Department, Georgia State University, Atlanta, Georgia.
Emma Lazarus Federation Papers, Jacob Rader Marcus Center, American Jewish Archives, Cincinnati, Ohio.
National Association for the Advancement of Colored People Papers, Library of Congress, Washington, D.C.
National Urban League Papers, Library of Congress, Washington, D.C.
Claude Pepper Papers, Claude Pepper Library, Florida State University, Tallahassee, Florida.
Ruth W. Perry Papers, Special Collections Department, University of South Florida Library, Tampa, Florida.
Robert W. Saunders Papers, Special Collections Department, University of South Florida Library, Tampa, Florida.
Southern Regional Council Papers, Atlanta University Center Archives, Atlanta, Georgia, microfilm edition.
Transport Workers of America Papers, Robert F. Wagner Labor Archives, New York University, New York City, New York.
U.S. Community Service Administration Records, Record Group 381, U.S. National Archives and Records Center, Southeast Region, Atlanta, Georgia.
U.S. District Court Records, Record Group 21, U.S. National Archives and Records Center, Southeast Region, Atlanta, Georgia.
Fuller Warren Papers, Florida State Archives, Tallahassee, Florida.
Women's International League for Peace and Freedom Records, Swarthmore College Peace Collection, Swarthmore, Pennsylvania, microfilm edition.
Shirley M. Zoloth, Clipping Scrapbook, 1957–1959, in author's possession.

Interviews Conducted by Author

Marilynn Bloom, August 6, 2002.
Thalia [Stern] Broudy, July 30, 2002, February 11, 2003.
Jack D. Gordon, October 25, December 4, 6, 14, 2001, March 13, 2002.
Matilda "Bobbi" Graff, May 18, September 30, 1992, January 29, 1993, April 26, 1994, December 28, 1998, December 19, 2000, December 26, 2001, March 8, 2002.
Ruth Greenfield, August 13, 2002.
Robert Kunst, February 4, 2003.
Libby Strauss, December 23, 2002.
Stella Suberman, February 7, 2002.
Cindy Thorner, December 18, 2002.
Leonard Turkel, April 25, 2002.
Milton Zoloth, August 23, 1991, December 14, 1992, December 15, 2000, July 23, 2001.
Shirley Zoloth, August 13, 23, 1991, May 5, October 2, December 14, 1992.

Interviews Conducted by Others

John O. Brown, "Straight Talk with Audrey Finkelstein," WLRN radio interview, May 1,

1997, archived in Florida State Archives, Tallahassee, Florida, copy in author's possession.

Matilda "Bobbi" Graff, videotaped interview with Gregory Bush, August 19, 1992, copy in author's possession.

Matilda "Bobbi" Graff, videotaped interview, University of Miami, Focus 51 Program, December 4, 1992, copy in author's possession.

Albert D. Moore, "Conversations with A. D. Moore," videotaped interview, Miami-Dade School Board, 2001, copy in author's possession.

Albert D. Moore, "Straight Talk with Audrey Finkelstein," WLRN radio interview, May 8, 1997, archived in Florida State Archives, Tallahassee, Florida, copy in author's possession.

James Nimmo, videotaped interview with Gregory Bush, 1987, copy in author's possession.

Books and Articles

Abrams, Charles. *Forbidden Neighbors: A Study of Prejudice in Housing*. New York: Harper, 1955.

Adams, Frank T. *James A. Dombrowski: An American Heretic, 1897–1983*. Knoxville: University of Tennessee Press, 1992.

Adams, Maurianne, and John Bracey, eds. *Strangers and Neighbors: Relations between Blacks and Jews in the United States*. Amherst: University of Massachusetts Press, 1999.

American Jewish Committee. *American Jewish Yearbook, 1947–1948*. Philadelphia: Jewish Publication Society of America, 1947.

———. *On Three Fronts: Thirty-Ninth Annual Report, 1945*. New York: American Jewish Committee, 1946.

American Jewish Congress. "Proceedings of the Convention." *Congress Record* 11 (June 1958), 1–2, 7–8.

Anderson, Alan B., and George W. Pickering. *Confronting the Color Line: The Broken Promise of the Civil Rights Movement in Chicago*. Athens: University of Georgia Press, 1986.

Anderson, Jervis. *Bayard Rustin: Troubles I've Seen*. Berkeley: University of California Press, 1998.

Anhalt, Diana. *A Gathering of Fugitives: American Political Expatriates in Mexico, 1948–1965*. Santa Maria, Calif.: Archer Books, 2001.

———. "Resuscitating Corpses: Memories of Political Exile in Mexico." In *Red Diapers: Growing Up in the Communist Left,* ed. Judy Kaplan and Linn Shapiro, 176–83. Urbana: University of Illinois Press, 1998.

Antler, Joyce. "Activists and Organizers: Jewish Women and American Politics." In *Jews in American Politics,* ed. L. Sandy Maisel, 231–49. Lanham, Md.: Rowman and Littlefield, 2001.

———. "Between Culture and Politics: The Emma Lazarus Federation of Jewish Women's Clubs and the Promulgation of Women's History, 1944–1989." In *U.S. His-*

tory as Women's History: New Feminist Essays, ed. Linda K. Kerber, Alice Kessler-Harris, and Kathryn Kish Sklar, 267–95, 424–29. Chapel Hill: University of North Carolina Press, 1995.

Bain, Leslie B. "Red Hunt in Miami: Who Formed the Posse?" *The Nation* 179 (August 7, 1954), 110–12.

Baldwin, Neil. *Henry Ford and the Jews: The Mass Production of Hate*. New York: PublicAffairs, 2001.

Barkun, Michael. *Religion and the Racist Right: The Origins of the Christian Identity Movement*. Chapel Hill: University of North Carolina Press, 1994.

Barnard, Hollinger F., ed. *Outside the Magic Circle: The Autobiography of Virginia Foster Durr*. Tuscaloosa: University of Alabama Press, 1985.

Barnebey, Faith High. *Integrity Is the Issue: Campaign Life with Robert King High*. Miami: E. A. Seemann Publishing Co., 1971.

Bartley, Numan V. *The Rise of Massive Resistance: Race and Politics in the South during the 1950s*. Baton Rouge: Louisiana State University Press, 1969.

Bates, Beth Tompkins. "A New Crowd Challenges the Agenda of the Old Guard in the NAACP, 1933–1941." *American Historical Review* 102 (April 1977), 340–77.

Bates, Daisy. *The Long Shadow of Little Rock*. New York: McKay, 1962.

Bauman, Mark, and Berkley Kalin, eds. *The Quiet Voices: Southern Rabbis and Black Civil Rights, 1880s to 1990s*. Tuscaloosa: University of Alabama Press, 1997.

Bayor, Ronald H. *Race and the Shaping of Twentieth-Century Atlanta*. Chapel Hill: University of North Carolina Press, 1996.

"Beachhead in Miami," *Ebony* 6 (March 1951), 96–97.

Belfrage, Cedric. *The American Inquisition, 1945–1960*. Indianapolis: Bobbs-Merrill, 1973.

Belknap, Michal R. *Cold War Political Justice: The Smith Act, the Communist Party, and American Civil Liberties*. Westport, Conn.: Greenwood Press, 1997.

Bell, Inge Powell. CORE *and the Strategy of Non-Violence*. New York: Random House, 1968.

Belth, N. C. *Barriers: Patterns of Discrimination against Jews*. New York: Anti-Defamation League, 1958.

Berger, Morroe, and Joseph B. Robinson. *Civil Rights in the United States in 1949: A Balance Sheet of Group Relations*. New York: American Jewish Congress and NAACP, 1950.

Berman, William C. *The Politics of Civil Rights in the Truman Administration*. Columbus: Ohio State University Press, 1970.

Bernstein, Barton J. "The Ambiguous Legacy: The Truman Administration and Civil Rights." In *Politics and Policies of the Truman Administration*, ed. Barton J. Bernstein, 269–314. Chicago: Quadrangle Books, 1970.

"Bigotry and Bombs in Florida." *Southern Patriot* 10 (January 1952), 1, 4.

Blanchard, William. *Racial Nationalism: Principles and Purposes*. Live Oak, Fla.: White Front Publishing Co., Inc., 1938.

Blumberg, Rhoda Lois. *Civil Rights: The 1960s Freedom Struggle*. Rev. ed. Boston: Twayne, 1992.
Bodan, Susan, and James R. Robinson. *1959 Miami Interracial Action Institute: Summary and Evaluation*. New York: Congress of Racial Equality, 1960.
"The Bomb Heard around the World." *Ebony* (April 1952), 15–16, 21–23.
"Bombings and Hate Sheets: A Program to Combat Lawlessness." [American Jewish Congress] *Congress Bi-Weekly* 25 (December 22, 1958), 15–19.
Bond, Julian. "Introduction." In *Strangers and Neighbors: Relations between Blacks and Jews in the United States*, ed. Maurianne Adams and John Bracey, 1–13. Amherst: University of Massachusetts Press, 1999.
Borstelmann, Thomas. *The Cold War and the Color Line: American Race Relations in the Global Arena*. Cambridge, Mass.: Harvard University Press, 2001.
Bracey, John, and August Meier. "Towards a Research Agenda on Blacks and Jews in United States History." *Journal of American Ethnic History* 12 (spring 1993), 60–67.
Braden, Anne. "The Civil Rights Movement and McCarthyism." *The Guild Practitioner* 37 (fall 1980), 109–16.
———. *House Un-American Activities Committee: Bulwark of Segregation*. Los Angeles: National Committee to Abolish the House Un-American Activities Committee, 1964.
———. *The Wall Between*. 2d ed. Knoxville: University of Tennessee Press, 1999.
Breitman, George. *Jim Crow Murder of Mr. and Mrs. Harry T. Moore*. New York: Pioneer Publishers, 1952.
Brinkley, Douglas. *Rosa Parks*. New York: Viking, 2000.
Broadwater, Jeff. *Eisenhower and the Anti-Communist Crusade*. Chapel Hill: University of North Carolina Press, 1992.
Broun, Heywood. "Up Pops the Wizard." *The New Republic* 99 (June 21, 1939), 186–87.
Brown, Sarah Hart. "Congressional Anticommunism and the Segregationist South: From New Orleans to Atlanta, 1954–1958." *Georgia Historical Quarterly* 80 (winter 1996), 785–816.
———. "Pensacola Progressive: John Moreno Coe and the Campaign of 1948." *Florida Historical Quarterly* 68 (July 1989), 1–26.
———. *Standing against Dragons: Three Southern Lawyers in an Era of Fear*. Baton Rouge: Louisiana State University Press, 1998.
Buhle, Paul. "Themes in American Jewish Radicalism." In *The Immigrant Left in the United States*, ed. Paul Buhle and Dan Georgakas, 77–118. Albany: SUNY Press, 1996.
Buhle, Paul, and Robin D. G. Kelley. "Allies of a Different Sort: Jews and Blacks in the American Left." In *Struggles in the Promised Land: Toward a History of Black-Jewish Relations in the United States*, ed. Jack Salzman and Cornel West, 197–229. New York: Oxford University Press, 1997.
Bunche, Ralph J. *The Political Status of the Negro in the Age of FDR*. Chicago: University of Chicago Press, 1973.
Burns, Stewart, ed. *Daybreak of Freedom: The Montgomery Bus Boycott*. Chapel Hill: University of North Carolina Press, 1997.

Burran, James A. "Urban Racial Violence in the South during World War II: A Comparative Overview." In *From the Old South to the New: Essays on the Transitional South,* ed. Walter J. Fraser Jr. and Winifred B. Moore Jr., 167–77. Westport, Conn.: Greenwood Press, 1981.

Button, James W. *Blacks and Social Change: Impact of the Civil Rights Movement in Southern Communities.* Princeton: Princeton University Press, 1989.

Camp, Helen C. *Iron in Her Soul: Elizabeth Gurley Flynn and the American Left.* Pullman: Washington State University Press, 1995.

Campbell, Clarice T. *Civil Rights Chronicle: Letters from the South.* Jackson: University Press of Mississippi, 1997.

Carey, Gordon R. "Action Institute Aids Miami Campaign." CORE-*lator* 78 (fall 1959), 1–2.

Carleton, William G., and Hugh Douglas Price. "America's Newest Voter: A Florida Case Study." *Antioch Review* 14 (December 1954), 441–57.

Carlson, John Roy. *The Plotters.* New York: Dutton, 1946.

Carson, Clayborne. "Blacks and Jews in the Civil Rights Movement." In *Jews in Black Perspectives: A Dialogue,* ed. Joseph R. Washington Jr., 113–31. Rutherford, N.J.: Fairleigh Dickinson University Press, 1984.

―――. "Civil Rights Reform and the Black Freedom Struggle." In *The Civil Rights Movement in America,* ed. Charles W. Eagles, 19–32. Jackson: University Press of Mississippi, 1986.

Caute, David. *The Great Fear: The Anti-Communist Purge under Truman and Eisenhower.* New York: Simon and Schuster, 1978.

Chafe, William H. "The Civil Rights Revolution: The Gods Bring Threads to Webs Begun." In *Reshaping America: Society and Institutions, 1945–1960,* ed. Robert H. Bremner and Gary W. Reichard, 67–100. Columbus: Ohio State University Press, 1982.

―――. *Civilities and Civil Rights: Greensboro, North Carolina, and the Black Struggle for Freedom.* New York: Oxford University Press, 1980.

Chappell, David L. *Inside Agitators: White Southerners in the Civil Rights Movement.* Baltimore: Johns Hopkins University Press, 1994.

Chase, Harold W. *Security and Liberty: The Problem of Native Communists, 1947–1955.* Garden City, N.Y.: Doubleday, 1955.

Clark, James C. "Civil Rights Leader Harry T. Moore and the Ku Klux Klan in Florida." *Florida Historical Quarterly* 73 (October 1994), 166–83.

Clark, Kenneth B. "Candor about Negro-Jewish Relations." *Commentary* 1 (February 1946), 8–14.

Cohen, Naomi W. *Not Free to Desist: The American Jewish Committee, 1906–1966.* Philadelphia: Jewish Publication Society of America, 1972.

Cohen, Richard. "Decision in Miami." [American Jewish Congress] *Congress Bi-Weekly* 28 (May 1, 1961), 10–12.

Cohn, David H. "The Development and Efficacy of the Negro Police Precinct and Court of the City of Miami." M.A. thesis, University of Miami, 1951.

Colburn, David R. "Florida's Governors Confront the *Brown* Decision: A Case of the

Constitutional Politics of School Desegregation, 1954–1970." In *An Uncertain Tradition: Constitutionalism and the History of the South,* ed. Kermit L. Hall and James E. Ely, 326–55. Athens: University of Georgia Press, 1989.

———. *Racial Change and Community Crisis: St. Augustine, Florida, 1877–1980.* New York: Columbia University Press, 1985.

Colburn, David R., and Richard K. Scher. *Florida's Gubernatorial Politics in the Twentieth Century.* Tallahassee: Florida State University Press, 1980.

Collier-Thomas, Bettye, and V. P. Franklin, eds. *Sisters in the Struggle: African American Women in the Civil Rights-Black Power Movement.* New York: New York University Press, 2001.

Collins, LeRoy. "But in Florida—We Cannot Wash Our Hands." In *We Dissent,* ed. Hoke Norris, 100–15. New York: St. Martin's Press, 1962.

———. "How It Looks from the South." *Look* 92 (May 27, 1958), 90–99.

Congress of Racial Equality. *Nonviolence in Theory and in Action.* New York: Congress of Racial Equality, n.d., ca. 1959.

Cony, Ed. "Miami Race Plan." *Wall Street Journal* (December 9, 1958), 1, 18.

Cook, James Graham. *The Segregationists.* New York: Appleton-Century-Crofts, 1962.

Cook, Robert. *Sweet Land of Liberty: The African-American Struggle for Civil Rights in the Twentieth Century.* London: Longman, 1998.

"CORE's Furthest South Group." *CORE-lator* 76 (spring 1959), 4.

Crawford, Vicki L., Jacqueline Anne Rouse, and Barbara Woods, eds. *Women in the Civil Rights Movement: Trailblazers and Torchbearers, 1941–1965.* Bloomington: Indiana University Press, 1993.

Critchlow, Donald T. "Communist Unions and Racism." *Labor History* 17 (spring 1976), 230–44.

Current, Gloster B. "Martyr for a Cause." *The Crisis* 59 (February 1952), 73–81.

Curry, Constance, et al. *Deep in Our Hearts: Nine White Women in the Freedom Movement.* Athens: University of Georgia Press, 2000.

Dade County Council on Community Relations, Community Planning Committee. *Dade County Schools and Desegregation.* Miami: Dade County Council on Community Relations, 1958.

Dade County Council on Human Relations. *Community Audit of Human Rights in Greater Miami.* Miami: Dade County Council on Human Relations, 1958.

Dalfiume, Richard M. *Desegregation of the U.S. Armed Forces: Fighting on Two Fronts, 1939–1953.* Columbia: University of Missouri Press, 1969.

———. "The 'Forgotten Years' of the Negro Revolution." *Journal of American History* 55 (June 1968), 90–106.

Davis, David Brion. "Jews and Blacks in America." *New York Review of Books* 46 (December 2, 1999), 57–63.

Davis, Lenwood G. *Black-Jewish Relations in the United States, 1752–1984.* Westport, Conn.: Greenwood Press, 1984.

Deal, Borden. "The Sign on the Highway." In *We Dissent,* ed. Hoke Norris, 141–56. New York: St. Martin's Press, 1962.

deGale, Anabelle. "Shirley Zoloth, Played Key Role in Desegregation." *Miami Herald*, October 21, 1999.

Deming, Barbara. "The Ordeal of SANE." *The Nation* 192 (March 11, 1961), 200–5.

Diner, Hasia R. *In the Almost Promised Land: American Jews and Blacks, 1915–1935.* Westport, Conn.: Greenwood Press, 1977.

Dinnerstein, Leonard. "American Jews and the Civil Rights Movement." *Reviews in American History* 30 (March 2002), 136–40.

———. *Antisemitism in America.* New York: Oxford University Press, 1994.

———. "Southern Jewry and the Desegregation Crisis, 1954–1970." *American Jewish Historical Quarterly* 62 (March 1973), 231–41.

———. *Uneasy at Home: Antisemitism and the American Jewish Experience.* New York: Columbia University Press, 1987.

Dittmer, John. *Local People: The Struggle for Civil Rights in Mississippi.* Urbana: University of Illinois Press, 1994.

Dollinger, Marc. "'Hamans' and 'Torquemadas': Southern and Northern Jewish Responses to the Civil Rights Movement, 1945–1965." In *The Quiet Voices: Southern Rabbis and Black Civil Rights, 1880s to 1990s,* ed. Mark K. Bauman and Berkley Kalin, 67–94. Tuscaloosa: University of Alabama Press, 1997.

———. *Quest for Inclusion: Jews and Liberalism in Modern America.* Princeton: Princeton University Press, 2000.

Donner, Frank J. *The Age of Surveillance: The Aims and Methods of America's Political Intelligence System.* New York: Knopf, 1980.

———. "The Congressional Pillory." *The Nation* 192 (February 18, 1961), 143–46.

———. "The Miami Formula: An Exposé of Grass-Roots McCarthyism." *The Nation* 180 (January 22, 1955), 65–71.

———. *The Un-Americans.* New York: Ballantine Books, 1961.

Draper, Alan. *Conflict of Interest: Organized Labor and the Civil Rights Movement in the South, 1954–1968.* Ithaca: ILR Press, 1994.

Dudziak, Mary L. *Cold War Civil Rights: Race and the Image of American Democracy.* Princeton: Princeton University Press, 2000.

———. "Desegregation as a Cold War Imperative." *Stanford Law Review* 41 (November 1988), 61–120.

Due, Tananarive, and Patricia Stephens Due. *Freedom in the Family: A Mother-Daughter Memoir of the Fight for Civil Rights.* New York: Ballantine Books, 2003.

Dukess, Karen, and Richard Hart. "The Invisible Man." *Miami Herald, Tropic Magazine* (February 16, 1992), 12–21.

Dunn, Hampton. "Miami's Jack Orr First Dixie Politician to Support Openly Integration Move." *Tampa Daily Times,* July 28, 1956.

Dunn, Marvin. *Black Miami in the Twentieth Century.* Gainesville: University Press of Florida, 1997.

Dykeman, Wilma, and James Stokely. "McCarthyism under the Magnolias." *The Progressive* 23 (July 1959), 6–10.

———. *Neither Black nor White.* New York: Rinehart, 1957.

Eagles, Charles W. "The Civil Rights Movement." In *A Companion to the American South*, ed. John B. Boles, 461–73. Malden, Mass.: Blackwell, 2002.
———. *Jon Daniels and the Civil Rights Movement in Alabama*. Chapel Hill: University of North Carolina Press, 1993.
———. "Toward New Histories of the Civil Rights Era." *Journal of Southern History* 66 (November 2000), 815–48.
"Editorial: Governor Fuller Warren." *The Crisis* 59 (February 1952), 102–3.
Emmons, Caroline. "'Somebody Has Got to Do That Work': Harry T. Moore and the Struggle for African-American Voting Rights in Florida." *Journal of Negro History*, 82 (spring 1997), 232–43.
Eskew, Glenn T. *But for Birmingham: The Local and National Movements in the Civil Rights Struggle*. Chapel Hill: University of North Carolina Press, 1997.
Evans, Sara. *Personal Politics: The Roots of Women's Liberation in the Civil Rights Movement and the New Left*. New York: Knopf, 1979.
Fairclough, Adam. "Historians and the Civil Rights Movement." *Journal of American Studies* 24 (December 1990), 387–98.
———. *Race and Democracy: The Civil Rights Struggle in Louisiana, 1915–1972*. Athens: University of Georgia Press, 1995.
Fairfield, William S. "Florida: Dynamite Law Replaces Lynch Law." *The Reporter* 7 (August 5, 1952), 31–34.
Farmer, James. "Foreword." In *Bridges and Boundaries: African Americans and American Jews*, ed. Jack Salzman, 12–14. New York: Braziller, 1992.
———. *Lay Bare the Heart: An Autobiography of the Civil Rights Movement*. New York: Arbor House, 1985.
"Father Theodore R. Gibson." *The Crisis* 68 (February 1961), 91–92.
"Fight to Defend Philly Schools Continues." [Pennsylvania Civil Rights Congress] *Let Freedom Ring* 1 (December 1953–January 1954), 3.
"Fighting the Klan." *Southern Patriot* 4 (May 1946), 7.
Findlay, James F., Jr. *Church People in the Struggle: The National Council of Churches and the Black Freedom Movement, 1950–1970*. New York: Oxford University Press, 1993.
Finkle, Lee. "The Conservative Aims of Militant Rhetoric: Black Protest during World War II." *Journal of American History* 60 (December 1973), 692–713.
Fleming, Harold. "The Price of a Cup of Coffee." *The Reporter* 22 (May 12, 1960), 25–26.
"Florida: First Fruits." *Time* (December 22, 1952), 18.
"Florida: Klan Vs. Conscience." *Southern Patriot* 10 (March 1952), 1.
Florida Legislative Investigation Committee. *Communism and the NAACP*. Atlanta: Georgia Commission on Education, 1958.
Ford, Carole Bell. *The Girls: Jewish Women of Brownsville, Brooklyn, 1940–1995*. Albany: SUNY Press 2000.
Forman, Seth. "The Unbearable Whiteness of Being Jewish: Desegregation in the South and the Crisis of Jewish Liberalism." *American Jewish History* 85 (June 1997), 121–42.
Forster, Arnold. *A Measure of Freedom: An Anti-Defamation League Report*. Garden City, N.Y.: Doubleday, 1950.

Forster, Arnold, and Benjamin Epstein. *The Troublemakers: An Anti-Defamation League Report.* Garden City, N.Y.: Doubleday, 1952.

Fosl, Catherine. *Subversive Southerner: Anne Braden and the Struggle for Racial Justice in the Cold War South.* New York: Palgrave Macmillan, 2002.

France, Royal W. "Miami Miasma." [American Civil Liberties Union] *Rights* 2 (November 1954), 4–6.

Franklin, V. P., Nancy L. Grant, Harold M. Kletnick, and Genna Rae McNeil, eds. *African Americans and Jews in the Twentieth Century: Studies in Convergence and Conflict.* Columbia: University of Missouri Press, 1998.

Freeman, Joshua B. *In Transit: The Transport Workers Union in New York City, 1933–1966.* New York: Oxford University Press, 1989.

Fried, Richard M. *Nightmare in Red: The McCarthy Era in Perspective.* New York: Oxford University Press, 1990.

Friedly, Michael, and David Gallen. *Martin Luther King, Jr.: The FBI File.* New York: Carroll and Graf Publishers, 1993.

Friedman, Murray. "The Civil Rights Movement and the Reemergence of the Left." In *African Americans and Jews in the Twentieth Century: Studies in Convergence and Conflict,* ed. V. P. Franklin, Nancy L. Grant, Harold M. Kletnick, and Genna Rae McNeil, 102–22. Columbia: University of Missouri Press, 1998.

———. *What Went Wrong? The Creation and Collapse of the Black-Jewish Alliance.* New York: Free Press, 1995.

Frommer, Morris. "The American Jewish Congress: A History, 1914–1950." Ph.D. diss., Ohio State University, 1978.

Fuchs, Lawrence H. *The Political Behavior of American Jews.* Glencoe, Ill.: Free Press, 1956.

Gaines, Kevin. "The Historiography of the Struggle for Black Equality Since 1945." In *A Companion to Post-1945 America,* ed. Roy Rosenzweig and Jean-Christophe Agnew, 211–34. Cambridge, Mass.: Blackwell, 2002.

Gardner, Michael R. *Harry Truman and Civil Rights: Moral Courage and Political Risks.* Carbondale: Southern Illinois University Press, 2002.

Garfinkel, Herbert. *When Negroes March: The March on Washington Movement in the Organizational Politics for FEPC.* Glencoe, Ill.: Free Press, 1959.

Garrow, David J. "The FBI and Martin Luther King." *The Atlantic Monthly* 290 (July–August 2002), 80–88.

———. *The FBI and Martin Luther King Jr.: From "Solo" to Memphis.* New York: Norton, 1981.

George, Paul S. "Criminal Justice in Miami, 1896–1930." Ph.D. diss., Florida State University, 1975.

———. "Policing Miami's Black Community, 1896–1930." *Florida Historical Quarterly* 57 (April 1979), 434–50.

———. *Visions, Accomplishments, Challenges: Mount Sinai Medical Center of Greater Miami, 1949–1984.* Miami Beach: Mount Sinai Medical Center, 1984.

Geyer, Elizabeth. "The 'New' Ku Klux Klan." *The Crisis* 63 (March 1956), 139–48.

Glazer, Nathan. "The Peace Movement in America." *Commentary* 29 (April 1961), 288–96.

———. *The Social Basis of American Communism.* New York: Harcourt, Brace and World, 1961.

Goings, Kenneth W., and Gerald L. Smith. "'Unhidden' Transcripts: Memphis and African American Agency, 1862–1920," *Journal of Urban History* 21 (March 1995), 372–94.

Goldberg, J. J. *Jewish Power: Inside the American Jewish Establishment.* Reading, Mass.: Addison-Wesley, 1996.

Golden, Harry L., and Julian Scheer. "Klan without Hoods." [American Jewish Congress] *Congress Weekly* 23 (March 23, 1956), 5–8.

Goldfield, David. "A Sense of Place: Jews, Blacks, and White Gentiles in the American South." *Southern Cultures* 3 (spring 1997), 58–79.

Goldner, Sanford. *The Jewish People and the Fight for Negro Rights.* Los Angeles: Committee for Negro-Jewish Relations, 1953.

Gornick, Vivian. *The Romance of American Communism.* New York: Basic Books, 1977.

"Governor Collins and the Sit-ins." *The Reporter* 22 (April 14, 1960), 26.

Graff, Matilda. "A Child Is Born in Fear." *National Guardian* (September 27, 1954), 6.

———. "The Historic Continuity of the Civil Rights Movement." Unpublished manuscript, 1971. Reproduced as part II of this book.

———. "What's Behind the Anti-Negro Terror." *National Guardian* (August 29, 1949), 1.

Graham, Hugh Davis. *Crisis in Print: Desegregation and the Press in Tennessee.* Nashville: Vanderbilt University Press, 1967.

Green, Ben. *Before His Time: The Untold Story of Harry T. Moore, America's First Civil Rights Martyr.* New York: Free Press, 1999.

Green, Henry A. *Gesher Vakesher, Bridges and Bonds: The Life of Leon Kronish.* Atlanta: Scholars Press, 1995.

Greenberg, Cheryl. "The Black-Jewish Alliance, 1930–1955: Revisiting the 'Golden Age' Hypothesis." Unpublished paper, Society for the Scientific Study of Religion, 1993.

———. "The Southern Jewish Community and the Struggle for Civil Rights." In *African Americans and Jews in the Twentieth Century: Studies in Convergence and Conflict,* ed. V. P. Franklin, Nancy L. Grant, Harold M. Kletnick, and Genna Rae McNeil, 123–64. Columbia: University of Missouri Press, 1998.

Greene, Melissa Fay. *The Temple Bombing.* Reading, Mass.: Addison-Wesley, 1996.

Grill, Johnpeter Horst, and Robert L. Jenkins, "The Nazis and the American South in the 1930s: A Mirror Image?" *Journal of Southern History* 58 (November 1992), 667–94.

"Groundless Fears." [American Jewish Congress] *Congress Bi-Weekly* 27 (October 10, 1960), 3–4.

Guzman, Jessie Parkhurst, ed. *Negro Year Book, 1941–1946.* Tuskegee, Ala.: Tuskegee Institute, 1947.

Hall, Joe. "Statement of Joe Hall, Superintendent of Schools, Dade County, Fla." *Conference Before the United States Commission on Civil Rights,* 109–20. Washington, D.C.: U.S. Government Printing Office, 1960.

Halpern, Ben. "The Roots of American Jewish Liberalism." *American Jewish Historical Quarterly* 66 (December 1976), 190–214.
Hampton, Henry, and Steve Fayer, eds. *Voices of Freedom: An Oral History of the Civil Rights Movement from the 1950s through the 1980s*. New York: Bantam Books, 1990.
Harap, Louis. "Nightmare in Miami." *Jewish Life* 9 (December 1954), 4–9.
Haynes, John E. *Red Scare or Red Menace? American Communism and Anticommunism in the Cold War Era*. Chicago: Ivan R. Dee, 1996.
Heale, M. J. *American Anticommunism: Combatting the Enemy Within, 1830–1970*. Baltimore: Johns Hopkins University Press, 1990.
———. *McCarthy's Americans: Red Scare Politics in State and Nation, 1935–1965*. Athens: University of Georgia Press, 1998.
Heilman, Samuel C. *Portrait of American Jews: The Last Half of the 20th Century*. Seattle: University of Washington Press, 1995.
Herman, Arthur. *Joseph McCarthy: Reexamining the Life and Legacy of America's Most Hated Senator*. New York: Free Press, 2000.
Hertzberg, Arthur. *The Jews in America: Four Centuries of an Uneasy Encounter*. New York: Simon and Schuster, 1989.
Heyrock, Jim. *Prejudice or Privilege?* Miami: Greater Miami Chapter, American Jewish Committee, 1969.
Higham, Charles. *American Swastika*. New York: Doubleday, 1985.
Hill, Robert A., ed. *The Marcus Garvey and Universal Negro Improvement Association Papers*. 7 vols. Berkeley: University of California Press, 1983–1990.
Holden, Anna. *A First Step Toward School Integration*. New York: Congress of Racial Equality, 1958.
Honey, Michael K. *Black Workers Remember: An Oral History of Segregation, Unionism, and the Freedom Struggle*. Berkeley: University of California Press, 1999.
———. "Labor, the Left, and Civil Rights in the South: Memphis during the CIO Era, 1937–1955." In *Anti-Communism: The Politics of Manipulation*, ed. Judith Joel and Gerald M. Erickson, 57–85. Minneapolis: MEP Publications, 1987.
———. *Southern Labor and Black Civil Rights: Organizing Memphis Workers*. Urbana: University of Illinois Press, 1993.
Horne, Gerald. *Black and Red: W.E.B. Du Bois and the Afro-American Response to the Cold War, 1944–1963*. Albany: SUNY Press, 1986.
———. "The Case of the Civil Rights Congress: Anti-Communism as an Instrument of Social Repression." In *Anti-Communism: The Politics of Manipulation*, ed. Judith Joel and Gerald M. Erickson, 119–41. Minneapolis: MEP Publications, 1987.
———. "Civil Rights Congress." In *Encyclopedia of the American Left*, ed. Mari Jo Buhle, Paul Buhle, and Dan Georgakas, 134–35. Urbana: University of Illinois Press, 1992.
———. *Communist Front? The Civil Rights Congress, 1946–1956*. Rutherford, N.J.: Fairleigh Dickinson University Press, 1988.
———. "The Red and the Black: The Communist Party and African-Americans in Historical Perspective." In *New Studies in the Politics and Culture of U.S. Commu-*

nism, ed. Michael E. Brown, Randy Martin, Frank Rosengarten, and George Snedeker, 199–237. New York: Monthly Review Press, 1993.

Horowitz, Daniel. *Betty Friedan and the Making of* The Feminine Mystique: *The American Left, the Cold War, and Modern Feminism*. Amherst: University of Massachusetts Press, 1998.

Howe, Irving. *World of Our Fathers*. New York: Harcourt Brace Jovanovich, 1976.

Hunter, Tera W. "Domination and Resistance: The Politics of Wage Household Labor in New South Atlanta." *Labor History* 34 (spring-summer 1993), 205–20.

Hutchinson, Earl Ofari. *Blacks and Reds: Race and Class in Conflict, 1919–1990*. East Lansing: Michigan State University Press, 1995.

Isserman, Maurice. "The 1956 Generation: An Alternative Approach to the History of American Communism." *Radical America* 14 (March-April 1980), 43–51.

———. *If I Had a Hammer: The Death of the Old Left and the Birth of the New Left*. New York: Basic Books, 1987.

———. *Which Side Were You On? The American Communist Party during the Second World War*. Middletown, Conn.: Wesleyan University Press, 1982.

Jacobstein, Helen L. *The Segregation Factor in the Florida Democratic Gubernatorial Primary of 1956*. Gainesville: University of Florida Press, 1972.

Jenkins, Philip. *The Cold War at Home: The Red Scare in Pennsylvania, 1945–1960*. Chapel Hill: University of North Carolina Press, 1999.

———. *Hoods and Shirts: The Extreme Right in Pennsylvania, 1925–1950*. Chapel Hill: University of North Carolina Press, 1997.

Jones, Lewis W. *Cold Rebellion: The South's Oligarchy in Revolt*. London: Macgibbon and Kee, 1962.

Joseph, Peniel E. "Waiting till the Midnight Hour: Reconceptualizing the Heroic Period of the Civil Rights Movement, 1954–1965." *Souls: A Critical Journal of Black Politics, Culture, and Society* 2 (spring 2000), 6–17.

"Jury Investigating Florida Terrorism Indicts Four." *Southern Patriot* 11 (January 1953), 3.

Kapur, Sudarshan. *Raising Up a Prophet: The African-American Encounter with Gandhi*. Boston: Beacon Press 1992.

Katagiri, Yasuhiro. *The Mississippi State Sovereignty Commission: Civil Rights and States' Rights*. Jackson: University Press of Mississippi, 2001.

Katz, Milton S. *Ban the Bomb: A History of SANE, the Committee for a Sane Nuclear Policy, 1957–1985*. Westport, Conn.: Greenwood Press, 1986.

Kaufman, Jonathan. *Broken Alliance: The Turbulent Times between Blacks and Jews in America*. New York: Scribner's/Macmillan, 1988.

Kelley, Robin D. G. *Hammer and Hoe: Alabama Communists during the Great Depression*. Chapel Hill: University of North Carolina Press, 1990.

———. "'We Are Not What We Seem': Rethinking Black Working-Class Opposition in the Jim Crow South," *Journal of American History* 80 (June 1993), 75–112.

Kellogg, Peter J. "Civil Rights Consciousness in the 1940s." *The Historian* 42 (November 1979), 18–41.

Kennedy, Randall. "Contrasting Fates of Repression: A Comment on Gibson v. Florida Legislative Investigation Committee." In *Secret Agents: The Rosenberg Case, McCarthyism, and Fifties America*, ed. Marjorie Garber and Rebecca Walkowitz, 265–73. New York: Routledge, 1995.

Kennedy, Stetson. "Inside the Confederate Army." [New York] *Sunday Compass Magazine* (August 17, 1952), 1.

———. *The Klan Unmasked*. Boca Raton: Florida Atlantic University Press, 1990.

———. "The Ku Klux Klan: What to Do about It." *The New Republic* 114 (July 1, 1946), 928–30.

———. "Miami: Anteroom to Fascism." *The Nation* 173 (December 22, 1951), 546–47.

———. "Murder by Bombing." *The Nation* 174 (January 5, 1952), 4.

———. *Southern Exposure*. Garden City, N.Y.: Doubleday, 1946.

Kimbrough, Mary, and Margaret W. Dagen. *Victory without Violence: The First Ten Years of the St. Louis Committee of Racial Equality (CORE), 1947–1957*. Columbia: University of Missouri Press, 2000.

King, Desmond. "'The Longest Road to Equality': The Politics of Institutional Desegregation under Truman." *Journal of Historical Sociology* 6 (June 1993), 119–63.

King, Richard. "The Role of Intellectual History in the Histories of the Civil Rights Movement." In *Race and Class in the American South Since 1890*, ed. Melvyn Stokes and Rick Halpern, 159–80. Oxford: Berg, 1994.

Klehr, Harvey, and John Earl Haynes. *The American Communist Movement: Storming Heaven Itself*. New York: Twayne, 1992.

Knebel, Fletcher, and Ben Kovicar. "The Negro in Florida: One Man's Progress and the Fight Ahead." *Look* 23 (April 14, 1959), 34–37.

Konvitz, Milton R. *Expanding Liberties: Freedom's Gains in Postwar America*. New York: Viking Press, 1966.

———. "Jews and Civil Rights." In *The Ghetto and Beyond: Essays on Jewish Life in America*, ed. Peter I. Rose, 270–89. New York: Random House, 1969.

———, ed. *Law and Social Action: Selected Essays of Alexander H. Pekelis*. Ithaca, N.Y.: Cornell University Press, 1950.

Korn, Bertram Wallace, ed. *Retrospect and Prospect: Essays in Commemoration of the Seventy-Fifth Anniversary of the Founding of the Central Conference of American Rabbis, 1889–1964*. New York: Central Conference of American Rabbis, 1965.

Korstad, Robert, and Nelson Lichtenstein. "Opportunities Found and Lost: Labor, Radicals, and the Early Civil Rights Movement." *Journal of American History* 75 (December 1988), 786–811.

Kosak, Hadassa. *Cultures of Opposition: Jewish Immigrant Workers in New York City, 1881–1905*. Albany: SUNY Press, 2000.

Krause, Allen. "Rabbis and Negro Rights in the South, 1954–1967." In *Jews in the South*, ed. Leonard Dinnerstein and Mary Dale Palsson, 360–85. Baton Rouge: Louisiana State University Press, 1973.

Krueger, Thomas A. *And Promises to Keep: The Southern Conference for Human Welfare, 1938–1948*. Nashville: Vanderbilt University Press, 1967.

"The Ku Klux Klan Tries a Comeback." *Life* 20 (May 27, 1946), 42–44.
Lardner, George Jr. "Miami Declares War: An Epidemic of 'Law and Order.'" *The Nation* 206 (February 19, 1968), 231–34.
Lawrence, David. "Home-taught Values and the Homeless." *Miami Herald*, April 14, 1991.
Lawson, Steven F. "The Florida Legislative Investigation Committee and the Constitutional Readjustment of Race Relations, 1956–1963." In *An Uncertain Tradition: Constitutionalism and the History of the South*, ed. Kermit L. Hall and James E. Ely, 296–325. Athens: University of Georgia Press, 1989.
———. "Freedom Then, Freedom Now: The Historiography of the Civil Rights Movement." *American Historical Review* 96 (April 1991), 456–71.
———. "Martin Luther King, Jr., and the Civil Rights Movement." *Georgia Historical Quarterly* 71 (summer 1987), 243–60.
Lawson, Steven F., and Charles Payne. *Debating the Civil Rights Movement, 1945–1968.* Lanham, Md.: Rowman and Littlefield, 1998.
Lawson, Steven F., David R. Colburn, and Darryl Paulson. "Groveland: Florida's Little Scottsboro." *Florida Historical Quarterly* 65 (July 1986), 1–26.
Layton, Azza Salama. *International Politics and Civil Rights Policies in the United States, 1941–1960.* Cambridge: Cambridge University Press, 2000.
Leonard, Richard D. *Call to Selma: Eighteen Days of Witness.* Boston: Skinner House Books, 2002.
Lenox, Teresa. "The Carver Village Controversy." *Tequesta: The Journal of the Historical Association of Southern Florida* 50 (1990), 39–51.
Lerner, Gerda. *Fireweed: A Political Autobiography.* Philadelphia: Temple University Press, 2002.
Levine, Daniel. *Bayard Rustin and the Civil Rights Movement.* New Brunswick, N.J.: Rutgers University Press, 2000.
Levine, Esther. "Southern Jewish Views on Segregation." In *Strangers and Neighbors: Relations between Blacks and Jews in the United States*, ed. Maurianne Adams and John Bracey, 524–27. Amherst: University of Massachusetts Press, 1999.
Lewis, David Levering. "Parallels and Divergences: Assimilationist Strategies of Afro-American and Jewish Elites from 1910 to the Early 1930s." *Journal of American History* 71 (December 1984), 543–64.
———. "Shortcuts to the Mainstream: Afro-American and Jewish Notables in the 1920s and 1930s." In *Jews in Black Perspectives: A Dialogue*, ed. Joseph R. Washington Jr., 83–97. Rutherford, N.J.: Fairleigh Dickinson University Press, 1984.
Lichtenstein, Alex. "Exclusion, Fair Employment, or Interracial Unionism: Race Relations in Florida's Shipyards during World War II." In *Labor in the Modern South*, ed. Glenn T. Eskew, 135–57. Athens: University of Georgia Press, 2001.
———. "Putting Labor's House in Order: The Transport Workers Union and Labor Anti-Communism in Miami during the 1940s." *Labor History* 39 (February 1998), 7–23.
———. "'Scientific Unionism' and the 'Negro Question': Communists and the Trans-

port Workers Union in Miami, 1944–1949." In *Southern Labor in Transition, 1940–1995*, ed. Robert H. Zieger, 58–85. Knoxville: University of Tennessee Press, 1997.

Lieberman, Robbie. *The Strangest Dream: Communism, Anticommunism, and the U.S. Peace Movement, 1945–1963*. Syracuse: Syracuse University Press, 2000.

Liebman, Arthur. *Jews and the Left*. New York: Wiley, 1979.

———. "The Ties That Bind: The Jewish Support for the Left in the United States." *American Jewish Historical Quarterly* 66 (December 1976), 285–321.

Liebman, Charles S., and Steven M. Cohen. "Jewish Liberalism Revisited." *Commentary* 102 (November 1996), 51–53.

Linfield, Michael. *Freedom Under Fire: U.S. Civil Liberties in Times of War*. Boston: South End Press, 1990.

Ling, Peter J., and Sharon Monteith, eds. *Gender in the Civil Rights Movement*. New York: Garland Publishing, Inc., 1999.

Lipset, Seymour Martin, and Earl Rabb. *Jews and the New American Scene*. Cambridge, Mass.: Harvard University Press, 1995.

Lowi, Theodore. "Southern Jews: The Two Communities." *Jewish Journal of Sociology* 6 (July 1964), 103–17.

Lynn, Susan. "Gender and Post World War II Progressive Politics: A Bridge to Social Activism in the 1960s USA." *Gender and History* 4 (summer 1992), 215–239.

———. *Progressive Women in Conservative Times: Racial Justice, Peace, and Feminism, 1945 to the 1960s*. New Brunswick, N.J.: Rutgers University Press, 1992.

Lyons, Paul. *Philadelphia Communists, 1936–1956*. Philadelphia: Temple University Press, 1982.

McAuliffe, Mary Sperling. *Crisis on the Left: Cold War Politics and American Liberals, 1947–1954*. Amherst: University of Massachusetts Press, 1978.

McCoy, Donald R., and Richard T. Ruetten. "The Civil Rights Movement, 1940–1954." *Midwest Quarterly* 11 (October 1969), 11–34.

———. *Quest and Response: Minority Rights and the Truman Administration*. Lawrence: University Press of Kansas, 1973.

MacDonnell, Francis. *Insidious Foes: The Axis Fifth Column and the American Home Front*. New York: Oxford University Press, 1995.

MacDougall, Curtis D. *Gideon's Army*. 3 vols. New York: Marzani and Munsell, 1965.

McMillen, Neil R. *The Citizens' Council: Organized Resistance to the Second Reconstruction, 1954–64*. Urbana: University of Illinois Press, 1971.

McWilliams, Carey. "The Klan: Post-War Model." *The Nation* 163 (December 14, 1946), 691–94.

———. *A Mask for Privilege: Anti-Semitism in America*. Boston: Little, Brown, 1948.

Mantinband, Charles. "Integration and the Southern Jew." [American Jewish Congress] *Congress Weekly* 25 (June 16, 1958), 9–11.

Marable, Manning. *Race, Reform, and Rebellion: The Second Reconstruction in Black America, 1945–1982*. Jackson: University Press of Mississippi, 1984.

Marker, Jeffrey M. "The Jewish Community and the Case of Julius and Ethel Rosenberg." *The Maryland Historian* 3 (fall 1972), 105–21.

Marshall, F. Ray. *The Negro and Organized Labor.* New York: Wiley, 1965.
Martin, Charles H. "The International Labor Defense and Black America." *Labor History* 26 (spring 1985), 165–94.
Marx, Gary T. *Protest and Prejudice: A Study of Belief in the Black Community.* New York: Harper and Row, 1967.
Maslow, Will. "Negro-Jewish Relations." In *Freedom Now: The Civil Rights Struggle in America,* ed. Alan F. Westin, 297–301. New York: Basic Books, 1964.
Mason, Gilbert R. *Beaches, Blood, and Ballots: A Black Doctor's Civil Rights Struggle.* Jackson: University Press of Mississippi, 2000.
Medoff, Rafael. *Jewish Americans and Political Participation: A Reference Handbook.* Santa Barbara, Calif.: ABC-CLIO, 2002.
Meier, August, and John Bracey. "The NAACP as a Reform Movement, 1909–1965: 'To Reach the Conscience of America.'" *Journal of Southern History* 59 (February 1993), 3–30.
Meier, August, and Elliott M. Rudwick. *Black Detroit and the Rise of the UAW.* New York: Oxford University Press, 1979.
———. "The Boycott Movement against Jim Crow Streetcars in the South, 1900–1906." *Journal of American History* 55 (March 1969), 756–75.
———. "Communist Unions and the Black Community: The Case of the Transport Workers Union, 1934–1944." *Labor History* 23 (spring 1982), 165–97.
———. *CORE: A Study in the Civil Rights Movement.* New York: Oxford University Press, 1973.
Meyerowitz, Joanne. "Beyond the Feminine Mystique: A Reassessment of Postwar Mass Culture, 1946–1958." *Journal of American History* 79 (March 1993), 1455–82.
"Miami Klan Tries to Scare Negro Vote." *Life* (May 15, 1939), 27.
"Miamians Stage Anti-Mundt Rally." *The Florida Progressive* 1 (July 1950), 3.
"Miami's 'Red' Terror Takes on an Anti-Semitic Hue." *National Guardian* (September 27, 1954), 6.
Miller, Jake C. "Harry T. Moore's Campaign for Racial Equality." *Journal of Black Studies* 31 (November 2000), 214–31.
Miller, Loren. *The Petitioners: The Story of the Supreme Court of the United States and the Negro.* New York: Meridian Books, 1967.
"'Miracle' Occurs at Miami Beach." *Southern Patriot* 11 (October 1953), 4.
Mohl, Raymond A. "Black Immigrants: Bahamians in Early Twentieth-Century Miami." *Florida Historical Quarterly* 65 (January 1987), 271–97.
———. "Making the Second Ghetto in Metropolitan Miami, 1940–1960." *Journal of Urban History* 21 (May 1995), 395–427.
———. "The Pattern of Race Relations in Miami since the 1920s." In *The African American Heritage of Florida,* ed. David R. Colburn and Jane L. Landers, 326–65. Gainesville: University Press of Florida, 1995.
———. "The Settlement of Blacks in South Florida." In *South Florida: The Winds of Change,* ed. Thomas D. Boswell, 112–39. Miami: Association of American Geographers, 1991.

———. "'South of the South': Jews, Blacks, and the Civil Rights Movement in Miami, 1945– 1960." *Journal of American Ethnic History* 18 (winter 1999), 3–36.
Moody, Anne. *Coming of Age in Mississippi*. New York: Dell Publishing, 1976.
Moore, Deborah Dash. *At Home in America: Second Generation New York Jews*. New York: Columbia University Press, 1981.
———. "Jewish Migration in Postwar America: The Case of Miami and Los Angeles." *Studies in Contemporary Jewry* 8 (1992), 102–17.
———. "Reconsidering the Rosenbergs: Symbol and Substance in Second Generation American Jewish Consciousness." *Journal of American Ethnic History* 8 (fall 1988), 21–37.
———. "Separate Paths: Blacks and Jews in the Twentieth-Century South." In *Struggles in the Promised Land: Toward a History of Black-Jewish Relations in the United States*, ed. Jack Salzman and Cornel West, 275–93. New York: Oxford University Press, 1997.
———. *To the Golden Cities: Pursuing the American Jewish Dream in Miami and L.A.* New York: Free Press, 1994.
Morgenroth, Florence. "Organization and Activities of the American Civil Liberties Union in Miami, 1955–1966." M.A. thesis, University of Miami, 1966.
Morris, Aldon D. "Black Southern Student Sit-in Movement: An Analysis of Internal Organization." *American Sociological Review* 46 (December 1981), 744–67.
———. "Centuries of Black Protest: Its Significance for America and the World." In *Race in America: The Struggle for Equality*, ed. Herbert Hill and James E. Jones, 19–69. Madison: University of Wisconsin Press, 1993.
———. *The Origins of the Civil Rights Movement: Black Communities Organizing for Change*. New York: Free Press, 1984.
———. "A Retrospective on the Civil Rights Movement: Political and Intellectual Landmarks." *Annual Review of Sociology* 25 (1999), 517–39.
Morris, Joe Alex. "The Truth about the Florida Race Troubles." *Saturday Evening Post* (June 21, 1952), 24–25, 50, 55–58.
Morris, Milton D., and Gary E. Rubin. "The Turbulent Friendship: Black-Jewish Relations in the 1990s." *Annals of the American Academy of Political and Social Science* 530 (November 1993), 42–60.
Murray, Hugh T., Jr. *Civil Rights, History-Writing, and Anti-Communism: A Critique*. New York: American Institute for Marxist Studies, 1975.
Naison, Mark. "The Communist Party in Harlem in the Early Depression Years: A Case Study in the Reinterpretation of American Communism." *Radical History Review* 3 (fall 1976), 68–95.
———. *Communists in Harlem during the Depression*. Urbana: University of Illinois Press, 1983.
Nelson, Jack. *Terror in the Night: The Klan's Campaign against the Jews*. New York: Simon and Schuster, 1993.
Newton, Bert C. *Uncle Tom's Cadillac: Not with Simon Legree but the NAACP*. Jacksonville, Fla.: Guild Press, 1956.

Newton, Michael. *The Invisible Empire: The Ku Klux Klan in Florida*. Gainesville: University Press of Florida, 2001.
Nolan, William A. *Communism versus the Negro*. Chicago: Regnery, 1951.
Norrell, Robert J. *Reaping the Whirlwind: The Civil Rights Movement in Tuskegee*. New York: Alfred A. Knopf, 1985.
North, Joseph. *Behind the Florida Bombings*. New York: New Century Publishers, 1952.
Olson, Lynne. *Freedom's Daughters: The Unsung Heroines of the Civil Rights Movement from 1830 to 1970*. New York: Scribner's, 2001.
Owen, George Earle. "Cross-Burning in Miami." *Christian Century* 66 (March 9, 1949), 313–14.
"Pattern of Violence." *New South* 4 (March 1949), 3–5.
Patterson, William L. *The Man Who Cried Genocide*. New York: International Publishers, 1971.
———, ed. *We Charge Genocide: The Crime of the Government against the Negro People*. 2d ed. New York: International Publishers, 1951.
Payne, Charles M. *I've Got the Light of Freedom: The Organizing Tradition and the Mississippi Freedom Struggle*. Berkeley: University of California Press, 1995.
———. "Men Led, but Women Organized: Movement Participation of Women in the Mississippi Delta." In *Women in the Civil Rights Movement: Trailblazers and Torchbearers, 1941–1965*, ed. Vicki L. Crawford, Jacqueline Anne Rouse, and Barbara Woods, 1–11. Bloomington: Indiana University Press, 1993.
Pease, Frank. *Program and Platform, American Defenders*. Coral Gables: American Defenders, 1938.
Peck, Jim. *Cracking the Color Line: Non-Violent Direct Action Methods of Eliminating Racial Discrimination*. New York: Congress of Racial Equality, n.d., ca. 1959.
———. *Freedom Ride*. New York: Simon and Schuster, 1962.
Peltason, J. W. *Fifty-Eight Lonely Men: Southern Federal Judges and School Desegregation*. New York: Harcourt, Brace and World, 1961.
Perlmutter, Nathan. "Bombing in Miami: Anti-Semitism and the Segregationists." *Commentary* 25 (June 1958), 498–503.
Perry, Ruth. "Along Freedom's Road." *Miami Times* (June 15, 1957), 2.
"Philadelphia Fights Back against Witch-hunters in Its Schools." *National Guardian* (April 19, 1954), 7.
Phillips, Kimberley L. *AlabamaNorth: African-American Migrants, Community, and Working-Class Activism in Cleveland, 1915–45*. Urbana: University of Illinois Press, 1999.
Phillips, William M. *An Unillustrious Alliance: The African American and Jewish American Communities*. Westport, Conn.: Greenwood Press, 1991.
Pillar, E. A. *Time Bomb*. New York: Arco Publishing Company, 1945.
Pintzuk, Edward C. *Reds, Racial Justice, and Civil Liberties: Michigan Communists during the Cold War*. Minneapolis: MEP Publications, 1997.
Polsgrove, Carol. *Divided Minds: Intellectuals and the Civil Rights Movement*. New York: Norton, 2001.

Poore, Caroline Emmons. "Striking the First Blow: Harry T. Moore and the Fight for Black Equality in Florida." M.A. thesis, Florida State University, 1992.
Poveda, Tony. "The Rise and Fall of FBI Domestic Intelligence Operations." *Contemporary Crises* 6 (April 1982), 103–18.
Preece, Harold. "The Klan Declares War." *New Masses* 57 (October 16, 1945), 3–7.
Price, Hugh D. *The Negro and Southern Politics: A Chapter in Florida History.* New York: New York University Press, 1957.
Pritchett, Wendell. *Brownsville, Brooklyn: Blacks, Jews, and the Changing Face of the Ghetto.* Chicago: University of Chicago Press, 2002.
Proudfoot, Merrill. *Diary of a Sit-in.* New Haven, Conn.: College and University Press Publishers, 1962.
Quill, Michael J. *Michael J. Quill Answers the Rantings of the Edwards-Smolikoff Open Letter.* New York: Transport Workers Union of America, 1948.
Rabby, Glenda Alice. *The Pain and the Promise: The Struggle for Civil Rights in Tallahassee, Florida.* Athens: University of Georgia Press, 1999.
Radosh, Ronald, and Joyce Milton. *The Rosenberg File: A Search for the Truth.* New York: Holt, Rinehart, and Winston, 1983.
Raines, Howell. *My Soul Is Rested: Movement Days in the Deep South Remembered.* New York: G. P. Putnam's Sons, 1977.
Ralph, James R., Jr. *Northern Protest: Martin Luther King, Jr., Chicago, and the Civil Rights Movement.* Cambridge, Mass.: Harvard University Press, 1993.
Record, Wilson. *The Negro and the Communist Party.* Chapel Hill: University of North Carolina Press, 1951.
———. *Race and Radicalism: The NAACP and the Communist Party in Conflict.* Ithaca, N.Y.: Cornell University Press, 1964.
"'Red' Terror in Dade County, Florida." *National Guardian* (August 2, 1954), 1, 5.
Reddick, L. D. "Anti-Semitism among Negroes." *Negro Quarterly* 1 (summer 1942), 112–22.
Reed, Linda. *Simple Decency and Common Sense: The Southern Conference Movement, 1938–1963.* Bloomington: Indiana University Press, 1991.
Reed, Merl E. *Seedtime for the Modern Civil Rights Movement: The President's Committee on Fair Employment Practice, 1941–1946.* Baton Rouge: Louisiana State University Press, 1991.
Ribuffo, Leo P. *The Old Christian Right: The Protestant Far Right from the Great Depression to the Cold War.* Philadelphia: Temple University Press, 1983.
Rich, Marvin. "Miami Experiences Racial Stalemate." *The Progressive* 24 (February 1960), 36–37.
Rischin, Moses. *The Promised City: New York's Jews, 1870–1914.* Cambridge, Mass.: Harvard University Press, 1962.
Ritchie, M.A.F. "The Fourth 'R' in Miami: A City Works at Human Relations." *New South* 7 (March-April 1952), 1–8.
Roberts, Dorothy. "Feuds among the Fascists." *New Masses* 57 (November 20, 1945), 12–15.

Robinson, Armstead L., and Patricia Sullivan, eds. *New Directions in Civil Rights Studies.* Charlottesville: University Press of Virginia, 1991.

Robinson, Jo Ann. *The Montgomery Bus Boycott and the Women Who Started It.* Knoxville: University of Tennessee Press, 1989.

Robinson, Joseph B., et al. *Assault upon Freedom of Association: A Study of the Southern Attack on the National Association for the Advancement of Colored People.* New York: American Jewish Congress, 1957.

Robnett, Belinda. *How Long? How Long? African-American Women in the Struggle for Civil Rights.* New York: Oxford University Press, 1997.

Rogers, Kim Lacy. "Oral History and the History of the Civil Rights Movement." *Journal of American History* 75 (September 1988), 567–76.

———. *Righteous Lives: Narratives of the New Orleans Civil Rights Movement.* New York: New York University Press, 1993.

Rogoff, Leonard. *Homelands: Southern Jewish Identity in Durham and Chapel Hill, North Carolina.* Tuscaloosa: University of Alabama Press, 2001.

Rorabaugh, W. J. *Kennedy and the Promise of the Sixties.* Cambridge: Cambridge University Press, 2002.

Rose, Peter I. "Blacks and Jews: The Strained Alliance." *Annals of the American Academy of Political and Social Science* 454 (March 1991), 55–69.

Rosen, Gladys. "The Rabbi in Miami—A Case History." In *"Turn to the South": Essays on Southern Jewry,* ed. Nathan Kaganoff and Melvin I. Urofsky, 33–40. Charlottesville: University Press of Virginia, 1979.

Rosen, Sumner M. "The CIO Era, 1935–55." In *The Negro and the American Labor Movement,* ed. Julius Jacobson, 188–208. Garden City, N.Y.: Anchor Books, 1968.

Rosenberg, Al. "Officials Put 'Squeeze' on Miami Y.P.A." *The Florida Progressive* 1 (July 1950), 4.

———. "This Thing Called 'Fear.'" *The Florida Progressive* 1 (January 1950), 3–4.

Ross, B. Joyce. *J. E. Spingarn and the Rise of the NAACP, 1911–1939.* New York: Atheneum, 1972.

Rothman, Stanley, and S. Robert Lichter. *Roots of Radicalism: Jews, Christians, and the New Left.* New York: Oxford University Press, 1982.

Rubin, Ellis S. *Report on Investigation of Subversive Activities in Florida.* Miami: American Legion, 1955.

Ruchames, Louis. "Jewish Radicalism in the United States." In *The Ghetto and Beyond: Essays on Jewish Life in America,* ed. Peter I. Rose, 228–52. New York: Random House, 1969.

Rupp, Leila J., and Verta Taylor. *Survival in the Doldrums: The American Women's Rights Movement, 1945 to the 1960s.* New York: Oxford University Press, 1987.

Rustin, Bayard. "Montgomery Diary." *Liberation* 1 (April 1956), 7–10.

Salmond, John A. "'The Great Southern Commie Hunt': Aubrey Williams, the Southern Conference Educational Fund, and the Internal Security Subcommittee." *South Atlantic Quarterly* 77 (autumn 1978), 433–52.

Salzman, Jack, ed. *Bridges and Boundaries: African Americans and American Jews.* New York: Braziller, 1992.

Salzman, Jack, and Cornel West, eds. *Struggles in the Promised Land: Toward a History of Black-Jewish Relations in the United States.* New York: Oxford University Press, 1997.

Saunders, Robert W. *Bridging the Gap: Continuing the Florida NAACP Legacy of Harry T. Moore, 1952–1966.* Tampa: University of Tampa Press, 2000.

Schrecker, Ellen. *Many Are the Crimes: McCarthyism in America.* Boston: Little, Brown, 1998.

Schultz, Debra L. *Going South: Jewish Women in the Civil Rights Movement.* New York: New York University Press, 2001.

Schwartz, Anita. "Ethnic Identity among Left-wing American Jews." *Ethnic Groups* 6, no. 1 (1984), 65–84.

Sears, James T. *Lonely Hunters: An Oral History of Lesbian and Gay Southern Life, 1948–1968.* Boulder: Westview Press, 1997.

Seney, Ed. "John B. Orr—The Man Who Shocked the State." *The Miamian Magazine* (December 1956), 20–21.

Shapiro, Edward S. "Anti-Semitism Mississippi Style." In *Anti-Semitism in American History,* ed. David A. Gerber, 129–51. Urbana: University of Illinois Press, 1986.

———. *A Time for Healing: American Jewry since World War II.* Baltimore: Johns Hopkins University Press, 1992.

Shapiro, Herbert. *White Violence and Black Response: From Reconstruction to Montgomery.* Amherst: University of Massachusetts Press, 1988.

Sheskin, Ira M. *Demographic Study of the Greater Miami Jewish Community: Summary Report.* Miami: Greater Miami Jewish Federation, 1984.

Sides, Josh. "'You Understand My Condition': The Civil Rights Congress in the Los Angeles African-American Community, 1946–1952." *Pacific Historical Review* 67 (May 1998), 233–57.

Simonhoff, Harry. "The Anti-Semitic Crusade in Miami Between 1935–1940." *Jewish Floridian* (April 21, 1950), 3.

Singer, David G. "An Uneasy Alliance: Jews and Blacks in the United States, 1945–1953." *Contemporary Jewry* 4 (spring/summer 1978), 35–50.

Sitkoff, Harvard. "Harry Truman and the Election of 1948: The Coming of Age of Civil Rights in American Politics." *Journal of Southern History* 37 (November 1971), 597–616.

———. *A New Deal for Blacks: The Emergence of Civil Rights as a National Issue, The Depression Decade.* New York: Oxford University Press, 1978.

———. "Racial Militancy and Interracial Violence in the Second World War." *Journal of American History* 58 (December 1971), 661–81.

Skotnes, Andor. "'Buy Where You Can Work': Boycotting for Jobs in African-American Baltimore, 1933–1934." *Journal of Social History* 27 (summer 1994), 735–61.

Smith, Charles U., ed. *The Civil Rights Movement in Florida and the United States.* Tallahassee: Father and Son Publishing, Inc., 1989.

Smith, Charles U., and Lewis M. Killian. *The Tallahassee Bus Protest.* New York: Anti-Defamation League, 1958.
Solomon, Gus J. *The Jewish Role in the American Civil Rights Movement.* London: World Jewish Congress, 1967.
Solomon, Mark. *The Cry Was Unity: Communists and African Americans, 1917–1936.* Jackson: University Press of Mississippi, 1998.
Sorin, Gerald. *The Prophetic Minority: American Jewish Immigrant Radicals, 1880–1920.* Bloomington: Indiana University Press, 1985.
Stark, Bonnie. "McCarthyism in Florida: Charley Johns and the Florida Legislative Investigation Committee, July 1956 to July 1965." M.A. thesis, University of South Florida, 1985.
Staub, Michael E. *Torn at the Roots: The Crisis of Jewish Liberalism in Postwar America.* New York: Columbia University Press, 2002.
Strong, Donald S. *Organized Anti-Semitism in America: The Rise of Group Prejudice during the Decade 1930–40.* Washington, D.C.: American Council on Public Affairs, 1941.
Sullivan, Patricia. *Days of Hope: Race and Democracy in the New Deal Era.* Chapel Hill: University of North Carolina Press, 1996.
"Sunny Florida." *The Crisis* 35 (June 1928), 203–4.
Svonkin, Stuart. *Jews against Prejudice: American Jews and the Fight for Civil Liberties.* New York: Columbia University Press, 1997.
Swerdlow, Amy. *Women Strike for Peace: Traditional Motherhood and Radical Politics in the 1960s.* Chicago: University of Chicago Press, 1993.
Taft, Aldon C. "Miami Spurns Integration." *Christian Century* 72 (October 19, 1955), 1220.
Talmadge, Herman E. *You and Segregation.* Birmingham: Vulcan Press, 1955.
"Tempest in Miami." *The Nation* 179 (July 24, 1954), 61–62.
Theoharis, Athan. *Chasing Spies: How the FBI Failed in Counterintelligence but Promoted the Politics of McCarthyism in the Cold War Years.* Chicago: Ivan R. Dee, 2002.
———. *Spying on Americans: Political Surveillance from Hoover to the Huston Plan.* Philadelphia: Temple University Press, 1978.
Theoharis, Jeanne F., and Komozi Woodard, eds. *Freedom North: Black Freedom Struggles Outside the South, 1940–1980.* New York: Palgrave Macmillan, 2003.
Thornton, J. Mills, III. *Dividing Lines: Municipal Politics and the Struggle for Civil Rights in Montgomery, Birmingham, and Selma.* Tuscaloosa: University of Alabama Press, 2002.
Toby, Jackson. "Bombing in Nashville: A Jewish Center and the Desegregation Struggle." *Commentary* 25 (May 1958), 385–89.
Trillin, Calvin. "State Secrets." *The New Yorker* (May 29, 1995), 54–64.
Tscheschlok, Eric. "'So Goes the Negro': Race and Labor in Miami, 1940–1963." *Florida Historical Quarterly* 76 (summer 1997), 42–67.
Tushnet, Mark V. *Making Civil Rights Law: Thurgood Marshall and the Supreme Court, 1936–1961.* New York: Oxford University Press, 1994.

———. *The NAACP's Legal Strategy against Segregated Education, 1925–1950.* Chapel Hill: University of North Carolina Press, 1987.

Tyson, Timothy B. *Radio Free Dixie: Robert F. Williams and the Roots of Black Power.* Chapel Hill: University of North Carolina Press, 1999.

Ullrich, Bernice. "Civil Rights Being Violated." *Miami Herald,* October 11, 1954.

U.S. House of Representatives. Committee on Un-American Activities. *Investigation of Communist Activities in the State of Florida.* Washington D.C.: U.S. Government Printing Office, 1955.

———. *Report on Civil Rights Congress as a Communist Front Organization.* House Report No. 1115. Washington, D.C.: U.S. Government Printing Office, 1947.

Vought, Kip. "Racial Stirrings in Colored Town: The UNIA in Miami during the 1920s." *Tequesta: The Journal of the Historical Association of Southern Florida* 60 (2000), 56–76.

Wagy, Tom R. *Governor LeRoy Collins of Florida: Spokesman of the New South.* Tuscaloosa: University of Alabama Press, 1985.

Waldron, Martin. "Dade's Token Gesture." *Tampa Tribune,* August 16, 1959.

Washburn, Patrick S. *A Question of Sedition: The Federal Government's Investigation of the Black Press during World War II.* New York: Oxford University Press, 1986.

Webb, Clive. "Closing Ranks: Montgomery Jews and Civil Rights, 1954–1960." *Journal of American Studies* 32 (December 1998), 463–81.

———. *Fight against Fear: Southern Jews and Black Civil Rights.* Athens: University of Georgia Press, 2001.

Weigand, Kate. *Red Feminism: American Communism and the Making of Women's Liberation.* Baltimore: Johns Hopkins University Press, 2001.

———. "The Red Menace, the Feminine Mystique, and the Ohio Un-American Activities Commission: Gender and Anti-Communism in Ohio, 1951–1954." *Journal of Women's History* 3 (winter 1992), 70–94.

Weintraub, Ruth G. *How Secure These Rights? Anti-Semitism in the United States in 1948: An Anti-Defamation League Survey.* Garden City, N.Y.: Doubleday, 1949.

Weisberg, Jacob. "Cold War without End." *New York Times Magazine* (November 28, 1999), 116–23, 155–58.

Weisbord, Robert G., and Arthur Stein. *Bittersweet Encounter: The Afro-American and the American Jew.* New York: Schocken Books, 1970.

Weiss, Nancy J. *Farewell to the Party of Lincoln: Black Politics in the Age of FDR.* Princeton: Princeton University Press, 1983.

Wenger, Beth S. *New York Jews and the Great Depression: Uncertain Promise.* New Haven, Conn.: Yale University Press, 1996.

Whitfield, Stephen J. *American Space, Jewish Time.* Hamden, Conn.: Archon Books, 1988.

———. "Blood and Sand: The Jewish Community of South Florida." *American Jewish History* 82 (1994), 73–96.

———. "Famished for Justice: The Jew as Radical." In *Jews in American Politics,* ed. L. Sandy Maisel, 213–30. Lanham, Md.: Rowman and Littlefield, 2001.

———. *Voices of Jacob, Hands of Esau: Jews in American Life and Thought.* Hamden, Conn.: Archon Books, 1984.
Wilhoit, Francis M. *The Politics of Massive Resistance.* New York: Braziller, 1973.
Winfrey, Lee. "What Miami's Peaceseekers Try to Do." *Miami Herald,* April 28, 1963.
Winkler, Allan M. "The Philadelphia Transit Strike of 1944." *Journal of American History* 59 (June 1972), 73–89.
Wisenberg, Sandi. "Left on the Beach." *Miami Herald, Tropic Magazine* (July 21, 1985), 10–15.
Wittner, Lawrence S. "The National Negro Congress: A Reassessment." *American Quarterly* 22 (winter 1970), 883–901.
———. *Rebels against War: The American Peace Movement, 1941–1960.* New York: Columbia University Press, 1969.
Yaffe, David. *The American Jews: Portrait of a Split Personality.* New York: Random House, 1968.
Zangrando, Robert L. *The NAACP Crusade against Lynching, 1909–1950.* Philadelphia: Temple University Press, 1980.
Zellner, Dorothy M. "Red Roadshow: Eastland in New Orleans, 1954." *Louisiana History* 33 (winter 1992), 31–60.
Zoloth, Shirley M. "The Miami CORE Story." *CORE-lator* 77 (summer 1959), 2.
———. "Miami Integration: Silence Causes Failure." *Southern Patriot* 17 (December 1959), 1–3.

Index

Afro-American Life Insurance Company, 190
Air Force Base Elementary School, 197, 199
Alien Registration Act (1940), 42
Amalgamated Clothing Workers Union, 17, 36
American Civil Liberties Union (ACLU). *See* Florida Civil Liberties Union
American Confederate Army, 214n35
American Defenders, 36
American Jewish Committee, 13, 18, 21, 33, 55
American Jewish Congress, 47; anticommunist stance of, 7; and Bible-reading case, 26–27, 128; and civil rights, 13–14, 18–19, 31; in Miami, 3, 32, 33, 34; and Miami CORE, 55, 157, 191; and school desegregation, 149; Women's Division of, 48
American Jewish Yearbook, 16
American Student Union, 36
American Veterans Committee (AVC), 3, 26, 31, 105
Amsterdam News, 20
Anti-Defamation League (ADL), 13, 18, 29, 31, 33, 34, 55. *See also* Florida ADL
Anti-Semitism: among blacks, 19–20, 56; during CORE sit-ins, 54, 165; and Jewish defense organizations, 18–19; and Ku Klux Klan, 24–25, 28–29; in Miami area, 14, 20–22, 31, 52, 54; in postwar era, 20–22, 29–30; and southern Jews, 34, 55, 58; in Soviet Union, 66; and synagogue bombings, 23–24, 28–29; and white supremacy, 25–30
Armstrong, P. D., 134
Atkinson, Arthur A., 26, 201–2
Atlanta, Ga., 6, 128

Bain, Leslie, 125
Baltimore, Md., 21, 154, 184
Bandell, Louis, 79
Barenblatt v. United States (1959), 173
Barr, Alice, 13, 147, 150, 152, 157, 158, 162, 167, 172, 174, 180, 181, 190
Bauman, Mark K., 6
Bayer, Bill, 157, 161
Benemovsky, Leah Adler, 38
Better Business Bureau, 176
Bibb, Joseph D., 20
Bible-reading controversy, 26–27, 128, 134–35, 201–2
Biderman, Peg, 168, 174, 180, 181, 182, 190–91
Bilbo, Theodore, 81
Birmingham, Ala., 6, 28, 39, 80
Blanchard, William, 21
Bloom, Marilynn, 48, 130
Bodan, Susan, 194
Bond, Julian, 14
Boykin, Frank W., 119
Braden, Anne, 69
Brautigam, George, 26, 121–22
Brick, Mary, 163
Brooklyn, N.Y., 36, 39
Brooklyn College, 66–67
Brown, John O.: as CORE spokesman, 154–55, 156, 165, 166, 185, 191, 193; and meetings with store managers, 152–53, 157, 161, 166, 175–76; and Miami CORE, 52, 53, 54, 147–48, 149, 156–58, 163–65, 174–78, 180, 182; and Miami NAACP, 49, 53, 173; and school desegregation, 49, 53, 135–37
Brown v. Board of Education of Topeka, Kansas (1954), 5

Burdine's Department Store, 56, 150, 167, 168, 171, 174, 176, 178, 185–86, 193, 234n94
Burnett, Hattie, 168
bus boycotts, 5, 49
Bush, Gregory, 9

Caldwell, Millard F., 95, 96
Caplan, Jonah, 194
Carbonell, Jose, 107
Carey, Gordon: and Miami CORE, 51–52, 57, 147–48, 149, 155–56, 182, 191; and Miami Interracial Action Institute, 55–56, 179, 181
Carlson, John Roy, 16, 23
Carson, Clayborne, 18
Carver Village controversy, 23–24, 29
Central Conference of American Rabbis, 18
Central Life Insurance Company, 190
Chamber of Commerce. *See* Miami Chamber of Commerce
Charlotte, N.C., 28
Chicago Defender, 19–20
Civil Rights Congress (CRC): in Los Angeles, 37; in Miami, 36–47, 87–95; in Michigan, 36, 37, 65; and NAACP, 41, 43; origins of, 37; papers of, 9; and William L. Patterson, 4, 40, 43, 44, 45, 61, 91; and racial justice, 37–38, 91. *See also* Miami CRC
civil rights movement: Cold War and, 35, 60–61, 68, 80–81, 96; interpretations of, 4–5, 7–8, 13–14, 34–35; Jews and blacks and, 6–7, 13–14, 15–20, 30–32; and Jewish organizations, 13–14, 18–19, 31–32; labor unions and, 15, 17–18, 39, 41, 57; and McCarthyism, 7–8, 25–26, 35, 42–43, 45–46, 61, 68, 96, 112–18, 121–22; in postwar era, 15, and southern Jews, 6–7. *See also* Miami CRC; Miami CORE; Miami NAACP; school desegregation; sit-ins
Clark, Kenneth B., 19
Coe, John M., 8, 38, 39, 46, 87
Cohen, Joseph, 121
Colescott, James A., 22–23
Collier, Tarleton, 80
Collier's, 95
Collins, LeRoy: and Commission on Race Relations, 58; political ambitions of, 57–58; and school desegregation, 48–49; and sit-ins, 29–30, 32, 57–58, 146
Commentary, 19, 28
Commission on Justice and Peace, 18
Commission on Law and Social Action, 19
Committee to Abolish Racial Discrimination, 17
Committee for Negro-Jewish Relations, 18
Committee for Nonviolent Action (CNVA), 129
Communist Control Act (1954), 43
Communist Party, 36–37, 39; in Miami, 65–66, 106–7
Concerned Parents for Peace, 67
Congress of Industrial Organizations (CIO), 17
Congress of Racial Equality (CORE): anticommunist position of, 16; in Detroit, 67; field agents for, 50–52, 55–56, 57, 149–50; origins of, 51; papers of, 9, and James R. Robinson, 50–51, 52, 57, 182. *See also* Miami CORE
Cony, Ed, 25
Coral Gables Jewish Center, 73
Coughlin, Charles E., 20
Council on Community Interrelations, 18–19
Cousins, S. A., 193
Crisis, 95, 97
Curry, Ruby, 182

Dade County Association of Intergroup Relations Officers (CAIRO), 173
Dade County Citizens Committee for Better Schools, 127
Dade County Commission, 49
Dade County Council on Community Relations (DCCCR), 49–50, 125, 126, 127, 133, 144, 149
Dade County Council on Human Relations, 127; meetings on school desegregation, 145–47; report on public accommodations, 137–44
Dade County Property Owners Association, 24
Dade County School Board, 50, 134–35, 195–97, 199

Dade County United Fund, 129
Daily Worker, 46
Delray Beach Citizens for Social Responsibility, 67
DETCOM, 66
Detroit, Mich., 37
Diaz, John A., 212n22
Dinnerstein, Leonard, 6, 19, 34
Dixon, Howard, 130
Dollinger, Marc, 6, 34
Dombrowski, James, 149–50, 155, 180, 222n82
Donner, Frank J., 8, 16
Drexel University, 125
Dudziak, Mary L., 61

Eagles, Charles W., 4
Eastern Airlines, 39
Eastland, James O., 112–13
Ebony, 99
Economic Opportunity Program, Inc. (EOPI), 7, 129–30
Edge, Earl, 181, 182
Edison Center Civic Association, 24
Eisenhower, Dwight D., 16
Eldridge, David, 28, 126
Emanuel, Victor, 42, 90
Emma Lazarus Federation of Jewish Women's Clubs, 3, 31
Ervin, Richard W., 137, 146

Fair Employment Practices Committee (FEPC), 15, 81
Farmer, James, 13–14, 51
Faubus, Orval, 145
Federal Bureau of Investigation (FBI): 24, 38, 39, 42, 45, 48; and Bobbi Graff, 36, 42, 65–66, 108–12, 116–18, 216n50
Fellowship of Reconciliation (FOR), 51
Fiery Cross, 21
Fisher, Bella, 30
Fisher, Bernice, 51
Florida ADL, 28
Florida A&M University, 55, 95
Florida Civil Liberties Union, 3, 27, 48, 157; and Bible-reading suit, 26, 128; Jews and, 26, 31–32
Florida Concerned Democrats, 7
Florida Council on Human Relations (FCHR), 27, 49–52, 127, 144
Florida Council for Racial Cooperation, 155
Florida East Coast Railroad, 139, 188
Florida International University, 131
Florida Legislative Investigation Committee (FLIC), 26, 28, 101, 128, 216n49
Florida Mobilization Committee to End the War in Vietnam (Florida MOBE), 129
Florida Progressive, 40
Florida Progressive Party, 3, 39–40, 81–83, 85–86, 92. *See also* Progressive Party
Florida Public Officers Association, 79
Florida Pupil Assignment Law, 146, 148–49, 165, 199
Florida Supreme Court, 38, 42, 46, 114, 116, 117
Floridians for Universal Health Care, 67
Flynn, Elizabeth Gurley, 38
Fried, Richard M., 16
Fulford Elementary School, 197, 199
Futch, Truman, 120

Gaines Housing Corporation, 84–85
Garroway, Dave, 185, 192
Garvey, Marcus, 4, 5, 39
Gertman, Jessie, 198
Gibson, Theodore, 44–45, 49, 57, 194

Gordon, Barbara: and EOPI, 130; and Miami CORE, 50, 53, 54, 58, 155–56, 172, 174, 179–80, 182; and Orr campaign, 48, 126–27
Gordon, Jack: and Bible-reading suit, 26–27, 201–2; and Burdine's, 224n93; and Florida ACLU, 26; and Florida MOBE, 129; and Florida Senate campaign, 128, 131; and Miami CORE, 167, 176, 178; and Orr campaign, 27–28, 48, 126–27; and school board campaign, 26, 57, 128, 200, 201–2, 203; and WILPF, 129–30; on Shirley Zoloth, 127, 131
Gordon, Jerry, 79
Gornick, Vivian, 60

Governor's Commission on Race Relations, 32
Graff, Emanuel, 43, 73–74, 107, 111, 116–17; background of, 1, 36, 65, 75–76; and black housing, 84–85; civil rights activity of, 79; and labor organizing, 41, 75–76
Graff, Matilda "Bobbi," 1–2, 4, 8–9, 35, 48, 59, 60; and Civil Rights Congress, 36–47, 66, 87–95; civil rights memoir of, 71–119; and Communist Party, 36, 65–66, 106–7; in Detroit, 36, 65–67, 75–77; early years of, 36, 65; and FBI, 66, 108–12, 116–18, 216n50; and flight to Canada, 46, 117–18; and Groveland case, 41–42, 43, 44, 88–89, 92–93, 96–97, 119–21, 122; and NAACP, 44–45, 46, 66, 95–101; and Parent-Teacher Association, 103–5; Progressive Party, 39–40, 44, 66, 81–87; retirement years of, 67–68; and voter registration campaign, 46, 99–100
Graham, Edward, 5, 85, 86, 194
Greater Miami Jewish Federation, 34
Greater Miami Ministerial Association, 201
Greater Miami Right to Work Committee, 41
Greenberg, Cheryl, 6, 18, 32, 34
Greensboro, N.C., 13, 57
Greyhound Bus Terminal, 188–89
Gropper, Gail, 39
Groveland case, 41–42, 43, 44, 88–89, 92–93, 96–97, 119–21, 122

Hadassah, 125
Hall, Joe, 136
Hawthorne, Ira D., 24
Headley, Mrs. Walter, 104
Headley, Walter, 24, 86
Heilman, Samuel C., 13–14
Henderson, Florence, 131
Hendrix, Bill, 24, 25, 214n35
Herrell, W. C., 148–49, 173
High, Robert King, 32, 58
Holden, Anna, 182
Holland, Sidney, 34
Holland, Spessard L., 126
Hoover, J. Edgar, 16, 65, 66
Horne, Gerald, 37

Howard, Ishmael, 13, 150, 151, 158, 163, 182
Howell, Hirsh, 181, 182, 174
Hunter, J. W., 120
Hutcheson, Sumner, 147

Industrial Union of Marine and Shipbuilding Workers of America, 39
Internal Security Act (1950), 43
International Labor Defense, 37
International Ladies Garment Workers Union, 17
International Workers Order, 31, 38
Interracial Action Institute, 55–56, 58
Irvin, Walter Lee, 97
Isserman, Maurice, 60
Ivory, Jack, 147, 152

Jackson-Byron's Department Store, 55–56, 168–69, 172, 185, 193
Jackson, Miss., 6
Jacksonville, Fla., 28
James, Otis, 174, 180
Jet, 177
Jewish Community Center, 38, 101–2
Jewish Cultural Center, 38, 101–3
Jewish Floridian, 21
Jewish Labor Committee, 17, 33
Jewish People's Fraternal Order, 3, 38
Jewish Veterans Committee, 3
Johns, Charley, 173
Johns Committee, 173. *See also* Florida Legislative Investigation Committee
Johnson, Lyndon B., 7, 129
Jones, Fred, 73
Jordan-Marsh Department Store, 167

Kaman, Charles, 182
Kaplan, Lillian, 130, 152, 157, 158, 159–61, 162, 166, 174, 180, 181, 182, 191
Kennedy, Stetson, 16, 21, 24, 207n6
Khaki Shirts of America, 21
King, Martin Luther, Jr., 30, 34, 51, 178, 182, 190
Knight Manor, 23, 83
Korean War, 45, 47
Korstad, Robert, 15

Kraslow, David, 102–3
Kress's Department Store, 150, 157, 158, 160–61, 172, 183, 185
Ku Klux Klan: and anti-Semitism, 28–29; and black housing, 23–24; and black voting, 22; John Roy Carlson on, 23; and Carver Village controversy, 23–24; James A. Colescott and, 22–23; and Groveland case, 41–42, 88–91; Bill Hendrix and, 24, 25; Stetson Kennedy on, 24–25; and labor activists, 39, 77–78; in Miami, 5, 14, 20–21, 22–24, 28–29, 30, 31, 77–78, 79, 86–87, 98; and Miami bombings, 23–24, 28–29; and Harry T. Moore murder, 24, 41–42, 97–99; in Orlando, 41–42; in postwar era, 16, Progressive Party and, 40, 83; and school desegregation, 196; and White Citizens Councils, 7; and white supremacy, 22–24, 26, 28–29
Kunst, Robert, 55

Lang, Daniel, 179, 194
Laundry Workers Union, 77
Layton, Azza Salama, 61
Lazere, Haskell, 149
Leiner, Gert, 148
Lerner, Gerda, 226n9
Lewis, David Levering, 17
Lewis, Florence, 198
Lichtenstein, Nelson, 15
Life, 22
Lindley, William, 79
Little Rock, Ark., 145
Los Angeles, Calif., 18, 37
Loutit, Henry L., 155

MacGregor, Angus, 134
Marshall, Thurgood, 30, 98
Martin, Marjorie, 174, 175, 181
McCain, James T., 51, 55, 57, 58, 148, 149, 155, 181, 182, 191
McCall, Willis, 41, 97
McCarran Act (1950), 43, 45, 86, 94, 115
McCarthy, Eugene, 7
McCarthy, Joseph, 7
McCarthyism: and civil rights movement, 7–8, 35; in Miami, 25–26, 35, 112–19

McCrory's Department Store, 151, 153–54, 156, 157, 158–59, 161–62, 174, 182, 183–85, 192–93
McGill, Ralph, 145
McGovern, George, 7, 128, 131
McInerney, James M., 93
McWilliams, Carey, 16
Meyer, Phil, 165, 185, 189–90, 193
Meyers, Anna Brenner, 134–35, 202
Miami, Fla.: black housing in, 83–85; bombings in, 23–24, 28–29; changing population of, 2–3, 25, 183; CORE in, 50–58, 147–48, 150–94; CRC in, 36–47, 87–95; HUAC in, 7, 46, 116, 118; Ku Klux Klan in, 5, 14, 20–21, 22–24, 28–29, 30, 31, 77–78, 79, 86–87, 98; NAACP in, 5, 26, 28, 32, 35, 44–45, 46, 49, 52, 66, 95–101; peace movements in, 3, 55, 128–29; politics and elections in, 22, 26–28, 39–40, 48, 126–27, 128, 131; Progressive Party in, 39–40, 44, 47, 66, 81–83, 85–86, 92; tourism in, 57–58, 146, 183; voter registration campaigns in, 22, 32, 99–100; War on Poverty in, 129–30; white supremacy in, 22–26; WILPF in, 3, 27, 31, 47, 105, 125–26, 127, 133–34
Miami ACLU, 31–32. *See* Florida Civil Liberties Union
Miami Beach, Fla., 14, 21, 25, 33, 34, 38
Miami Beach Convention Bureau, 142
Miami bus station, 140
Miami Chamber of Commerce, 166, 167, 171, 174, 175–76, 184, 185
Miami CRC: FBI and 108–12, 116–17; Bobbi Graff and, 1–2, 33, 39–47, 66, 87–95; and Groveland case, 41–42, 43, 44, 88–89, 92–93, 96–97, 121; and Ku Klux Klan, 41–42, 89–91; and labor organizing, 39, 41, 84–85; and Miami police, 41, 42, 92; and Harry T. Moore, 45; and NAACP, 44–45, 46, 66, 94; James Nimmo and, 38–39, 42; origins of, 38, 87; and Progressive Party, 38–39; Charles Smolikoff and, 38–39, 42; weaknesses of, 43–44; and witch hunts, 38, 42, 43, 45–46, 66, 68, 112–29. *See also* Civil Rights Congress

260 · INDEX

Miami CORE: Interracial Action Institutes of, 55–56, 58, 177–80, 181, 186, 190–91; minutes of, 147–48, 156–59, 161–63, 166–67, 174–75, 180–82; origins of, 50–51, 147–48; report on, 182–87; Report on Racial Discrimination of, 187–89; sit-in reports of, 150–56, 159–61, 163–66, 168–72; Shirley Zoloth and, 1–2, 35, 50–58, 147–48, 150–94. *See also* Congress of Racial Equality

Miami Daily News, 24, 29, 42, 57, 89, 114, 121, 126, 198

Miami Herald, 23, 33, 34, 102, 114, 185, 189

Miami Marlins, 181

Miami NAACP: John Brown and, 49, 52, 53; and CORE, 52; Florida Legislative Investigation Committee, 25–26, 28, 35, 101, 216n49; Theodore Gibson and, 44–45, 49; Bobbi Graff and, 46, 66, 85–86, 94–101; Edward Graham and, 85–86; and and Groveland case, 44, 88–89; impact of Cold War on, 7; and Jews, 32, 33; legal action by, 5, 32, 49, 98, 197; and Miami CRC, 45, 46, 66, 85–86, 94–95; and Harry T. Moore, 45, 97–98; John Orr and, 28; right-wing attacks on, 26, 35, 101; Robert Saunders and, 101; voter registration campaign of, 46, 99–100, 150; weaknesses of, 44. *See also* National Association for the Advancement of Colored People

Miami NOW. *See* National Organization of Women for Equality in Education

Miami Progressive, 40

Miami Register, 179

Miami Shipbuilding Corporation, 39

Miami Times, 156

Miami Transit Company, 49

Miami WILPF. *See* Women's International League for Peace and Freedom

Michigan Civil Rights Congress, 36, 37

Mitchell, Dot, 135

Monteith College, 71

Montgomery Bus Boycott, 5, 49, 51

Moore, Albert D., 54, 157–58, 161, 174, 179, 180, 181, 190

Moore, Deborah Dash, 6, 26, 33, 34

Moore, Harry T., 5, 24, 41, 45, 95, 96–97, 122

Moore, Richard V., 155

Mount Sinai Hospital, 32

Mundt, Bill, 96

Naison, Mark, 37

Nashville, Tenn., 28, 50

Nation, 46, 125

Nation and Race, 21

National Association for the Advancement of Colored People: anticommunist position of, 7, 16, 35, 44, 46, 95–96; and Civil Rights Congress, 41, 44; Florida State Conference of, 45, 95–97; and Groveland case, 41, 96; and Jewish organizations, 14, 17, 19; legal action by, 15, 26, 45; membership increases during 1940s, 15; and Harry T. Moore, 24, 41, 45, 95–97; right-wing attacks on, 26, 29–30; Roy Wilkins and, 26, 30, 44, 49. *See also* Miami NAACP

National Association of Intergroup Relations Officials, 173

National Citizens League of America, 20

National Committee for a Sane Nuclear Policy (SANE), 3, 48, 128–29

National Conference of Christians and Jews, 31

National Council of Jewish Women, 3, 31, 32, 48, 127, 198–201

National Federation for Constitutional Liberties, 37

National Guardian, 41, 46, 69, 88, 119–21

National Jewish Community Relations Advisory Council, 16, 18

National Maritime Union, 17

National Organization for Women, 32, 67

National Organization of Women for Equality in Education, 32, 98

National Negro Congress, 37

National Peace Action Coalition, 79

National Urban League, 5, 7, 16, 17, 33, 35, 179

Negro Citizens Service League, 5

Negro Uplift Association, 5

Negro Voters League, 22

Negro Young Democratic Club, 150

New Orleans, La., 80

New York, N.Y., 18, 21
Nickerson, O. L., 40
Nimmo, James, 38–39, 40, 41, 42, 43–44, 77–78, 116, 121
Nixon, Richard M., 7

Opa Locka, Fla., 84
Opa Locka Naval Training Station, 107
Operation Dixie, 18–19, 80
Orchard Villa Elementary School, 50, 52, 53, 57, 182, 194–97, 199
Orr, John B., 27–28, 40, 48, 50, 126–27, 128

Pan-American Airways, 39, 78
Painter's Union, 85
Pallott, William L., 138
Parent-Teacher Association, 103–5
Patterson, William L., 4, 37, 40, 43, 44, 45, 61, 91
Paul Robeson Club, 41
Payne, Jesse James, 95
Pease, Frank, 20
Pelley, William Dudley, 20
People's Coalition for Peace and Justice, 67
Pepper, Claude, 78, 125, 126
Perlmutter, Nathan, 28–29
Perrine, Corinne, 196
Perry, Ruth W., 26, 28, 30
Philadelphia, Pa., 18, 21, 47; witch hunt in, 125–26
Phillips, Earnestine, 168–69, 172
Physicians for Social Responsibility, 67
Piller, E. A., 16
Pintzuk, Edward, 37
Pittsburgh Courier, 20, 23, 212n35
Polsgrove, Carol, 8
Progressive, 35
Progressive Party: in Miami, 39–40, 44, 47, 66, 81–83, 85–86, 92; and Henry A. Wallace, 39–40, 47, 66, 82–83, 125. *See also* Florida Progressive Party
Progressive Voters League, 5, 45, 95
Preece, Harold, 16
Price, Hugh, 13–14
Prieto, Baldomero, 196
Puryear, R. W., 155

Quigg, H. Leslie, 22

Rabinowitz, Selma, 48, 126–27
Randolph, A. Philip, 15, 18
Ray, Raymond, 172
Reddick, L. D., 19
Reichenbach, Jack, 172
Resnick, Edward, 128, 174
Resnick, Phyllis, 128, 168, 180
Retail Merchant's Association, 152–53, 154, 166
Richards Department Store, 169–71, 185, 193
Rischin, Moses, 60
Roberts, Dorothy, 16
Robinson, James R.: and Miami CORE, 52, 57, 182; and origins of national CORE, 50–51; letters from Shirley Zoloth, 153–56, 172–73, 175–80, 189–91
Roosevelt, Franklin D., 15
Rose, Peter I., 14
Rosenberg, Alfred P., 27, 40, 121
Rosenberg spy case, 45
Roth, Burnett, 31
Royal Canadian Mounted Police, 118
Royal Castle Restaurant, 172, 185, 193
Russell, Helen, 24
Rustin, Bayard, 18, 51

SANE. *See* National Committee for a Sane Nuclear Policy
Saunders, Robert, 101
Seaboard Airline Railroad, 139, 187–88
Schlafrock, Max, 46, 113
Schomburg Library, 9
school desegregation, 48–50, 52, 99, 126–28, 147, 149, 194–97; and American Jewish Congress, 149; and LeRoy Collins, 48–49; and Jack Gordon, 57, 128; and Miami CORE, 52; and Miami NAACP, 49; and Miami WILPF, 47–48, 127, 133–34; and National Council of Jewish Women, 127, 198–201; at Orchard Villa Elementary School, 50, 52, 57, 182, 194–97; and Orr campaign, 48–50, 126; and Shirley Zoloth, 49–50, 57, 133–37, 194–97
Schwartz, Evelyn, 198

Schwartz, Sid, 172
Sellers, Tim, 121
segregation: in hotels, 21–22, 141; in housing, 23–24; patterns in Miami, 14, 137–44, 183; in public transportation, 139–40, 187–89; in restaurants, 141–42, 183; in retail stores, 143; in theaters, 140–41. *See also* school desegregation; sit-ins
Seymour, Rozalind, 172, 182
Shapiro, Edward S., 16
Sheiner, Leo, 46, 101, 113
Shenandoah Elementary School, 103
Shepherd, Samuel, 97, 120
Shipbuilders Union, 77–78
Shuttlesworth, Fred, 193
Sides, Josh, 37
Simpson, Mildred, 158, 162, 163, 167, 182
Sipser, Rose, 147, 157, 167, 180
Sir John Hotel, 162, 190
sit-ins: in 1950s, 207n1; in Miami, 53–57, 150–94; television coverage of, 53, 154, 157, 161, 165, 166, 184–85, 186, 192, 193
Sitkoff, Harvard, 37
Skop, Morris A., 73
Smathers, George, 125
Smith Act (1940), 42, 92–93, 115
Smolikoff, Charles, 38–39, 77–78, 114
Society for Humanistic Judaism, 67
Soller, Fannie, 47
Soller, Max, 65
Solomon, Sam, 5
Southern Christian Leadership Conference, 81
Southern Conference Educational Fund (SCEF): 24, 46, 69, 72, 78, 81, 113, 128, 155, 180, 222n82
Southern Conference for Human Welfare, 80–81, 95, 96, 101
Southern Patriot, 24, 69, 81, 155, 180, 194–97
Southern Regional Council, 27
Southern Women for Peace, 3, 47
Stein, Arthur, 19
Stephens, Patricia, 55
Stephens, Priscilla, 55
Stern, Philip, 128
Stern, Thalia: and Bible-reading suit, 26, 128; and EOPI, 130; and Miami CORE, 50, 52, 53, 58, 148, 155, 163, 174–75, 178, 180; and

Orr campaign, 48, 127; and peace movement, 128–29
Stewart, W. B., 155
Stoner, Jesse B., 16, 207n6
Stoner Anti-Jewish Party, 207n6
Subversive Activities Control Board, 43
Svonkin, Stuart, 13–14
Swanson, Don, 202

Tallahassee Bus Boycott, 49, 55
Tampa, Fla., 83
Tannen, Harold, 90, 101
Temple Beth-El (Miami), 28
Theoharis, Athan, 16
Thomas, Ernest, 120
Thomas, Norman, 47
Thorner, Cindy, 128
Thorner, Robert, 128
Thouvenelle, B. E., 170–71
Till, Emmett, 66
Transport Workers Union, 18, 39, 78
Truman, Harry S, 15, 96
Turkel, Leonard, 48, 128, 175, 181

Ullrich, Bernice, 47, 48, 125
United Auto Workers, 17
United Nations, 47, 61, 76
Universal Negro Improvement Association (UNIA), 4, 5, 39
University of Chicago, 51
University of Miami, 9, 82, 121, 130, 131, 140
University of Wisconsin, 53
Uphaus v. Wyman (1959), 173
U.S. Department of Justice, 19, 93–94, 111
U.S. House of Representatives, Committee on Un-American Activities (HUAC), 43, 81; hearings in Miami, 7, 46, 116, 118; hearings in Philadelphia, 47, 48
U.S. Senate, Subcommittee on Internal Security, 7, 43, 46, 113
U.S. Supreme Court: *Brown* decision of, 25, 137, 145, 148, 199; on interstate travel, 51; on Miami golf case, 98–99; on Miami NAACP, 49; on state witch hunts, 172–73; on white primary, 96

Velde Committee, 116, 118. *See also* U.S.

House of Representatives, Committee on Un-American Activities
Volunteers in Service to America (VISTA), 129
Voter registration campaigns: in Miami, 22, 32, 99–100

W. T. Grant Store, 56, 152–54, 156, 157, 158–59, 162, 163, 166, 167, 174, 183–85, 192–93
Walgreen Drug Store, 158, 172, 185, 193
Wallace, Henry A., 39, 40, 45, 47, 66, 82–83, 96, 125
War on Poverty: in Miami, 129–30
Ward, E. A., 147
Wark, J. D., 157, 166
Warren, Fuller, 29, 42, 97
Wayne State University, 67, 68
Webb, Clive, 6, 34
Weisbord, Robert G., 19
Wheatherley, Richard, 129
Wheatley, Harry, 158
White Citizens Councils, 7, 25, 29, 145, 196
White Front, 20–21
Whitfield, Stephen J., 60
Wilkins, Roy, 26, 30, 44, 49
Williams, Charles, 147, 158, 163
Williams, Franklin H., 121
Wisconsin State Historical Society, 9, 131
Wolff, Milton, 43–44
women: new postwar roles of, 3–4, 59
Women Strike for Peace, 3, 129
Women's International League for Peace and Freedom (WILPF); in Miami, 3, 27, 31, 47, 105, 125–26, 127, 133–34; in Philadelphia, 125; Shirley Zoloth and, 47–48, 125–26, 127, 133–34
Women's Zionist Organization of America (Hadassah), 125
Woolworth's, 13, 54, 150, 151, 153–54, 156, 157, 160, 174, 176–77, 183, 185–86
Workmen's Circle, 3, 33, 36, 47
World Assembly for Peace, 67
Wyland, Ben F., 155

Yaffe, Doris, 130
Young People's Socialist League, 47
Young Progressives, 36

Zoloth, Barbara, 54–55
Zoloth, Milton, 1, 180; background of, 47, 125; and CORE sit-ins, 13, 167, 174–75, 182
Zoloth, Shirley M., 1–2, 4, 8–9, 35, 59–60; activism of, 59–60, 125–31; civil rights writings of, 133– 203; CORE-*later* article of, 191–93; and EOPI, 129–30; and Gordon school board campaign, 57, 128, 200, 201–3; letters to James R. Robinson, 153–56, 172–73, 175–80, 189–91; and Miami CORE, 35, 50–58, 147–48, 150–94; and National Council of Jewish Women, 48, 127, 198–203; and Orr campaign, 48, 50, 126–27; and peace movement, 48, 128–29; in Philadelphia, 47, 125–26; Report on Miami CORE, 182–87; retirement years of, 131; and school desegregation, 47–50, 126–28, 133–37, 145–47, 194–201; and WILPF, 47–48, 125–26, 127, 133–34

Raymond A. Mohl is professor of history at the University of Alabama at Birmingham. He is the author of *The New City: Urban America in the Industrial Age, 1860–1920* (1985), co-editor of *The New African American Urban History* (1996), and editor of *The Making of Urban America*, 2d ed. (1997).

www.ingramcontent.com/pod-product-compliance
Lightning Source LLC
Chambersburg PA
CBHW022108150426
43195CB00008B/319